The Croix de Feu and its successor, the Parti social français, stood at the centre of the political conflict in the turbulent final years of the French Third Republic. Membership peaked at 750,000 in 1937 and at the time the movement was widely regarded as the counterpart of fascism in Germany and Italy. However, until recently there has been relatively little debate concerning the question of whether France possessed an indigenous mass fascist movement in the 1930s. *From liberalism to fascism* is based largely on archival research. Dr Passmore's innovative conceptual approach places French fascism in the wider context of the history of French conservatism, using a micro-study of a crisis of the liberal-conservative tradition in Lyon to reflect national trends. Thus his study goes beyond the traditionally held opinion that fascism in France was a result of economic crisis, middle-class discontent and the fear of communism, and challenges the hitherto accepted views of French social and economic structures in the early part of the twentieth century.

From liberalism to fascism

The right in a French province, 1928–1939

From liberalism to fascism

The right in a French province, 1928–1939

Kevin Passmore
University of Wales Cardiff

CAMBRIDGE
UNIVERSITY PRESS

PUBLISHED BY THE PRESS SYNDICATE OF THE UNIVERSITY OF CAMBRIDGE
The Pitt Building, Trumpington Street, Cambridge CB2 1PR, United Kingdom

CAMBRIDGE UNIVERSITY PRESS
The Edinburgh Building, Cambridge CB2 2RU, United Kingdom
40 West 20th Street, New York, NY 10011–4211, USA
10 Stamford Road, Oakleigh, Melbourne 3166, Australia

© Kevin Passmore 1997

First published 1997

Printed in the United Kingdom at the University Press, Cambridge

Typeset in Plantin 10/12 pt

A catalogue record for this book is available from the British Library

Library of Congress cataloguing in publication data
Passmore, Kevin.
   From liberalism to fascism: the right in a French province, 1928–1939 / Kevin
Passmore.
      p.   cm.
   Includes bibliographical references and index.
   ISBN 0 521 58018 8 (hc)
   1. Lyon Region (France) – Politics and government. 1. France – History –
1914–1940. 3. Croix de Feu (Organization; France) – History. 4. Parti social
français – History. 5. Fascism – France-Lyon region – History – 20th
century.   I. Title
   DC801.L967P37   1997
   944'.58230815 – dc20   96–43847 CIP

ISBN 0 521 58018 8 hardback

CE

This book is dedicated to Kathy, Joe and Emily

Contents

Illustrations

Preface

The view that fascism is a phenomenon with roots in France, if not yet widely accepted, has in recent years become a respectable subject for debate amongst historians. Most would admit that there is a grain of truth in Zeev Sternhell's contention that figures such as Déroulède and Barrès contributed to the emergence of fascism, and perhaps even invented it. Robert Paxton's view that the Vichy regime, although not fascist, leaned in that direction, and needed no prompting from the occupying power to engage in antidemocratic and antisemitic measures, has become the orthodox framework for interpretation of that regime. Yet the question of whether France in the 1930s possessed an indigenous mass fascist movement has received comparatively little attention. This is surprising, given that the Croix de Feu and its successor, the Parti social français, possessed perhaps three-quarters of a million members at the movement's peak in 1937, and were seen as fascist by the left and even by many right-wingers. Until the late 1980s historians were content to accept René Rémond's contention that the Croix de Feu/PSF were 'Bonapartist', a peculiarly French form of authoritarianism that had nothing to do with fascism. At last, however, with the publication in 1995 of Robert Soucy's *French Fascism: The Second Wave*, a study of the Croix de Feu based on extensive archival research has appeared It calls into question many of the received ideas on which discussions of the Croix de Feu/PSF have rested. For Soucy there is no doubt that the movement represented a French fascism.

My intention is that this book should be part of the ongoing debate about fascism in France. Soucy's book focussed upon classification of the Croix de Feu. Whilst this book has as its central theme the nature of fascism, its particular contribution is an analysis of the league in its historical context. My aim was to go beyond the vague generalisations about economic crisis, middle-class discontent and fear of communism to which historians have hitherto confined themselves. It is to be hoped that the account of the reasons for the emergence of the Croix de Feu will be useful even to those who do not accept the arguments about fascism. Nevertheless, in explaining this crisis, it was especially important to make a delicate distinction between the conditions which produce a fascist movement and those which allow it to gain power. To meet these objectives I found it necessary to delve deeply into the history of the French right, for it was out of a crisis of conservatism that fascism emerged: hence the lengthy discussions of little-studied movements such as the Fédération républicaine, the Alliance démocratique and the Parti démocrate populaire. It was also essential to reassess dominant views of French social structure, in particular Stanley Hoffman's notion of the 'stalemate society'. If Hoffman's contention that France in this period was characterised by an unshakable social consensus is accepted, then it would be difficult to explain why a fascist movement should have emerged. The introduction to the book therefore includes a brief critique of the theoretical assumptions of Hoffman's approach. It also includes an introduction to the theory of 'social closure', a more 'historical' alternative to the sociology of Emile Durkheim and Talcott Parsons that inspired Hoffman. The book does not represent a defence of 'closure theory' as an approach to history. But the conceptual introduction does provide a framework for the book itself and especially for the critique of Hoffman that runs through it.

It is perhaps also necessary to justify the book's concern with the thorny problem of whether a movement can be described as 'fascist'. It could be argued that instead of putting a label on the Croix de Feu, we should limit ourselves to examining the movement in its specifically French context. It might be added that a desire to label the Croix de Feu as 'fascist' arises from political prejudice. There are, however, three reasons why a conceptual approach to fascism is essential to the study of this period. First, historians should certainly attempt to be conscious of, and limit, their political and other prejudices. But the fact remains that the questions we ask necessarily arise partly out of such preconceptions. This does not, however, absolve us from ensuring the internal coherence of our arguments and conclusions, from confronting our questions with evidence, or from exposing our work to the criticism of others. The historian therefore does not aim to tell the 'truth' but to achieve relative objectivity from a point of view – our views are not objective, but some answers to particular questions are better than others. It is therefore as possible for an antifascist to write usefully on fascism as it is for a conservative to advance the discipline of constitutional history. As historians we cannot prevent the asking of particular questions. (Though we might want to do so as citizens and/ or moralists – but of course historians are no better at citizenship or morality than anyone else.) Once a question is asked we can either choose to ignore it or denounce it on moral grounds, or, as historians, we can treat it on its merits.

Secondly, once the question of fascism is posed, the historian then has to ask whether it is a *useful* way of describing a particular movement. Is it more useful than concepts such as 'authoritarian conservatism' or 'totalitarianism'? Such issues are decided by asking how much of what we know is revealed, explained or obscured by the concept in question. We might want to discard the definition altogether, or we might want to modify it. If we conclude that the Croix de Feu was fascist it does not mean that we are taking an essentialist position – that by giving a movement a name we are somehow 'reflecting' its real nature. All we are saying is that this concept is a relatively useful means of making sense of what we know. To say that the Croix de Feu is fascist does not therefore rule out the possibility that this concept will be superseded. And crucially, neither does it mean that we cannot simultaneously use other definitions. The Croix de Feu could for example both be fascist *and* belong to a broader group of populist movements.

Thirdly, it follows from the above that there is no reason why we should not be concerned *both* with the political definition of the Croix de Feu and with analysis of the movement in its context. On the one hand, using the concept of fascism reveals, arguably of course, certain important features of the Croix de Feu. Perhaps more importantly, using the concept of fascism permits comparison. This is impossible without concepts which extend beyond particular instances. Otherwise it would be impossible for historians to ask whether the rise of Nazism in Germany was part of European or world developments. On the other hand, questions of this nature do not rule out an examination of the origins and nature of the Croix de Feu in its French specificities. This latter type of analysis is possible because the concept of fascism does not, as we have seen, claim to capture the essence of fascism; it is necessarily partial and of use only from a certain point of view, depending on the questions we ask. To claim that the Croix de Feu is fascist and therefore that it has important features in common with Nazism or Italian fascism does not mean that we have said everything there is to say about the movement. So in looking at the specific features of the Croix de Feu we must simultaneously deploy many other concepts.

One final explanation of the book's scope is necessary. I am aware that it is marked by my own location within a period in which European politics have changed radically. I researched the book at a time when the British miners' strike of 1984–5 turned my attention towards class struggles and collisions of economic interests, and completed it in the period following the collapse of the Berlin Wall, which seemed above all to underline the multidimensional and indeterminate nature of political conflict. I am therefore particularly conscious that I have not done justice to the gender dimension of French politics and society in the early twentieth century. This is not because of a lack of sources, or because I was unaware of the importance of gender. The reason is quite simply that at the time that I undertook the research for the book I lacked the conceptual tools that would have permitted me to ask appropriate questions of my material. Nevertheless, the conceptual framework of the book does in principle allow the possibility of incorporating gender into the analysis. Closure theory, as will be explained in the introduction, is based on the assumption that a common set of concepts can be used to examine all forms of social conflict, whether based on race, property, gender or any other criterion. It could perhaps be argued that closure theory contributes to the achievement of Joan Scott's ambition to place gender on the same theoretical footing as class and race (see her *Gender and the Politics of History* (New York, 1988), 30).

This book has been made possible by the assistance of a number of institutions and persons, whose help I gratefully acknowledge. I owe a great debt to the supervisors of my Ph.D. thesis on which this book is based, Gwynne Lewis and Roger Magraw. In France, I am indebted to Monsieur Yves Lequin, who made available to me the resources of the Centre Pierre Léon. Jean-Luc Pinol, Annie Grange, Régis Ladous and Pierre-Yves Saunier provided me with hospitality and encyclopaedic knowledge of the Rhône and its history. Gratitude is also owed to the staff at the Bibliothèque nationale de France, the Archives nationales de France, the Archives départementales du Rhône, the Bibliothèque municipale de Lyon and the Musée Gadagne. Monsieur Gilles de la Rocque kindly allowed me to see his father's papers and helped in countless other ways, even though he would not agree with the conclusions reached in this book. Thanks also to those active in the political movements of the 1930s who provided me with interviews: Marcel Brunet, Jacques Darodes, Roger Fulchiron and Claudius Dériol. My ideas about France in the 1930s were developed during many discussions with Richard Vinen. Steve Rigby introduced me to the theory of 'social closure', which provides the intellectual framework for much of what follows. I am equally indebted to the anonymous readers who provided invaluable and constructive criticism. Ian Dennis is to be thanked for drawing the maps and diagrams. I must also acknowledge the financial assistance of the British Academy, the Society for the Study of French History, the Department of History at the University of Warwick, and the School of History and Archaeology at the University of Wales College of Cardiff. The Department of History at the University of Manchester permitted me to continue with my research at a difficult moment by providing me with employment.

Finally, I wish to thank my colleagues in the History and Welsh History Section at the University of Wales College of Cardiff – especially Garthine Walker, Chris Williams, Andy Croll and Jonathan Osmond who all commented helpfully on parts of the manuscript – for providing the intellectually invigorating and friendly environment in which this book has been completed.

The author wishes to acknowledge that modified extracts from the following journal articles appear in some chapters of this book: 'Business, corporatism and the crisis of the French Third Republic: the example of the silk industry in Lyon', *Historical Journal* (1995), 959–87; 'Boy-scouting for grown-ups? Paramilitarism in the Croix de Feu and Parti Social Français', *French Historical Studies* 19 (1995), 527–57. 'The French Third Republic. Stalemate society or cradle of fascism?', *French History* 7 (1993), 417–49 and 'The Croix de Feu: Bonapartism, national-populism or fascism?' *French History* 9 (1995), 93–123 are reproduced by permission of the editor © Oxford University Press.

Abbreviations

ACS	Alliance des chambres syndicales lyonnaises (federation of small businesses)
AF	Action française
AICA	Association industrielle, commerciale et agricole (Lyon branch of CGPF)
AJG	Archives Justin Godart
ALP	Action libérale populaire
CFTC	Confédération française des travailleurs chrétiens
CGPF	Confédération générale de la production française
CGT	Confédération générale du travail
CRCCL	Compte rendu des travaux de la Chambre de commerce de Lyon
CSIM	Chambre syndicale des industries métallurgiques du Rhône
FNC	Fédération nationale catholique
JAC	Jeunesse agricole chrétienne
JOC	Jeunesse ouvrière chrétienne
JP	Jeunesses patriotes
PDP	Parti démocrate populaire
PPF	Parti populaire français
PSF	Parti social français
PVCCL	Procès verbaux de la Chambre de commerce de Lyon
SFS	Syndicat des fabricants de soieries de Lyon
SPF	Syndicats professionnels français (trade union wing of PSF)
TMF	Syndicat des tisseurs mécaniques à façon (large sub-contracting weavers)
UCS	Union des chambres syndicales lyonnaise (big business federation)
UF	Union fédérale des commerçants, artisans et petits commercants de la Croix Rousse (small shopkeepers organisation – founded the Front économique in 1932)
UMAC	Union des mutilés et des ancien combattants du Rhône
UNC	Union nationale des combattants

UNSA	Union nationale des syndicats agricoles
USE	Union du Sud-est des syndicats agricoles (conservative agricultural union)
USIC	Union sociale des ingénieurs chrétiens
VN	Volontaires nationaux (part of the Croix de Feu)

1 Introduction

In April 1928 Raymond Poincaré led the right to its second and last clear majority under the Third Republic. Once the Radical-Socialist Party conference of November 1928 had ordered its representatives to leave an administration too reactionary for its tastes (the 'coup d'Angers'), conservatives took sole responsibility for government. The left meanwhile had been reduced to disarray by the fiasco of the Cartel des gauches government of 1924 to 1926; the extreme right, which had briefly flourished during that period, was also in decline. Many conservatives believed themselves to be on the threshold of a new era.

Yet 1928 proved to be yet another false dawn in the history of the right. In both parliament and country it remained as fragmented as it had ever been. The system of proportional voting by list which had been used for the elections of 1919 and 1924 had imposed an unusual degree of electoral discipline on the right. But since negotiations between tendencies were carried on informally by political barons, extra-parliamentary political organisation withered away. In parliament the deputies of the right were dispersed in five groups in the legislatures of both 1919 and 1924. The restoration of two-round single-member constituency voting in 1928 meant that local complexities could once again come to the fore. Party structures also revived. There were, however, three distinct movements within the parliamentary right: the Catholic Fédération républicaine, the secular Alliance républicaine démocratique and the recently formed Christian democratic Parti démocrate populaire (PDP). None of these was able to unite the right in the Chamber of Deputies, where there were now six groups of the right and centre-right.

Poincaré and especially his successor André Tardieu endeavoured to stabilise the Republic through a programme of moderate reforms. The result was only to open up cracks within the right-wing coalition and even the Republic itself. Tardieu failed to transcend the deep historical and socio-economic divisions of the French right. Instead of building a strong conservative party on the British model, his position was

1

undermined by elements within his own majority, principally the right wing of the Fédération républicaine. Governments succeeded each other with the tedious monotony typical of the Third Republic. There also developed extra-parliamentary opposition among conservative supporters, who were organised in the Défense paysanne and the Fédération des contribuables. Together with the onset of the world economic crisis, these tensions led to the return to power of the left in May 1932. Disarray was such that there were now no fewer than ten conservative groups in the Chamber.

Return to opposition at least gave conservatives a common enemy, and in the following twenty months all were apparently united in disgust at the inability of a succession of Radical-led governments to implement a deflationary economic policy. On 6 February 1934, following the implication of several Radical politicians in the Stavisky scandal, various organisations of the extreme right demonstrated on the Place de la Concorde. Fifteen people were killed and 2,000 injured. On the following day the Radical Prime Minister Daladier resigned. His party switched its support to a government of the right under ex-President Gaston Doumergue. Subsequent events, however, showed that the unanimity of the right had been superficial. The right was no more able than the Radicals had been to elaborate a coherent economic strategy. The left meanwhile reorganised around the new issue of antifascism. On 14 July 1935 the Radicals joined the Parti socialiste (SFIO) and the Communist Party in the Popular Front. Successive conservative governments under Doumergue, Pierre-Etienne Flandin and Pierre Laval failed to master the political, economic and international situation. Many of their supporters therefore turned to antiparliamentary leagues, of which the Croix de Feu was by far the most important.

Even the electoral victory of the Popular Front in May 1936 and the mass strikes which greeted the installation of Léon Blum as Prime Minister failed to cement conservative unity. Although the number of right and centre parliamentary groups was reduced to five, a reorganisation of the right outside parliament merely added to the scrum of competing parties. The Croix de Feu became the Parti social français (PSF). Its new strategy of seeking power through the electoral system led to conflict with the established conservative parties. The situation on the far right was further complicated by the formation of the Parti populaire français (PPF), led by the ex-communist, Jacques Doriot. Neither parliamentary nor extreme right played a central role in the defeat of the Popular Front. On the eve of war both supported an increasingly authoritarian government led by Daladier. The rule of the 'fusilleur du 6 février' was accepted only because there was no alternative.

Thus the history of the French right in the interwar years was marked by weak leadership, division in the Chamber of Deputies and extreme volatility on the part of an electorate that was difficult to contain within sketchy party structures. The purpose of this book is to account for this pattern. Did these divisions reflect fundamental material and/or ideological cleavages? Were they merely superficial, masking a deeper unity? How is the periodic emergence of movements of the extreme right to be accounted for? What implications does this chronic fissiparousness of the right have for our understanding of the Third Republic? How, if at all, did the regime cohere if those most committed to stability were unable to realise their avowed aim of creating a united political movement?

Conservative divisions and republican society

The obligatory starting point for those interested in these questions is with René Rémond. Inspired by André Siegfried and François Goguel, Rémond explains the history of the right in terms of subterranean traditions and mentalities. Whereas Goguel sees a single right-wing 'mentality' marked by a concern for order and liberty, Rémond detects three irreducible elements within French conservatism throughout the period from 1815 to the present day, each 'with its own system of thought, temperament and clientele'. The first is a reactionary and traditionalist strand descended from Ultraroyalism. The second is a liberal-conservative tradition which originated in the July Monarchy. The third is Bonapartism, which reconciled democracy and authority in a manner unique to France. Amongst its capacities is the ability to absorb and neutralise movements of the antidemocratic extreme right. So fascism has never found fertile ground in France. No single idea united the three rights, not even defence of the status quo. The task of the historian is to trace the successive forms taken by each tendency.[1]

There is no need to rehearse the objections to Rémond's views in detail.[2] Most important, fixing the essential characteristics of the right in the first half of the nineteenth century allows little room for new responses to new problems. As chronological distance from the founding years increases, it becomes ever more difficult to fit individual movements into any of the three categories. In consequence Rémond's

---

[1] René Rémond, *Les Droites en France* (1981); André Siegfried, *Tableaux des partis en France* (1930); Emmanuel Berl, *La Politique des partis* (1931); François Goguel, *La Politique des partis sous la Troisième République* (1946).
[2] Roger Martelli, 'Peut-on connaître la droite? Approches critiques', *Cahiers d'histoire de l'institut Maurice Thorez* 20-1 (1977), 15–19.

method becomes increasingly anticontextual. The essential components of each tradition are regarded as constant in all periods, while other features of particular movements are dismissed as a product of historical contingency. Nevertheless, Rémond's approach does have two advantages. First it emphasises that there is no single characteristic which defines the right across all periods. The concept of the 'right' gains meaning only in opposition to the 'left' in a given historical context. Secondly, there can be little doubt that something akin to Rémond's traditions has helped to define the history of the right. The problem lies rather in the assumption that the traditions exist in the real world in a pure form and that they are internally coherent. It is more appropriate to regard them as useful abstractions; ideal types which serve as a means of illuminating the nature of movements which in practice constructed their identities from a great variety of material – not always French in origin. Not only did Rémond's traditions overlap, but they also underwent significant changes and became subdivided. Such changes resulted first from the fact that the traditions in question were only ever partly embodied in historical groups and individual actors, and secondly from reinscription in new historical conjunctures. Thus traditionalists came to accept capitalism and aspects of liberal economics. Similarly the adaptation of liberal-conservatism to mass politics involved fundamental conflicts within a tradition torn between abstract commitment to sovereignty of the people on the one hand and the desire for class protection and fear of the 'law of number' on the other. Finally, by the 1930s the Bonapartist tradition had become intertwined with European fascism.

Prominent among Rémond's intentions was to contest a Marxist view which saw the right's fundamental purpose as defence of the dominant social class. In the early nineteenth century, Marxists argued, the right had been identified with the declining aristocracy. The struggle to eliminate the last vestiges of the *ancien régime* meant that the Republican bourgeoisie was on the left, and could therefore enlist the support of workers and peasants. In the longer term this conflict between feudalism and capitalism was increasingly circumscribed by assimilation of the aristocracy into capitalism and the development of popular struggles. For Sanford Elwitt and Herman Lebovics the turning point came in the 1890s when Catholic landowners and anticlerical businessmen are said to have joined forces in the face of the emergent socialist threat. By the 1930s the class struggle had been simplified still further. The left, led by the Comintern, confronted a bourgeoisie in which international monopoly capital was preponderant. That there was still no single party of the right had little significance beyond the fact that diverse vocabularies were used to broaden electoral appeal. The same assumptions underlie the Marxist approach to fascism. Since the bourgeoisie is seen as a bloc, then the whole of the right must have turned to fascism in the mid-1930s. Leagues and parties are said to have united around Gaston Doumergue's 'fascist' proposals for constitutional reform put forward in 1934. Behind this movement, inevitably, was monopoly capital, manipulating the discontent of the petty bourgeoisie in order to secure undisputed control over the state for itself.[3]

Again there is no need to linger over well-known weaknesses. The modern right is certainly a significant component of a broad dominant class. Yet it cannot be identified exclusively with defence of capitalism. Other sources of social power such as the 'credentials' of the professions and gender must also be taken into account. These in turn cannot be analysed separately from political and ideological cleavages, of which the clerical/anticlerical struggle was the most important. Even in the 'economic' domain unity should not be taken for granted, for a variety of conceptions of society struggled for supremacy. Also the failure of the right to unite in response to the crisis of 1936 shows that one cannot assume a reflex of class defence. A further problem is that the Marxist view emphasises manipulation by the powerful and therefore neglects the impact on the right of socially subordinate groups.

I shall argue that there was a dynamic of unity and disunity within the right. The fact that all components of the right were, as Marxists insist, united in antisocialism, was insufficient to create political unity because various fractions of the ruling class sought to oppose socialism in different ways and disagreed even on what to defend. Challenge from the left sometimes revealed the 'fundamental unity' of the right, but, depending on context, was just as likely to cause intra-conservative conflict, as in crisis conditions competing groups redoubled their efforts to defend their own solutions. This was because of the legacy of ideological divisions identified by Rémond, together with differences of economic interests. Disunity is a feature of conservatism in all countries. But in France difficulties were especially great because of two inter-related problems. The first was the divisive legacy of the French Revolution, evident particularly in the clerical/secular struggle. The second derived from the uneven pace of French industrialisation, which created a structural imbalance in the economy and kept alive, as late as

---

[3] Martelli, 'Peut-on connaître la droite?'; M. Margairaz, 'La Droite et l'état en France dans les années trente', *Cahiers d'histoire de l'institut Maurice Thorez* 20–1 (1977), 91–136; Sanford Elwitt, *The Third Republic Defended: Bourgeois Reform in France* (London and Baton Rouge, 1986); Herman Lebovics, *The Alliance of Iron and Wheat in the Third French Republic, 1860–1914: The Origins of the New Conservatism* (Baton Rouge and London, 1988).

the 1950s, a series of contradictory visions of social organisation. It is, of course, far from original to stress the importance of economic or ideological conflict in French history.[4] This has not prevented many historians from reducing one source of division to the other, or from dismissing one type of conflict altogether. Pierre Birnbaum, for example, interprets French history in the light of a conflict between two universalist imaginary communities: one Catholic, the other based on fidelity to the French Revolution.[5] Sanford Elwitt on the other hand argues that labels such as 'clerical' and 'anticlerical' are useful only for keeping track of ministries. They reveal nothing of what happened at the more fundamental level of social politics.[6] In reality, the fragmentary nature of the right can be grasped only if the inseparability of cultural and economic divisions in the minds of historical agents is kept in mind.

The emphasis in this book is therefore upon the fragmentary and ill-disciplined nature of right-wing politics. Neither Goguel's 'political' temperaments' nor his defence of capitalism provided the right with a fundamental unity. In some respects the interpretation advanced here is closer to that of Jacques Bainville, who argued that the forces of order in the Third Republic comprised a series of isolated and leaderless groups. Only in exceptional periods was a Clemenceau or Poincaré able to impose unity.[7] This view, however, raises the question of social cohesion, since it is usually assumed that the right plays a central role in binding society together, and indeed that society must 'cohere' if it is to be viable. Bainville, writing from a royalist perspective, felt that, without a 'head', society, especially a democratic society, must sooner or later degenerate into anarchy. Modern historians have also assumed that conservative movements were essential to social cohesion, but differ from Bainville in the belief that the Third Republic *did* provide the necessary consensus and that the right was essential to its production. This is true of Stanley Hoffman's influential notion of the 'stalemate society'. This concept derives from the sociology of Talcott Parsons and Durkheim, who argued that a 'common culture' permits social groups to enjoy mutually beneficial relationships.[8] For Hoffman there was in the

[4] Malcolm Anderson, *Conservative Politics in France* (1974), 22–3.
[5] Pierre Birnbaum, *'La France aux français': histoire des haines nationalistes* (1993), 9–16, 83–6.
[6] Elwitt, *The Third Republic Defended*, 290.
[7] Jacques Bainville, *The French Republic* (1935).
[8] Stanley Hoffman, 'Paradoxes of the French political community', in *In Search of France: Renovation and Economic Management in the Twentieth Century* (New York, 1963). Examples of the influence of Hoffman include Richard F. Kuisel, *Capitalism and the State in Modern France* (Cambridge, 1981); F. Monnet, *Refaire la république: André Tardieu, une dérive réactionnaire* (1933), especially 172. For the influence of Hoffman on writings about the failure of fascism in France see note 10.

Third Republic a psycho-social compromise between bourgeoisie and small producers, excluding only the extreme left and extreme right. It was based on the idea of limiting economic change in order to preserve peasants and small business as an element of social stability. Later historians have agreed that stability was guaranteed partly by the impregnation of the right with the values of the stalemate society. This deep-seated social compromise was far more important than political and ideological struggles. Indeed, for Hoffman 'political life came close to the model of a pure game of parliamentary politics . . . played in isolation from the nation at large by a self-perpetuating political class'.[9] Hoffman's idea of a compromise between capitalists and small producers has been taken over by some Marxist historians, who give the right, as political representative of the dominant class, a still greater role in manufacturing 'hegemony'. It is argued that in the 1890s an alliance of landowners and capitalists used protectionism and an ideology of 'national labour' to incorporate the petty bourgeoisie and sections of the working class into social compromises which lasted until their destruction by the Popular Front in the 1930s. Thus both Hoffman and the Marxists dismiss political and ideological conflicts over issues such as Church and state as irrelevant to basic social compromises. In so doing they exaggerate the stability both of the Third Republic and of the right and make it hard to explain why so many conservatives should have turned to antiparliamentarian movements in the 1930s.[10]

As an alternative to these views I shall follow the approach of Abercrombie, Hill and Turner in their book *The Dominant Ideology Thesis*, who argue that the importance of a 'dominant ideology' or 'common culture' in holding society together has been overemphasised. They argue that governments are seldom loved or supported by the masses, and that increasingly in modern society the ruling class itself is ideologically fragmented. The failure of subordinate classes to overthrow the system owes less to ideological incorporation than to political

---

[9] Monnet, *Refaire la république*.

[10] Some have sought to escape this difficulty by following Hoffman's view that the leagues represented merely an alternative authoritarian means of preserving a stalemate society threatened from 'outside' by economic crisis and Germany. Marxists on the other hand argue that the rise of the leagues was a response to the threat from the left in 1934–5. In both cases the roots of the leagues in the overlapping ideological and material divisions of the right are neglected. P. Milza, *Le Fascisme français, passé et présent* (1987), 224–5; Zeev Sternhell, *La Droite révolutionnaire: les origines françaises du fascisme* (1978) 30, note 3; Allen Douglas, *From Fascism to Libertarian Communism: Georges Valois against the Third Republic* (Berkeley, 1993), xvii–xix; Martelli, 'La Droite et l'état'; Lebovics, *The Alliance of Iron and Wheat*, 190. Some of the same assumptions may be detected in the work of the non-Marxists R. Soucy, *French Fascism: The Second Wave* (Yale, 1995) and W. D. Irvine, 'Fascism in France. The strange case of the Croix de Feu', *Journal of Modern History*, 63 (1991), 271–95.

constraint, the 'dull compulsion of economic necessity', and the capacity of the system to generate *some* reward for all groups.[11] This does not mean that the ideological strategies of the right are of no significance. On the contrary, it will be argued that the instability of the Republic resulted precisely from the belief of conservatives that society *should* cohere. Unversed in modern social theory, the various factions of the right believed that France could be saved from anarchy only if they could convert both elites and masses to their point of view. The problem was that ideas of how to achieve cohesion differed fundamentally and, when coupled with incompatible material interests, led to conflict. Bainville's view that only overthrow of the Republic could preserve France from chaos is a particularly striking example of the problem, for royalists like him were regarded as dangerous subversives by other conservatives. Thus whereas conservative politics have most often been analysed in relation to the construction of hegemony, my concern is with the disruptive effects of ideology and material interest on the ruling elites and on society as a whole.

Difficulties were especially acute in the 1930s, when the economy ceased to deliver sufficient material recompense.[12] At this late stage divergent ideological and economic strategies took on a new importance as competing factions of the dominant classes redoubled their efforts to defend threatened advantages. Furthermore, we shall see that there was an authoritarian potential within the ideologies of all the main components of the right, so that a belief in the necessity of a reinforcement of authority developed within a broad spectrum of political opinion. It was from these circumstances that the Croix de Feu issued. It will be argued that the league represented a mobilisation of conservative rank-and-file in response to the divisions of the established right.[13] Besides being a response to division, the league was also a product of long-term class, religious and political conflicts within the right. This book will seek to place the Croix de Feu within this context, and will therefore also re-examine the supposed stability of French society.

---

[11] Lebovics, *The Alliance of Iron and Wheat*, 7–8. Nicholas Abercrombie, Stephen Hill and Bryan S. Turner, *The Dominant Ideology Thesis* (1980).

[12] Frank Parkin, *Marxism and Class Theory: A Bourgeois Critique* (1979), 83.

[13] In other words a socio-political crisis does not result from disruption of previously stable arrangements. Rather it consists in the fact that the normal heterogeneity of interests and activities becomes intolerable for one reason or another. If my view is correct, then the arrival in power of a fascist movement owes less to its ability to manufacture a new hegemony (as Althusserian scholars have argued, for example David Abrahams in *The Collapse of the Weimar Republic: Political Economy and Crisis* (New York, 1986) than to political factors.

Definitional issues

It is customary when discussing fascism to begin with definitional questions. Yet historians have generally been content to take the concepts of the right and conservatism as given.[14] Since one of my chief purposes is to explore the nature of the relationship between the right and the extreme right, such an approach will not do here. Although this book is not intended as a defence of a particular form of social theory, the understanding of conservative politics it presents is nevertheless heavily indebted to the neo-Weberian notion of 'social closure'.[15] A brief introduction to this theory is therefore essential. The starting point is that the right was bound up with the struggle of advantaged groups to 'exclude' the non-privileged from access to resources and reward. 'Exclusionary social closure' involves the defence not just of material resources like the means of production and land, but also the means of coercion and access to knowledge. A variety of 'codes of exclusion' can be used to monopolise these advantages. They include legal titles to property, aristocratic birth, gender, membership of a communal group such as a religion or race, or possession of 'credentials' such as the educational qualifications necessary for exercise of the professions. In order to enforce exclusionary closure a combination of economic, legal, institutional, ideological and linguistic strategies can be used. Conservative movements may be implicated in all of these, but their particular goal as political parties is the enforcement of exclusionary systems by means of state power. Thus conservatives may defend property and inheritance laws, the legal monopolies of the professions and perhaps exclusive rights of men or of ethnic or religious groups. It is however essential to bear in mind that parties represent only one of a number of ways in which exclusionary closure can be maintained. For example informal rules such as membership of a religious or ethnic group can be used to limit job opportunities. Similarly the power of capitalists does not necessarily depend on the presence in government of friendly political parties. Big business in particular possesses immense institutional and financial power, and so can co-exist even with social

[14] Exceptions are Jean-Charles Petitfils, *La Droite en France de 1789 à nos jours* (1973); Roger Eatwell and Noël O'Sullivan (eds.), *The Nature of the Right: American and European Politics and Political Thought Since 1789* (1989).
[15] Parkin, *Marxism and Class Theory*; Raymond Murphy, *Social Closure: The Theory of Monopolisation and Exclusion* (Oxford, 1988); for the first systematic application of closure theory to history see S. H. Rigby, *English Society in the Later Middle Ages: Class, Status and Gender* (1995); for a discussion of multiple forms of power see M. Mann, *The Sources of Social Power* I: *A History of Power from the Beginning to A.D. 1760*, (Cambridge, 1986).

democratic regimes as long as the latter leave intact basic guarantees of property. Nevertheless, powerful groups usually *believe* that they need the support of political parties. This, as we shall see, is a source of conflict.

Where conditions are favourable exclusionary closure may provoke a counter-struggle on the part of excluded groups to 'usurp' the same rewards. Usurpationary closure often involves mass mobilisation, and may lead to conflict with the state. Usurpationary closure is usually associated with the left. A third type of closure combines both exclusion and usurpation: 'dual closure' is the process by which certain groups simultaneously attempt to usurp the advantages of the elites and close off opportunities to subordinate groups. Dual closure reflects the fact that in modern society power and its rewards are not confined to a small group. With the growth of knowledge-based activities, the expansion of the state and the separation of ownership and control of capital, power is diffused throughout society.[16] Many people therefore occupy contradictory locations within social relations. A classic example is that of white-collar workers, a group which will figure extensively in this book. They benefit from advantages in the labour market due to possession of credentials and share the delegated power of capitalism or the state, but at the same time are exploited as wage-earners and are subject to bureaucratic supervision.

Viewing the right in the light of closure theory has a number of advantages. First, closure theory takes account of the fact that left and right must be understood in historical terms and in opposition to each other. Exclusionary closure must be conceived of as a *process*, which has to be actively created and recreated through struggle with the excluded. All post-tribal societies are based on exclusionary closure. But only in the modern world is there a political struggle to modify the distribution of power through the capture of state power, and the precise objects of this struggle vary according to context. Second, closure theory emphasises conflict and overcomes the excessive reliance of the stalemate society thesis upon consensus. Third, it provides an alternative to the Marxist identification of political conflict exclusively with capitalism. It admits the importance of capital/labour conflict, but allows for other dimensions of power and resistance, and for conflict within each of them.

A further important advantage of closure theory is therefore that it illuminates the divisions of conservatism. Although all on the right are by definition opposed to the left, the specific advantages defended are diverse, and may result in conflicts of interest. Capitalists, for example,

[16] Eric Olin Wright, *Capital, Crises and the State* (1978).

may attack the privileges of doctors in order to reduce the pressure of health care costs upon wage and tax bills. Similarly the professions may seek to expand opportunities for themselves by gaining the right to regulate and inspect private firms. Diversity of outlook also derives from the fact that social groups pursue a complex mixture of material and ideal ends. It is therefore impossible to distinguish classes from status groups on the grounds that the former seek material reward, the latter prestige: doctors may engage in struggle about fees; trade unions may be concerned with skill – partly an ideal notion. Even where a group purports to be based on a single criterion, such as class or Catholicism, it must nevertheless be analysed in the context of all the contradictions of society, none of which is primary. These rather abstract points can be made clearer by an example. In the Third Republic some businessmen used Catholic paternalism to exploit status divisions within the work-force. This does not, however, mean that Catholicism should be regarded as secondary to defence of capitalism. The businessman's view of the economy was shaped by Catholicism, and his view of the Church was shaped by material interest. Private Catholic schools played a part in the monopolisation of knowledge and access to careers in the business hierarchy; Catholic values also defined sections of the business class through marriage alliances and the transmission of property. So Catholicism was combined with material interest to produce a frame-work for group cohesion and for recognition of allies and enemies. Thus for the Catholic businessman an anticlerical industrialist could not be a reliable defender of property, whilst a Catholic socialist could not be a genuine supporter of the faith. It cannot be assumed that a common economic position will necessarily cause a group to unite against those who oppose its 'objective' interests.

The notion of 'dual closure' further illuminates intra-conservative conflict, and indeed both the far right and interwar Christian democracy will be examined partly in terms of this concept. Many individuals and groups occupy ambiguous positions within the right because they seek simultaneously to defend their position against the left and to usurp the advantages defended by the conservative elites. White-collar workers, organised in Catholic trade unions, were a case in point. The concept of dual closure can be extended to take account of conflict related to location within multiple networks of closure. Thus a politically weak section of the dominant class might seek to ally with subordinate groups in order to pursue a struggle against another section of the dominant class. Alternatively indigenous workers might use French citizenship to close off opportunities to immigrants. Whether such workers support the right depends upon historical context. Where they do so, it means that they place more emphasis upon the advantages to be gained by excluding immigrants than upon collective struggles against employers.

The notion of dual closure also casts further doubt upon the use of ideological incorporation as a means of explaining the support of subordinate groups for the right. The previously mentioned worker does not so much internalise the dominant ideology as appropriate parts of it in order to further his/her own interests, and this may lead to conflict within the right. For example conservative workers may develop their own stake in the dominant ideology, which constrains the freedom of the elites: a worker who attributes relative advantage to Catholicism shared with his/her boss, is likely to be suspicious of an employer who seeks to set aside religion in the interests of unity with non-Catholic business. Conflict is further exacerbated because different sections of the conservative masses are 'incorporated' into different dominant ideologies. The concept of dual closure reveals, then, that general social struggles continue *within the right* in an altered form, constantly calling into question efforts to defend the interests of the privileged. The identity of the right is constantly undermined by the fact that it contains within itself something of that which it purports to resist – the usurpationary struggles of the left. This points to one final strength of closure theory: it allows for the fluidity of the boundary between left and right. Many movements, such as the Radical-Socialist Party, do not fit easily into the left/right division.

A potential objection to identification of the right with exclusionary closure is that some sources of privilege are defended as much by the left as by the right. In our period many left-wingers were prepared to discriminate on the basis of gender, citizenship and age. The solution to this problem is that the right/left division should be not regarded as an *objective* reflection of exclusionary and usurpationary closure. Rather it is related to political conflict at a given historical moment. Sources of reward have to be defended politically only if they are contested politically – that is where they involve conflict over state power. Gender was a principle of exclusionary closure in the Third Republic, and was contested in daily life. It also contributed to the shaping of political struggles – as Joan Scott argues, it was a means of signifying power.[17] But it was less important in explaining the left/right division than was class or religion because most politicians of left and right accepted the dominant view of women's position in society and because of the notorious weakness of French feminism.[18] More generally, we have seen that there was not one, but several rights. The left therefore defines itself

[17] Joan Scott, *Gender and the Politics of History* (New York, 1988), 42–3.
[18] Murphy, *Social Closure*, 111–21.

in opposition to a right which does not possess a fixed meaning. A particular group could therefore be situated on the left according to the issues of the day, but possess affinities with the right on others.[19] This underlines once again the fluidity of the left/right boundary, and the difficulties faced by both sides in defining their frontiers.

Drawing the strands of the argument together, it is possible to see within the right a dynamic of unity and division. The right must be understood in terms of efforts to monopolise reward in a society of scarcity and to oppose the usurpationary struggles of the left. This, however, engenders conflict within the right. This is because individuals and groups defend different and often multiple sources of reward conceived in different ways; because of the conviction of the various factions of the elites that they must legitimate their power and impose their own views of the world upon society as a whole, and because many conservatives pursue dual closure strategies, engendering a usurpationary struggle within the right. For these reasons there is a double conflict among the various factions of the ruling class and between the elites and the conservative rank-and-file. This struggle is ongoing, so it is ahistorical to see the right in terms of compromise around a single issue such as protectionism or a set of values such as those of the stalemate society. It involves economic, social, political, ideological and organisational questions which in the minds of the protagonists are inseparable.

A typology of the right and extreme right

In the light of these reflections it is possible to elaborate a fourfold typology of conservative parties that can be depicted on two axes (see Figure 1). One represents the authority/democracy opposition: the extent to which right-wing movements tolerate the pluralism and diversity (structured nevertheless by power) which normally characterise society or seek to impose cohesion through coercion. Between the poles of authority and democracy are movements that combine acceptance in principle of popular sovereignty with constraints upon its functioning in practice (such as constitutional monarchy, limited suffrage or strong executive rule).[20] The second axis shows the elite/popular opposition.

---

[19] A semantic distinction could be made between the term 'conservative', which could be applied in a restricted sense to an individual or group that supports exclusionary closure in one of its forms, and 'right-wing', which is historically defined. Thus, it might make sense to describe left-wing views on race and gender as 'conservative', but it would be a contradiction in terms to describe them as 'right-wing.' Left and right make sense only in opposition to each other.

[20] For this reason the typology which follows uses the broader term 'constitutional' rather than 'democratic'.

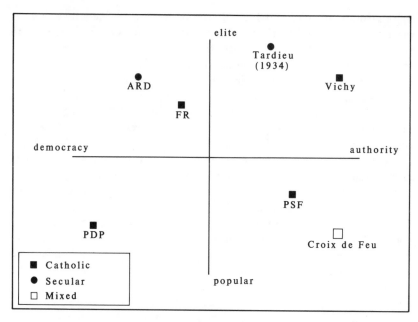

Figure 1   Typology of conservative parties

Elitist conservative movements are based largely on exclusionary closure, and claim that a narrowly defined group is qualified to govern in the interests of all. Popular movements of the right combine exclusionary with usurpationary closure. They lay greater emphasis on the direct expression of the will of the people.[21] This populist claim to represent the people gives expression to a contradiction latent within modern societies between the governed and the established authorities. Populism is not therefore a rhetorical device used to manipulate the masses, and neither can it be reduced to an expression of the interests of the petty bourgeoisie.[22] A third dimension represented on the diagram illustrates the fact that parties of all types could be situated within either Catholic or secular networks (or systems of 'communal closure'). Thus both the Catholic Fédération républicaine and the secular Alliance démocratique are included under the constitutional-elitist heading, although they came into conflict on the religious issue. It must be emphasised that in practice the three oppositions represented on the diagram are inseparable. For example, the nature of the 'popular'

---

[21] Ernesto Laclau, 'Fascism and ideology' and 'Towards a theory of populism', both in Laclau, *Politics and Ideology in Marxist Theory* (1977).
[22] Irvine, 'Fascism in France', 287–8.

changes as it is combined with either democracy or authoritarianism, or with the religious or secular. So fascists and Christian democrats, for example, conceive of the people in radically different ways.

Certain limitations of the typology should be kept in view. First, the range of conservative movements is vast and there is little point in discussing types of right-wing movement that did not exist in Third Republican France. Second, the parties of the left cannot be represented on the same axes. This is because the left, like the right, was fragmented by its situation within the multi-dimensional conflicts of French society. The left therefore combined opposition to the right with multiple affinities. For example the moderate left and right agreed on democracy, while both socialists and communists shared the secularism of the Alliance démocratique. Finally, no movement falls neatly into any of the categories. Indeed, the presence of different kinds of conservative within the same movement is a central reason for conflict. The four types of movement described below never exist in a pure form.

1 The constitutional-elitist right

The individuals, parties and movements within this category accepted parliamentary democracy, but also claimed that the social elites were best suited to govern. They depended on informal social networks for cohesion amongst themselves and on a mixture of apathy, toleration and deference rather than party organisation for mass support. Many of the deputies of the constitutional-elitist right possessed no formal extra-parliamentary organisation at all. Even the main parties of the parliamentarian right, the Fédération républicaine and especially the Alliance démocratique were not firmly implanted in the country at large, while their deputies sat in a variety of parliamentary groups. Politically they sought to balance democracy and pluralism against individual liberty and the need for order – in other words they feared that thorough democratisation would threaten their privileges. Such movements were either anticlerical and liberal-conservative as in the Alliance démocratique, or drew upon aspects of traditionalism as in the Catholic Fédération républicaine. One cannot, however, see these two strands of the democratic-elitist right, as Rémond does, literally as representatives of the Revolutionary and counterrevolutionary traditions.[23] No-one in the parliamentary right wanted a return to the ancien régime; no-one wanted a complete break with the past either. It is more useful to see these two families as operating within rival systems of communal

---

[23] See also Eatwell and O'Sullivan, The Nature of the Right, 63–8.

closure, Catholic and lay. Furthermore clericalism and anticlericalism were combined with divergent economic interests to produce a multitude of groupings, within and across parties.

2 The constitutional-popular right

By definition all movements of the right seek to monopolise access to reward. Constitutional-popular groups also engage in usurpationary struggle. They therefore combine antisocialism with social reformism, antielitism, anticapitalism and populism. Their claim to represent the people is expressed in an aspiration towards mass organisation and in the fact that they draw upon both excluded sections of the elites and subordinate elements within the right. The chief example of this type of movement in the Third Republic was the Christian democratic PDP. There was much overlap between elitist and popular conservatism. On the one hand the PDP included elements that attempted to push it in a conservative direction; on the other the Fédération républicaine and Alliance démocratique included reformist elements. On the secular side of French politics the nearest equivalent to the PDP was the Radical-Socialist Party. The latter hesitated between centre-left and centre-right, pulled one way by its reformism and anticlericalism, the other by its antisocialism.

3 The authoritarian-elitist right

A similar distinction between elitist and populist movements can be made within the authoritarian right. In times of crisis the social elites may become disillusioned with constitutional methods and turn to an authoritarianism based on the institutions of state, army and economy. We shall see that in the late Third Republic many of the leaders of the constitutional-elitist right were attracted by authoritarianism of this kind, the best known being André Tardieu. The Vichy regime was to represent a more antidemocratic version of the authoritarian-elitist right. Individuals, groups and regimes in this category distrusted mass mobilisation, but sometimes appealed symbolically to the people against the current or recently deposed holders of power. Their relations with the fourth type of right-wing movement were therefore ambiguous.

4 The authoritarian-populist right and fascism

Authoritarian-populism differs from authoritarian-elitism in the claim to express the opposition of the people to the 'establishment'. And whereas authoritarian-elitists exercise rule through existing institutions, authoritarian-populist movements combine this with the mass mobilisation typical of the left and of constitutional-popular movements. But they differ from the latter in that they conceive of the people as a totality rather than in pluralist terms. Fascism can be regarded as a sub-type of the authoritarian-populist right. It adds to the characteristics of authoritarian-populism a more extreme opposition to democracy and pluralism and a drive to impose an historically defined world-view by means of mass mobilisation expressed in paramilitarism. In this respect there is something qualitatively different about fascism, which is captured in Roger Griffin's description of it as a form of populist ultra-nationalism which he terms 'palingenetic'. Members of such movements possess a sense of living through an imminent turning point in history, in which the agents of decadence in both the left and the establishment would be swept away.[24]

A particular focus of this book will be upon the Croix de Feu, a league which gained perhaps 400,000 members by the time of its dissolution by the Popular Front government in June 1936. Until recently most agreed with René Rémond that this movement was not fascist, but a metamorphosis of the Bonapartist tradition.[25] Robert Soucy and William Irvine have recently challenged this consensus, arguing that the Croix de Feu and even its more moderate successor the PSF were fascist.[26] I shall suggest that whether or not they regard it as fascist, historians have exaggerated the conservatism of the Croix de Feu and underestimated its populism. What has been at issue is rather whether a supposed combination of authoritarianism and conservatism, on which all agree, made the league fascist.[27] The view advanced here is that the

[24] My view draws upon Laclau 'Fascism and ideology'; Geoff Eley, *Reshaping the German Right: Radical Nationalism and Political Change after Bismarck* (New York, 1980); Geoff Eley, 'What produces fascism: preindustrial traditions or a crisis of the capitalist state?', *Politics and Society* 12 (1983), 53–82; R. Griffin, *The Nature of Fascism* (1992).

[25] Rémond, *Les Droites en France*, 195–230; Milza, *Fascisme français*; K.-J. Müller, 'French fascism and modernisation', *Journal of Contemporary History* 9 (1976), 75–100; G. Howlett, 'La Rocque, the Croix de Feu and the Parti Social Français' (D.Phil. thesis, Oxford, 1986); Philippe Burrin, 'Le fascisme', in Jean-François Sirinelli (ed.), *Histoire des droites en France* (1992), I, 634.

[26] R. Soucy, *French Fascism. The Second Wave, 1933–1939* (Yale, 1995); R. Soucy, 'French fascism and the Croix de Feu: a dissenting interpretation', *Journal of Contemporary History* 26 (1991), 159–88; R. Soucy, *French Fascism: The First Wave, 1924–1933* (Yale, 1986); R. Soucy, 'The nature of fascism in France' *Journal of Contemporary History* 1 (1966), 27–55; W. D. Irvine, 'Fascism in France'; M. Margairaz, 'La Droite et l'état en France dans les années trente', *Cahiers d'histoire de l'institut Maurice Thorez*, 20–1 (1977), 91–136.

[27] Rémond, *Les Droites en France*, 199–202; Burrin, 'Le fascisme', 634; Irvine, 'Fascism in France'; Soucy, 'Fascism in France'; Roger Austin, 'The Conservative Right and the Far Right in France. The Search for Power', in Martin Blinkhorn (ed.), *Fascists and*

Croix de Feu must be seen as an authoritarian-populist movement, which combined radicalism and reaction in a specific way. This was possible because the Croix de Feu emerged from a crisis of the right, as rank-and-file conservatives mobilised against leaders unable to deal with economic crisis, or the threat from the left or from Germany. Furthermore, it will be argued that the Croix de Feu was fascist, for it was also marked by paramilitarism and a palingenetic myth.

This book will endeavour to explain how and why a fascist movement could have emerged within a single French department, the Rhône – a department moreover where the right had traditionally been marked by a tolerant and parliamentarian liberal-conservatism. The potential drawbacks of a departmentalised history of France are well known.[28] The Rhône is certainly unique in ways that will emerge in the course of the chapters that follow; generalisation from a single case is always hazardous. But with nearly a million inhabitants and as the site of the Lyonnais conurbation, France's second city, the department has considerable importance in its own right. Local politicians such as Edouard Herriot, partly because he was mayor of Lyon, played significant roles in national politics. Moreover, the social structures and landscapes of the rural parts of the Rhône – the mountains of the west, the polycultural Lyonnais plateau and the wine-producing Beaujolais – were varied enough for it to serve as a microcosm of the nation as a whole.

The following chapter places the Lyonnais liberal tradition within the historical development of the right in France and the Rhône since the foundation of the Third Republic. The precariousness of the liberal-conservative 'hegemony' is demonstrated by means of a critique of the Marxist view of this period. The chapter also shows that there was no basic social consensus; rather there was a patchwork of conflicting social groups structured by conflicting sources of social power. The interpenetration of ideological and material conflict is investigated further in the two following chapters. Chapter three shows how the structural imbalance in the Lyonnais economy, together with the Church's re-Christianisation project, led to the emergence of reformist business movements and Catholic trade unions, both of which eroded the predominance of liberal-conservatism in Lyon. Chapter four shows how integration into the market, development of peasant sociability and

Conservatives: The Radical Right and the Establishment in Twentieth Century Europe (1990), 179–80.

[28] J. Rougerie, 'Faut-il départementaliser l'histoire de la France?', *Annales ESC* 21 (1966), 178–93.

social Catholicism undermined rural notables, whether liberal-conservative or Catholic. Chapter five examines the impact on the right of the conservative reformism associated with André Tardieu in 1930–1. It will be argued that the failure of these reforms should not be seen as an example of the resistance of the stalemate society to change, but as a result of long-term conflicts in French society. For this reason opposition to Tardieu led to the first signs of a populist mobilisation within the right, which later issued into fascism. Chapter six examines the impact of the economic crisis on the right, showing that although in some senses less serious than in Germany, it nevertheless exacerbated the tensions of a society already riven by chronic divisions. The development of a diffuse authoritarianism, particularly evident in the vogue for corporatism, will be described. It will be suggested that this provided fertile ground for authoritarian political movements of many types, some fascist. Chapter seven shows how in 1932–6 already weakened conservative parties were torn apart by the impossible demands of their supporters and by political polarisation. Some of their supporters turned to the Popular Front; others, especially after the failure of Doumergue, began to think in terms of extra-legal action. Chapter eight examines the rise of the Croix de Feu. The movement will be seen as one of several possible responses to the crisis of the right, and it will be argued that it was fascist, above all because through its paramilitary mobilisations it engaged in a radical drive against both the left and the conservative establishment. The movement will also be situated in the economic and ideological divisions of French society. Chapter nine analyses the response of the right to the Popular Front government, with particular reference to the PSF – the political party created following the dissolution of the Croix de Feu by the government in June 1936. It will be suggested that the PSF ceased to be fascist but remained a movement of the non-fascist authoritarian-populist right, for the fascist option had been dealt a decisive defeat by the events of June 1936. Yet the divisions of the French conservative constituency which had given rise to the Croix de Feu remained. So as the PSF moved away from paramilitary activism it lost the Croix de Feu's ability to transcend the divisions of the right, and was therefore the cause of new conflicts. Had the elections scheduled for 1940 taken place the right might have made significant gains. It is less likely that a coherent majority would have emerged. With or without defeat and occupation, the right was therefore kindly disposed to a dose of authoritarian rule.

2   From France to the Rhône

Until 1870 politics in the Rhône were dominated by liberal constitutional monarchists who found their ideal in the July Monarchy and then
rallied to the Empire. But in the first decade of the Third Republic the
right was marginalised by the triumph of the Republicans, who won
every parliamentary seat in the department from 1876 until 1889.[1] In
the 1890s a Republican liberal-conservatism known to contemporaries
as 'Progressisme' and led by Edouard Aynard began to regain ground. It
soon won a dominant position on the right, though it never seriously
threatened the left. In 1904 the Progressiste Fédération des comités
républicains du sixième arrondissement appeared. It was extended to
cover the whole of the conurbation and then the department, and in
1905 adhered to the Fédération républicaine, which had been founded
in Paris in November 1903 by Eugène Motte to regroup the anti-
Dreyfusard majority of the Opportunists.[2] From the turn of the century
until the rise of the Croix de Feu the Fédération was to be the
predominant conservative party in the Rhône. It regularly elected three
or four of the department's twelve (thirteen from 1928) deputies and
gradually improved its share of the vote over the next decades.

To make sense of the crisis of the Lyonnais right in the 1930s it is

[1] André Latreille (ed.), *Histoire de Lyon et du lyonnais* (Lyon, 1956); André Latreille, 'Lyon
sous le régime republicain', in *Histoire de Lyon*, III: *De 1815 à 1940*, ed. A. Kleinclausz *et
al.* (Lyon, 1952); A. J. Tudesq, *Les Grands Notables en France (1840–1849)* (1964),
166–8, 284–91; Pierre Gric, pseudonym of Georges Rieussec, *Les Courants politiques du
Rhône, types et silhouettes* (Lyon, 1934); Laurent Bonnevay, *Histoire politique et administrative du conseil général du Rhône.* II: *1790–1940* (Lyon, 1946); Francois Delpech, 'La
Presse et les partis à Lyon de l'avènement des républicains à l'esprit nouveaux', *Cahiers
d'histoire* 16 (1971), 27–38; G. Garrier, *Paysans du Lyonnais et du Beaujolais* (Grenoble,
1973), 515–17.

[2] Laurent Jauffret, 'Quelques grands bourgeois lyonnaises' (mémoire de maîtrise, Lyon II,
1987), 114–28; Joseph Buché, *Essai sur la vie et l'œuvre de Edouard Aynard (1837–1913)*
(1921); J. Prévosto, 'Les Elections municipales à Lyon de 1900 à 1908', *Revue d'histoire
moderne et contemporaine* (1979), 51–78; Bonnevay, *Conseil général du Rhône*, 49–50;
L'Union républicaine, 17 May 1932; W. D. Irvine, *French Conservatism in Crisis: The
Republican Federation of France in the 1930s* (Baton Rouge and London, 1979), 1–3;
Fonds Louis Marin, AN 317 AP 70.

necessary to understand the conditions in which the Fédération emerged as the dominant conservative party. This raises some broad questions about the right in the 1890s, a period widely regarded as the cradle of modern conservatism. For Herman Lebovics and Sanford Elwitt this period saw the coming together of moderate Republican businessmen and royalist landowners in response to rural discontent, labour troubles and the emergence of organised socialism. Particular emphasis is given to the Méline tariff of 1892. Landowners and businessmen saw protectionism as a means to raise prices and blunt the edge of working-class and especially peasant discontent, at the cost of industrial dynamism – an argument that owes a debt to Hoffman's stalemate society thesis. The goodwill created by tariff negotiations is said to have prepared the ground for a favourable response to the Pope's appeal in 1892 for royalists to 'rally' to the Republic. The high point of collaboration came with Méline's 'ministry of social pacification' of 1896–8, which was supported by ex-Royalists in the hope that their commitment to order would earn concessions for the Church. Elwitt sees in the same period a convergence of Catholic Le Playists and lay Solidarists on the social question. Republicans abandoned the liberal view that working-class discontent could be assuaged by social mobility and universal suffrage. Catholics and secularists now agreed that the working class was a fact of life and that its problems must therefore be 'managed'.[3]

Lebovics and Elwitt correctly stress the importance of antisocialism to the remaking of the right in the 1890s. Yet mere awareness of the socialist threat did not necessarily create political unity. This was partly because the co-existence of advanced capital and an industrial proletariat with a mass of peasants and small entrepreneurs presented the right with a confusing series of options. Some, as Lebovics and Hoffman suggest, sought to oppose socialism through alliance with petty producers. But there was more than one way of achieving this goal. Peasants and artisans could be defended either by measures against large capital or by modernisation of small business through, for example, co-operatives. An alternative for those favourable to big business was to identify the petty bourgeoisie with shareholding, and perhaps to couple this with an appeal to workers through social reform paid for by expanding production. Alternatively, conservatives could stick with the liberal conviction that social mobility in a 'classless society' would assuage discontent. Matters were rendered still more complex by the way in which economic divisions were related to the clerical/anticlerical conflict. Religious or lay

---

[3] Elwitt, *The Third Republic Defended*; Lebovics, *The Alliance of Iron and Wheat*.

values were combined with divergent attitudes to questions of political economy to produce complex vertical and horizontal divisions within the right.

Thus in Lyon the Progressistes retained their faith in liberalism, combining this with a profound commitment to Catholicism. This divided them from potential allies in the rest of France for many conservatives shared neither the liberalism nor the Catholicism of their Lyonnais counterparts. Within Lyon the influence of Progressisme among the bourgeoisie was contested on the left by the appeal of Radicalism, and on the right by Catholic nationalism. Also attracted to the latter were parts of the conservative rank-and-file. In some cases the nationalists were prepared to accept limitations on industrialisation in order to win peasant support. Thus the example of the Rhône suggests that the 1890s did not see the installation of a conservative hegemony in the sense that wide sections of society internalised a set of core values. Indeed, the instability of conservative politics derived precisely from the belief of each group that it possessed the antidote to socialism.

Although the above remarks suggest that French conservative politics were too complex to be reduced to Rémond's three traditions, the emergence of the Fédération in the Rhône can nevertheless be seen as an example of the transmission of the Orleanist tradition to the moderate republicans. For Rémond Progressisme resembled Orleanism in that both had originated on the left, and as a result brought together liberalism and conservatism, maintenance of the principles of 1789 and defence of order: to the July Monarchy's *juste milieu* corresponded the Progressiste slogan of 1902, 'neither revolution nor reaction'. Both were tolerant in their attitude to religion; both were more interested in political and economic liberty than in social reform, and were supported by business.[4] Rémond's view of French liberalism is refined in the work of Pierre Rosanvallon.[5] He argues that it was marked by a deep distrust of democracy, and that figures such as Guizot and Taine wished to ensure that government was monopolised by those possessed of superior 'capacities', who would rule as representatives of a unitary nation. Even though Gambetta saw democracy as a means of resolving the social question, he still saw the *institueurs* as the guides of the people. Rosanvallon suggests, in an argument which has something in common with that of Lebovics and Elwitt, that in the 1890s liberals abandoned the notion of an indivisible society of isolated individuals with a common higher interest. Instead they accepted that society was the locus of an inevitable class conflict that must be contained. The example of

[4] Rémond, *Les Droites*, pp. 161–2.
[5] Pierre Rosanvallon, *Le Moment Guizot* (1985).

the Rhône, replicated in other parts of France, suggests however that the 'libéralisme capacitaire' of Guizot and Gambetta survived well beyond the 1890s. Indeed, this longevity helps to explain the crisis of the right in the 1930s, when liberal politicians struggled to reconcile their belief in rule by an enlightened elite with the rise of corporate bodies. The Orleanist tradition was not, however, transmitted unproblematically to the Progressistes. Rather it was marked by the particular social and ideological circumstances of the region. In particular, Progressisme combined liberalism, elitism and a profound commitment to Catholicism in a highly distinctive way.

Nevertheless, social and political conflict did not take the form of an anarchic struggle of interest groups, for it was conditioned by the distribution of power and by the predominant 'codes of exclusion'. In the Third Republic three forms of exclusion were based primarily on legal sanction. Access to the means of production was limited by the rules of private property; access to state power was controlled by a combination of wealth, credentials and republican values; certain professions, such as lawyers and doctors, enjoyed legal monopolies.[6] Women were excluded from full ownership of property, and could not vote or hold office. Social relations were also conditioned by the clerical/anticlerical struggle, which should be seen as a form of communal closure. In this network of power relations a republican man who owned a bank was particularly well endowed with opportunities (though he might occasionally have fretted about the extent of Catholic royalist influence in the army, or worried that his wife might be seduced in the confessional). Wealthy Catholics were in a more ambiguous situation. They possessed economic and social power, and the Church had control over significant parts of the private education system. Catholics could therefore become lawyers, doctors or engineers. Although in the 1900s Republicans tried to prevent them from doing so, Catholics were able to move directly from the *grandes écoles* to the upper reaches of the administration. But many less senior positions in the administration were closed to them, and even the wealthiest had little chance of becoming government ministers. Thus Catholics defended private property and private education, but were largely excluded from political power. This is why elements within the Catholic right were open to populism. It is in the light of this fragmented society that we must look at the right in the Rhône. But first it will be necessary to provide the reader with a brief outline of the administrative, geographical and social features of the Rhône department.

---

[6] M. Larkin, *Religion, Politics and Preferment in France since 1890* (Cambridge, 1995).

The Rhône

The Rhône is the smallest department outside the Paris region. But it had in the 1930s a population of about 900,000, of which around 70% lived in the agglomeration of Lyon, while 12% resided in smaller towns such as Villefranche, Tarare and Givors. The rest lived in communes with populations of less than 2,000.[7] For administrative purposes the department was divided into two arrondissements: Villefranche in the north and Lyon to the south.[8] These arrondissements were subdivided into twenty-one cantons, which were important as constituencies for local elections. Below this level were 269 communes (Maps 1 and 2). The commune of Lyon was split into seven municipal arrondissements and twelve cantons. This study will also use the polling districts of Lyon and Villeurbanne as a unit of analysis (Maps 3–5). Whereas in the case of Marseille urbanisation had been accompanied by the absorption of suburban communes, those surrounding Lyon remained autonomous.

The area comprising Lyon and its satellite communes is divided into three by the Rhône and Saône rivers, each corresponding with a distinct phase of urbanisation. The oldest part of the city – the 5th arrondissement – lies on the right bank of the Saône, with the narrow streets of Vieux Lyon at the foot of the river cliffs. In the 1930s Vaise, to the north, was industrial, while the south was bourgeois or petty bourgeois. Between the two rivers lay the second phase of the city's growth. The apartments of the nobility and the rentier class were traditionally located between Bellecour and Ainay (districts 204–8), where religious institutions such as the Catholic University were also found. The commercial classes lived further to the north. Still further north was the historic centre of the silk industry, the Croix-Rousse, where in the interwar years white-collar workers had taken over from weavers. The third phase of urbanisation took place in the late nineteenth century as the left bank of the Rhône was gradually made safe from flooding. The bourgeois residences of the Brotteaux (6th arrondissement) contrast with industrial La Guillotière (7th arrondissement). Expansion of the commune of Villeurbanne also dated from the second half of the nineteenth century. Its population grew from 9,000 in 1876 to 56,000 in 1936. Finally, the 1920s witnessed the explosive growth of a belt of industrial communes stretching from Vaulx en Velin in the east to Oullins in the south-west.

[7] The exact population is unknown because from 1900 until 1936 census returns for the commune of Lyon were systematically falsified. J. Bienfait, 'La Population de Lyon à travers d'un quart de siècle de recensements douteux (1911–1936)', *Revue de géographie de Lyon* 1–2 (1968), 63–132.

[8] For the history of the administrative boundaries of the Rhône see M. Gardin et al., *Paroisses et communes de France: le Rhône* (1978).

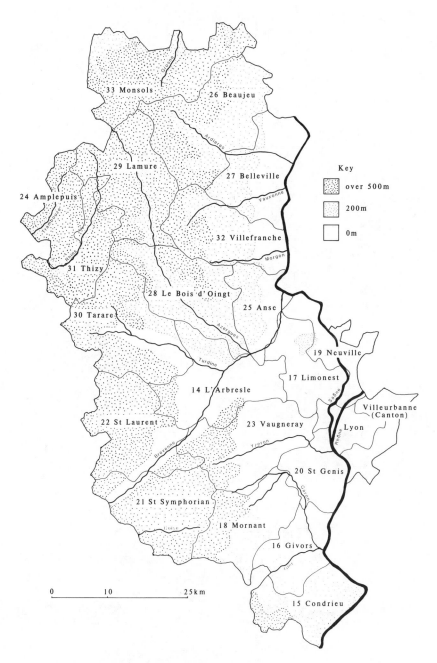

Key

over 500m

200m

0m

33 Monsols

26 Beaujeu

29 Lamure

27 Belleville

24 Amplepuis

32 Villefranche

31 Thizy

28 Le Bois d'Oingt

25 Anse

30 Tarare

19 Neuville

17 Limonest

14 L'Arbresle

Villeurbanne
(Canton)

22 St Laurent

23 Vaugneray

Lyon

20 St Genis

21 St Symphorian

18 Mornant

16 Givors

15 Condrieu

0   10   25km

Map 1   Cantons of the Rhône

Map 2   Communes of the Rhône

Cantons and communes of the Rhône

Canton
14 L'Arbresle
15 Condrieu
16 Givors
17 Limonest
18 Mornant
19 Neuville
20 St Genis Laval
21 St Symphorien sur Coise
22 St Laurent de Chamousset
23 Vaugneray
24 Amplepuis
25 Anse
26 Beaujeu
27 Belleville
28 Le Bois d'Oingt
29 Lamure
30 Tarare
31 Thizy
32 Villefranche
33 Monsols

Canton/Commune
30 1 Affoux
33 2 Aigueperse
19 3 Albigny
25 4 Alix
25 5 Ambérieux
24 6 Amplepuis
15 7 Ampuis
30 8 Ancy
25 9 Anse
14 10 L'Arbresle
32 11 Arbuissonnas
32 13 Arnas
21 14 Aveize
26 15 Avenas
33 16 Azolette
28 17 Bagnols
26 18 Beaujeu
27 19 Belleville sur Saône
25 20 Belmont
14 21 Bessenay
14 22 Bibost
32 23 Blacé
28 24 Le Bois-d'Oingt
31 25 Bourg-Thizy
20 27 Brignais
23 28 Brindas
13 29 Bron
22 30 Brullioles
22 31 Brussieu
14 32 Bully
19 33 Cailloux sur Fontaines

19 34 Caluire et Cuire
33 35 Cenves
27 36 Cercié
29 37 Chambost-Allières
22 38 Chambost-Longessaigne
28 39 Chamelet
17 40 Champagne
20 43 Chaponost
23 44 Charbonnières les Bains
27 45 Charentay
20 46 Charly
25 47 Charnay
16 48 Chassagny
17 49 Chasselay
28 50 Châtillon-d'Azergues
18 51 Chaussan
25 52 Chazay-d'Azergues
26 53 Chenas
29 54 Chenelette
28 56 Chessy les Mines
14 57 Chevinay
26 58 Chiroubles
17 59 Civrieux d'Azergues
29 60 Claveisolles
32 61 Cogny
21 62 Coise
17 63 Collanges au Mont d'Or
15 64 Condrieu
27 65 Corcelles
31 66 Cours
23 67 Courzieu
19 68 Couzon au Mont d'Or
23 69 Craponne
24 70 Cublize
19 71 Curis
17 72 Dardilly
30 73 Dareizé
32 74 Denicé
30 75 Dième
14 76 Dommartin
27 77 Dracé
21 78 Duerne
26 79 Durette
16 80 Echalas
17 81 Ecully
26 82 Emeringes
14 83 Eveux
26 84 Fleurie
19 85 Fleurieu sur Saône
14 86 Fleurieux sur l'Arbresle

19 87 Fontaines Saint Martin
19 88 Fontaines sur Saône
23 89 Francheville
28 90 Frontenas
16 91 Givors
32 92 Gleizé
29 93 Grandris
23 94 Grézieu la Varenne
21 95 Grézieu le Marché
16 96 Grigny
22 99 Haute-Rivoire
20 100 Irigny
28 101 Jarnioux
30 102 Joux
26 103 Juliénas
26 104 Jullié
31 41 La Chapelle de Mardore
21 42 La Chapelle sur Coise
20 142 La Mulatière
14 250 La Tour de Salvagny
31 262 La Ville
32 105 Lacenas
25 106 Lachassagne
29 107 Lamure
27 108 Lancié
26 109 Lantignié
21 110 Larajasse
28 6 Le Breuil
32 151 Le Perréon
28 111 Légny
14 112 Lentilly
26 12 Les Ardillats
17 55 Les Chères
15 97 Les Haies
22 98 Les Halles
30 147 Les Olmes
30 174 Les Sauvages
28 113 Létra
25 114 Liergues
32 115 Limas
17 116 Limonest
17 117 Lissieu
15 118 Loire sur Rhône
15 119 Longes
22 120 Longessaigne
25 121 Lozanne
25 122 Lucenay
26 124 Marchampt
17 125 Marcilly-d'Azergues
25 126 Marcy

23 127 Marcy-l'Etoile
31 128 Mardore
31 129 Marnand
24 130 Meaux
23 131 Messimy
21 132 Meys
16 133 Millery
28 134 Moiré
33 135 Monsols
16 136 Montagny
32 137 Montmelas Saint
        Sorlin
22 138 Montromant
22 139 Montrottier
25 140 Morancé
18 141 Mornant
19 143 Neuville sur Saône
14 144 Nuelles
27 145 Odenas
28 146 Oingt
18 148 Orliénas
20 149 Oullins
33 150 Ouroux
20 152 Pierre-Bénite
19 153 Poleymieux
23 154 Pollionay
21 155 Pomeys
25 156 Pommiers
31 158 Pont-Trambouze
30 157 Pontcharra sur
        Turdine
25 159 Pouilly le Monial
29 160 Poule
33 161 Propières
26 162 Quincié
19 163 Quincieux
29 164 Ranchal
26 165 Regnié
18 166 Riverie
32 167 Rivolet
19 168 Rochetaillé
24 169 Ronno
18 170 Rontolon
14 171 Sain Bel les Mines
32 172 Salles
14 173 Sarcey
14 175 Savigny
18 76 Soucieu en Jarrest
14 177 Sourcieux les Mines
22 178 Souzy
16 179 St Andéol le Château
18 180 St André la Cote
30 181 St Appolinaire
33 182 St Bonnet des
        Bruyères
29 183 St Bonnet le Troncy

33 185 St Christophe
33 186 St Clément de Vers
22 187 St Clément les Places
30 188 St Clément sur
        Valsonne
17 191 St Cyr au Mont d'Or
32 192 St Cyr le Chatoux
15 193 St Cyr sur Rhône
17 194 St Didier au Mont
        d'Or
18 195 St Didier sous
        Riverie
26 196 St Didier sur
        Beaujeu
27 197 St Etienne des
        Oullières
27 198 St Etienne la
        Varenne
13 199 St Fons
30 200 St Forgeux
22 203 St Genis
        l'Argentière
20 204 St Genis Laval
23 205 St Genis les
        Ollières
27 206 St Georges de
        Reneins
19 207 St Germain au Mont
        d'Or
14 208 St Germain sur
        l'Arbresle
33 209 St Igny de Vers
33 210 St Jacques des Arrêts
27 211 St Jean d'Ardières
16 213 St Jean de Touslas
25 212 St Jean des Vignes
31 214 St Jean la Bussière
32 215 St Julien
14 216 St Julien sur Bibost
28 217 St Just d'Avray
27 218 St Lager
18 219 St Laurent d'Agny
28 222 St Laurent d'Oingt
22 220 St Laurent de
        Chamousset
23 221 St Laurent de Vaux
30 223 St Loup
33 224 St Mamert
30 225 St Marcel l'Eclairé
16 226 St Martin de Cornas
21 227 St Martin en Haut
18 228 St Maurice sur
        Dargoire
29 229 St Nizier
        d'Azergues
14 231 St Pierre la Palud

17 232 St Rambert l'île
        Barbe
19 233 St Romain au Mont
        d'Or
30 234 St Romain de Popey
15 235 St Romain en Gal
16 236 St Romain en Gier
18 237 St Sorlin
21 238 St Symphorien sur
        Coise
28 239 St Vérand
24 240 St Vincent de Reins
18 184 Ste Catherine sous
        Riverie
15 189 Ste Colombe
23 190 Ste Consorce
22 201 Ste Foy l'Argentière
20 202 Ste Foy les Lyon
28 230 Ste Paule
18 241 Taluyers
27 242 Taponas
30 243 Tarare
23 244 Tassin la Demi-Lune
28 245 Ternand
28 246 Theizé
29 247 Thel
31 248 Thizy
23 249 Thurins
33 251 Trades
15 252 Trèves
15 253 Tupin et Semons
30 254 Valsonne
23 255 Vaugneray
13 256 Vaulx en Velin
32 257 Vaux en Beaujolais
26 258 Vauxrenard
13 259 Venissieux
20 260 Vernaison
26 261 Vernay
28 265 Ville sur Jarnioux
22 263 Villecheneve
32 264 Villefranche
13 266 Villeurbanne
26 267 Villié Morgon
20 268 Vourles
23 269 Yzeron

Map 3   Lyon and Villeurbanne

The population of Vénissieux, for example, rose from 8,000 in 1921 to 16,000 ten years later. By this time only 9% of the adult male population had been born in the commune, while 44% were of foreign extraction.[9] Meanwhile, new residential zones appeared to the west. In communes such as Ecully, Tassin la Demi-Lune and St Cyr, peasant farms and the summer residences of the Lyonnais elites were swamped by commuter bungalows.

The rural part of the department consists of four natural regions.[10] The Monts du Beaujolais and the Monts du Lyonnais are in general inhospitable. Steep slopes, acid soils, long cold winters, hot summers and unpredictable rainfall ensured that only potatoes and rye could be cultivated with real success. Forest often covers the slopes and crests of the mountains. There are few exceptions to this bleak picture. The relatively broad valleys of the Azergues and Turdine rivers are more suited to agriculture than the gorge-like Brévenne. In the interior of the mountains, especially towards the south, gently rolling hills also provide

[9] P. Vidélier, 'Images d'une banlieue ordinaire dans l'entre deux guerres' (unpublished paper).
[10] Geographical descriptions from Garrier, *Paysans du Lyonnais*, 15–38.

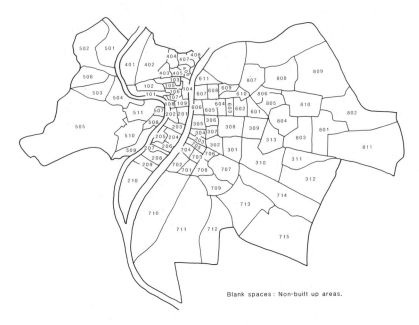

Blank spaces : Non-built up areas.

Map 4   Lyon and Villeurbanne: polling districts, 1928–35

a less difficult environment. Livestock farming progressed in those areas in the interwar period. Both mountain ranges were areas of dispersed peasant farmers, many of them tenants, and all but a few of them Catholic. The major difference between the Monts du Beaujolais and the Monts du Lyonnais is the omnipresence of the textile industry in the former.

The third region, the Beaujolais, can be divided into two. Close to the river is the flood plain of the Saône, where the land is suitable for polyculture, particularly grain and stock raising. The Beaujolais proper is relatively featureless in its southern part, and is more hilly to the north. The first hills bordering the Monts du Beaujolais are the domain of the vine. The best-quality wines are produced in the north. The climate also favours the vine, though late frosts and hailstorms are always a danger. This was an area of small independent producers, aristocratic and bourgeois landowners, and sharecroppers. The only town of any importance is industrial Villefranche.

Finally, the Lyonnais plateau stretches from the Azergues in the north to the Gier in the south. In the west it is bounded by the Monts du Lyonnais and in the east by the cliffs of the Rhône–Saône valley. As its

Map 5   Lyon and Villeurbanne: polling districts, 1936–9

name suggests, the macro-relief of the plateau is raised and fairly flat. But its surface is dissected by a host of streams running in deep wooded valleys. Mechanisation is consequently difficult. As late as 1949 sledges were often used instead of carts.[11] The proximity of a large urban market compensated for poor soils and frequent frosts and droughts. Vegetables and above all fruit could therefore be produced on a commercial scale. Almost all of the land was farmed by small and medium peasant proprietors; large property was rare. The eastern border of the plateau shades into the residential suburbs of the Lyonnais *banlieue*.

Conservatism and society, 1870–1914

Progressisme and the elites

Progressisme originated in the support of a small group of wealthy bourgeois for republicanism in the 1860s and 1870s. Many Progressistes

[11] P. Guiot, *Thurins: démographie d'une commune rurale de l'ouest lyonnais* (1949).

were drawn from an elite of big capitalists that had begun to emerge from an economy hitherto dominated by merchant-manufacturing. Aynard and Henri Germain, for example, had interests in silk and banking.[12] Such men also dominated the Chamber of Commerce. From Aynard's election in 1890 until 1924, the presidents of this powerful body also occupied important positions in the Fédération républicaine. Some Progressistes, like Auguste Isaac, were converts from Orleanism. Others, like the banker Morin-Pons, were Protestants. Electoral support came initially from the 6th arrondissement of Lyon, regarded by many as the home of the progressive bourgeoisie (in contrast to the monarchist 2nd). Then in the 1890s Aynard and his followers began to make headway in the department as a whole. The causes were not particular to Lyon. Royalism was thrown into crisis by the failure of Boulangism; many of its supporters were therefore willing to accept the Ralliement. This brought more conservative individuals into the Progressiste fold, such as Alphonse Gourd who won the parliamentary seat for the 2nd arrondissement in 1898, and brought with him a campaign for reinforcement of the state.[13] It would be wrong, however, to identify the Progressiste elite exclusively with capitalism. Members of the professional classes also rallied to the Progressiste standard. The lawyer Laurent Bonnevay, deputy of Tarare from 1902, was typical. The rise of Progressisme may also have owed something to the shift to the right of doctors, as their professional status was increasingly recognised by the state.[14] Aynard defined his ruling class in terms designed to unite capitalists, professionals and academics. It comprised those who were

better educated, masters of the sciences or arts, or better provided with borrowed or legitimately acquired resources, who have the demanding task of directing labour, burdened with all the risks and responsibilities inherent in this task. These are the superior minds, the directors of labour, those burdened with great responsibility, those who gave you [the socialists] universal suffrage.[15]

Progressisme was the party of an elite possessed of property and education. In our terms it represented an example of the constitutional-elitist right, based on exclusionary closure.

The quotation also suggests that Aynard espoused a brand of liberalism which defined the nation in terms of formally equal

---

[12] For Henri Germain see Jean Bouvier, *Le Crédit lyonnais* (1961).

[13] Delpech, 'Presses et partis à Lyon'; J. Joly (ed.), *Dictionnaire des parlementaires françaises* (7 vols., 1962–72); C. Ponson, *Les Catholiques lyonnais et la Chronique sociale* (Lyon, 1979), 50-2, 54.

[14] Jack D. Ellis, *The Physician Legislators of France: Medicine and Politics in the Early Third Republic, 1870–1914* (Cambridge, 1990).

[15] Edouard Aynard, *Discours prononcés à la Chambre des députés pendant la législature de 1889 à 1893* (undated), 17 November 1892, 195-7.

individuals, possessed of a common interest, led by the most gifted among them – an example of Rosanvallon's *libéralisme capacitaire*. Fidelity to liberalism was also expressed in Aynard's view that religion was a private matter, and in the commitment of most of the Lyonnais elites to free trade. Aynard, like most French politicians, certainly idealised the petty bourgeoisie. But he did not seek state intervention on their behalf. Rather he saw small property in terms of the liberal principle of free enterprise, a rung on the ladder of social mobility.[16] His ideal, moreover, was an alliance of small shareholder and big capitalist, not rural artisan and family business. A critic of a supposed lack of dynamism in the French bourgeoisie, Aynard denounced Méline's ruralism in the name of big business, industrial progress and the French Revolution.[17]

Elwitt sees Aynard as a participant in a Le Playist consensus concerned with managing working-class discontent. He was certainly involved in Le Playist organisations. But his interpretation of the doctrine was liberal. It was enough for the employer to try to avoid lay-offs in difficult times for the 'industrial family' to become a reality. Aynard's idea of social reform did not go beyond the protection of child labour – adults, male or female, were responsible individuals whose right to work could not be restricted. Aynard condemned both the solidarist Paul Deschenel and the Catholic reformer De Mun in the name of liberalism.[18] Democracy and mass education, said Aynard, made possible a classless society in which the elite would be renewed by merit. Social mobility was the only remedy for working-class discontent.[19]

That the dominant conservative group in one of the most populous departments in France should have retained its commitment to liberalism is in itself a significant exception to the Lebovics thesis. There were other examples in the rest of France. Léon Say, of the Rouen sugar family, was one who remained devoted to liberalism. Another was the Roubaix cotton manufacturer Eugène Motte. Like Aynard, Motte kept his distance from Catholic integrism, preferring to confine religion to private life. These examples are all the more significant because Motte and Say played a significant part in the Progressiste movement alongside Méline, an illustration of the depth of disagreement within the

---

[16] D. Gordon, 'Liberalism and socialism in the Nord: Eugène Motte and Republican politics in Roubaix, 1898–1912', *French History* 2 (1989), 312–43.

[17] Aynard, *Discours 1889 à 1893*, 17 November 1892, 4–5; *Discours prononcés à la Chambre des députés pendant la législature de 1893 à 1913* (undated), speech of 25 June 1896, 541–3.

[18] Elwitt, *The Third Republic Defended*, 236; Jauffret, 'Quelques grands bourgeois lyonnaises', 114–28.

[19] Aynard, *Discours 1889 à 1893*, speech of 17 November 1892, 195–7; Aynard, *Discours 1893 à 1913*, 25 June, 1896, 530–6.

movement over questions of political economy. Indeed, the Méline tariff had taken account of such divergences by making important concessions to free traders. It is difficult then to see protectionism as the cement of an hegemonic bloc.[20]

Neither was Progressisme in the Rhône the political arm of the dominant classes as a whole. Substantial sections of the bourgeoisie supported the Radical-Socialist Party. The strength of the latter was symbolised above all by Edouard Herriot's occupation of the mayoralty of Lyon from 1905 until 1957, apart from temporary deposition during the Second World War. Herriot's political awakening in the Dreyfus Affair illustrates perfectly the complex motives which determined the political allegiances of the French bourgeoisie. It is impossible to disentangle the material and ideal interests which led him, as a young lycée professor, deeply committed to the belief that it was the duty of an intellectual elite to guide the people, to condemn the Philistinism of the antiDreyfusards. In the Ligue des Droits de l'Homme Herriot found like-minded professors, lawyers and doctors. By the 1930s the more established professions, especially lawyers and doctors, leaned more to the right. Still, however, Radicalism retained the allegiance of the less secure professions, such as *instituteurs* and pharmacists. Similarly, the wealthiest businessmen were loyal to the right, but many smaller employers supported the Radicals, again for a mixture of reasons. In smaller towns bosses had long battled with the clergy over issues such as Sunday working. For such people anticlericalism represented much more than a tool for manipulation of the masses; it was part of the way in which they defined themselves.[21]

Thus a large proportion of the Lyonnais bourgeoisie, as in France as a whole, was beyond the reach of the right. Furthermore, the pro-Radical bourgeoisie had its own views of the social question, shaped again by the seamlessness of material and ideal interests. Many Radicals believed that the best way to relieve working-class discontent was through democracy, *lay* education, social mobility and ultimately the abolition of the salariat. Léon Bourgeois's doctrine of solidarism modified but did not overturn this wisdom: the role of the state was to remove obstacles to individual

---

[20] D. Gordon, 'Liberalism and Socialism in the Nord'; J. Garrigues, 'Léon Say: un libéral sous la Troisième République', *Revue historique* 579 (1991), 119–41; M. Smith, *Tariff Reform in France, 1860–1900: The Politics of Economic Interest* (Cornell, 1980), 196–235.

[21] Serge Berstein, *Edouard Herriot, ou la République en personne* (1985), 36–40; Serge Berstein, 'La Politique sociale des Républicains', in *Le Modèle républicain*, ed. Serge Berstein and Odile Rudelle (1992), 189–208; Judith Stone, *Bourgeois Reform in France* (1984); Sabine Jessner, 'Edouard Herriot in Lyons: some aspects of his rôle as Mayor', in *From Ancien Régime to Popular Front*, ed. C. K. Warner (New York and London, 1969).

mobility. This was the kind of Radicalism espoused by Herriot. His municipality endeavoured to further individual enterprise by investing in infrastructural projects such as the Bron aerodrome and the Port Rambaud. His social welfare measures protected those unable to make their way in the market economy and provided opportunities for workers to rent cheap housing. Significantly, however, his plans to build a new hospital led to a storm of accusations from conservatives, who were equally fearful of socialism, that he was undermining the charitable activity of the Church. So in spite of the fundamental hostility of Herriot to socialism, he was divided from Catholic conservatives by his belief that only the action of the *secular* state could solve the social problem.

Aynard's optimistic liberal-conservatism was also contested on its right. The *Nouvelliste*, a daily newspaper founded in 1884, remained within the monarchist tradition (though it professed neutrality on the question of the regime). In terms of economic doctrine and antipathy to socialism the *Nouvelliste*'s ideas were indistinguishable from those of the Progressistes. It differed in its suspicion of democracy and in a snobbish contempt for republican parvenus. Unlike the Progressistes, who separated religious and economic spheres, the *Nouvelliste* combined the same attachment to classical liberalism with the integrist view that religion should suffuse all aspects of life, reconciling the two in the belief that Adam Smith had merely discovered the laws through which God regulated the world. The *Nouvelliste* therefore denounced the Progressistes for their lukewarm support of the Church. This was all the more serious because the *Nouvelliste*, thanks to the support of the clergy, built up a large circulation. The Progressistes were never able to establish a newspaper able to compete with it, even in the interwar period, which was one reason why religious issues remained central to the political agenda.[22]

To the right of the *Nouvelliste* (although increasingly indistinguishable) were the heirs of Legitimism, who combined Catholic integrism with an antiliberalism inspired by a conservative social Catholicism. They reacted to the victory of the republicans in the 1870s by forming a network of non-political organisations. These included the Catholic University (1877), the Association catholique des patrons lyonnais (1871) and De Mun's Œuvre des cercles catholiques d'ouvriers (1871) which protected a few healthy working-class islands from the socialist contagion. These organisations used the immense institutional power of the Church to influence social and political life. The ability to maintain power in unfavourable circumstances was illustrated by the career of the

---

[22] L. Vaucelles, *Le Nouvelliste de Lyon et la défense religieuse, 1879–1889* (1971).

lawyer Charles Jacquier (1848–1928). A one-time Legitimist, he combined involvement in Action française with devotion to the cause of the
Church. He became doyen of the Faculté catholique de droit, and, in
1925, president of the powerful Rhône branch of the Fédération national
catholique (FNC).[23] This was part of a restoration of the influence of the
long-moribund Legitimist tradition in Lyonnais politics in the late 1920s.
Another product of the 1880s was the agricultural association, l'Union
du sud-est (USE). Far from merging with or even tolerating Republican
elites, the Catholic landowners who sponsored it aimed to integrate the
peasantry into a Catholic and hierarchical society.[24] In this their aim was
identical to that of similar organisations in Brittany which endeavoured
to isolate peasants from the invasive republican state.[25]

Progressisme and the masses

Just as Progressisme failed to unite the elites, so it had limited success in
establishing 'hegemony' over the masses – not just over the left, but even
over its own supporters. Lebovics maintains that protectionism was
coupled with ideological idealisation of small property to bind the
peasantry and lower middle class to the emergent bourgeois bloc. There
can be no doubt that *some* sections of the elites pursued such a strategy,
and in many cases it may have been successful. The problem however
was that other conservative groups combined material interest and lay or
clerical values in conflicting ways. The result was to reinforce the
divisions of the right and to facilitate the development of autonomous
movements of rank-and-file conservatives.

In France as a whole the means by which conservatives won mass
support varied widely, but nowhere could it be said, without qualification, that the elites had inculcated a body of ruling ideas into their
supporters. In some areas Catholicism was essential to the right. In
Maine-et-Loire nobles and peasants shared both Catholicism and
memories of the Vendée rebellion against the French Revolution. But
conservatism there was not dependent on the nobility – indeed where
nobles were numerous the left often prospered. Rather the right
flourished in areas where peasant sociability had been channelled into
Catholic organisations. Peasants voted for nobles only as long as they
remained the best defenders of religion, and bought into the dominant

---

[23] Ponson, *Les Catholiques lyonnais*, 19–51.
[24] Gilbert Garrier, 'L'Union de sud-est des syndicats agricoles avant 1914', *Mouvement
social* 67 (1969), 17–28; Garrier, *Paysans du Lyonnais*, 518–22.
[25] S. Berger, *Peasants against Politics: Rural Organisation in Brittany, 1911–1967* (Cambridge, Mass., 1972).

ideology only to the extent that it matched their own interests. In the interwar period some peasants in the Cholet area of the department were to turn to the left-wing Christian democracy represented by the *Jeune république*, for this movement was able to combine Catholicism with an economic programme more in tune with peasant aspirations.[26] In the Hérault and Gard departments, as Gérard Cholvy has shown, right-wing voting was most likely in areas where Catholics were involved in a long-term struggle with Protestantism for control of political and social life. Catholic nobles were able to exploit these conflicts, particularly through charitable organisations, but they had not created them. Here too the 1920s were to reveal, with the progress of Christian democracy, how conditional the loyalty of the peasants and workers to the nobles had been.[27] In other areas of France secular values were more important to the right than Catholicism. Republicans had in the 1870s won small producers with promises of railways and market opportunities. The market had in turn been linked to republican education by the notion that it provided the key to material success and social mobility.[28] Where republicans shifted to the right – often they were to form the nucleus of the Alliance démocratique – their conservatism crystallised around defence of status, future prospects and the lay values traditionally associated with Republicanism.[29] Thus in both clerical and anticlerical cases conservative supporters had developed their own stake in the 'dominant ideologies', thereby limiting the freedom of the elites. This became evident at the time of the Ralliement in 1992–3. Through the Ralliement the Church intended to encourage monarchists to accept the Republic and thereby make common cause with defenders of order within the regime. This goal was not easy to realise. For example, in the Pas-de-Calais the moderate anticlerical republican Charles Jonnart, a future founder of the Alliance démocratique, initially welcomed the

---

[26] Jean-Luc Marais, 'Pourquoi le Maine-et-Loire n'est-il pas devenu républicain au début de la IIIe République?' *Annales de Bretagne* 99 (1992), 441–54; Jean-Luc Marais, 'La Défence de l'Anjou chrétien', in *Le Diocèse d'Angers* ed. François Lebrun (1981); Jean-Luc Marais, *Les Sociétés d'hommes: histoire d'une sociabilité du 18e siècle à nos jours, Anjou, Maine, Touraine* (Vauchretiene, 1986), 139–46, 163–6.

[27] Gérard Cholvy, 'Religion et politique en Languedoc mediterranéen et Roussillon à l'époque contemporaine', in *Droite et gauche de 1789 à nos jours* (Montpellier, 1975), 33–74.

[28] Elwitt, *The Making of the Third Republic*; Berstein, 'La Politique sociale des républicains'.

[29] The Alliance démocratique candidate in a Senate election in the Gironde, a businessman, stated: 'As the son of a worker, educated in the communal school, then as a scholarship student at the *lycée*, I have contracted a debt towards our democratic and republican institutions, to which I am firmly attached' (E. Ginestous, *Histoire politique de Bordeaux* (Bordeaux, 1945)). S. Berstein, 'La Culture républicaine dans la première moitié du XXe siècle', in *Le Modèle républicain*, ed. Berstein and Rudelle, 167–9.

Ralliement, and even declared his willingness to contemplate the presence of the Christian Brothers in state schools. A rank-and-file reaction forced him to change his mind. The Ralliement foundered in Catholic areas for analogous reasons. Formerly royalist constituencies certainly regarded socialism as a threat, but to religion and community as well as property. They could not believe that acceptance of the anticlerical Republic would help them to defend their way of life.[30]

Again the Rhône throws a particularly interesting light on the complex mixture of material and ideal interests that determined mass support for the right. In the previously cited examples there was a clear division between clerical suspicion of the Republic and anticlerical republican conservatism. Aynard, however, sought to marry Republicanism and Catholicism. Like many Progressiste leaders he was a practising Catholic and favoured toleration of all faiths. He went further in his sponsorship of private Catholic schools which preached republican ideas of 'promotion sociale'.[31] His goal was to create an antisocialist front by reconciling Catholics and republicans, but on a basis very different from that described by Lebovics. The effect was therefore to exacerbate the divisions of conservatism. Aynard had in fact created a parallel route to social mobility which depended on Catholic rather than lay values. So a white-collar worker who believed he owed his status to having obeyed the Church's strictures against the cabaret was unlikely to feel that alliance with anticlericals would protect him from socialist levelling. This made Aynard a prisoner of his ideological strategies. He responded positively to the Ralliement and was one of a small band of Catholics to espouse the Dreyfusard cause and to vote for Waldeck-Rousseau in 1899. Yet as Dreyfusardism turned into an assault on Catholic education, Aynard had no choice but to join the opposition and to fight the separation of church and state.[32] Here again there were parallels in other parts of France. Eugène Motte in the Nord built an alliance with the lower-middle-class groups by combining religion with liberal and Republican ideas of social mobility, expressed in the slogan 'God, small

---

[30] D. Shapiro, 'The Ralliement in the politics of the 1890s', St Antony's Papers, 13 (1962), 13–48; J. Vavasseur-Desperrier, 'L'Implantation locale d'un grand notable du Pas-de-Calais, Charles Célestin Jonnart (1857–1927)', Revue du Nord 288 (1990), 907–27; M. Schmidt, Alexandre Ribot: Odyssey of a Liberal in the Third Republic (The Hague, 1974); Christian Estève, 'Le Souvenir de la Révolution dans le Cantal. L'exemple du ralliement et son échec partiel', Revue historique 187 (1992), 391–417; Cholvy, 'Religion et politique', pp. 68–9.

[31] Aynard, Discours 1893 à 1913, speech of 24 June, 1910, (247–69); Ponson, Les Catholiques lyonnaises, 106, 130–4; Marc du Pouget, 'Laurent Bonnevay, un notable libéral et social', in Cent ans de catholicisme social, ed. J.-D. Durand et al., 163–4.

[32] J.-M. Mayeur, 'Les Catholiques Dreyfusards', Revue historique 261 (1978); G. Laperrière, La Séparation à Lyon (1904–1908) (Lyon, 1973).

business and liberty', but it was split apart by a revival of anticlericalism in 1910.[33]

Aynard's difficulties underline the conditional nature of mass support for Progressisme in the Rhône. This question will be dealt with more fully in the two chapters which follow. Suffice it for the moment to note that conservative voters, in spite of apparent passivity, were never fully incorporated into the Progressiste bloc. This was most evident in those parts of the department where landowners and priests remained powerful. In the Monts du Lyonnais peasants voted for Progressistes in parliamentary elections only because the arrangement of constituency boundaries gave them little chance of electing candidates more sympathetic to their views. In local contests they voted for crypto-royalists or later the Action libérale populaire (ALP). In the Beaujolais, in a conflict which resembled that between 'blues' and 'whites' in Brittany, the urban republican right of Villefranche struggled for supremacy with an aristocratic rural conservatism which preferred the ALP. Aynard struck a deeper chord among the relatively prosperous Catholic peasant proprietors of the Lyonnais Plateau. His blend of liberalism and Catholicism had greater appeal in an area where religious values seemed to preserve wealthier peasants from land subdivision, permitting them to take advantage of growing market opportunities. A similar argument can be applied to conservative white-collar workers of Lyon, where, as we shall see, ideas about social mobility were particularly important in the silk industry. But even in Lyon and on the plateau, support for Progressisme remained dependent on economic prosperity and the Church's willingness to tolerate the political primacy of liberalism.

Furthermore, from the 1890s a more popular conservatism began to emerge, usually leaning more towards authoritarian-populism than to the constitutional-popular right. This was made possible partly by the problematic relationship between the Catholic church and the Lyonnais elites. There is some truth in Lebovics's contention that the Ralliement should be seen as an attempt to unite the propertied classes, but once again shared antisocialism was insufficient to create a deeper community of ideas. The Church did not oppose socialism simply because it feared for its wealth. The power of the Church rested to just as great an extent on resisting the secularising thrust of the left. So many Catholics saw the Ralliement as part of a drive to return the de-Christianised popular classes to the Catholic fold. They linked acceptance of the democratic Republic with the endorsement in the encyclical *Rerum Novarum* of social reform and Christian trade unions, which it regarded both as a

[33] D. M. Gordon, 'Liberalism and socialism in the Nord'.

means of assuaging the grievances of the proletariat and of demonstrating the Church's concern with their plight. Together these changes paved the way for the Christian democratic groups which sprang up in many parts of France during the 1890s, and which fed into the popular nationalist movements of the turn of the century.[34] In Finistère, for example, Christian democracy enabled the clergy to take over leadership of the peasantry, alarming nobles and the Church hierarchy with their demagogic antisemitism.[35] In Paris the shift to the right of the shopkeeper movement described by Philip Nord owed much to the mobilisation of formerly passive Catholic traders by the Catholic populist Union nationale of abbé Garnier.[36] Lyon too was a leading centre of Christian democracy.[37] And here too the 'nouvelles couches catholiques' often moved from Christian democrat groups like the Union nationale into the nationalist movements which flourished at the time of the Dreyfus Affair.[38]

Nationalism varied in complexion from the proto-fascist Grand occident de France to the Ligue de la patrie française, which combined populism with affinities to the constitutional-elitist right. After the Dreyfus Affair, as the separation of Church and state dominated political life, the energies of many nationalists were diverted into the more moderate and elitist ALP. The same dialectic of popular mobilisation and elite attempts to profit from it lay behind all of these movements. On the one hand, the nationalists won support from groups which combined antisocialism with a struggle to bite into the privileges of the elites (in other words they pursued a strategy of 'dual closure'). The Church's support for trade unions found favourable ground thanks to the growth of white-collar employment, and Catholic trade union leaders like Auguste Gruffaz doubled as radical right activists.[39] On the other hand, the search of antirepublican Catholic elites, resentful of their exclusion from political power, for popular appeal provided a significant impetus for nationalism. Representatives of wealthy Catholic families like the Lucien-Bruns were present in most nationalist movements, as

[34] J.-M. Mayeur, *L'Abbé Lémire* (1966); Christian Ponson, *Les Catholiques lyonnais* (Lyon, 1979); Estève, 'Le Souvenir de la Révolution'.

[35] S. Berger, *Peasants against Politics*, 42–54.

[36] P. Nord, *Paris Shopkeepers and the Politics of Resentment* (Princeton, 1986); the same can perhaps be said of L. Berlanstein, 'Parisian white collar employees and nationalism in the *Belle époque*', in *Nationhood and Nationalism in France from Boulangism to the Great War*, ed. R. Tombs (1991).

[37] Ponson, *Les Catholiques lyonnaises*, 62–7.

[38] Stephen Wilson, 'Catholic Populism at the time of the Dreyfus Affair. The Union nationale', *Journal of Contemporary History* 9 (1975), 667–705.

[39] Stephen Wilson, 'The antisemitic riots of 1898 in France', *Historical Journal* 19 (1976), 787–806; Ponson, *Les Catholiques lyonnais*.

well as the ALP.[40] Some of them were attracted by Méline's notion of an
alliance of bourgeoisie and peasantry. At the turn of the century the
cotton manufacturers of the Monts du Beaujolais, in the face of the
socialist threat and in a bid to avoid hours regulation, began to disperse
their production into the countryside, cultivating a passéist myth of an
harmonious bucolic society.[41] The role played by silk merchant-
manufacturers, dependent on artisans for production, such as Victor
Perret (senior) in the ALP suggests here too a fear for the future of petty
production.[42] The attitude of the Progressiste elites towards nationalism
was more complex. They feared its radicalism and perhaps also its
distrust of unrestrained industrialisation. Even Gurnaud, leader of the
relatively moderate La Patrie, saw the Progressistes as 'reactionary'. Yet
nationalism presented a challenge of which the Progressistes were
obliged to take account. The Progressiste deputy Gourd was seen at one
meeting of La Patrie. In December 1902 Aynard fused the Progressiste
L'Express de Lyon with the journal of La Patrie.[43] Although the marriage
was troubled and short-lived, it revealed that the pre-eminence of
Progressisme on the right was insecure.

In view of these difficulties it is not surprising that the antisocialist front
of the 1890s was shattered by the Dreyfus Affair and the subsequent
revival of anticlericalism.[44] Moreover, it was around the issues of this
period that the conservative parties which dominated the right until
1940 were formed. The Fédération républicaine, Alliance démocratique
and ALP were all created in this period, as were the main parties of the
left. This was another reason why the religious conflict remained
important in the 1930s. The right did from time to time rediscover
unity, but there was at best an indirect relationship to the strength of the
challenge from the left. All sections of the right and many Radicals (but
not all of the bourgeoisie) rallied to governmental use of force against
strikers. But this does not prove the existence of 'hegemony' or
'consensus'. Even in times of deep crisis Catholics and laïques sometimes
had difficulty in recognising each other as conservatives. Thus Clemenceau was able to throw the right into confusion by alleging a secret

---

[40] AN F[7] 13 256, for example fifty royalists attended a meeting of La Patrie in March
1901.
[41] J.-P. Houssel, La Région de Roanne et le Beaujolais textil face à l'économie moderne, 2 vols.
(Lille, 1979), I, 147–50.
[42] Ponson, Les Catholiques lyonnais, 40–2.
[43] AN F[7] 13 256; Laperrière, La Séperation à Lyon, 87–92.
[44] G. Le Béguec and J. Prévotat, 'L'Eveil à la modernité politique', in Sirinelli, Histoire des
droites, I, 213–89; M. Winock 'Le mythe fondateur: l'affaire Dreyfus', in Le Modèle
républicain, ed. Berstein and Rudelle 131–45.

alliance of CGT and ALP in 1906 – a year of considerable industrial unrest.[45] In the Nord in 1910 Eugène Motte saw the destruction of his alliance with the Radicals, thanks to a resurgence of anticlericalism.[46] The perceived weakness of the established right encouraged some rank-and-file conservatives to take matters into their own hands, as the emergence of nationalism and Christian democracy shows. Before 1914, however, the radical right remained relatively marginal and the Republic was in no immediate danger of collapse. This was not because of a compromise between bourgeoisie and petty producers, cemented by protectionism. It survived because of relative prosperity, the left's powerlessness and the judicious use of force.

Conservatism and society in the 1920s

The right emerged triumphant from the elections of 1919.[47] The system of departmental lists and proportional representation used in that year encouraged the formation of broad coalitions. Since the socialists and the Radicals were deeply divided, this placed the right in an advantageous position. The Alliance démocratique took the initiative of proposing a 'Bloc national', which would stretch from the ALP and Fédération to the Radicals and those socialists still attached to the wartime Union sacrée. A compromise on the religious question formed part of the Bloc's programme, and suggested that fear of Bolshevism had at last made possible elite unity. In parliament in 1920 the deputy Pierre Forgeot, although not a believer himself, urged Briand to use the Church as a weapon against Bolshevism.[48]

Unity, however, was far from complete. On 7 November, on the initiative of their new national president, Edouard Herriot, the Radicals withdrew from the Bloc, although some departmental federations still participated in its lists. Elsewhere, unable to accept the Bloc's commitment to laïcité, dissident conservative lists were organised. The Bloc proved as incapable of organising itself as a coherent force in parliament as it had in the country. Partisans of the Bloc were spread over four groups. The Gauche républicaine démocratique (96), Républicaines de gauche (61) and Action républicaine et sociale (46) were linked to the Alliance démocratique. The Entente républicaine démocratique (ERD)

---

[45] B. F. Martin, 'The formation of the Action Libérale Populaire. An example of party formation in the French Third Republic', *French Historical Studies* 9 (1976), 660–89.
[46] Gordon, 'Liberalism and socialism in the Nord'.
[47] Jean-Marie Mayeur, *La Vie politique sous la Troisième République, 1870–1940* (1984), 251–69.
[48] H. W. Paul, *The Second Ralliement: The Rapprochement betweem Church and State in France in the Twentieth Century* (Washington, 1967), 58.

(183) grouped Catholic deputies close to the ALP and the Fédération, along with nationalists like Maurice Barrès. The Fédération was divided between liberals like Auguste Isaac, reformists like Laurent Bonnevay and Christian democrats.[49] The right wing of the Bloc was particularly discontented, for it never gained the influence it expected, and denounced a succession of governments for their unwillingness to cut ties with the Radicals. The first administrations, led by Millerand and Leygues, were based on groups from the ERD to the Radicals, but came to grief over reparations. Subsequent administrations inclined more to the centre. This caused conflict within the ERD, where Laurent Bonnevay was viewed by some as a traitor for having joined the left-leaning Briand government (January 1922–January 1923). Raymond Poincaré, prime minister for the rest of the life of the parliament, was also criticised for combining a nationalist policy, particularly evident in the occupation of the Ruhr, with a domestic policy more favourable to the Radicals. In view of these tensions it is not surprising that the right fought the elections of 1924 in a rather more dispersed order than it had those of 1919. The socialists and Radicals, in contrast, had formed the Cartel des gauches. So this time an electoral system that rewarded broad alliances permitted the left to win a majority.

The sorry tale of the Cartel's attempts to grapple with an apparently intractable financial crisis has often been told.[50] Herriot's adminstration lasted ten months before being overthrown by the Senate. Over the next fifteen months six governments came and went in rapid succession. More important from the present perspective was the right's response. In the short term it sought to contain the radicalism of the Cartel by working with centre politicians like Joseph Caillaux. Most conservatives also agreed that the best way to undermine the Cartel was to portray it as a matrix of socialism and revolution, and thus to detach the Radicals from the Cartel. In order to co-ordinate the right, Alexandre Millerand created the Ligue républicaine nationale in November 1924. Beyond this, however, strategies differed, and the hardening of divisions within the right was reflected in a certain revival of party organisations. The Fédération républicaine became a more activist organisation when Louis Marin succeeded Auguste Isaac as president in 1924. Under Marin the Fédération shifted to the right, and was therefore able to absorb the electorate of the ALP, the one prewar party of the right that did not revive. The Fédération sought either dissolution of parliament and new elections, or failing that a

[49] Mayeur, La Vie politique, 291.
[50] Jean-Noël Jeannenney, Leçon d'histoire pour une gauche au pouvoir: la faillite du Cartel (1975); François de Wendel en république: l'argent et le pouvoir (1976).

'Union nationale' majority stretching from the Radicals to themselves. This strategy was viewed with some suspicion by the centre right, out of a republican aversion to use of the President's right of dissolution. To Union nationale the moderate right preferred an alliance of Radicals and centre-right ('concentration républicaine), which would combine antisocialism with republicanism and secularism. The centre-right too became a little more firmly organised, for the term 'Alliance démocratique', out of use since 1914, reappeared in 1927. Meanwhile, a new Christian democratic party, the PDP, was founded in 1924. It too preferred a coalition of centres to a right-wing bloc. In the event, it was the Union nationale that won out with the return of Poincaré in July 1926. But in spite of the electorate's approval of this solution in the general elections of 1928, the roots of the crisis of the 1930s were already present.

During the 1920s the structural imbalance in the French economy had been aggravated. The economy grew rapidly. The development of new large engineering, electrical and chemical plant threw into even sharper relief the continuing importance of small producers.[51] This posed with greater urgency the problems which had long troubled the right regarding the nature of industrialisation and the place of workers, peasants and small entrepreneurs in French society. Historians are divided on the question of whether or not small production constituted a barrier to growth. But at the time businessmen such as Louis Renault certainly thought that it did.[52]   Similar views were current in the electricity industry, where they were propagated by managers like Auguste Detœuf of Alsthom and Ernest Mercier of the electrical giant CGE. In 1926 Mercier and Detœuf set up Redressement français to promote 'neocapitalism'. This involved concentration, integration, rational use of labour and raw materials, high consumption, disciplined competition by means of ententes, freer trade and an end to state protection of small business.[53] Workers would be won over by prosperity and social reform; small producers by rural public works.[54]

---

[51] François Caron, *An Economic History of Modern France* (1979), especially 230–1; T. Kemp, 'French economic performance: some new views reconsidered', *European History Quarterly* 15 (1985), 474–5.

[52] P. Fridenson, *Histoire des Usines Renault I: Naissance de la grande entreprise*, (1972), 133–4.

[53] R. F. Kuisel, *Ernest Mercier, French Technocrat* (Los Angeles, 1967); Kuisel, 'Auguste Detœuf, conscience of French industry', *International Review of Social History* 20 (1975), 149–74; Kuisel, *Capitalism and the State in Modern France: Renovation and Economic Management in the Twentieth Century* (Cambridge, 1981).

[54] Kuisel, *Mercier*, chapter 4; P. Fridenson, 'L'Idéologie des grands constructeurs dans l'entre-deux-guerres', *Mouvement social* 81 (1972), 52–68; S. Schweitzer, *De l'Engrenage à la chaîne: les Usines Citroën, 1913–1935* (Lyon, 1983), 86.

For Monnet neocapitalists were an elite standing outside the stalemate society.[55] We shall see, however, that although the influence of Redressement itself was limited, similar reforming ideas were present in many sections of society, creating a considerable potential for conflict. This was all the more true because the strategies of Redressement contrasted with efforts of other groups to recruit small producers as allies against Bolshevism. This strategy had been promoted by some in the Bloc national, and resulted in a system of tax exemptions and cheap credit for artisans. Small producers were also exempted from the Eight Hour Law of 1919.[56] These measures did not stabilise the regime. Rather the attempt to create a 'stalemate society' engendered conflict, particularly as big business resented the unfair advantages of artisans.[57]

Furthermore, religious divisions remained entangled with economic conflicts. Mercier, like many electrical employers, leaned towards the anticlerical lay centre-right and even the Radicals.[58] As a Protestant married to a niece of Captain Dreyfus, he was almost by necessity on the advanced wing of the bourgeoisie.[59] Many within the Fédération, on the other hand, were opposed to Redressement on both economic and ideological grounds. The party included a number of bosses of insurance companies, mining, heavy metallurgical and textile concerns, all with an historical connection to the aristocracy and therefore to Catholic royalism – the ancestor of the Fédération. The same industries also had relatively high labour costs, or in the case of the textile industry a difficult market position which pushed up its marginal costs. Religion and material interest together reinforced their opposition to social reform.[60] Such pressures helped push the Fédération to the right in the 1920s. It would, however, be a mistake to see a simple dichotomy

---

[55] Monnet, *Refaire la république*, 172.

[56] Some of those responsible for such measures, such as Clémentel, saw organisation of small producers as a step to modernisation. Mere preoccupation with small producers did not necessarily imply a Malthusian outlook. S. Zdatny, *The Politics of Survival: Artisans in Twentieth Century France* (Oxford, 1990), chapter 1.

[57] Kevin Passmore, 'Business, corporatism and the crisis of the French Third Republic. The example of the Silk industry in Lyon', *Historical Journal* 38 (1995), 959–87.

[58] The Alliance démocratique programme of 1927 combined the usual concern with small producers with a call for increased production as the best social policy, encouragement of business mergers and industrial rationalisation (D. G. Wileman, 'P. E. Flandin and the Alliance républicain démocratique', *French History* 4 (1990), 169).

[59] M. Burns, *Dreyfus, a Family Affair, 1789–1945* (1991).

[60] Irvine, *French Conservatism in Crisis*, 19–21; D. Higgs, *Nobles in Nineteenth Century France* (Baltimore and London, 1987), chapter 4; Jeanneney, *de Wendel*, 445. The same kinds of employers also dominated the peak employers' association, the CGPF: I. Kolboom, *La Revanche des patrons: le patronat français face au Front populaire* (1986), 67–104; H. W. Ehrmann, *Organized Business in France* (Princeton, 1957), 16–29.

between Catholic suspicion of modernisation and republican faith in progress. Many anticlericals were suspicious of rationalisation, while in the Rhône ideas resembling those of neocapitalists developed in association with social Catholicism.

Thus although the violent struggles of the Separation period had subsided the clerical/anticlerical division remained an important structurant of political life. There was, moreover, a big expansion in Catholic education between the wars. Paradoxically the more conciliatory attitude of the Church to the Republic also ensured that religious conflict remained central to politics.[61] In the 1920s the Church abandoned the myth that a fundamentally Catholic population could be brought back to the true path by elimination of Jews, Protestants and Freemasons. The hierarchy now felt that it would have to defend its interests within the Republic through mass pressure groups like the FNC, founded in 1924 to oppose the anticlerical measures of the Cartel. By the beginning of the 1930s the FNC had lost some of its momentum, thanks to the fall of the Cartel, papal suspicion of its nationalism, and the fact that the Church was now more interested in working through the politically 'neutral' Action catholique. Now that the FNC ceased to offer a platform for Catholic nationalists like Philippe Henriot, Xavier Vallat and Victor Perret, they turned to the Fédération républicaine as an alternative means of mobilising the Catholic people. They were advantaged by the fact that the FNC had liberated the organisational resources of the Church, permitting Catholic populists to use the parish network for political purposes. Difficulties were compounded by the fact that even though it now accepted the Republic, the Church still insisted on unity of the faithful in religious matters and turned a blind eye to political divergences within its lay organisations. This provided Catholics who were suspicious of the Republic with organisational resources (as in the case of the previously mentioned Charles Jacquier). We shall see that in Lyon these developments made the Fédération more dependent than ever upon the Church, and provided a major reason for its move towards Catholic nationalism.[62]

The emergence of a mass Catholic movement also benefited Christian democrats, a development which increased conflict within the parishes

---

[61] G. Jacquemart, *Catholicisme* (1956), IV, 235; Paul, *The Second Ralliement*; N.-J. Chaline, *Des Catholiques normandes sous la Troisième république: crises, combats, renouveau* (Roanne, 1985). J.-C. Delbreil, *Centrisme et démocratie-chrétienne en France: le Parti démocrate populaire des origines au MRP* (1990), especially 174–87; J. McMillan, 'Catholicism and nationalism in France. The case of the Fédération nationale catholique, 1924–1939', in *Catholicism in Britain and France since 1789*, eds. N. Atkin and F. Tallet, (1996), 151–63.

[62] See pages 150–1.

and within the right. Specialist Catholic Action groups for workers and peasants (the JAC and JOC respectively) created in the late 1920s were another product of the hierarchy's new commitment to parish mobilisation, and also of the desire of some sections of the elites to use small producers as allies against socialism. But Catholic Action militants believed too that re-Christianisation depended upon demonstrating the efficacy of Catholic solutions to the problems of exploited social groups, and were sometimes ready to play down religious issues in order to reach them. Social Catholicism was therefore suspect to Catholic elites on both religious and social grounds. In the 1920s conflicts were relatively limited.[63] But in Brittany the Syndicats des cultivateurs-cultivants of abbé Mancel mobilised tenants and sharecroppers, to the annoyance of both landowners and the royalist Archbishop of Rennes.[64] In the Nord the CFTC was a source of concern to textile employers who sought its condemnation by the Pope.[65] Such tensions often lay behind the progress of the PDP, formed in 1925. Needless to say, the ambition of its founders to form a non-confessional reformist conservative party could not be achieved. The only alternative was to encroach on the terrain of the Fédération in departments such as Meurthe-et-Moselle, Finistère and the Nord.[66] The PDP itself won only a handful of seats, but it also enjoyed significant support in the left wing of the Fédération républicaine.[67]

Thus in the 1920s conservative politics remained as unstable as ever. Furthermore, the fact that professional and other forms of corporate organisation had been given a boost by the war economy had institutionalised religious conflict.[68] Redressement français was one of a host of such organisations formed in this period, from the Confédération générale de la production française (CGPF), through Chambers of Agriculture and Trades to non-economic pressure groups like veterans' associations and the FNC. Particularly significant is that these bodies crystallised within existing Catholic and lay networks. Redressement grew out of the solidarist tradition; specialist Catholic Action groups infiltrated a variety of professional bodies. The largely lay artisan

---

[63] *La Nation*, 15 January 1930; G. Gayet, 'L'Union du sud-est des syndicats agricoles' (mémoire de maîtrise, Lyon II, 1972), 75–8; A. Tardieu, *Sur la Pente* (1935), xxxvi.

[64] P. Barral, 'Les Syndicats bretons de cultivateurs-cultivants', *Mouvement social* 67 (1969), 147–71; Delbreil, *Centrisme et Démocratie-Chrétienne*, 244–6.

[65] M.Launey, *La CFTC. Origines et développement, 1919–1940* (1986), 109–206.

[66] Delbreil, *Centrisme et Démocratie chrétienne*; J.-C. Delbreil, 'Les Démocrates-chrétiens en Lorraine dans l'entre-deux-guerres', *Cahiers lorrains* 4 (1987), 419–47.

[67] Conflict with nationalists was one reason for the secession of the pro-PDP 'Groupe Pernot' in 1932. See Irvine, *French Conservatism in Crisis*, 59–60.

[68] C. S. Maier, *Recasting Bourgeois Europe: Stabilisation in France, Germany and Italy after World War One* (Princeton, 1975).

movement was disrupted by a Catholic and conservative tendency based on Alsace.[69] Thus the old constraints upon conservative politicians which resulted from the linkage of material interest with lay or Catholic values were reinforced by the growth of associations.[70] The complexity of the pressure groups with which the right had to reckon was in turn increased. The Radicals added to the problem as they gradually abandoned their role as guardians of the republican ideal in order to defend the interests of the (anticlerical) petty bourgeoisie.[71]

This was part of a wider crisis of the liberal state. Interest groups are not a danger to liberal democracy where they are well integrated with political parties.[72] But in interwar France an exceptionally incoherent body of organisations aimed to influence government policy in mutually contradictory ways. The parliamentary right, the main organisations of which had been formed during the Dreyfus Affair, was ill equipped to synthesise these conflicting interests.[73] Many conservatives were deeply suspicious of organisations intermediate between nation and state. This was particularly true of those who espoused Rosanvallon's 'liberalisme capacitaire'. It also, paradoxically, applied to those on the right wing of the Fédération who favoured corporatism, for they aimed to discipline rather than liberate the energies of the associations. Those, like the Christian democrats, who envisaged a genuine democratisation of social life were excluded from political power. More typical was André Tardieu who combined limited acceptance of professional associations with faith in rule by an enlightened elite. Tardieu also betrayed his suspicion of pluralism by ascribing the blame for social conflict to conspirators within the Radical Party. There was nevertheless some truth in the conviction that the growing preoccupation of the Radicals with special interests added to the crisis of parliament. The right in general believed that Radicalism owed its entrenchment in the machinery of state to manipulation of patronage and control over the 'mares stagnantes' created by *scrutin d'arrondissement*. It was also felt that the pivotal parliamentary position of the Radicals gave petty producers an undue influence on state policy. In 1919 Louis Renault had already asked whether the plethora of middlemen in French commerce was a

[69] Zdadtny, *Artisans*, 54–60.
[70] In the Lorraine leaders of the Fédération, such as Louis Marin and François de Wendel, were personally indifferent to Catholicism, but were nevertheless electorally dependent upon the Church (Jeanneney, *de Wendel*, 436–9).
[71] S. Berstein, *Histoire du Parti radical*, 2 vols. (1980, 1982).
[72] Juan B. Linz, 'Some notes toward a comparative study of fascism in sociological historical perspective', in *Fascism. A Reader's Guide*, ed. W. Laqueur (Berkeley, 1976), 40–1.
[73] J.-L. Pinol, '1919–1958. Le Temps des droites?' in *Histoire des droites*, I: 310.

consequence of the political system.[74] With their inability to decide between left and right the Radicals became the scapegoats for weaknesses in the Republican system that were in reality more general. Hostility to Radicalism, moreover, could in certain circumstances, spill over into antiparliamentarianism.

The ramifications of this crisis in the Rhône will be examined in detail in the following chapters. For the moment it is sufficient to note that the elections of 1919 had confirmed Progressiste domination of the right. Fédération members took the lion's share of places on a list which also included the Alliance démocratique, ALP and Independent Radicals. Aynard having died in 1913, leadership passed to his close associates, Auguste Isaac and Laurent Bonnevay. In public at least harmony reigned. In the unusual conditions of this election, seven out of twelve members of the conservative list were elected. With the exception of Fleury-Ravarin, who preferred the Républicains de gauche, all but one of them sat in the Chamber with the Catholics of the ERD. As heirs of Aynard's belief in toleration, Isaac and Bonnevay were well placed to serve as token Catholics in the ministries of Millerand and Briand in 1920. Isaac became Minister of Commerce, and played an important role in organising resistance to the strikes of May 1920. He ensured that a strike-breaking organisation, the Union civique, first created in Lyon, was imitated all over France. In Lyon the Union civique was supported by a broad range of political and social organisations from a variety of traditions. For Maurice Moissonier and André Boulmier these developments confirmed the emergence in the city of organised monopoly capitalism, which dominated the petty bourgeoisie and merged with the state.[75]

In reality, antisocialist unity had been as difficult to realise in the Rhône as in the rest of France. Not surprisingly in view of Herriot's hostility to the Bloc, Aynard's dream of an alliance with the Radicals in Lyon remained unrealised. In 1919 in spite of the best efforts of Weitz, president of the Comité républicain de commerce et de l'industrie, a Bloc list had proved impossible to bring about, thanks to the refusal of Herriot to accept the participation of Gourd.[76] Meanwhile conflict within the right continued. The social conservatism of Isaac and Gourd contrasted with Bonnevay's reformism. Business interests had manœuvred, unsuccessfully, to evict the latter from the conservative list.[77]

[74] Fridenson, *Histoire des usines Renault*, 133–4.
[75] Maurice Moissonnier and André Boulmier, 'La Bourgeoisie lyonnaise aux origines de l'Union civique de 1920?', *Cahiers d'histoire de l'institut de recherches marxistes* 4 (1980–1), 106–31.
[76] Gric, *Les Courants politiques*, 56–7; Berstein, *Edouard Herriot*, 69–75.
[77] Marc du Pouget, 'Laurent Bonnevay, un notable libéral et social', in *Cent ans de catholicisme social à Lyon et en Rhône-Alpes*, ed. J.-D. Durand *et al.* (1992), 116.

The gap between the two wings of Progressisme was increased by Isaac's preoccupation with demographic issues and by Gourd's belief in a strong presidency on the American model.[78] Although the main conservative groups were able to maintain unity for the elections of 1924, votes were lost to a 'Concentration républicaine' list which grouped moderate right-wingers and dissident Radicals. This was one reason for the total defeat of the right in the Rhône: not a single conservative was elected.

Latent tensions within the Lyonnais right became visible in the years after the elections of 1924, and will be examined in subsequent chapters. For the moment it is necessary to point out two aspects of this crisis. First, in the late 1920s the Fédération fell victim to internal division. Bonnevay became engaged in a running polemic with Marin, largely about the latter's allegedly negative attitude to the Locarno treaties. As a result Bonnevay ceased active involvement in the Fédération. More seriously, Auguste Isaac resigned as national leader of the Fédération after defeat in the elections of 1924. Isaac subsequently withdrew from political life in protest against the nationalism of his successor, Louis Marin. In Lyon a power struggle developed within the Fédération. On one side stood the new departmental president, François Peissel. He was a moderate who favoured the international policy of Briand, the conservative reformism of Tardieu and aspects of social Catholicism. In spite of this Peissel enjoyed the support of liberal grandees like Isaac. No doubt this was because Peissel was infinitely preferable to his rival, Victor Perret. The latter was an ally of Louis Marin, to whose hard line in international affairs Perret added an equally intransigent attitude to social reform and an ambiguity towards parliamentary democracy. Both Perret and Peissel, then, broke with the liberal tradition embodied in Isaac. By mid-1932 Perret's faction had established complete control over the Fédération.

The result, however, was that the Fédération saw its position of pre-eminence challenged by the Alliance démocratique and the PDP. From 1928, as Figure 2 reveals, the centre-right vote increased. A major reason was the desertion of moderate Fédération deputies such as Bonnevay (Tarare) and J.-B. Delorme (Givors) to the Alliance démocratique. Like the Fédération, the Alliance was a product of the Dreyfus Affair, grouping those moderate Republicans who had rallied to Waldeck-Rousseau's government of Republican Defence. Although Aynard had played a part in the formation of the Alliance, only a few individuals, such as the deputy Fleury-Ravarin, had been associated with it before the war.[79] Even Fleury-Ravarin was elected under the umbrella

---

[78] Ladous, 'Auguste Isaac', 131–58.
[79] G. Lachapelle, *L'Alliance démocratique* (1935).

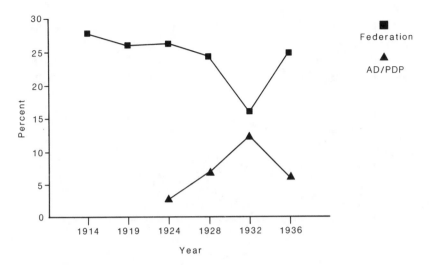

Figure 2   The Rhône: the rise of the centre-right, 1914–36

of the Fédération. But as the Fédération shifted to the right, sections of the liberal elites together with the anticlerical and progressive bourgeoisie turned to the Alliance démocratique. The latter developed especially in the 6th arrondissement where it took over the mantle of progressive conservatism from the Fédération. Alongside the lay centre-right there also emerged the new Christian democratic party, the PDP. Its Lyon branch was formed a few days after its founding conference in Paris, on 15 and 16 November 1924.[80] Although it never achieved the electoral success of the Alliance, the PDP too was to become a source of concern to the Fédération, not least because it enjoyed the support of Peissel.

The left

The emphasis in this book is upon the divisions of the right. This is not, however, to deny the importance of conflict between left and right. On the contrary, the very intensity of antisocialism encouraged competing conservative groups to impose their particular world-views on their rivals. This was all the more true because of the exclusion of much of the Catholic right from political power in the Third Republic. In this sense the Rhône represents a microcosm of France as a whole, for nationally too conservatives remained in a minority throughout the interwar period

[80] J. Raymond-Laurent, *Le Parti démocrate populaire* (Le Mans, 1965); J.-C. Delbreil, *Centrisme et démocratie chrétienne*, 23–35.

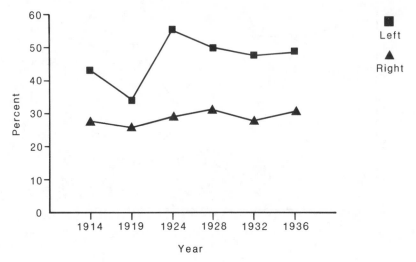

Figure 3   The Rhône: left and right shares of the registered electorate, 1914–36

(see Figure 3). In the Rhône, except in 1919, the right never won more than 33% of those eligible to vote, and never elected more than four or five of the department's twelve and later thirteen deputies. The right's performance on the municipal council of Lyon was equally poor. In 1935, its best year, it won only fourteen out of fifty-four seats. With the exceptions of Amplepuis and Cours all the smaller industrial towns were also held by the left. Only the Conseil général functioned intermittently as a counterweight to the left.[81]

Until 1936 the left in the Rhône was dominated by Radicalism and more particularly by Edouard Herriot. Three times prime minister and mayor of Lyon for half a century, Herriot provides a classic example of the way in which individuals could build a powerful position through accumulation of offices straddling legislature and executive. Small towns and the popular areas of Lyon provided the best electoral support for Radicalism, but it also had substantial backing in wealthy areas of the city, even winning the bourgeois 2nd and 6th arrondissements in the municipal elections of 1925. Radicalism also remained a force in some working-class areas, winning the seat of La Guillotière from the socialists

---

[81] Mainly because use of cantonal boundaries in local elections led to an overrepresentation of rural areas. In 1936 thirteen constituencies in the agglomeration represented an average of 10,874 electors, while twenty mainly rural cantons englobed an average of 4,961 voters.

in 1932 *législatives*. The Lyonnais Radical Party was distinguished in particular by possession of a dense network of committees, based particularly on the café society of the mixed popular quarters of the city – Herriot's own 1st arrondissement was typical. In the late 1930s membership figures of up to 8,000 were claimed in the 3rd arrondissement. These committees, in both town and countryside, were run above all by public-sector white-collar workers, shopkeepers and artisans. Although most professionals voted for the right, lawyers, doctors and professors were also prominent among the party's activists. Thus, unusually for the Radical Party, a powerful notable co-existed with a well-organised body of militants. The latter were usually some way to the left of Herriot, except perhaps in working-class Villeurbanne and La Guillotière, where the SFIO was the main opponent of Radicalism.

Tensions within Radicalism were increased by the further progress of socialism after the Great War. The SFIO had dominated the political life of Villeurbanne since the turn of the century, apart from a brief communist interlude. The key figure in the socialist hegemony was Dr Joly, elected mayor in 1925 and deputy in 1928. He was on the reformist wing of the party and deeply anticommunist. He found allies in other areas of Lyon, such as André Philip who was to win the 7th arrondissement from the Radicals in 1936. In 1928 the SFIO took over from the Radicals as the dominant party in the wine-growing Beaujolais, where it appealed to small proprietor wine-growers and sharecroppers suffering from falling prices. Local deputy Armand Chouffet was on the left of the party.

One of the principal aims of the right, perhaps *the* goal, was to detach the Radicals from the SFIO. French conservatives everywhere were perplexed by Radicalism, unable to comprehend why a party based on the property-owning middle classes should resist participation in a right-wing bloc. Herriot presented an even more difficult puzzle because in 1926 he had abandoned the Cartel strategy he had pursued since 1919. He concluded that the socialists could not be relied upon to commit themselves wholeheartedly to left unity, and that in future left-wing governments would have to be more respectful of financial orthodoxy. Hence in 1926 he agreed, in order to save the Franc, to participate in Poincaré's Union nationale government. In Lyon (as in the rest of France) this earned Herriot the hostility both of many Radical activists and of the SFIO. The latter presented him with a particular problem, for socialists were in a majority on the municipal council. From 1926 he was obliged to use his immense personal popularity to fight off socialist attempts to oust him from the mayoralty. The municipal elections of 1929 confirmed the balance of forces on the council and Herriot was re-elected mayor only with the 'malevolent neutrality' of the socialists. Matters came to a head in 1931 when, after a quarrel over the designation of delegates for a senate election, Herriot resigned his seat on the council. Placing himself at the head of a Radical list in the socialist stronghold of the 3rd arrondissement, he was triumphantly re-elected. He now had an impregnable majority on the Conseil municipal. Thanks to this triumph he returned to the presidency of the national party.

The right, naturally, was delighted with this breach with the socialists. But in fact it had been a victory for the policy of 'Radicalism alone'. Herriot resisted all efforts to replicate the Union nationale in the Rhône, and indeed had resigned from the City Council partly in order to avoid reliance on right-wing votes. Those who favoured Union nationale were forced to leave the party – Etienne Grammont in 1928 and Charles Lambert in 1932. As national President of the party, Herriot refused formal alliance with the socialists for the 1932 election campaign, but invited them to rally to his 'Republican programme' and categorically rejected an alliance with the right. In the Rhône republican discipline functioned satisfactorily in all six seats where there was a *ballotage*.[82]

The right was mystified by such behaviour. In 1933 after Radicals and socialists had combined to defeat the right in a municipal by-election, *L'Union républicaine* commented 'once again we see the Radical-Socialists, partisans of property and wealth, allied to socialists who openly declare themselves to be against property and for the International'.[83] Many conservatives felt that in order to separate Radicals and socialists they had simply to make greater efforts to demonstrate that the latter were enemies of property. This belief showed a fundamental misconception of the nature of French politics. Bourgeois Radicals *were* antisocialist, but there was no reason why this should have led them to join a right-wing alliance. On the contrary, they adhered to a set of Republican values which were conceived partly as an antidote to socialism.

Conclusion

A similar failure to perceive the complexities of French politics is shared by some modern historians of the right. The example of the Rhône suggests that the late Third Republic was not characterised by an

---

[82] The previous paragraphs are based on numerous press reports, particularly in *Lyon républicain* and on Berstein, *Edouard Herriot*; Berstein, *Histoire du Parti radical*; M. Soulié, *La Vie politique d'Edouard Herriot* (1962); E. Herriot, *Jadis* (1948).

[83] *L'Union républicaine*, 22 January 1933.

alliance of property owners around protectionism, ruralism and anti-socialism. Although antisocialism was a common denominator among conservatives, it is more difficult to use the term 'hegemony' which implies internalisation of dominant ideas by wide sections of society. There was a multiplicity of conservative groups each shaped by the economic and religious divisions of French society. Thus Aynard's liberal individualism divided him from Méline's ruralism on the national level, and from the *Nouvelliste* and social Catholics locally. The loyalties of the bourgeoisie were divided between these right-wing groups and the Radicals. Nor did the Progressistes succeed in 'incorporating' the conservative masses in the strong sense of the term. The support of peasants and white-collar workers was conditional on prosperity and defence of the Church. After the Great War the liberal elite was increasingly threatened by economic conflict and by the new strategies of the Church, which contributed also to the mobilisation of subordinate social groups within the right. The problems of Lyonnais conservatism were, moreover, ramifications of a national crisis which was beginning to undermine the parliamentary system.

It is more convincing to see Lyonnais conservatism as an example of persistence of the Orleanist tradition, transmitted first to Aynard's pre-1914 Fédération and then to the Alliance démocratique. But the liberal tradition was modified as it was reinscribed in changing historical contexts. It also became subdivided as the Orleanism represented by the *Nouvelliste* merged with Legitimism. Although both Aynard and the *Nouvelliste* were recognisably liberal, there was a political chasm between the latter's belief in limited suffrage and constitutional monarchy as a means of perpetuating a wealthy oligarchy, and Aynard's belief in an elite renewed by democratic education. In the 1920s Aynard's *libéralisme capacitaire* – which survived much longer than Rosanvallon allows – came into conflict with the left-liberal notions of association. Indeed, Aynard's liberalism rendered conservatives ill equipped to deal with the interwar crisis, which was to expose the fragility of the Progressiste hold over both elites and masses. It is to the origins of this crisis in town and country that we now turn.

3   Urban society in the Rhône

Writers of greater and lesser talent portrayed Lyon as a city of individualism, secrecy, materialism and fear of the envy of others.[1] In the 1920s liberal individualism certainly retained a powerful institutional and cultural position in spite of the relative decline of the silk industry with which it had traditionally been associated. This tradition was represented by Catholic silk manufacturers such as Auguste Isaac and Henry Morel-Journal. The first, like Aynard, had also occupied leading positions in the Fédération républicaine. Mass support for liberal-conservatism had been provided in particular by white-collar workers, who shared liberal ideas about social mobility. The extent to which either elites or conservative masses (let alone those outside the right) were incorporated into a 'dominant ideology' should not, however, be exaggerated. The liberal elite defined itself in terms of a set of social, political and religious values which excluded important sections of the dominant classes within Lyon and divided it from some sections of the ruling elites in France as a whole. Neither did electoral support for liberal-conservatism imply unqualified endorsement. Rather support for liberalism depended on favourable market conditions, opportunities for social mobility, the ability of the elites to contain the socialist threat and the tacit support of a Church which was increasingly inclined to turn its long-standing antiliberalism into practical action.

Well before the world economic crisis affected France, liberal-conservatism was in difficulties. This crisis must be placed in the context of the national developments outlined in chapter two. The imbalance in the French economy was reflected in the Rhône by sectoral diversification and by growing contrasts between large-scale monopoly capitalism, medium-sized family business, and a paradoxical strengthening of the old putting-out system in the silk industry. State intervention, never confined simply to protection of declining sectors, aggravated such

[1] Pierre Drieu la Rochelle, *Secret Journal and Other Writings* (Cambridge, 1973), 14–15; A. Demaison, 'Visites à la presse de province (V), Bourgogne et région lyonnaise', *Revue des deux mondes* (1929).

56

problems. The elites were divided over how to confront the problems of social and economic change along lines which resembled the national opposition between Redressement français and those who wished to preserve petty production as an element of stability in the social system. Thus in the Lyonnais engineering industry, anticlericalism and neo-capitalism came together as they did in Redressement français; those most opposed to neocapitalism were to be found in the right wing of the Catholic Fédération républicaine (to be discussed in chapter five). But debates in Lyon were given a peculiar twist by the Catholicism of many businessmen. Economic programmes were entangled with the Church's efforts to re-Christianise France by working through particular social groups, business included. The Church also aimed to overcome class divisions among Catholics and French people in general, but the effect was nevertheless to undermine mass support for the Catholic and liberal elite through the formation of rival business ideologies and Catholic trade unions, which were especially successful among white-collar workers. The success of Christian trade unionism also resulted from declining social mobility and a reaction to feminisation of white-collar employment, both of which also helped to weaken the liberal idea of social mobility. In many respects the social and economic ideas of the CFTC resembled those of the more advanced neocapitalists, at least in its Catholic Lyonnais version. But other sections of the CFTC, especially in the silk industry, were linked to the Catholic reaction against neocapitalism, which drew support from the merchant manufac-turing branch of the silk industry.

Precisely because the example of the Rhône was in many senses unique it throws light on the nature of Third Republican society. It suggests that the sources of change ('modernisation' for some historians) in the Third Republic were to be found within the social system itself, not an extra-societal elite. This in turn casts doubt on the notion that French society was characterised by an unshakable social consensus, or that the major purpose of the right was to defend existing social arrangements.[2] But before examining these themes it will be necessary to introduce the political and social structures of urban society in the Rhône and to say something of the position of the Catholic Church.

Social space, political space

Jean-Luc Pinol divides the agglomeration of 1936 into four types of social space (see Map 6).[3] Type 3 is characterised by the strong presence

---

[2] Kuisel, *Capitalism and the State*, 272–80; Monnet, *Refaire la république*, 356.
[3] J.-L. Pinol, *Espace sociale et espace politique: Lyon à l'époque du Front populaire* (Lyon,

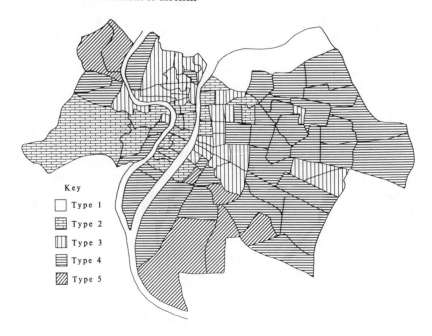

Key

☐ Type 1

▦ Type 2

▥ Type 3

▤ Type 4

▨ Type 5

Map 6   Lyon and Villeurbanne: social space, 1936

of workers. It includes four suburban communes (not shown on the map) – Vénissieux, Oullins, St Fons and Pierre-Bénite; most of Villeurbanne; the northern part of the 5th arrondissement (Vaise); and much of the 3rd and 7th. Often the proportion of workers in the electorate was extremely high, reaching 80% of the adult male population in Vénissieux in 1931.[4]

In type 2 there is no clear predominance of any social group, though white-collar workers and artisans are somewhat overrepresented. It includes the Croix-Rousse and parts of the left bank of the Rhône. The situation is complicated by type 4, which is marked by overrepresentation of public-sector white-collar workers. In these districts both the ruling classes and the private-sector salariat are underrepresented. Socially the districts of type 4 belong either with working-class or unsegregated areas. So the tripartite division of space is not really disrupted.

1980), 104–10. The method used was hierarchical cluster analysis. Four suburban communes – Bron, Vaulx en Velin, Ste-Foy-les-Lyon and Pierre Benite – all characterised by an overrepresentation of farmers, do not fall into these categories.
[4] P. Videlier, *Vénissieux d'A à Z* (Lyon, 1984); M. Bonneville, *Naissance et métamorphose d'une banlieue ouvrière: Villeurbanne. Processus et formes d'urbanisation*, (Lyon, 1978), 63.

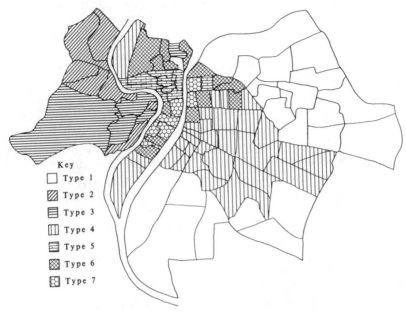

Key
☐ Type 1
▨ Type 2
☰ Type 3
▥ Type 4
☰ Type 5
▨ Type 6
▨ Type 7

Map 7   Lyon and Villeurbanne: typology of political space, 1936

The ruling classes are concentrated chiefly in the centre of the city: in the presqu'île from Perrache in the south to the Terreaux in the north; along the *quais* of the Rhône, especially in the 6th arrondissement, and on the Boulevard des Belges, bordering the Parc de la Tête d'Or (also in the 6th). Elites are also well represented in the Point du Jour (5th arrondissement), and in the suburban communes of the west such as Ecully, Tassin la Demi-Lune and Ste Foy les Lyon. The remainder of the population in wealthy districts consists of categories closely linked to them: clergy, students, higher-grade white-collar workers and middle managers.

Map 7 summarises Pinol's 'typologies of political orientations'. Broadly speaking the tripartite division of social space coincides with voting behaviour. The main bastions of conservative voting are types 6 and 7, overwhelmingly situated in bourgeois districts. The right was also overrepresented in type 5 (1st arrondissement) and type 3 (5th arrondissement), but was unable nevertheless to compete with Radicals and socialists respectively. The one exception to the bourgeois–right equation was the Croix-Rousse, a socially mixed area in which conservatism was predominant. The probable explanation is that religious practice was greater and the parish network better established than in areas with a similar social make up on the left bank of the Rhône. In the latter area the urbanisation of the late nineteenth century had run ahead of the Church's capacity to adapt. Thus Catholicism was as important to voting behaviour in the city as in the countryside. In general the right achieved no more than average scores in socially mixed districts (type 4), where the Radicals alone achieved scores that were a little better than average. Finally, the right did badly in working-class areas. Vaise was a socialist bastion (type 2); the southern part of the 7th arrondissement, Villeurbanne, and (not shown on the map) the eastern suburbs of St Fons, Bron and Vénissieux (type 1) shifted from socialism to communism in 1936. These generally unsurprising patterns are confirmed by Pinol's analysis of political and social variables, which shows a positive relationship between conservative vote and the presence of businessmen, the liberal professions, senior managers and higher-grade white-collar workers.

To some extent other factors cross-cut class position. There was a positive correlation between the conservative vote and the presence of older electors and those born in towns or cities. *Quartier* also plays a significant role in that political polarisation is less marked in socially mixed areas.[5] The latter phenomenon helped to sustain Radicalism in the city, whereas in towns like Roubaix where the middle class was weaker it had been squeezed almost out of existence. Nevertheless the explosion of the working-class *banlieue* between the wars kept alive bourgeois fears of proletarian insurrection. Suburbs such as Vénissieux were seen almost as foreign countries. Such sentiments were reinforced by the crowding together of immigrants in conditions of indescribable poverty.[6]

The fact of polarisation must also be qualified by the diversity of bourgeois districts. In the last decades of the previous century there had been an exodus of wealthy bourgeois, reputedly the younger and more dynamic, from the presqu'île (2nd arrondissement) towards the newly urbanised Brotteaux (6th).[7] In the interwar years much was still made of a cultural and political opposition between the traditionalist 2nd arrondissement (Ainay in particular) and the more open attitudes of the Brotteaux bourgeoisie. This is a central theme in Jean Dufourt's 1934 satirical novel *Calixte*, and was echoed by journalists.[8] Pinol, basing his findings on the membership of elite *cercles* and on differences in

---

[5] Pinol, *Espace sociale*, 125–52.   [6] Videlier, *Vénissieux*.
[7] J.-L. Pinol, 'Mobilités et immobilismes d'une grande ville: Lyon de la fin du XIX siècle à la seconde guerre mondiale' (doctorat ès lettres, Lyon II, 1989), 184.
[8] Jean Dufourt, *Calixte* (Lyon, 1934), 19–22; Demaison, 'Presses de Province'.

occupational structure, suggests that by the 1930s the 2nd–6th opposition was declining.[9] This is undoubtedly true. But it nevertheless remains essential to an understanding of bourgeois culture and Lyonnais politics. Practising Catholics and the old bourgeoisie of rentiers, traders and merchant-manufacturers were more numerous in the 2nd arrondissement, which was also the site of the Faculté catholique.[10] Over half of the 128 noble households listed in the 1936 edition of the *Annuaire Tout-Lyon* still lived in their traditional *quartier* between Place Bellecour and Ainay in the 2nd. (Certain of the western suburbs, especially Ecully and Tassin la Demi-Lune, possessed the same social mix as the 2nd arrondissement – many bourgeois had second homes in these communes.) The 6th arrondissement, in contrast, was home to Republican institutions like the Prefecture. There was a certain Protestant presence. In 1936 the Brotteaux remained the preferred residence of industrialists, engineers and senior managers. In the late nineteenth century it had been here that the more adventurous sections of the bourgeoisie had rallied to the Republic and later founded the Fédération républicaine. In the 1920s, as the Fédération républicaine drifted to the far right, many of the same groups turned to the Alliance démocratique. The 6th was the only area in the department in which this party was well organised, while the Fédération re-established itself there only with some difficulty. The diversity of elites in the Rhône becomes still more apparent when medium-sized industrial towns are considered. Apart from monopolisation of the dyeing industry of Villefranche and the Beaujolais mountains by the multinational Gillet group, local businessmen remained dominant. None of the cotton towns of the Beaujolais possessed close links with Lyon. The cotton merchants of Villefranche were part of a circuit that included Alsatian weavers and local dyers, while the metallurgical industry of the sub-prefecture was dependent upon the vine.

In sum, the relationship between voting patterns and social structures reveals a level of social polarisation which brought home to the privileged classes the need for unity in defence of property. If the presence of a socialist threat was sufficient to create bourgeois unity, then it ought to have existed in Lyon. But to achieve this unity the elites had to win support in socially mixed areas where social antagonisms were less intense, and overcome cultural divisions within the different parts of the city. This was all the more difficult because of the way in which religious and political divisions were related to the complexities of the Lyonnais economy.

[9] Pinol, 'Mobilités et immobilismes', 239–64, 408.
[10] Pinol, *Espace sociale*, 80–4.

The Catholic Church

The history of the right in the Rhône, as it is in the rest of France, is inseparable from the immense power of the Catholic Church. Religious practice was highest in the countryside. In the mountainous west attendance at mass was often nearly unanimous; in the Beaujolais there was considerable anticlericalism, though almost nowhere in rural areas did the level of Easter practice fall below one third of adult males. In Lyon only about one in ten attended Easter communion. But attendance was considerably higher in the bourgeois 2nd and 6th arrondissements, whilst the industrial suburbs almost entirely escaped the reach of the Church. Perhaps the best measure of the influence of the Church is that in 1928 there were 25,810 pupils in state primary schools compared to 12,232 in Catholic establishments. In absolute terms this was the highest in France.[11]

The political weight of the Church owed as much to its organisational power as it did to the extent of religious practice. There was a dense network of clerical and lay institutions centred on the parish, which endeavoured to take charge of the lives of the faithful. These were, of course, organised in an hierarchical fashion and the Church insisted unwaveringly on the unity of all believers in matters of faith. Yet the Church rarely acted as a body, for just as economic classes were cross-cut by religious divisions, so Catholics were divided by politics, class and other issues. Broadly speaking, however, it is possible to divide Catholics into conservatives and progressives.

The conservative wing of the Church was represented above all by Cardinal-Archbishop Maurin, in position from 1917 until 1937. Politically Maurin was reputed to favour Action française. He was supposed to have refused a request from the pope to announce the banning of Maurras's writings, and during the ensuing controversy he spoke up in favour of the AF student group. He distrusted the social Catholic *Chronique sociale* and was rumoured to have sought papal condemnation of the Catholic trade union movement. Maurin's views were shared by many of the senior laity. Such people were well represented in the Congrégation des messieurs de Lyon, a kind of Catholic freemasonry, which was active in the struggle against the Cartel and the Social Insurance legislation of 1928 and 1930. Conservatives were also numerous in the upper reaches of the Ligue de défense catholique, the Lyon branch of the pressure group, the FNC, the parish-based Cercles d'hommes, and the Faculté catholique. Conservatives

[11] G. Le Bras, 'Notes statistiques et d'histoire religieuse', *Revue d'histoire de l'Eglise de France* 6 (1933), 503–5; *Le Nouvelliste*, 5 January 1928.

were also to be found at the summit of institutions autonomous of the Church, such as the *Nouvelliste* and the agricultural trade union, the USE. Yet in the longer term the influence of royalism within the Church was declining. Maurin bowed to the wishes of the papacy as far as AF was concerned, and in a series of pastoral letters urged Catholics to cut ties with the movement. A renewal of the higher clergy after 1926 also helped ensure fidelity to the papal line. Action Française found itself denied access to the *Nouvelliste* and its activists became less influential within the Cercles d'hommes. The chief beneficiary of these changes was to be the Fédération républicaine right led by Victor Perret.[12]

Since the 1890s Catholic conservatives had been challenged by a more popular social Catholicism which, as we have seen, issued from the Christian democracy which had been stimulated by the Ralliement. At the centre of this network was a review, *La Chronique sociale*, founded in 1892 and the Secretariat social, which became autonomous from the *Chronique* in 1907. The latter built up a mini-empire of which the most important components were the Fédération des groupes d'études sociales, study groups based in the parishes, and the Semaines sociales which organised courses on social issues. Between the wars the *Chronique* played a significant role in the organisation both of Catholic trade unions and of the new specialist Catholic Action groups, of which the most important were the Jeunesse ouvrier chrétien and the Jeunesse agricole chrétienne – all of these were to have a significant, if indirect, political impact. Intellectual backing was provided by Jesuit theologians such as Valensin at Fourvière and Lubac at the Institut catholique.[13]

In the interwar years there were deep tensions between these two strands of Lyonnais Catholicism. Both, however, shared an integrist conception of Catholicism – the belief that public life should be moralised by the actions of Christians in the *cité*. Disagreement related to the issue of *how* Catholicism should be lived. Conservatives stressed elite-dominated charity and action through quasi-political organisations like the FNC. The *Chronique*, especially with the rise of Catholic Action after 1926, hoped to re-Christianise the nation partly through conversion

---

[12] A. Dansette, *Histoire religieuse de la France contemporaine* II: *Sous la Troisième république* (1952), 341, 393; Paul, *The Second Ralliement*, 151, 160; AN F[7] 13 226, various reports; *Semaine religieuse de Lyon*, 25 January 1929; A. Latreille and X. de Montclos, 'Forces religieuses et attitudes politiques dans la région Rhône-Alpes à la veille de la IIe guerre mondiale', in *Eglises et chrétiens dans la deuxième guerre mondiale*, ed. X. de Montclos (Lyon, 1978); Jacques Gadille, 'Le Temps des guerres et du concile (1914–1965)', in *Le Diocèse de Lyon*, ed. Jacques Gadille (1983), 271–99.

[13] Ponson, 'La Chronique sociale de Lyon en 1940', in *Eglises et chrétiens*, ed. de Montclos; Joseph Folliet, *Notre Ami, Marius Gonin* (Lyon, 1944); Bruno Dumons, 'Prédicateurs et directeurs spirituels des élites catholiques lyonnaises (1890–1950)', *Revue historique* 192 (1995), 99–120.

by example – they were much enamoured of retreats, intended to sustain the necessary spirituality. It was also believed that the Christian message could be spread by preaching Catholic solutions to social questions. This would be the task of elites drawn from each social milieu and organised in specialist Catholic Action. Most important for our purposes, these two conceptions of Christianity gave rise to divergent political perspectives. On the one hand, although the *Chronique* was formally apolitical, it aimed to detach the Church from reactionaries and formed part of a network which included the Christian democrat PDP and the left wing of the Fédération républicaine. On the other hand, Conservatives favoured the Perret wing of the Fédération. Both therefore contested the position of the Lyonnais liberal elite. Although Catholic values were essential to the way in which people like Isaac defined themselves, their view that religion was a private affair divided them from integrists of any colour. Isaac, for example, was hostile to clerical involvement in politics, and dismissed social Catholicism on the grounds that the suffering of the workers was not always undeserved and owed much to heredity. Apart from involvement in raising funds for private schools, conservatives of Isaac's ilk rarely played a significant role in Church institutions. In this tension between liberalism and the two wings of Social Catholicism lay a major reason for the crisis of liberal-conservatism in Lyon in the 1930s, especially as it was entangled with disputes concerning the nature of industrialisation and the organisation of society.[14]

From merchant-manufacturing to monopoly capitalism

The prosperity of Lyon had been built on trading and manufacture of silk products. The *fabrique* at its apogee in 1870 employed nearly half of all the workers in Lyon and possessed some 120,000 looms in the region.[15] Chemicals and machine building had been dependent on the silk industry. In structural terms the silk industry was still based on handlooms, master artisans (*façonniers*) and putting out by merchant-manufacturers (*fabricants de soieries*), though an elite of thread traders (*marchands de soies*) with interests in banking had emerged by the 1860s. By the interwar years the Rhône economy had been transformed. It was now characterised by large-scale capital and the manufacture of artificial textiles, chemicals and motor vehicles. The proportion of the active

---

[14] R. Ladous, 'Auguste Isaac et la tradition républicaine', in *Cent ans de catholicisme social à Lyon et en Rhône-Alpes*, ed. J.-D. Durand *et al.* (Lyon, 1992).

[15] Yves Lequin, *Les Ouvriers de la région lyonnaise (1848–1914)* (1972); Pierre Cayez, *Métiers Jacquard et hauts fourneaux* (Lyon, 1978).

population employed in the textile industry fell from 14% in 1906 to 11% in 1936, while the numbers employed in metallurgy rose from 5% to 10%. The relative importance of older industries such as leather and furniture also declined. Meanwhile plant employing more than 500 workers rose in number from thirteen to twenty-three.[16]

Fundamental changes took place within the silk industry. In spite of its relative decline the *fabrique* still employed an estimated 100,000 workers in twelve departments and accounted for 11% of the value of French exports. Although the number of looms had fallen to 50,000 by 1931, productivity in all branches of the industry was very much higher than in 1914.[17] Weaving had been almost completely mechanised by 1914 and improved considerably in efficiency during the interwar years.[18] As a result factory weaving progressed. A new breed of *fabricants-usiniers* not only owned their own factories, but controlled the whole production process from purchase of thread to sale of finished cloth.[19] Since the late nineteenth century dyeing too had been concentrated in large factories, thanks to the large amounts of capital needed for the new roller method. Mass production advanced further with the use of artificial fibres from the early 1900s. Consumption of rayon surpassed that of natural silk by 1928. A number of large artificial-fibre factories were built in suburban communes surrounding Lyon during the 1920s.[20]

Artificial-fibre manufacturers joined the more important *fabricants-usiniers*, dyers and chemical interests in an overlapping business elite.[21] A key position was occupied by the Gillet corporation, which dominated the dyeing industry in the Rhône and in much of France. Because of its interests in chemical production the company was also able to invest in the new artificial-fibre industry, sometimes in collaboration with groups such as Usines du Rhône.[22] Although Gillet had begun as a local

---

[16] Pinol, '*Mobilités et immobilismes*', 287, 293–6; Kevin Passmore, 'The right and extreme right in the department of the Rhône 1928–1939' (Ph.D., University of Warwick, 1992), 62–5.

[17] A. Isaac, 'Les Cahiers de l'industrie française. La soie', *Revue des deux mondes* (1930), 89–106.

[18] Lequin, *Les Ouvriers*, 76–85; M.-L. Bourgeon, 'Repartition des métiers de tissage de la soie au service de la fabrique lyonnaise en 1937–8, *Etudes rhodaniennes* 14 (1938), 229; Laferrère, *Lyon, ville industrielle*, 177–8; Isaac, 'Les cahiers', 89, 92.

[19] CRCCL, 1935, 148. In 1928 such businessmen represented 30% of the membership of the SFS, and possessed an average of 181 looms in 1936.

[20] Pinton, 'La Soie artificielle à Lyon', *Etudes rhodaniennes* 6 (1930), 242–3; Isaac, 'Les cahiers', 95–7.

[21] M. Laferrère, *Lyon, ville industrielle: essai de géographie et de techniques industrielles* (1960), 187, 205.

[22] Laferrère, *Lyon, ville industrielle*, 192–3; Marcel Peyronnet, *La Dynastie des Gillets: les maîtres de Rhône-Poulenc* (1979), 201–8.

concern it had moved its headquarters to Paris. So it was often *marchands de soie* such as Morel-Journel who played the leading role in the Lyonnais business elite. Thanks to traditional involvement in banking, *marchands de soies* were also able to participate in the capital-hungry artificial-textile industry.[23] This elite represented the descendants of the Progressistes.

Lyon's economy had begun to diversify in the 1860s. But the decisive impetus was imparted by the Great War. Chemical companies such as Usines du Rhône and Saint Gobain expanded rapidly thanks to the transfer of activities from the occupied north, making St Fons, to the south-west of Lyon, the principal centre of the French chemical industry. Rhône-Poulenc, created by fusion of the Usines du Rhône with Poulenc Frères in 1928, was one of the largest companies in France.[24] Metallurgy too expanded as a result of the war, mainly in Villeurbanne, Vénissieux, Bron and Oullins. In 1918 metallurgy employed 45,000 workers, compared to 25,000 at the outbreak of hostilities; the postwar maximum of 44,446 was reached in 1930.[25] Of these, 11,000 were accounted for by the vehicle manufacturer Berliet, which in 1917 had completed the construction of a new factory at Vénissieux, larger than that of Henry Ford in Detroit.[26] The electrical equipment industry had also grown. Les Câbles de Lyon, for example, began by supplying the electricity generating industry and new tram companies in the 1900s. In a development typical of this industry it was in 1912 absorbed by the CGE.[27] These very large firms were at the centre of a complex of engineering firms making a range of products from machine tools, through construction equipment to machinery. Heavy metallurgy, on the other hand, was less common, although there were blast furnaces in Givors run by Fives-Lille and Prénat.[28]

In spite of these spectacular changes, the triumph of big capital was incomplete. In some sectors family firms remained the rule. A good example was the cotton industry, which employed several thousand

---

[23] Pinton, 'La Soie artificielle', 237; J. Perret, 'Dans la banlieue industrielle de Lyon: Vaulx en Velin', *Etudes rhodaniennes* 8 (1937), 24–33. Laferrère, *Lyon, ville industrielle*, 210–12; M. Bonneville, *Naissance et métamorphose d'une banlieue ouvrière: Villeurbanne. Processus et formes d'urbanisation* (Lyon, 1978), 17, 51; Laferrère, *Lyon, ville industrielle*, 210–12, 226; Peyronnet, *La Dynastie des Gillets*, 108–9.

[24] Laferrère, *Lyon, ville industrielle*, 445–9; Peyronet, *La Dynastie des Gillets*, 97–109; E. Herriot, *Lyon pendant la guerre* (Lyon, 1919).

[25] Figures from CRCCL; E. Fougère, *L'Effort industriel de Lyon pendant la guerre*, (Lyon, 1919).

[26] Saint-Loup, *Marius Berliet, l'inflexible* (1962); Laferrère, *Lyon, ville industrielle*, 304–10 and 361–81; Vidélier, *Vénissieux*.

[27] Laferrère, *Lyon, ville industrielle*, 319–28.

[28] *Lyon Républicain*, 29 December 1935.

workers in Villefranche and the Beaujolais mountain towns of Thizy, Tarare, Amplepuis and Cours.[29] Dyeing and finishing had been concentrated under the wing of the Gillet group.[30] Weaving, in contrast, was dominated by medium to large self-financing family firms, able to prosper because it was possible to accumulate looms a few at a time. The Beaujolais cotton industry was also marked by technological backwardness. Looms were out-dated; in Tarare, 63% of motive power still came from steam in 1926.[31] The survival of the Beaujolais cotton industry depended partly on isolation in safe home and colonial markets.[32] This was just the kind of industry which had supported Méline in the 1890s and which was attacked by neocapitalists in the 1920s. In fact to some extent the cotton industry compensated for lack of automation by its flexible structures, making use of artisan labour in the countryside to produce varied cloths and finishes. This flexibility was partly based on home weaving, which had been reviving since the turn of the century as factory owners sought to escape regulation and trade unions.[33] In this respect the cotton industry anticipated modern 'post-Fordist' methods, so it is difficult to say whether it was 'traditional' or 'modern'.[34] Whatever the case, such firms had little to gain from the rationalisation, standardisation and social reform preached by the neocapitalist movement. A similar pattern could be found in the leather industry where the number of cobblers declined as mass-produced rubber-soled men's shoes (often foreign) invaded the market.[35]

Family firms were also numerous in the metallurgical industries.[36] Some produced specialised machine tools in relatively short series. Others were engaged in repair and maintenance. Total integration of large metallic construction factories was in fact rare.[37] They were provided with semi-finished products by eighty foundries of which in

[29] C. Albout, 'Démographie et industrialisation d'une région rurale de la fin du XVIIe siècle à nos jours: le canton de Tarare' (mémoire de maîtrise, Lyon II, 1970); H. Velu, 'Villefranche en Beaujolais', *Etudes rhodaniennes* 14 (1938), 46–71; J. -P. Payant, 'Etude démographique d'une cellule industrielle en Haut Beaujolais: Thizy et Bourg-de-Thizy de 1836 à nos jours', (mémoire de maîtrise, Lyon II, 1974); Houssel, *La Région de Roanne et le Beaujolais*; *Le Nouveau Journal*, 3 January 1928, on Thizy; Henri Bordas, 'Tarare', *Annales de géographie* 33 (1930).

[30] Vélu, 'Villefranche', 51; Laferrère, *Lyon, ville industrielle*, 225–6 and note 286.

[31] *La Voix sociale*, July/August 1930; Bordas, 'Tarare', 47–8.

[32] Albitreccia, 'L'Industrie du coton', *Annales de géographie* 8 (1933), 237.

[33] Houssel, *La Région de Roanne*, 147–8; Bordas, 'Tarare', 48; Albitreccia, 'L'Industrie du coton'.

[34] Charles Sabel and Jonathon Zeitlin, 'Historical alternatives to mass production: politics, markets and technology in nineteenth century industrialisation', *Past and Present* 108 (1985), 173–6.

[35] CRCCL, 1928, 714, 718; Bonneville, *Villeurbanne*, 49, 728–9).

[36] Laferrère, *Lyon, ville industrielle*, 305.

[37] Bonneville, *Villeurbanne*, 57, 61; Pinol, *Espace social*, 101–2.

1935 twenty-four employed less than ten workers.[38] Edmond Weitz, president of the metallurgy employers' association, saw founders as part of a supple and harmonious ensemble permitting Lyon to sustain its reputation for quality production.[39] Here too mass production co-existed with flexible production. Relations within this system were not always as harmonious as Weitz maintained. Many small and even medium firms were in a position of dependence thanks to the subcontracting system.[40] In the metallurgical industry there was a potential anticapitalism even in quite large firms.

Business structures were particularly complex in the silk industry, especially in the weaving sector. Here the emergence of big capital contrasted with the survival of the merchant-manufacturing system. In 1928, 278 out of 399 (70%) members of the Syndicat des fabricants de soieries de Lyon (SFS), and perhaps 300 non-unionised *fabricants*, possessed no factories of their own.[41] They purchased thread from *marchands de soies* and had it woven and dyed by *façonniers*. The latter were either factory-owning *gros façonniers* or rural home weavers. In 1936 one in five of all looms in the region were operated by home weavers.[42] This apparently anachronistic system survived partly because its flexibility allowed the industry to adapt to rapidly changing patterns of demand in the market for luxury goods.[43] It also had the advantage that with no fixed capital of their own, *fabricants* were able to pass on the effects of the frequent slumps inherent in luxury markets by forcing weavers to accept contracts at lower prices.[44] One reason for recovery of home weaving after the war was rural electrification and the inexpensiveness of converting handlooms. This meant that home weavers were no longer confined to the production of luxury goods, but could compete with factories in the weaving of cheaper cloths.[45] Finally, and most important in the present context, home weaving benefited from postwar attempts to sustain the artisanate as a bulwark against communism.[46] The result, as we shall see, was conflict, for factory weavers (whether *gros*

---

[38] PVCCL, 14 February 1935; CRCCL, 1935.

[39] *Lyon républicain*, 15 December 1935; Bonneville, *Villeurbanne*, 57.

[40] Bonneville, *Villeurbanne*, 62.

[41] *Compte rendu annuel des travaux du Syndicat des Fabricants de Soieries de Lyon* (hereafter CRSFS), 1928; S. Garcin, 'La Fabrique lyonnaise de soieries de 1900 à 1929' (mémoire de maîtrise, Lyon II, 1969).

[42] M.-L. Bourgeon, 'Répartition des métiers de tissage de la soie au service de la fabrique lyonnaise en 1937–8', *Etudes rhodaniennes* 14 (1938), 215–34.

[43] Sabel and Zeitlin, 'Historical alternatives to mass production', 173–6; Laferrère, *Lyon, ville industrielle*, 96; Isaac, 'Les Cahiers', 104.

[44] H. Bertrand, *Soierie lyonnaise: chardonne et soie ordinaire. Evolutions récentes; situation actuelle* (Lyon, 1930), 80–1.

[45] Isaac, 'Les Cahiers', 100.   [46] Bertrand, *Soierie lyonnaise*, 46.

façonniers or *fabricants-usiniers*) resented what they saw as the unfair competition of home weavers.[47] *Fabricants non-usiniers* viewed such attacks on home weaving as a threat to their own existence. They idealised the artisanate and attacked 'American methods' (though they continued to exploit home weavers and refused their demands for minimum price (*tarif*)).

Thus, the Second Industrial Revolution produced in the Rhône a complex mixture of business structures. Standardised mass production in large factories was the rule only in chemicals and artificial fibres. More often large production units co-existed with, or were integrated into, a flexible production system. Such was the case in cotton, metallurgy, leather goods and especially silk. So there was a potential conflict between two different philosophies of production, one based on standardisation and rationalisation, the other based on flexibility and quality. Often such tensions led to anticapitalism, even in relatively large firms, aggravated in some cases by a subcontracting system which was common not only in the silk industry, but in metallurgy, clothing and furniture. In the silk industry *gros façonniers* were particularly prone to anticapitalism because of their historic opposition to the *fabricants* who provided them with work. Medium-business anticapitalism was to lead many into the Croix de Feu and PSF. Finally, business differed in its relationship to the artisanate, some regarding it as essential to flexible production or as a barrier against socialism, while others saw it as an anachronism and a source of unfair competition. Thus we can see in the Rhône some of the fundamental dilemmas of Third Republican society.

The changes described above were bound in some way or other to have had a political impact. But conflicts in business are impossible to comprehend without also taking into account politics, culture and ideology. Business institutions in the Rhône were dominated by the successors of Aynard, who remained more or less faithful to his version of Catholic liberal-conservatism. This elite had been immeasurably strengthened by the economic changes detailed above. Yet by the late 1920s the liberal hegemony was threatened by a modernising and reformist challenge from the engineering industry which gained some sympathy from sections of the elite itself, and by changes in the social practice of the Church. There was also a reaction against neocapitalism from sections of the silk and other industries, which was also inseparable from Catholic hostility to liberalism.

---

[47] PVCCL, 7 February 1929.

The liberal tradition

The origins of the liberal tradition were in the political, social and economic conjuncture of the late eighteenth and early nineteenth centuries. In the 1920s liberalism still formed an essential part of an ideological apparatus that preceded individuals and, along with economic and social conditions, structured their lives. Aspects of production in the silk industry can be seen as sustaining the liberal world-view. But these same features of the industry were also a *product* of the activities of businessmen raised in the liberal tradition. These passively inherited economic and ideological structures explain the reproduction of the liberal tradition. But at the same time these structures were embodied – partially and often in a contradictory way – in the consciousness of individuals who were therefore able actively to modify them.

The combination of individualism and discretion that marked the *soierie* was related to rapid changes in fashions and a constant search for new fabrics, which dictated secrecy and rapidity in design and execution.[48] Such attitudes helped to sustain a belief in the individuality of the consumer and indeed of Frenchmen in general. Self-reliance was in turn linked to a commitment to social mobility. The relative openness to talent of an industry which required no fixed capital reinforced the notion of rule by a meritocracy founded on the work ethic.[49] We shall see that the notion of social mobility was essential to the incorporation of white-collar workers into the liberal consensus. Another bulwark of the liberal tradition was the dependence of the *soierie* upon foreign markets and raw materials: 60% of production was exported in 1930, while French sericulture met only a fraction of raw material requirements. Although in the 1920s worries about Japanese competition were growing, the silk industry nevertheless continued a tenacious battle in defence of free trade. Allies in port towns and the wine trade were, however, insufficient to overcome the enormous weight of protectionist interests. The *fabrique* also resisted the neomercantilism of cotton and metallurgical industries.[50] The labour intensive nature of production reinforced distrust of social reform. For most employers the only means of improving the lot of the workers was to reduce production costs and thereby make cheaper goods available. Trades unions were seen at best as an unavoidable evil. Unable or unwilling to dip into their pockets, the

[48] Laferrère, *Lyon, ville industrielle*, 188; Bertrand, *Soierie lyonnaise*, 187.

[49] P. Gillet, *Edmund Gillet 1873–1831: industriel, régent de la banque de France* (Lyon, 1932), 2.

[50] J. Laffey, 'Lyonnais imperialism in the Far East, 1900–1938', *Modern Asian Studies* 10 (1970), 225–40; J. Laffey, 'The roots of French imperialism in the nineteenth century: the case of Lyon', *French Historical Studies* 6 (1969), 45–67.

liberal elite touted religion and individual social mobility as remedies for working-class discontent.

The liberal tradition unashamedly favoured big business. This had been true since Aynard had denounced Jules Méline's view that the French were an essentially rural people. In the 1920s big firms unanimously endorsed cartels.[51] This represented a break with liberal individualism, but could be justified in terms of freedom of association. Cartelisation represented a potential for conflict with smaller firms. But before the 1920s conflict was limited – less by ideological incorporation than by prosperity, the institutional power of big-business and the extreme individualism of many small and medium businesses. *Fabricants non-usiniers* were particularly individualistic. Some distrusted association by employers on the grounds that it might encourage imitation by *façonniers*.[52] Many *non-usiniers*, moreover, were at the head of marginal concerns that relied on *façonniers* to make cloth quickly enough for them to sell before suppliers demanded payment.[53] The rapid turnover of such firms was reflected in the fluctuating membership of the Syndicat de fabricants de soieries (SFS), which rose from 372 in 1920 to 725 in 1929, and dropped back again to about 300 in 1937.[54] The resulting insecurity reduced their ability to express collectively any hostility they might have felt towards the business elites.

Another reason for the dominance of the liberal business elite was its entrenched institutional position. Leadership of the SFS was monopolised by the wealthiest *fabricant-usiniers*. Although they were in a majority within the SFS, individualistic *non-usiniers* accepted their exclusion from positions of power, perhaps also satisfied by the federal structure of the organisation.[55] The SFS was reputed to pull the strings of the powerful Chamber of Commerce. It is true that members often spoke as if this was the case.[56] Also the mode of election of the Chamber favoured the silk industry. The latter possessed eight out of twenty-three seats, while the engineering industry had only two.[57] In the elected bureau, where most decisions were made, the *fabrique* had a permanent majority. Yet the authority of the relatively broad and prestigious SFS was cited in order to legitimate what in reality was a very select group of

---

[51] CRCCL, 1928, 360–9.
[52] Geni, 'L'Organisation professionnelle de la fabrique lyonnaise de soieries: étude historique et critique', (thèse de droit, Grenoble, 1942), 139–41.
[53] Laferrère, *Lyon, ville industrielle*, 95, 97, 107.
[54] CRSFS, 1937; Geni, 'L'Organisation professionnelle', 52; CRSFS, 1937.
[55] Fonds Justin Godart, carton 1 (hereafter AJG, all documents from carton 1), Report of Daniel Isaac, 13 October 1935.
[56] PVCCL, 10 January 1929, 14 February 1935.
[57] *Le Nouveau Journal*, 26 March 1939.

wealthy businessmen. Indeed, certain SFS leaders were of unorthodox opinion and on that count excluded from the leadership of the Chamber. No *fabricant* was president from 1919 until 1937. With the support of allies in the wholesale trade and lesser industries the liberal elite of *marchands de soies, fabricants* and chemical manufacturers was able to isolate opposition from the engineering industry and a minority of *fabricants*. Five of the Chamber's six presidents since 1890 had presided over the Société d'économie politique, which was dedicated to the propagation of liberal principles.[58]

Control of the Chamber of Commerce was an enormous asset. Election in theory by all *patentés* (even though participation rates were very small) legitimated its mission of representing the general economic interest of the region to the government. Also, the Lyon Chamber was automatically granted a seat in the bureau of the Assembly of Presidents of Chambers of Commerce of France. This organisation too was designed to circumvent the 'rule of number'.[59] No other organisation could seriously dispute the claims of the Chamber. The Chambers of Tarare and Villefranche were dominated by conservative cotton manu-facturers and wine merchants whose opinions generally matched those of their fellows in Lyon – free trade excepted.[60] The big business Union des Chambres syndicales patronales lyonnaises (UCS) claimed to be the organisation that best synthesised the views of local employers.[61] In fact its role was mainly restricted to organisation of elections – always uncontested – to the Chamber of Commerce.[62] The local affiliate of the CGPF, the Association industrielle, commerciale et agricole (AICA), vegetated until June 1936.

Opposition to the liberal elites was doubtless also reduced by the prosperity of the 1920s and by the fact that the silk industry retained considerable economic weight. Both the chemical and engineering industries relied to some extent on supplying the textile industry.[63] Many engineers were to attribute the crisis of the 1930s to the downturn in the silk industry.[64] Also the political power of the electrical industry was reduced by the fact that the headquarters of the largest firms were in Paris. Marius Berliet, head of the most important local engineering concern, kept apart from *patronal* politics and did not even join an

---

[58] H. Morel-Journel, *Notes sur la Chambre de Commerce de Lyon à l'usage de ses membres* (Lyon, 1937).
[59] Morel-Journel's expression, PVCCL, 14 May 1936.
[60] *L'Industrie dans la région de Roanne, Thizy, et Cours* (April 1929).
[61] *Bulletin de l'Union des chambres syndicales lyonnais* (BUCCL), June 1928.
[62] Morel-Journal, *Notes sur la Chambre de Commerce*, 10.
[63] Bonneville, *Villeurbanne*, 15.
[64] *Lyon républicain*, 15 December 1935; PVCCL, 14 February 1935.

employers' association. By default this left Lyonnais institutions to the silk industry. For all of these reasons, even Edmond Weitz, an implacable opponent of the *soierie*, was obliged to recognise in 1930 that it 'remains the dominant industry of this city'.[65]

Just as the liberalism of the business elite potentially excluded sections of the capitalist class on economic grounds, so Catholicism defined its boundaries. In the language of closure theory the liberal elites used a combination of status criteria and legal control over private property to exclude competitors from access to resources, opportunities and reward. Aynard and his successors spoke of toleration and claimed that religion could be reconciled with liberalism by a separation of spiritual and social matters.[66] This was meant to make possible the unity of the elites, but this goal was hard to achieve in practice. On the one hand toleration excluded integrists (whether among the elites who controlled *Le Nouvelliste* or in the new Catholic Action movements, committed to re-Christianisation). On the other hand the liberal elite was divided from anticlericals such as Edmund Weitz, for the theoretical separation of religion and private life was hard to maintain in practice. Indeed, by making religion a question of personal choice Catholic values were linked to the ascetic qualities presumed to be necessary for economic success. Silk manufacturers in particular diffused an austere model of behaviour which synthesised the Jansenist strand in Lyonnais Catholicism and the liberal work ethic. For Auguste Isaac work was the 'law of God'.[67] For the novelist Henri Béraud Lyon was a town where avarice ruled and where wealth borrowed the visage of misery in order to disguise itself.[68] Dufourt satirised the predilection of silk merchants for unfashionable and worn clothing.[69] Charity, according to Dufourt, was designed not just to relieve poverty but to educate the humble in appropriate types of behaviour and to get oneself known in the best society.[70] Catholicism, although it was not to be expressed in public, was one of the keys to social acceptance. In *Calixte* Philippe is taken to task for hiding himself behind a pillar at mass.[71] Such affectations were part of a set of basic values which served to define the group and to exclude outsiders. It is not surprising that Protestant businessmen such as Weitz, let alone more recently enriched engineers, should have felt ill at ease in such a society.

The liberalism of the business elite resembled that of the CGPF

---

[65] PVCCL, 6 January 1930.
[66] *Le Nouvelliste*, 1 January 1932; Ladous, 'Auguste Isaac', 140–4; Aynard, *Discours 1893 à 1913*, 534, speech of 25 June 1896.
[67] *La Voix sociale*, 12 March 1922.   [68] Henri Béraud, *Ciel de suie* (1933), 1.
[69] Dufourt, *Calixte*, 64–6, 119.   [70] *Ibid.*, 121.
[71] Demaison, 'La Presse de province', 12; Dufourt, *Calixte*, 121–2.

leaders described by Henry Ehrmann.[72] Conservatism on social issues was combined with a belief in big business as the motor of progress. Liberal individualism was tempered only by commitment to cartels. It was, moreover, a liberalism based on individual initiative, tolerance and progress, not the restrictive Malthusianism described by Hoffman or Sauvy. But the position of the liberal elite was a fragile one. It did not rest on ideological incorporation of the elites or conservative masses, let alone the supporters of the Radicals or socialists. It depended on a constellation of social, economic and political factors which were threatened by the growing imbalance in the economy, by the efforts of the state in the 1920s to protect small producers, and by a problematic relationship between liberalism and the Catholic Church.

The crisis of liberalism

One source of tension was a new aggressiveness in promoting big business. The weaver Louis Guéneau denied that recent progress in the use of artificial fibres had been due to 'abnormal circumstances', and that the construction of new factories would lead to disaster. Natural silk, said Guéneau, had had its day.[73] Such beliefs had clear implications for smaller-scale producers of luxury goods. The weaver Henry Bertrand urged the exclusion from the SFS of firms with less than fifty to a hundred looms.[74] Even Morel-Journel, a pillar of the liberal establishment, complained privately that luxury goods served aesthetic and not industrial needs.[75] Such conflicts draw their significance from the attempts of governments, often Radical in composition, to protect small business in the 1920s. Morel-Journel and his big-business colleagues in the Chamber of Commerce unanimously condemned the unfair advantages of home weavers. It was said that whereas workers in factories refused to work more than eight hours, they were nevertheless prepared to work much longer shifts for higher pay in unregulated home workshops.[76]

This was accompanied by a questioning of aspects of liberalism, even within the silk industry. Some preached the virtues of collective organisation. Paul Charbin, as president of the SFS in 1928, believed that individualism was outmoded, and that the interdependence of modern firms prescribed association for purchase of raw materials,

---

[72] H. Ehrmann, *Organised Business in France* (Princeton, 1957), 28–9.
[73] Louis Guéneau, *La Soie artificielle* (1928); echoed by Fougère in *Le Nouveau Journal*, 6 April 1925; Bertrand, *Soierie lyonnaise*, 18.
[74] Bertrand, *Soierie lyonnaise*, 135ff.   [75] Morel-Journel, *Journal*, 11 November 1932.
[76] PVCCL, 7 February 1929.

manufacturing, sales, and defence of common interests.[77] Bertrand meanwhile appealed for respect of the rights of the trade unions. His view that establishment of good labour relations was conditional upon replacement of 'artisanal' and therefore ill-disciplined French workers by immigrant labour illustrates the link between co-operation with semi-skilled workers and standardised mass production.[78] Big firms were also distinguished by a pragmatic view of the Eight Hour Law. Thanks to the seasonal nature of their industry the majority of *fabricants* were implacably hostile to this measure. But many had nevertheless adapted to it by means of round-the-clock shift working, which permitted continuous utilisation of capital resources. Similarly, compulsory family allowances were reluctantly approved on the grounds that the private schemes of some large firms put them at a cost disadvantage in relation to smaller concerns.[79]

This interest in rationalisation, mass production and collaboration with workers was part of the movement in favour of industrial modernisation incarnated by *Redressement français*. One president of the SFS, Etienne Fougère, was a vice-president of this movement. Neo-capitalism must be seen partly as a reaction against state protection of small production in the 1920s, which in Lyon had contributed to the revival of merchant-manufacturing and to rivalry between large and small business. But economic tensions were only part of the story. The emergence of progressive business ideas owed as much to ideological and political developments as to economics. In Lyon the liberal and Catholic tradition gave a peculiar twist to neocapitalism. Formal links to Redressement were rare. Mercier's movement was rooted in an anti-clerical solidarist tradition with which few had much sympathy. Rather progressives among the elites drew upon aspects of the Catholic tradition, taking advantage in particular of the Church's new concern with the preoccupations of particular social groups. One consequence was the formation in 1928 of a Lyon section of the Catholic employers' group, the Confédération française de professions (CFP). Its meetings attracted members of the business elite such as Morel-Journel and the silk importer Charles Mouterde. Employers discussed the application of social Catholic doctrines to industry, the guiding principle being that rationalisation and efficiency depended partly on respect for 'la personne humaine'. The CFP was almost unique among employers' organisations in approving of the Social Insurance Laws of 1928 and 1930.[80]

---

[77] *Le Nouvelliste*, 31 March 1928.   [78] Bertrand, *Soierie lyonnaise*, 49, 147–8.
[79] PVCCL, 24 October 1929.
[80] Formed by a fusion of the Association des patrons lyonnais, close to the *Nouvelliste*, and the Union catholique lyonnais which was more moderate. *Le Nouvelliste*, 13 March 1928,

'Modernist' views were most common among the largest firms in the weaving branch, perhaps because of their long hostility to home producers. But a coherent reform movement did not emerge. Few subscribed to all of the ideas described above. Most big weavers in the Chamber of Commerce remained loyal to the liberal majority. Morel-Journel expressed his contempt for luxury production only in private. Commitment to mass production was not total, for even big firms wished to gain advantage from the prestige of Lyonnais luxury goods. Many tended in the 1920s to combine mass production of raw cloth with diversity of finishes, and to treat artificial fibres simply as a means to extend the variety of finishes. Older businessmen like Isaac were especially likely to favour high-quality production.[81] Others, however, went further in their questioning of the liberal tradition.

The new social practices of the Church also helped medium business to articulate grievances. Such firms were of particular importance to social Catholicism, which saw them as an element in a 'middle class' able to neutralise antagonism between capital and labour through some kind of corporate arrangement. Certain *gros façonniers*, such as Jean Monamy, leader of the TMF, were particularly interested in social Catholicism. Their progressivism derived from their long struggle against the *fabricants* who provided them with contracts. Monamy was often to be seen at meetings of the Catholic trade union, the Confédération française des travailleurs chrétiens (CFTC).

Metallurgists, often from a quite different cultural tradition, went furthest in their critique of liberalism. In 1927 Morel-Journel asserted at the Société d'économie politique that current business recession had shown that bosses should not be too individualist in agreeing contracts – in other words a plea for cartels. The next speaker, Weitz, of the engineering employers' association, went rather further. He ruled out the traditional liberal remedy of cutting costs through wage reductions or longer work days (an implicit endorsement of the Eight Hour law). Instead he called for rationalisation and collective organisation of production with negotiations between capital and labour. Government would create a favourable climate for business through moderate protectionism and intervention in the housing market.[82] In September 1928 Weitz signed a collective contract with the CGT and CFTC,

12 March 1929, 10 March 1930; C. Ponson, 'La "Chronique sociale" de Lyon en 1940', in *Eglises et chrétiens*, ed. de Montclos, 28; Bertrand, *Soierie lyonnaise*, 49, 147–8.

[81] Isaac, 'Les Cahiers', 91–2.

[82] *Salut Public*, 6/7 February 1927; CRCCL, 1928, 687–93; *Nouveau Journal*, 2 March 1925 reports that the CSIM was addressed by the moderate socialist Albert Thomas.

which included a permanent consultative organisation.[83] The metallurgy employers' association distributed family allowances and other benefits. The engineering industry was almost alone in patronal circles in accepting the Social Insurance Laws of 1928 and 1930.

Recognition of the rights of trade unions implied reinforcement of employers' organisations. Whereas the SFS was essentially a pressure group integrated into a lobbying system crowned by the Chamber of Commerce, the Chambre syndicale des industries métallurgiques du Rhône (CSIM) was designed to take its place in a system of collective bargaining. In this the CSIM was aided by Aymé Bernard's AICA. AICA had been established in 1918 to deal with postwar labour unrest and to implement the new system of collective contracts, something the Chamber of Commerce was ill equipped to do.[84] Since it was the metallurgical industry that was most affected by the strikes it inevitably took a leading role. AICA posed a direct challenge to the Chamber of Commerce, for it was led by progressives such as Weitz, Charbin and Fougère.[85] It sought to create a common front of all employers. But as working-class militancy declined in the 1920s AICA lost a vitality which it fully recovered only after June 1936.

The reformism of the engineering industry can be explained partly by economic interest, for it suffered from a shortage of skilled labour, whilst labour costs were relatively low.[86] But this is not the only explanation, for labour costs in the more conservative weaving and dyeing industries were also low. Equally important was that whereas the silk elite was largely recruited from a small group of old Catholic families, the roots of the engineering employers were in the anticlerical petty bourgeoisie of the late nineteenth century.[87] Weitz, moreover, resembled the enterprising textile manufacturer Hippolyte Simler in J.-R. Bloch's novel *Et compagnie*, in that he was of Alsatian and Protestant origin.[88] To the elites the very lifestyle of the newly rich metallurgists was an affront. In 1918 the Prefect, commenting on the enrichment of engineering

---

[83] E.-S. Massoubre, *Les Ententes professionnelles dans le cadre national et la doctrine économique* (1935).

[84] Georges Lefranc, *Les Organisations patronales en France du passé au présent* (1976); *Le Nouvelliste*, 6 June 1919.

[85] *Le Nouvelliste*, 26 February 1928.

[86] PVCCL, 18 February 1929: 25% in engineering generally, compared to up to 90% in some branches of the silk industry.

[87] P. Cayez, 'Quelques aspects du patronat lyonnais pendant la deuxième étape de l'industrialisation', in *Le Patronat de la seconde industrialisation*, ed. M. Lévy-Leboyer (1979); Pinol, 'Mobilités et immobilismes', 685–7.

[88] J.-R. Bloch, *Et Compagnie*, quoted in Claude Fohlen, 'The Industrial Revolution in France, 1700–1914', in *The Fontana Economic History of Europe*, ed. C. Cipolla, vol. IV, part 1 (1973), 38–9. Pinol, 'Mobilités et immobilismes', 467–8.

employers, spoke of 'exterior manifestations of luxury and well-being which has a great impact on a public opinion habituated to the traditional affectation of economy and simplicity which distinguishes the silk industry'.[89] This explains Morel-Journel's view of Weitz as impetuous and unreliable – characteristics at the antipodes of the self-image of the liberal elite. That the Catholic forgemaster Louis Prénat (representative of a group associated for a combination of historical and economic reasons with the formerly royalist right) felt the need to create a rival Catholic engineering association is revealing of the atmosphere pervading the main association. There are several exceptions to the Catholic/silk and anticlerical/engineering equations. Berliet, for example, combined Legitimism and an interest in American production methods. But these exceptions merely prove the rule that ideology and material interest were married to produce a multitude of competing groups.

In the light of these considerations it is not surprising that Weitz's efforts to breach the hegemony of the silk industry straddled politics and business. In February 1928 he denounced the 'industrial feudalism' of the silk industry in the Mascaraud committee which channelled business funds to centrist politicians, pointing out that he spoke for both engineering employers and the Alliance démocratique, of which he was departmental president.[90] In June 1929 he lobbied in the name of the 'heavy industries' for a seat in the bureau of the Chamber of Commerce.[91] Seven months later Weitz protested, on the occasion of the election of a new vice-president, about the exclusion of engineering and other industrial sectors from the leadership of the Chamber.[92] On this occasion the progressive *fabricant* Charbin was accepted as a compromise candidate. Two years later Weitz was behind a coup in which Morel-Journel was replaced as first vice-president by Charbin.[93] For his part Morel-Journel, very attached to the prestige of the Chamber, saw Weitz as an agent of the 'invasive' AICA.[94] There were similar conflicts in the Villefranche Chamber, where metallurgists and the retail trades agitated for a greater number of seats.[95]

The business conflicts detailed so far were essentially between two sections of large-scale capital: on the one hand the liberal establishment

[89] ADR 4m 234, report of 24 April 1918; Dufourt, *Calixte*, 22.
[90] *Le Nouvelliste*, 28 February 1928.
[91] Morel-Journel, *Journal*, 14 June 1929; PVCCL, 6 January 1930.
[92] PVCCL, 6 January 1930; Morel-Journel, *Journal*, 12 January 1932.
[93] Morel-Journel, *Journal*, 12 January 1932; PVCCL, 12 January 1932.
[94] Morel-Journel, *Journal*, 23 January and 2 May 1934.
[95] CRCCV, 29 August 1928, 28 December 1928, 19 June 1929, 30 October 1929, 27 November 1929.

and on the other the reformist metallurgical industries, with a minority of big *fabricants* like Charbin hovering between the two sides. Other points of view struggled to make themselves heard. In fact many businessmen were enamoured neither of cartelised liberal-capitalism nor of Weitz's brand of rationalising reformism and interventionism. One such group was represented by those consumption industries which remained wedded to quality production. Perhaps typical is Antoine Celle of the leather industry. He favoured economy in labour costs, the use of bonuses and a wise division of labour. But he also felt that 'he who desired the integral application of American methods in French factories would commit the same stupid error as the farmer of the Nord who wanted to grow cotton on his land'. On behalf of his own leather goods industry he bemoaned the trend towards rubber soles and mass production. Also worried about the trend towards uniform mass production were *fabricants non-usiniers* in the silk industry, dependent as they were upon home weavers. Their point of view was best represented by the president of the Church decoration and gold braid section of the SFS, Victor Perret. Perret was better known as leader of the Fédération républicaine. Since those he represented were largely excluded from the leadership of employers' associations, Perret's reaction against neo-capitalism took a political form and will be discussed in the following chapter. Small business interests were represented in the Chamber of Commerce by representatives of the Alliance des chambres syndicales lyonnaises. But its leaders, quite substantial businessmen, enjoyed a rather cosy relationship with the business establishment. Small business too was better represented politically through the Radical-Socialist Party. This left Catholic small business without a voice, especially as Catholic Action did not turn its attention in this direction until the mid-1930s. One group which did, however, begin in the 1920s to articulate a critique of the liberal establishment was the Catholic trade union movement, the CFTC.

The CFTC: a Trojan horse within the right?

The conservative elites in Lyon defined themselves in terms of business, liberal individualism and Catholicism. Employers in the engineering industry were therefore excluded for their combination of anticlericalism and left liberalism. Also denied any form of autonomous expression of their interests were non-business Catholics. This was true of elite groups such as lawyers, engineers and other professionals, which showed little consciousness of themselves as distinctive groupings. The Catholic Union social des ingénieurs chrétiens (USIC), for example, had a small membership which overlapped with patronal organisations. We shall see that such groups began to make a mark upon Lyonnais conservatism in the mid-1930s, often through social Catholic movements and later the Croix de Feu and PSF. In the 1920s and early 1930s, however, the main challenge to the elitist conception of conservatism came from Catholic trade unions, mainly dominated by white-collar workers. The elites promoted Catholicism in an effort to legitimate their power. But this destabilised the right because it gave space to the Church's efforts to defend its power. Also, subordinate groups absorbed the dominant ideology only partially and as a function of their own experience.

Liberalism and white-collar workers

This was particularly true of white-collar workers, a group which occupies a notoriously contradictory position within social relations. To a greater or lesser degree, they shared the delegated power of the capitalist but were also subject to managerial control and were excluded from ownership of property. Higher-grade employees especially were also able to exploit their relative scarcity in order to accumulate a 'cultural capital' which gave them advantages in the labour market and permitted exclusion of more subordinate groups. Because of their ambiguous position the political attitudes of white-collar workers varied from those on the left who saw themselves as part of a revolutionary proletariat to those on the right who endorsed Catholic trade unionism. In the 1920s the latter increasingly attempted to redefine the right in terms of their own ideal and material interests, especially through the Christian democratic movement.

We have seen that the ability of the liberal elites to transmit their values to subordinate groups was uneven. Success was greatest where the latter were able to use aspects of the dominant ideology to define themselves as superior to other sections of the dominated classes. This was true of the prosperous Catholic peasantry of the Lyonnais plateau. The same applied to many white-collar workers in the silk industry. In both cases liberal individualism was linked to possession of qualities needed for success in the market. It has been seen that turnover among *fabricants de soieries* was very high.[96] There were several well-publicised examples of those who were able to set up on their own. François Peissel had begun his working life in a silk packaging factory and ended it as a *commissionnaire en soieries* and Fédération deputy. This example is especially relevant because in his youth Peissel had been a trade unionist

---

[96] Laferrère, *Lyon, ville industrielle*, 97–8.

and always remained favourable to the CFTC.[97] Before 1914 the expansion of white-collar employment in all sectors – from 23% of the electorate in 1896 to 31% in 1911 – provided openings for sons of workers and shopkeepers.[98] White-collar workers themselves had a significant chance of becoming merchants and were protected against downward mobility.

The possibility of rising to a senior position and perhaps ultimately of setting up on one's own implied adhesion, outwardly at least, to the outlook of employers. This identification was positively encouraged by the conscious effort of employers to disseminate a model of dress and behaviour and by close contact of silk employees with their bosses. Offices of *fabricants* were generally modest, even dingy, affairs, where a small group of employees (almost exclusively male) could doubtless feel that they were participating in a common cause.[99] In *Calixte* Dufourt satirised the willingness of white-collar workers in certain prestigious silk firms to ape the manners of their employers and to accept meagre salaries in return for the chance to work their way up through the firm (*passer par la filière*).[100] In other words employees built up a kind of 'cultural capital'. This capital was tenuously related to ability to do the job – in *Calixte* Philippe was told by his employer that his diploma from a Parisian commercial college would be of little use. Rather there was a dual process in which employers set up 'codes of exclusion' designed to ensure that only properly socialised individuals rose to senior positions. Employees appropriated these codes and used them to set themselves off from competitors in the labour market, but could also use them as a means of creating solidarity against the employer. To this combination of Catholic and liberal values could be attributed the foresight necessary for the accumulation of savings needed to set up on one's own or for a comfortable retirement. Even the CFTC press described its own adherents as 'sober and hard-working', and was full of tirades against a society which worshipped only pleasure. That such views were often expressed in the context of attacks on the left is indicative of the inextricability of Catholicism, present or future status and political outlook.[101] The influence of liberal ideology outside the silk industry is more difficult to assess. But in the 1920s it was still common for bookkeepers and especially travelling salesmen to become self-employed. An insight into hiring policy comes from a study of the Trayvou factory

[97] Gric, *Les Courantes politiques*, 123–6.
[98] This and the following paragraph rely on Pinol, 'Mobilités et immobilismes', especially 456–7, 620–39 and 669–96.
[99] Dufourt, *Calixte*, 27.   [100] *Ibid.*, 27–8, 58–9.
[101] *La Voix sociale*, July–August 1926.

at La Mulatière – a rare example of an engineering firm run by Catholics.
It was said that it was sufficient to signal one's piety to managing director
Berthelon in order to be sure of employment.[102] It is significant that
about a dozen employees of Trayvou turn up in the Fédération
républicaine, of whom the majority were white-collar workers.

The CFTC and the ambiguities of social Catholicism

In the interwar years, however, the conditions on which this partial
incorporation of white-collar workers into the liberal-conservative right
had depended were already breaking down. First, in the interwar
period social structures became more rigid. The number of white-
collar workers in the electorate even fell a little: from 31% in 1911 to
30% in 1936. So there were fewer opportunities for working-class self-
improvement. A few white-collar workers rose to become representatives or technicians, but the chance of becoming an employer had
almost disappeared. Higher education, open only to sons of the
bourgeoisie, had become the main route to a career in management. In
other words the informally acquired credentials which had permitted a
degree of social mobility were replaced by expensive educational
requirements. Technical training was increasingly necessary for lower-
grade workers, but it fitted them only for positions below a certain
level. Stagnation in the number of male employees was associated with
growth in female employment.[103] This was explained partly by
proletarianisation of white-collar work, which also made male employees more conscious of separate interests. A CFTC bank worker
wrote of employees who were 'imprisoned in a situation of misery, shut
into a specialisation which leaves them ignorant of financial problems.
They are the common herd from which fortunes are squeezed for
others.'[104] Thus an interwar white-collar worker was more likely to
have been born to a white collar family, and would probably remain a
white-collar worker all his life. Catholic trade unions were looked to by
many as a means of defending collectively a threatened cultural capital
and of excluding women.

Alongside these structural factors must be placed the changing
strategies of the Church. The Conservative wing of Catholicism had
long been interested in trade unions. Its most lasting product was the

---

[102] François Robert, 'Trayvou 1909–39. Qualification, rationalisation et mobilité ouvrière'
(mémoire de maîtrise, Lyon II, 1986). Thanks to François Robert for allowing me to
see the interviews on which his study was based.
[103] Sylvie Zerner, 'De la Couture aux presses: l'emploi féminin entre les deux guerres',
Mouvement social 140 (1987), 9–25.
[104] *La Voix sociale*, 21 June 1925.

Corporation des employés de soierie, created in 1886.[105] It was linked to the Œuvre des cercles, founded in response to the Commune by the Legitimist Albert de Mun. The progressive Catholics of the *Chronique* also had many white-collar followers, so it was logical that it too should have founded a union in 1912.[106] After the war Gonin of the *Chronique* recruited the journalist Maurice Guérin to reconstitute local Catholic unions.[107] In March 1920 these were incorporated into the CFTC, which had been constituted nationally on 1/2 November 1919.[108]

Membership of the CFTC probably reached around 5,000 in the Rhône before the post-June 1936 expansion.[109] In 1922 women represented at least 68% of CFTC members. This was not at all typical of the CFTC nationally, and was perhaps due to the precocious implantation of female unions in Lyon.[110] Women nevertheless played a subordinate role in the CFTC: all departmental leaders were male, and most of them were white-collar workers. Female unions showed few signs of vitality. Indeed, one of the *raisons d'être* of the CFTC was to exclude women from the labour force. Even Mlle Coindre, leader of the Syndicat des dames employés, condemned female work as a symptom of the materialism evident in the cinema, literature and the arts. Women could not be forbidden to work, but the state should encourage them to return to the family.[111] Of the male manual unions only that in engineering had more than a sporadic existence, but with only fifty-four members in the region in 1922 it was numerically insignificant beside white-collar unions.

CFTC white-collar workers were most often draughtsmen, book-keepers or office workers in the silk industry. There was also a substantial minority of bank workers in the movement. The CGT recruited best among bank employees, the sales staff of the *grands magasins* and the office workers of the metallurgical industry.[112] Thus CFTC support came disproportionately from higher-grade and more independent employees. Raoul Duclos, head of the white-collar union, was chief accountant in a silk firm.[113] The Catholic/silk and metallurgy/

[105] *Ibid.*, July–August 1926; Ponson, *Les Catholiques lyonnais*, 176.
[106] Ponson, *Les Catholiques lyonnais*; Roullet, *L'Action sociale*.
[107] M. Launay, 'Le Syndicalisme chrétien en France, 1885 à 1940', (thèse d'état 1980), 1377–84.
[108] Launay, 'Le Syndicalisme chrétien', 1368ff.
[109] M. Launay, *La CFTC: Origines et développement, 1919–1940* (1986), 217, 401–2; 'Le Syndicalisme chrétien', 1473–4, 1519.
[110] Launay, 'Le Syndicalisme chrétien' 1488.
[111] *La Voix sociale*, October 1931.
[112] This analysis is based on results of Prud'homme elections in *La Voix sociale*, November 1929 and 1937.
[113] Launay, 'Le Syndicalisme chrétien', 1407.

anticlerical opposition found among employers was reproduced in the case of white-collar workers. There were doubtless many exceptions. There was for example a small core of CFTC activists among technical staff in the engineering and building industries. They had been recruited from former students of the CFTC's own Ecole d'apprentissage supérieure.[114] This proves again the rule that Catholic and anticlerical networks were related to status, career prospects and material interests to produce a diversity of groupings.

The network metaphor, the intersection of social class, sector of employment and parish structure, helps also to illuminate the ideological divisions of Catholic trade unions, and beyond that of bourgeois society and the right in the Rhône. Most CFTC activists lived in bourgeois and mixed areas of central Lyon.[115] These areas combined a strong parish network with high religious practice and the presence of large numbers of white-collar workers. The central point is that CFTC activism was not based on the enterprise but on the parish, which meant that militants acted both as white-collar workers and as Catholics. Only rarely did the Catholic unions possess an enterprise section. The exception was in certain big banks, but this was due to their concentration in the city centre. It is probable that just as many CFTC members came from smaller banks, where bosses were notorious for their hostility to unions of any tint.[116] It was in turn the nature of parish structures, themselves related to social structure and ideological traditions, that determined the tracks along which CFTC ideology travelled.

Thus the CFTC's conservative wing, essentially the silk employees of the Corporation, drew support from the 4th arrondissement, home of the traditional branch of the silk industry, of merchant-manufacturers like Victor Perret and of the once Legitimist Œuvre des cercles. The presence of the Corporation in the CFTC is a little incongruous. Guérin seems to have achieved a united front of Catholic trade unions only at the cost of allowing the Corporation to retain its separate existence rather than merge into the white-collar federation, and by making Gruffaz regional President.[117] Gruffaz admitted to a theoretical preference for mixed patron–worker unions over the CFTC formula of independence. He was reluctant to use the term 'syndicate', preferring 'profession' or 'corporation'.[118] He was suspicious of the 'furore' of unrestrained economic progress, which threatened to disorganise these

[114] *La Voix sociale*, July–August 1930.
[115] Its strongest sections were in Perrache, Bellecour and the Croix Rousse. *La Voix sociale*, March–April 1926.
[116] *La Voix sociale*, 15 July 1923, May 1927.
[117] Launay, 'Le Syndicalisme chrétien', 1387–8, 1410, 1437–41.
[118] *La Voix sociale*, October 1928, 21 October 1923.

fundamental units of society, as well as ignoring the varied tastes of the French consumer.[119] His understanding of self-improvement did not mean that anyone could become an employer simply because they possessed the necessary capital. Rather one had to learn a trade through a laborious apprenticeship to a particular station.[120] This was understood by Gruffaz's obituarist, who saw his special merit as having remained an *employé* all his life, and never to have desired anything else.[121] For Gruffaz it was not merely occupation of a post which determined a just salary, but the competence and moral worth of the occupier. He was therefore concerned that technical schools should provide students with a moral education.[122] Thus Gruffaz drew on the Catholic notion of vocation in order to echo the concern with acquisition of cultural capital described above, but linked it to protection of status rather than social mobility.

Gruffaz's views were also close to those *fabricants* who saw corporatism as a defence against the decline of the luxury industries and the artisanate. Gruffaz enjoyed a particularly close relationship with one such employer, Victor Perret, whose own senior employees appeared at meetings of the Corporation. The Corporation remained the 'faithful tenant' of the Association catholique des patrons, which had been presided over in the early 1900s by Perret's father. Gruffaz was also a member of the Fédération républicaine, of which Perret junior was President. Both Corporation and Fédération recruited from groups affiliated to the Œuvre des cercles.[123] Cardinal-Archbishop Maurin himself was sympathetic to Gruffaz's brand of trade unionism.[124] In the early 1920s it was rumoured that he had sought papal condemnation of the CFTC.[125]

The more left-leaning CFTC adherents were also recruited from the parishes, but from the Groupes d'études sociales, part of the *Chronique*'s mini-empire, rather than the Cercles d'hommes which nourished the Corporation and Fédération républicaine. Indeed, Guérin denounced the 'syndicat-cercle'. Relations were so close that in 1926 fusion of CFTC and Cercles d'études was envisaged.[126] These were stronger on the left bank of the Rhône, where the elites were more progressive and parishes more recently implanted. Progressives dominated the white-

---

[119] *Ibid.*, May 1927; April 1930.
[120] *Ibid.*, 16 December 1923, 10 May 1925.   [121] *Ibid.*, 1937.
[122] *Ibid.*, 1937, April 1930.
[123] *Ibid.*, September–October 1926 and November 1929.
[124] Launay, *La CFTC*, 76–9.
[125] Launay, 'Le Syndicalisme chrétien', 1493–1507; Launay, *La CFTC*, 256.
[126] In May 1926 one study group voted to transform itself into a section of the CFTC white-collar union (Launay, 'Le Syndicalisme chrétien', 1515–16).

collar and engineering federations. Their most lucid spokesman was Maurice Guérin.[127] The CFTC defended the Eight Hour Law and agitated for social insurance institutions free from patronal control. It played a leading role in the 1925 bank strike, after which a number of its militants were sacked. In some circumstances the CFTC was prepared to collaborate with the CGT and CGTU. But it remained firm in its hostility to communism as an ideology.[128] For the CFTC class conflict was to be contained by index linking of wages and institutionalised under the control of the state through a system of compulsory syndicalisation and collective bargaining. Class struggle was an inevitable feature of modern society, but it did not have to be pursued to the death.[129]

Such pronouncements caused the CGT and CGTU to characterise the CFTC as a bosses' union. There is some evidence to support this, for it had been formed in the midst of postwar antiBolshevik paranoia and some of its affiliates were subsequently formed, in the classic manner of 'yellow' unions, after the defeat of long and bitter strikes.[130] Some CFTC demands were traditional Catholic ones, such as the right of workers to a weekly rest day, and the belief that salaries should be high enough to permit women to stay at home. What is more, Guérin was as concerned as Gruffaz to relate white-collar work to possession of a certain lifestyle. He was among the first to denounce easy enjoyment and 'worship of the god of pleasure', which he believed had led to the triumph of the Cartel des gauches in 1924. From such tirades against women in low-cut dresses, men who believed that their dignity rested in the style of their socks, cinemas, dancing and the wearing of jewellery, it is possible to deduce the self-image of the Catholic trade unionist.[131] The difference was now that CFTC activists sought to *impose* through collective action a set of criteria intended to improve the position of Catholics in the labour market. Similarly the progressive CFTC retained faith in social mobility but believed that promotion prospects were to be defended collectively.[132] Hence for example the union's unsuccessful struggle to attach to the collective contract in the engineering industry a set of dispositions designed to improve the moral structure of the profession. Thus the CFTC sought to use this cultural capital to constitute competitors as subordinate. It was this appropriation of

[127] *La Voix sociale*, 20 January 1924; Launay, *La CFTC*, 24. Guérin left Lyon for a national post in 1927.
[128] *La Voix sociale*, January 1931; Launay, 'Le Syndicalisme chrétien', 1520.
[129] *Le Voix sociale*, December 1926.
[130] For example the tram company (Office des tramways lyonnais–OTL) union formed in 1928.
[131] *La Voix sociale*, July–August 1926.   [132] *Ibid.*, 1 January 1922, 21 June 1925.

aspects of the (locally) dominant ideology in order to exclude competitors which placed the CFTC within the right. Material issues and Catholicism were inseparable, so it was difficult for the CFTC to collaborate with the CGT even where interests apparently coincided.

Nevertheless, the emphasis on collective action and the commitment to a form of social democracy meant that the CFTC simultaneously contested the liberal-conservative hegemony.[133] Moreover, its ideas converged with those of the progressive-minded businessmen described above. The CFTC did not talk in terms of 'classlessness', as the liberal elites had, but saw social conflict as a fact of life. Maurice Guérin welcomed rationalisation as a means of diminishing the difficulty of work and of reducing the cost of goods – so long as the 'organised profession' ensured that harmful consequences were kept to a minimum.[134] The CFTC could boast some practical success, for along with the CGT it signed the collective contract in the engineering industry in 1928.[135] Yet the CFTC was scarcely the natural ally of the often anticlerical metallurgical employers. Catholic trade unions, to their annoyance, had at first been excluded from the negotiations for the collective contract. The CFTC was later permitted to sign, but its ideas on the moralisation of the profession were rejected. A spokesman for the engineering draughtsmen denounced the hypocrisy of bosses who permitted marital infidelity and attendance at the cinema, but refused paid holidays.[136]

The CFTC was more successful in establishing contact with progressive Catholic employers through the Confédération française des professions. Representatives of the *gros façonniers* in the silk industry were particularly willing to listen. Other Catholic employers were less keen on the CFTC, as the following extract from an open letter of Auguste Isaac reveals:

You, the CFTC, share with the socialists the misconception that the boss is always rich and that business is always good . . . Only today I have received a letter from a bourgeois woman which makes my heart bleed, in which she recounts how every day she is obliged to watch her daughters do their own cooking. Do you realise that the majority of housekeepers will no longer look after the children at night? The crisis of domestic service is no less serious than that of housing. Both result from multiple causes, but at the bottom one always finds the law of least effort.

---

[133] *Ibid.*, 12 March 1922. The main headline of the second issue of La Voix sociale (1 February 1922) was 'Le Libéralisme économique à l'assaut du syndicalisme chrétien'.
[134] *La Voix sociale*, March 1927.   [135] See pages 76–7.
[136] *La Voix sociale*, October 1930.

Isaac went on to argue against the CFTC's view that Catholic social teaching obliged backing for the Eight Hour Law. On the contrary, said Isaac, his own Catholicism had taught him that work was the law of man, that laziness was a sin and that he who did not use his talents to the full was ignorant of the laws of God.[137] Isaac's letter reveals then a deep class and cultural division within Catholicism, and illustrates perfectly that social and political conflict could be produced in France by the way in which religion was combined with divergent conceptions of political economy.

The emergence of Catholic trade unionism was then of great political importance. Its membership may have been limited in comparison with the 30,000 CGT members in the Rhône in 1935.[138] Nevertheless CFTC militants could get themselves heard through the Catholic press, particularly the *Croix du Rhône*. In the bank strike of 1925 the CFTC manifestly spoke for a large number of employees. Both wings of the CFTC were related to conflicts within the right. On the one hand the Corporation aligned itself with Victor Perret and his brand of traditionalism. On the other the majority wing of the CFTC, the *Chronique* and Œuvre des cercles were part of a political network which included the PDP and extended into the Fédération républicaine where it had the sympathy of the deputy Peissel. Like the JAC the CFTC was part of a crisis of conservatism in the Rhône. Both movements paved the way for the Croix de Feu.

Since the 1890s the liberal elites of Lyon had defined themselves in terms of liberalism, big business and a synthesis of the Victorian work ethic with Catholic asceticism. Belief in individualism and the career open to talent was also transmitted, partially at least, to elite groups such as engineers, managers and perhaps also the liberal professions. This combination of liberalism and Catholicism also appealed to white-collar workers within Lyon, who were able to use aspects of the dominant ideology to constitute themselves as superior to other sections of the subordinate classes. However, the position of the liberal elites depended on the maintenance of favourable economic conditions and on the willingness of the Church to tolerate the liberal hegemony.

In the interwar period both of these conditions were undermined. The Second Industrial Revolution and the impact of war created conflicts between new and old and large and small industries. Capitalist concentration and economic growth also changed the conditions within which white-collar workers were employed. At the same time the

---

[137] Auguste Isaac, open letter to the CFTC, *La Voix sociale*, 29 July 1922.
[138] A. Prost, *La CGT à l'époque du Front populaire* (1964), 212.

Church began to use its organisational resources in order to reach particular social groups. The new Catholic movements were based on the idea of class collaboration, but in practice they were unable to overcome divisions among Catholics, and reinforced divisions within the major socio-economic groupings. The result was a complex series of alignments which can be summarised as follows.

1 The liberal and Catholic elite retained support among big business in the silk, artificial-fibre, dyeing and chemical industries, and in a measure difficult to ascertain was endorsed by managers and professional groups.

2 Some sections of this elite, such as Paul Charbin, were half-tempted by neocapitalist ideas about rationalisation, organisation of social forces and reform. But they articulated these ideas through social Catholic groups rather than Redressement français.

3 Some Catholic businessmen, especially medium businessmen like the *gros façonniers*, adopted a more advanced version of social Catholicism, and connected with the views of the progressive wing of the CFTC and Christian democracy.

4 Employers in the engineering industry were opposed to the liberal and Catholic establishment on both religious and economic grounds. They were also divided from more progressive businessmen and the CFTC by the religious issue.

5 In opposition to neocapitalism there developed a right-wing Catholic reaction. This included many medium businessmen, the merchant-manufacturing wing of the silk industry and the conservative wing of the CFTC. The key figure was Victor Perret who played a vital role in both the SFS and the Fédération républicaine.

4   Rural society in the Rhône

A relatively insignificant 18% of the population of the Rhône lived in communes defined as rural; 64,000 economically active persons were occupied in agriculture. The figures confirm the predominantly urban and industrial nature of the department. Yet because of the advantage that conservative parties drew from overrepresentation in elected bodies, the rural world cannot be neglected. During the *Belle époque* the peasantry had provided much of the electoral backing for the wealthy notables who represented Progressisme in Parliament. But this did not mean that peasants had been incorporated into an 'hegemonic bloc'. Support among the peasantry was conditional, while in many areas the rural elites remained suspicious of Progressisme. First, in the Monts du Lyonnais and the Beaujolais voters backed the Progressistes in legislative elections only because the arrangement of constituency boundaries submerged the antirepublican minority. In both areas many wealthy aristocratic or bourgeois Catholic notables retained a hankering after monarchy. In the Lyonnais mountains they relied on the influence of the Church over isolated peasants. In the Beaujolais they depended on the ties of landowner and sharecropper as well as on the Church. Second, in the Beaujolais mountains, peasants were equally isolated and open to clerical influence. But here moderate republican industrialists were more powerful than nobles. So an elite-dominated Progressisme flourished, again with the tacit support of the Church. Thirdly, on the plateau there existed a peasant conservatism based on Catholicism, prosperity, market opportunity and loyalty to Progressiste notables. During the interwar period, in all three areas, the leadership of notables, whatever their political colour, was called into question, just as the position of the liberal elite had been undermined in urban society.

One cause was a strengthening of medium peasant farms: there was a fall of 36% in the number of holdings in the Rhône between 1912 and 1942, while average size increased from 6.5 to 9.5 hectares. The main

cause was the departure of small proprietors from the countryside.[1]
Before 1914 the rural exodus in the Rhône had been relatively
restrained. But losses in World War One, the resulting low marriage and
birth rates, together with high mortality, and the attraction of employment in an expanding industrial economy, caused depopulation to
gather pace.[2] Small peasants were least likely to have the capital
necessary for reconstruction of their holdings and were most likely to
limit families to a single child. Depopulation led in many areas to
domination of villages by medium peasants, as the pro-Radical rural
bourgeoisie, petty bourgeoisie and marginal proprietors departed. One
result was gradual conquest of the Conseil général by the right, for
medium peasants were mainly conservative. In the longer term depopulation contributed to peasant self-consciousness. Meanwhile tenants and
sharecroppers benefited from a shortage of competition for leases, which
may have assisted them in shaking off the domination of landowners.
Peasant isolation was also broken down by greater prosperity, improved
communications, involvement in new forms of sociability such as
veterans associations and integration into the market economy.

The market, however, was a mixed blessing, for increased specialisa-
tion and reliance on national and international markets also made
peasants vulnerable to price fluctuations. In the Beaujolais this caused
increasingly independent peasants to turn to the Parti socialiste
(SFIO), which preached the value of co-operatives and state support
for prices. In the mountains and on the plateau, on the other hand, the
peasant response to the market was formulated in the context of
Catholicism. In the 1920s the Church, as part of its re-Christianisation
drive, accentuated its critique of economic liberalism and attempted to
reach peasants through the JAC. At the end of the decade this
movement was beginning to come into conflict with established
agricultural syndicalism in the form of the USE. The JAC prepared the
way for the Croix de Feu and PSF.

This view of rural society calls into question Pierre Barral's contention
that conflict within the countryside was subordinate to a global hostility
to urban and industrial society.[3] The town/country opposition may have
been one of the conflicts which structured social relations, but the
peasantry were integrated via social Catholicism and socialism into
national political conflicts. More acceptable is Philippe Gratton's view

---

[1] Garrier, *Paysans du Lyonnais*, 463–91, 581–2. My analysis of peasant society draws its
conclusions to a considerable extent from the mass of data presented in this work.
[2] *Ibid.*, 619–35.
[3] Pierre Barral, *Les Agrariens français de Méline à Pisani* (1968), 14.

that the development of rural capitalism created inequalities in the position of large and small producers within the market.[4] In this sense peasants were an exploited class. But one cannot move directly from property and market relations to class formation, consciousness and socialist politics, as Gratton attempts to do. This is because class was not the only axis of monopolisation and exclusion in French society.[5] Peasants were potentially brought together by class interest, but at the same time pulled apart by the religious divide above all. This is why some peasants sought socialist solutions to their problems and others turned to social Catholicism. The result was both division of the peasantry and class conflict within the right. But it would be insufficient to say that class interests were 'mediated' by an ideological super-structure. Rather we should see rural politics in terms of a web of cross-cutting projects, which in the minds of historical actors were inseparable, of which liberation of peasants from market fluctuations was only one. Of equal importance was the attempt of the Church to re-Christianise the peasantry. So we could just as easily say that the communal solidarity of Catholics created a potential for collective action, but that Catholics were also pulled apart by class. Before analysing the resulting struggles it is necessary to provide a brief introduction to the conservative electorate in the department.

The conservative electorate

The election of 1932 was used to produce a typology of political orientations in the communes situated outside the agglomeration.[6] Fourteen types were produced, which have been regrouped into three categories according to whether there was predominance of right or left, or near equality of the two camps (Maps 8–10). The mean percentage of votes cast in each type, together with the number of communes in each type, is shown in Table 1.

It can be seen from Map 8 that almost all areas of right-wing predominance were located in the mountains. The conservative vote is highest in type 1, which is most often found in the interiors of the ranges, and where the average score of the right was no less than 89%. In type 2 it falls to a still impressive 74%. Type 3, in which conservative candidates gained on average 62%, is distinguished by a certain strength

[4] P. Gratton, *Les Paysans contre l'agrairisme* (1972).
[5] Murphy, *Social Closure*, 122–8.
[6] The method used is hierarchical cluster analysis (see M. J. Norusis, *SPSS-X Introductory Statistics Guide* (Chicago, 1988), 219–33. The technique involves grouping the communes into types according to similarities in voting patterns. Note that the separation of the fourteen types into three on the maps was not the result of statistical analysis, but was done to facilitate interpretation.

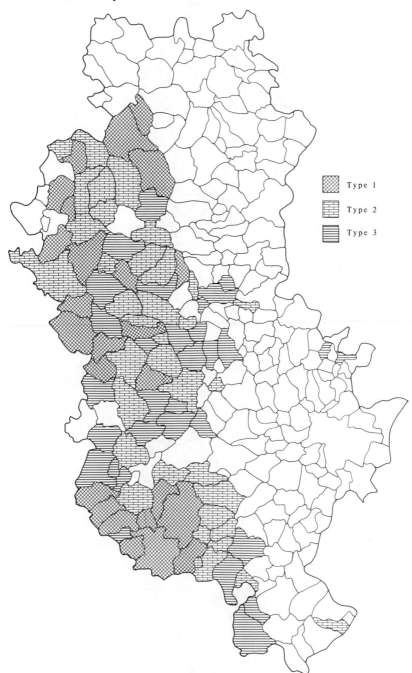

Map 8   The Rhône: typology of political space, 1932: the right

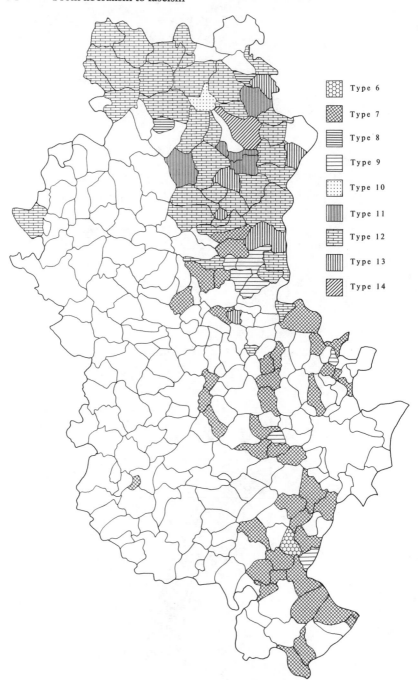

Map 9   The Rhône: typology of political space, 1932: the left

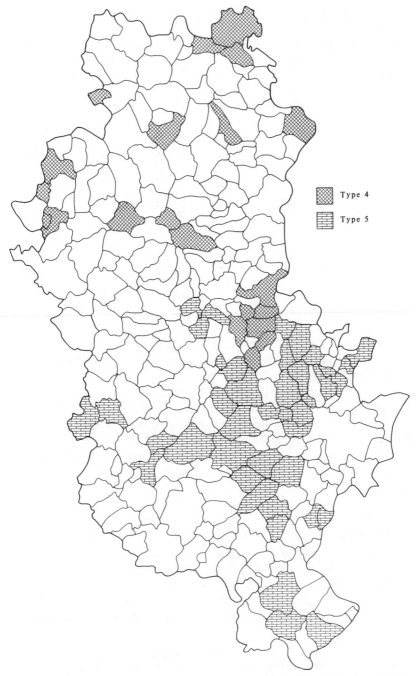

Map 10   The Rhône: typology of political space, 1932: equality of left and right

Table 1 *Typology of voting behaviour in 1932: mean percentage of votes cast by type*

Type	Number	Right	Radical	SFIO	PCF
1	25	89	6	4	1
2	37	74	16	8	2
3	32	62	28	8	3
4	22	52	10	33	4
5	41	51	40	6	3
6	1	14	81	1	4
7	42	38	43	13	5
8	2	9	45	46	0
9	7	27	35	31	8
10	1	5	0	93	2
11	4	23	12	64	1
12	36	37	12	49	2
13	7	9	45	46	1
14	1	26	14	38	22

of radicalism. Only in industrial towns and villages of the Beaujolais mountains (type 4), and the Brévenne valley (type 5), was the left able to challenge the right.

On the plateau two types predominate. Type 5, in which the right gained a small majority of votes (51%), represents a transition from conservative strength in the mountains to relative weakness in the more densely populated industrial east. It covers much of the west and north of the plateau, as well as the Brévenne valley. On the eastern fringe of the plateau and in isolated industrial centres like Sain Bel the conservative score falls to a still respectable 38% (type 7). The main rivals of the right in both cases were the Radicals.

The Beaujolais viticole, like mountainous Monsols to the north, was a bastion of socialism.[7] In the four communes of type 11, for example, the socialist vote was 64%, while in type 12, to which thirty-seven communes belong, it was 49%. Only in a few communes, mainly situated in the canton of Anse, were conservatives a match for the combined left, winning an average of 52% of the vote.

Contemporaries were in no doubt that this pattern was accounted for

---

[7] That a mountainous canton like Monsols was socialist is to be explained by the concentration of inhabitants in small villages where many were occupied in sawmills, and by the fact that many worked at harvest time for winegrowers in the Beaujolais.

by two variables: Catholicism and agriculture.[8] A report at the 1936 congress of the Fédération républicaine identified the Catholic peasantry as the main source of support for the party, admitted an inability to cross the Catholic/anticlerical divide, and reported a lack of success in small rural towns where the socialists could exploit their 'ridiculous tall story about the 200 families'.[9] The geography of conservatism lends considerable support to these views. It coincides broadly with the first surveys of religious practice in the department carried out in the mid-1950s. Height above sea level of a commune was shown to be the best predictor of religious practice.[10] Neither is there any reason to doubt the existence of a strong correlation between the agricultural population and right-wing voting. This relationship appears even at the lowest level of analysis. A report on the mountain commune of St Genis l'Argentière (St Laurent) divided the population into 800 farmers who were mainly conservative, and twenty-seven leftists employed in quarries and tile factories.[11] All the same, the correlation between conservatism and the peasantry must be qualified. Variables such as form and size of landholding, extent of involvement in the market, settlement patterns and sociability must also be taken into account. Some of these influences were examined by the method of multiple regression (for models and explanation of sources see appendix one).

In wine-growing areas the conservative vote was highest in communes where religious practice was high, where proprietors were numerous, where population was declining, where co-operative members were few, and where the proportion of land devoted to the vine was relatively low. Given that population loss led often to domination of villages by medium proprietors, and given also the appeal of the co-operative movement to smaller proprietors, it can be inferred that conservatism in the Beaujolais was an affair of Catholic polycultural medium and large peasant proprietors. This is confirmed by the nature of the left-wing vote in the same area. Radicalism did badly in areas where sharecropping was important, and was strong in communes with more stable populations. As Tony Judt has shown for the Var, Radicalism was stronger in socially mixed communes. It was therefore eroded by the rural exodus and by the growth of class antagonism. Socialism, on the other hand, was in the ascendant in the Beaujolais. The SFIO vote is best explained by monoculture of the vine

[8] B. M. E. Léger, *Les Opinions politiques des provinces françaises* (1934), 139–40.
[9] *L'Union républicaine*, 21 June 1936; Berstein, *Histoire du Parti radicale*, II, 308.
[10] *L'Archidiocèse de Lyon: situation démographique et religieuse*, 2 vols. (Lyon, 1958).
[11] ADR 4m, *Conseils municipaux*, dossier St Laurent de Chamousset, report of 16 April 1941; Henri de Farcy, *Paysans du Lyonnais: la vie agricole dans la vallée de l'Yzeron* (Lyon, 1950), 129–30.

and the presence of co-operative members. It is therefore reasonable to assume that socialism appealed to (anticlerical) small proprietors who saw in co-operatives a means of escaping subservience to the market. Particularly intriguing is the absence of correlation between either socialist or conservative votes and sharecroppers, for contemporary observers were impressed by the advance of socialism in this category.[12] Our results suggest that this traditionally deferential category was now divided in its loyalties.

In non-wine-growing communes the conservative vote is, as expected, closely associated with high religious practice. Other variables have relatively little impact on the conservative vote. But here too Radicalism shows the expected strength in communes with stable populations. On the plateau too, emigration of artisans and small proprietors strengthened the right and weakened Radicalism. Albert Pin shows that this was the explanation for the passage to the right of Messimy (Vaugneray) in 1919. The process was exemplified by mayor Jean Parrel, whose farm grew by renting, purchase and inheritance from little more than 5 hectares in 1919 to nearly 15 in 1939.[13] As in wine-growing communes, differentiation among the peasantry is problematic. Tenants are a relatively good indicator of conservative voting, whilst proprietors contribute to the explanation of the Radical vote. The direction of causation is hard to unravel. It could be that both religious practice and conservative voting were high in the mountains because tenants were relatively wealthy or perhaps open to landlord influence. But closer analysis shows that in the mountains most peasants, whether tenants or proprietors and whatever the size of their holdings, were conservative. In Ste Catherine (Mornant), where the right gained 162 of 183 votes cast, only fourteen tenants were inscribed on the electoral lists of the Chamber of Agriculture, compared with seventy proprietors. It can therefore be concluded that the power of conservative elites depended less on manipulation of dependent tenants than upon the influence of the Church on the isolated peasantry as a whole. On the plateau, on the other hand, peasants were not unanimously conservative. In Montagny (Givors) – interestingly a commune in which most peasants lived in the bourg – 63% of registered electors voted Radical and only 11% for the right; forty-one electors were listed as proprietors and only six as tenants/sharecroppers. Given the negative correlation between Radicalism and population loss, it would seem that it was mainly small proprietors, perhaps also engaged in non-agricultural pursuits, who voted for the Radicals.

---

[12] *Le Nouveau Journal*, 25 February 1935.
[13] Albert Pin, 'Un notable paysan de l'entre-deux-guerres: Jean-Marie Parrel' (mémoire de maîtrise, Lyon II, 1989).

In sum, conservatism rarely drew its electoral support from groups which were directly open to manipulation. Even in the Beaujolais its hold over sharecroppers was declining. The conservative electorate, all over the department, consisted largely of a growing class of polycultural Catholic medium peasants resident in communes increasingly dominated by agriculture. The elites, liberal-conservative or crypto-monarchist, could retain this support as long as there lasted a delicate alliance with the Church, and prosperity and peasant isolation endured.

The mountains

In the mountains the power of conservative notables had always been indirect, depending more on the loyalty of an isolated and relatively poor peasantry to the Church. This is why the right held the allegiance of both proprietors and tenants. Landowners were noble in the Monts du Lyonnais, so a crypto-monarchist variety of conservatism dominated. Bourgeois property was more common in the Monts du Beaujolais, especially around Tarare where businessmen and other wealthy residents of cotton towns owned land, permitting the moderate Republican conservatism of Laurent Bonnevay to flourish.

Most farmers owned and worked their own land, though tenants were more numerous in the mountains than anywhere else in the department. The great majority of farms were of about 12–14 hectares, though some were as small as 2 and others as large as 40.[14] Tenants were relatively privileged, for they were grouped in areas where conditions were better, such as the mountain interiors and the Azergues valley. In those parts of the mountains in which terrain permitted agricultural activity, farmers lived either in hamlets of two or three families or in isolated dwellings in the middle of farms. This, in other words, was the classic settlement pattern in areas of poor upland farming where farms had to be large.[15] Communication was not always easy, especially during the winter. The steep slopes of the mountain borders were a barrier. They split the commune of Thurins into two separate worlds. As late as 1949 dwellers in the upland part of the commune went to mass in Yzeron and to the market in St Martin en Haut. Only administrative reasons obliged them to descend to Thurins-bourg.[16] Dairy farmers in the cantons of St Symphorian and St Laurent were obliged by the insufficiency of the transport system to specialise in the production of cheese and butter

[14] Jean Guicherd and Charles Ponsart, *L'Agriculture du Rhône en 1926* (Lyon, 1927), 361.
[15] A. Perrin, 'Le Mont d'Or lyonnais et ses abords', *Etudes rhodanniennes* 3 (1927), 55–81; Guiot, *Thurins*.
[16] Guiot, *Thurins*.

rather than milk.[17] In these conditions it is hardly surprising that peasants pursued their own affairs without much thought for their neighbours. There was, for example, no co-operation among farmers for the hiring of labour, as there was in some parts of France.[18] It was said that until the appearance of the motor car the mountains were regarded by non-natives as equal in remoteness to the North Pole.[19]

Attendance at mass provided the only regular link between peasant families. Religious practice was indeed high. In the mountain interiors over 90% of men and women were regular attenders at mass. The Church idealised a region in which families were numerous, values were patriarchal, work was respected and gendarmes had little to do.[20] But deeper analysis reveals a number of significant changes which affected the relationship of peasants to notables. In 1932 a political activist wrote that 'after mass the men invade the cafés. For this is the only available opportunity for these honest men to get together to discuss their professional interests or those of the commune. For the rest of the week each is preoccupied by his own tasks and takes little notice of his neighbour.'[21] This quotation reaffirms the centrality of the Church to peasant sociability. But the fact that peasants were prepared to spend much of the day in the café is also important. In some parts of France declining attendance at vespers reflected the appearance of rival after-noon attractions and represented the first signs of de-Christianisation.[22] In the Rhône mountains things had not gone that far. But there are further reasons to suspect the existence of a more cohesive and independent peasantry.

First, progress of medium properties at the expense of small matched the general trend in the department. As elsewhere the cause was a decline in population. It was most evident in the Monts du Beaujolais, where silk and cotton weaving ceased from the late nineteenth century to provide supplementary income to peasants scraping a living from impoverished soils.[23] The communes of the Monts du Lyonnais were less affected. A natural surplus of births over deaths only just failed to compensate for emigration of the young.[24] But everywhere in the

[17] Garrier, *Paysans du Lyonnais*, 611–12.
[18] G. Le Bras, *Etudes de sociologie réligieuse* (1938), 153–4; G. Le Bras, 'Notes de statistique et d'histoire réligieuses', *Revue d'histoire de l'Eglise de France* 6 (1933), 503–5; G. Le Bras, *Introduction à l'histoire de la pratique religieuse en France*, 2 vols. (1942 and 1945); Farcy, *Paysans du Lyonnais*, 139–40; *L'Archidiocèse de Lyon*.
[19] Guicherd and Ponsart, *L'Agriculture du Rhône*, 365; Henri Lagardette, *Impressions beaujolais: de la résistance à la vigne* (Lyon, 1931).
[20] *La Croix du Rhône*, 29 May 1939.   [21] *L'Union républicaine*, 10 July 1932.
[22] Lagrée, *Religion et cultures en Bretagne*, 72.
[23] The worst-affected canton, Lamure, lost 42% of its population between 1906 and 1936.
[24] Garrier, *Paysans du Lyonnais*, 619–35;

mountains subdivision of land was halted, a major reason being the high cost of constructing new farm buildings.[25] This process coincided in many areas with the decline of rural weaving, which caused many areas to revert to dependence on agriculture alone. Even around industrial Tarare communes such as Dareizé and Joux returned to agriculture.[26] We shall see that in the interwar period most mayors were recruited from among peasant notables.[27]

Second, there are signs that the ties of dependence between landlord and tenant were weaker than ever. This was partly because of the difficulty of finding tenants. Rents were said in 1926 to be on average two and a half times their 1914 level, an increase far outstripped by inflation. Often land was sold to the tenant. Proprietors resident in Lyon often left total liberty to their tenants, not daring to increase a sometimes derisory rent.[28] Furthermore, many landowners were absent. One example was Alexandre La Bâtie, mayor of Montromand and leader of the Fédération républicaine in the canton. He was hardly ever in Montromand, and in 1937 found that his influence had been eroded by the PSF.

Thirdly dairy farming was beginning to transform the economy of the mountains. In the early 1920s peasants remained subsistence farmers. It was calculated in 1926 that the price of milk covered only half of production costs. Also, there were problems resulting from the over-population and mongrelisation of cattle, insufficient forage, and epidemics of foot and mouth disease. Yet matters gradually improved. After a two-year struggle by producers' associations, including an abortive strike in 1922, the price of milk was raised to a more satisfactory level by an accord with the wholesale trade in 1924. A marked improvement in productivity followed. In the Monts du Lyonnais, where transport was too poor for milk to be sent to Lyon, small cheese and butter factories were established.[29] The market, then, brought peasants into active involvement with each other and with agricultural syndicates.

Fourthly, a rising money income may have permitted a more diverse sociability. In the 1920s most communes possessed running water and electricity; supplies to remote hamlets now preoccupied the authorities. One consequence of the arrival of electricity was that peasants could listen to the radio. Little is known of the impact of radio on rural society,

[25] Guicherd and Ponsart, L'Agriculture du Rhône, 361.
[26] Albout, 'Démographie et industrialisation'.   [27] See chapter 6.
[28] Guicherd and Ponsart, L'Agriculture du Rhône, 362, 554, 586; Barral, Les Agrariens français, 191–4.
[29] Garrier, Paysans du Lyonnais, 609–12; Barral, Les Agrariens Français, 212–13.

but it is possible that receivers in the cafés frequented on Sunday afternoons formed a part of social life. Those peasants who had returned from the war joined veterans' groups: according to Antoine Prost it was the *mouvement ancien combattant* which took on the role of animator of social life in the countryside during the interwar years.[30] Such changes should not be exaggerated. But it does seem that the isolation of mountain dwellers both from each other and from the outside world was breaking down at a time when the influence of large landowners was declining for economic reasons. The mountains remained, nevertheless, overwhelmingly Catholic, so peasant self-consciousness was likely to be expressed within the right.

The plateau

In some respects peasant society on the plateau resembled that of the mountains. The settlement pattern was less dispersed, but still there were no large peasant villages to compare with those of Provence. To the north peasants typically lived in hamlets of five or six farms, situated on the steep sides of valleys. This is explained by the fractured topography, shortage of cultivatable land, abundance of sources of water and need for shelter from the sun. Only towards the southern edge of the plateau were there larger villages.[31] But even here bourgs often contained a largely non-agricultural population.[32]

Furthermore, all sources agree that peasants lived rather isolated lives. Farmhouses were often surrounded by high windowless walls which, in the view of a contemporary geographer, symbolised 'the hereditary desire for isolation, the fear of involvement in the lives of others and of allowing others to interfere in their own'. He also reports that in the 1920s there was much feuding between peasants.[33] Mutual aid was not unknown, but was limited to family and immediate neighbours. As in the mountains, attendance at mass on Sundays remained the primary form of social life. Without attaining the levels of the mountains, church attendance remained respectable, and was clearly related to the proportion of peasants in the population. Moreover, religious life was private. It did not involve collective ceremonies or the 'chants de foule' of Alsace or Brittany.[34]

But at this point similarity with the mountains ends. Population

---

[30] Antoine Prost, *Les Anciens Combattants et la société française*, 3 vols. (1977), II, 180–213.
[31] Garrier, *Paysans du Lyonnais*, 162–3.   [32] Guiot, *Thurins*, 113.
[33] Farcy, *Paysans du Lyonnais*, 107–9.
[34] *Ibid.*, 139–40: Vaugneray: 50% for men and 60% for women; Pin, 'Un Notable paysan', 35.

density was much higher; communications were easier. The proximity of an urban market compensated for unfavourable agricultural conditions. A decisive turning point in the plateau economy was the wine over-production crisis of 1907, from which time fruit, a much more profitable cash crop, began to replace wine.[35] Progress was halted during the war years, but between 1921 and 1931 prosperity returned as recovery was aided by state and private institutions. Even in the Bas Beaujolais, fruit began to supplant poorer-quality wines.[36] At first produce had been destined primarily for Lyon, but this market was easily saturated owing to ease of communication with the lower Rhône valley, and so peasants increasingly concentrated on good-quality production for a wide national and international market.[37] This further encouraged specialisa-tion – Chaponost and Irigny for example concentrated on strawberries. The difficulties presented by climate, terrain and soil meant that peasants were obliged to avoid putting all their eggs in one basket.[38] Intensive monoculture was largely confined to the *grande banlieue*, an area where vegetable production by small market gardeners was also important.[39] Nonetheless, fruit production helped break down peasant isolation. Most transported their own produce to railheads or even to markets in Lyon.[40] This was particularly true of market gardeners, who were both small traders and peasants, possessed of a strong collective identity.[41] Peasants were also exposed to price fluctuations in a world market. Heavy borrowing to finance investment in fruit production left them poorly equipped to face an economic downturn.[42]

This was all the more so because on the plateau the trend towards reinforcement of medium property was uneven. In many areas subdivi-sion of land continued unabated throughout the interwar period. This appears to have been particularly true in areas where fruit production was most profitable.[43] On the other hand the same areas were also likely to experience an influx of commuters, and small peasants were most vulnerable to the advance of urban property.[44] But some communes in

---

[35] André Cholley, 'Quelques remarques sur la culture et le commerce des fruits dans la banlieue de Lyon', *Etudes rhodaniennes* 3 (1927), 83–107; Garrier, *Paysans du Lyonnais*, 448–50.

[36] Cholley, 'Culture de fruits'; Garrier, *Paysans du Lyonnais*, 614.

[37] Cholley, 'Cultures de fruits', 88.   [38] *Ibid.*, 103–7.

[39] R. Jeantet and J. Willemain, 'La Banlieue maraîchère et la commerce des légumes à Lyon jusqu'en 1939', *Etudes rhodaniennes* 16 (1940) 221–74.

[40] Cholley, 'Culture de fruits', 84.

[41] Jeantet and Willemain, 'La Banlieue maraîchère', 250.

[42] Garrier, *Paysans du Lyonnais*, 614–15.

[43] Farcy, *Paysans du Lyonnais*, 73–4; Garrier, *Paysans du Lyonnais*, 550; Guiot, *Thurins*, 25.

[44] Guiot, *Thurins*; Garrier, *Paysans du Lyonnais*, 549.

close proximity to Lyon, such as Brignais, became almost entirely agricultural as the rural artisanate departed. In more westerly communes such as Messimy, however, there was both a growth in the number of medium farms and a tendency for the non-agricultural population to depart.[45] The tendency towards 'peasantisation' was uneven, but real.

The point to emphasise, however, is that on all parts of the plateau the social independence of the peasantry contrasted with vulnerability to the market. In some circumstances this might have led to socialism. But on the plateau conservatism derived from the relative prosperity of peasants raised in a Catholic, but not clerical, tradition. Republican notables like Aynard had grafted onto this Catholicism a democratic rhetoric which stressed the spirit of initiative of small property and presented railways as an opportunity for peasants to break into a wider market. This kind of thinking appealed especially to those medium peasants with sufficient land to be able to take advantage of new opportunities, and who saw their own Catholic values as essential to family stability, social status and avoidance of the consequences of inheritance laws – the 'bonnes familles' – of which the Parrel family in Messimy was a typical example.[46] Their value system was revealed in denunciations of materialism and love of luxury among people such as dairy maids.[47] The left, on the other hand, was associated with a (declining) rural petty bourgeoisie and small peasantry. Thus the Progressiste hegemony on the plateau was dependent on the goodwill of the Church, never enamoured of liberalism, and upon the maintenance of economic prosperity.

The Beaujolais

The anticlericalism, radicalism, and even socialism of the Beaujolais peasantry contrasted sharply with the relative passivity of farmers in the mountains and with the contentment of the proprietors of the plateau. Here the influence of the right was confined to large landowners, to some but not all of their sharecropping clientele and to Catholic medium proprietors, especially in the southernmost part of the Beaujolais where conditions were similar to those on the plateau. The Beaujolais was an area of class and cultural conflict, brilliantly satirised in Gabriel Chevallier's 1934 novel *Clochemerle*, for which the model was the village of Vaux en Beaujolais.[48] How is the weakness of the right in the Beaujolais to be accounted for?

First, contrasts in social structure were very marked. Large proprietors, sometimes bourgeois but most often aristocratic, dominated most

---

[45] Pin, 'Un Notable paysan', 113–41.   [46] *Ibid.*, 30–34.

[47] *Le Nouveau Journal*, 2 February 1926.   [48] G. Chevallier, *Clochemerle* (1934).

of the Beaujolais – with the exception of the most southerly part. Many
had been present for centuries; the Brac de la Perrière family had been
important landowners in St Lager since 1550. Nobles owned perhaps
half the land. The Comte de Fleurieu, for example, owned land in
Villefranche, Arnas, Anse and St Georges de Reneins. In 1914 he had
been the most important landowner in the department. Big properties
were worked by paid labour or most often by sharecroppers. This system
of 'vigneronnage' was unique to the Beaujolais and a small part of the
Maconnais. It was usual for the sharecropper to supply the labour of
himself and his spouse and to meet the cost of temporary workers taken
on during the vintage. Customarily his expenses were raised further by
the whole of the cost of minor equipment, by his duty to pay half the
cost of hay and straw and by the necessity to purchase food not produced
by himself. Theoretically, his only income was from the sale of half the
wine produced.[49]

Proprietors saw *vigneronnage* as a perfect example of class collaboration, lauding the sharecropper for his freedom from the servitude of the
worker, his willingness to have his say, and his courtesy tinged with
deference toward his 'monsieur'.[50] Gilbert Garrier shows, however, that
in the nineteenth century the position of sharecroppers was of strict
dependence. They were caught in a vicious circle of debt by the practice
common to most proprietors of advancing cash at the beginning of each
year, whilst poverty forced sale of wine at the moment when prices were
at their lowest. Sharecroppers were subject to daily surveillance.[51]

Yet as in the case of tenant farmers in the mountains dependence was
dissolving in the 1920s, thanks to growing difficulty in finding vignerons.
Consequently proprietors were forced to accord advantages to them. The
obligation to pay a fixed due for the use of pasture was reduced and in bad
years waived; premiums for accident and hail insurance were taken on by
the proprietor; hay and straw were paid for by the proprietor alone, wages
were paid for days spent planting new vines and permission was often
granted to cultivate an orchard.[52] Also, it is probable that inflation had
permitted sharecroppers to rid themselves of debts.[53] Finally contemporaries noted a tendency towards the absenteeism of some proprietors. It

[49] Jacques Burel, 'La Vignoble beaujolais' (thèse de droit, Lyon, 1941); Raymond Billiard,
Vigneronnage et vigneron beaujolais (Villefranche, 1938); Garrier, *Paysans du Lyonnais*,
268

[50] Billiard, *Vigneronnage et vigneron beaujolais*, 32–3; Guicherd and Ponsart, *L'Agriculture
du Rhône*, 374.

[51] Garrier, *Paysans du Lyonnais*, 268–9, 390–1.

[52] Guicherd et Ponsart, *L'Agriculture du Rhône*, 375; Billiard, *Vigneronnage et vigneron
beaujolais*; Garrier, *Paysans du Lyonnais*, 584–5.

[53] R. Estier, review of Garrier, *Paysans du Lyonnais*, *Cahiers d'histoire* 20 (1975), 489–99.

was said that such landlords had sufficient income from other sources not to worry about the excessive demands of sharecroppers, which put less fortunate proprietors in a difficult position. Supervision was often delegated to a manager, often with sad consequences for social peace.[54] Growing economic independence was, then, one of the reasons for the advance of socialism in the Beaujolais in the 1920s.

Conflict between sharecroppers and landowners was comparatively recent compared to the opposition of small independent wine producers to the axis of noble and curé – the type of conflict described in *Clochemerle*. Many small growers owned no more than a single hectare, and few had as many as four. Many laboured on the holdings of the more fortunate. It is noticeable that although there were independent winegrowers all over the Beaujolais, they leaned towards the left only in those areas where they lived in close proximity to the aristocracy, mainly the north. Another factor which divided small growers from large was changes in the nature of commercial wine-growing that had begun in the days of the phylloxera crisis. Since that period the vine had become increasingly concentrated in a few communes on the banks of the Rhône and above all in the Beaujolais.[55] Monoculture was accompanied by a tendency towards mass production from high-yield hybrid vines rather than the gamay for which the Beaujolais was famous. Big growers in particular sought to repair the neglect of the war years by planting high-production varieties with a view to an immediate profit. Small independent producers were worse affected by absence and death during the war, but did not have the capital necessary for replanting with hybrids. Many were forced to abandon the land. Those who adapted best were concentrated in areas where quality of wine was good enough to maintain profit levels – mainly the north. Small growers therefore accused large ones of exploiting the Beaujolais name in order to sell inferior products.[56] Like the fruit growers of the plateau, small *viticulteurs* were obliged to sell their wine immediately after the vintage, when prices were at their lowest.[57] During the downturn which began in the late 1920s such producers turned to co-operatives.[58]

One reason for this was a tradition of association among winegrowers. The pattern of settlement in the Beaujolais viticole is as dispersed as in many other areas of the department, with a predominance of large hamlets. In the Haut Beaujolais a handful of sharecropper cottages often surrounded the residence of a noble or bourgeois proprietor. But social

---

[54] Burel, 'Le Vignoble beaujolais', 59–60; Guicherd and Ponsart, *L'Agriculture du Rhône*, 375–6.
[55] Garrier, *Paysans du Lyonnais*, 595–6.   [56] *Ibid.*, 603–4 and 550n.
[57] Burel, 'Le Vignoble beaujolais', 37–9.   [58] Perrin, 'Le Mont d'Or', 598–9.

life was richer. *Viticulteurs* were never far apart and communication was easy. Market production had long accustomed winegrowers to contact with the outside world. The town of Villefranche was a source of new ideas. Contemporaries saw Beaujolais winegrowers as characterised by a mixture of conviviality, honest independence and egalitarianism, ever ready to co-operate in the search for solutions to the multitude of problems with which winegrowers were afflicted.[59]

A combination of subjection to the market, sociability and an historic opposition to aristocracy and Church explains the radical sympathies of small Beaujolais winegrowers. The right survived in two kinds of areas. First in the southern part of the Beaujolais, especially the canton of Anse. Here the rural exodus and the decline of small in favour of medium property was most pronounced, large domains were few, and monoculture of the vine less developed.[60] Conditions were not dissimilar to those on the plateau, and peasant conservatism was just as conditional. Secondly, the right retained the support of a dwindling number of sharecroppers.

Agricultural syndicalism

The Union du Sud-Est: from counterrevolution to pressure group

In the Beaujolais peasants raised in an anticlerical tradition turned to socialism. But in the rest of the department protest was contained within the right and developed first within the agricultural union movement. The Union du Sud-est des syndicats agricoles (USE) was officially constituted in October 1888. The initiative came from two Legitimist large proprietors in the Beaujolais, the Comte de St Victor and Emile Duport. Their aim was to defend Catholic and hierarchical conception of rural society. All those engaged in agriculture, regardless of class, would combine in a corporate defence of rural interests. Not surprisingly Republicans denounced a rebirth of feudalism. But in fact the foundation of the USE implied a recognition that the quasi-feudal ties of *vigneronnage* were insufficient to win mass support in the age of democracy. Peasants were to be reached through the provision of material services. Thus the first progress of the USE coincided with the phylloxera crisis.[61]

---

[59] Lagardette, *Impressions beaujolais*; A. Perrin, 'Les Coopératives vinicoles en Beaujolais', *Etudes Rhodaniennes* 19 (1944), 1–20.
[60] Garrier, *Paysans du Lyonnais*, 549–50 and 550n.
[61] Garrier, 'L'Union de sud-est des syndicats agricole'; Garrier, *Paysans du Lyonnais*, 518–22; Barral, *Les Agrariens français*, 107–13.

After the war the USE continued to expand. In 1935 there were 1,900 syndicates and 183,500 subscribers to its journal in the south-east. Of these the Rhône accounted for respectively 112 syndicates and 17,824 members spread across most of the department.[62] The only competitor of any importance was the Fédération des syndicats de défense viticole du Bas Beaujolais, presided by the Radical-Socialist senator Emile Bender, a reflection of political conflict in the Beaujolais. Large proprietors remained prominent in the leadership of the USE. Representing the department of the Rhône were members of noble families such as André Brac de la Perrière, the Comte de St Victor and the Comte de Leusse.[63] All three were from families which regularly appeared in the subscription lists of the local journal of Action française. Yet after the war the USE underwent fundamental changes as it inserted itself into the system of corporate representation (described on pp. 47–8). Its function was now to lobby for concessions within the Republic; therefore the USE's antirepublicanism was muted. This was reflected in the leadership of the USE. Alongside nobles were bourgeois proprietors such as vice-president Julien Riboud, who owned 200 hectares in the canton of Monsols, as well as vines in the Haut Beaujolais. He was the son of a banker. What is more, Riboud possessed impeccable Republican credentials. His father had been a part of the Aynard circle, and remained a director of the Aynard family bank. A more ambiguous figure was Felix Garcin, President of the USE since 1923. He was linked to the founding milieu of the syndicate because he combined a professorship of political economy at the Catholic University with the presidency of the board of the *Nouvelliste* and the directorship of a silk firm. Yet Garcin also maintained cordial relations with the Alliance démocratique politician André Tardieu. Julien Riboud was also a member of that party, as well as of the Fédération républicaine.[64] Contacts with politicians of the governmental centre-right were in fact the key to the USE's success as a pressure group. In the 1920s the USE operated more or less independently, cultivating its links with local deputies, but was most influential when Tardieu was Minister of Agriculture in 1929 and 1930. A pragmatic alliance with centre-right and centre-left politicians was typical of interest groups between the wars.

The USE's near monopoly of agricultural syndicalism in the Rhône

[62] *Annuaire de l'Union du sud-est des syndicats agricoles*, 1936.
[63] Some of the biographical information that follows is from Gerard Gayet, 'L'Union du sud-est des syndicats agricoles' (mémoire de maîtrise, Lyon II, 1972).
[64] Gayet, 'L'Union du sud-est', 92–145, states that in 1931 Garcin was offered the Agriculture Ministry by Tardieu.

also meant that it was able to make use of official bodies created in the 1920s. Thus the Conseil général, although in the hands of the left, had to award the presidency of the Departmental Agricultural Office (created in 1919), to a conservative *conseiller général* who played a secondary role in the USE.[65] Of greater significance was the USE's domination of the Rhône Chamber of Agriculture, set up in 1927. It was elected partly by direct suffrage, and partly by syndicates. The USE possessed 658 out of 770 mandates in the syndical college. Direct elections were always uncontested, for the USE put forward joint lists with pro-Radical bodies. Most Chamber personnel were drawn from the USE. Julien Riboud was its president. The need to conciliate Radical peasants was perhaps one reason for the eclipse of aristocratic leadership.[66] Control of the Chamber conferred upon the USE both economic and political advantages. It enabled the USE to channel government money to farmers. It also reinforced its legitimacy.[67]

The shift of the USE from counterrevolution to pressure group can also be seen in the USE's economic liberalism. In 1925 the USE spoke of the emergence in the countryside of a new elite based on success in the market.[68] True, the USE also appealed to the social Catholicism of La Tour du Pin, but its conception of 'mutual aid' went no further than insurance against fire and bad weather. Only under pressure from the rank-and-file in the 1930s did the USE adopt a more advanced corporatism.[69] In financial and economic policy the only exception to liberal principles was protectionism. It had no truck with the interventionist agricultural policy of the Radicals and socialists. The USE then owed much to the Orleanist tradition. Whereas Riboud adhered to the 'libéralisme aménagé' of the Progressistes, Garcin owed more to the curious blend of liberalism and integrism preached by *Le Nouvelliste*.[70]

We have seen that, within limits, this ideology was accepted by the peasantry. It was also accepted for pragmatic reasons by the mainly aristocratic landowners who had founded the USE, though they remained royalist malcontents at heart. But by the end of the 1920s the liberal leadership of the USE was under pressure. In the first place the USE *could* be seen as representing a narrow group of big farmers who did well out of the market system, and with increasingly tenuous links to the countryside. An enormous paper membership was used merely to legitimate lobbying activities. The only contact of the rank-and-file with

[65] Barral, *Les Agrariens français*, 209; Michel Augé-Laribé, *La Politique agricole de la France* (1942).

[66] Charles Gallet of the Alliance démocratique was also a member of the Chamber.

[67] Gayet, 'L'Union du sud-est', 118–23.   [68] *Le Nouveau Journal*, 7 March 1925.

[69] *La Croix du Rhône*, 12 April 1936.   [70] Gayet, 'L'Union du sud-est', 78.

the syndicate was through the co-operative fertiliser depot in the *chef-lieu* of the canton. There was, then, a potential gap between the USE and its members. The USE leadership found it difficult to bridge this gap because, whilst it was obliged to invoke the mass of the peasantry in support of its demands, it feared both a self-conscious peasant movement and the interventionist measures proposed by Radical spokesmen of the peasantry. The equivocal attitude of the USE towards the peasantry is best seen in its relations with the JAC.

The Jeunesse agricole chrétienne

Although the JAC was one of the first authentically peasant movements in France, the initiative for its creation came from outside rural society. It was a distant result of the Ralliement. Before 1914 rural study groups had grown out of the *Chronique sociale*.[71] They numbered less than a dozen before 1914. After the war the movement progressed, and in 1929 was integrated into the Jeunesse agricole chrétienne, one of a number of specialist movements designed to end the decline of Catholicism by making contact with workers and peasants in their own 'milieu'.[72] Total membership figures are unknown. Those given by the press were contradictory: 600 subscribers to the JAC press were reported in September 1931, but only 150 members in the department one year later.[73] By 1937 there were probably forty sections in the Rhône.[74] Although not numerically strong, the Jacistes were sure of an audience out of proportion to their numbers, for the columns of the widely read *Croix du Rhône* were open to them.

The JAC was also encouraged by the hierarchy, which ensured close clerical encadrement.[75] Catholic elites also patronised the JAC. Leaders of the USE, including Garcin himself, frequently gave talks to JAC groups.[76] Thanks to the sponsorship of Riboud, Jean-Marie Parrel, who was closely linked to the JAC, became the first authentic peasant to join the ruling circles of the USE.[77] The USE leadership encouraged the JAC in order to incorporate its leaders, contain its radicalism, and confine it to religious activities.[78] But the antiliberal JAC gained a momentum of its own, developing in ways which often horrified the elites.

[71] Folliet, *Marius Gonin*, 213–16; Ponson, *Les Catholiques lyonnais*.
[72] Folliet, *Marius Gonin*, 216; Adrien Dansette, *Destin du catholicisme français, 1926–1956* (1957).
[73] *Le Petit Montagnard de Tarare*, 6 September 1931 and 18 September 1932.
[74] *Le Nouvelliste*, 23 May 1937.
[75] Particularly from teaching orders at the Ecole Sandar.
[76] *Le Nouvelliste*, 4 May 1930.   [77] Pin, 'Un Notable paysan'.
[78] *Le Nouveau Journal*, 7 May 1925.

The JAC was led by a group which was a little set apart from the peasant masses. The first president of the Rhône federation was Claudius Delorme. His father combined the profession of surveyor with running the family farm, and was a relative of the local Fédération républicaine deputy Jean-Baptiste Delorme, also a prosperous working farmer. In other words, Claudius Delorme issued from a typical example of the Catholic and conservative 'bonnes familles' of the plateau. Young Claudius was educated at the Ecole Sandar, a Catholic agricultural college of which the staff were proponents of social Catholic ideas. In 1939 he came into possession of a few hectares at St Laurent d'Agny. From a rather different background was Delorme's successor in 1934, Joseph Bosse-Platière. The latter's father, Alexandre, was a leading activist of the Fédération républicaine in the Beaujolais. Bosse-Platière senior was a prosperous winegrower and ex-army officer. He enjoyed close relations with the agricultural elites of the Beaujolais, so the presence of his son also illustrates the dynamic of manipulation from above and pressure from below of which the JAC was a product.

There can be little doubt that the JAC rank-and-file were genuine peasants. The movement was at first confined to the plateau. Some were from communes such as Brignais and Chaponost which specialised in the intensive production of fruit. Others, like Caluire et Cuire, were zones of market gardening, for which from 1933 there was a specialist section.[79] These communes were all dominated by peasant proprietors.[80] It is also significant that two mountain communes sent delegates to the congress – Brullioles and St Genis l'Argentière. In the years which followed, the JAC expanded further into the mountains and the southernmost part of the Beaujolais. In all these areas the loyalty of the peasantry to notables had, for different reasons, been highly conditional. Significantly there was no sign of JAC activity in the northern Beaujolais. Here landowners dominated what was left of conservatism, while opposition to them was monopolised by the anticlerical left rather than partially contained within the right. The JAC can then be seen as a part of a crisis of notable politics on the right.

This is confirmed by the ideology of the JAC. The emphasis of Action catholique on proselytisation in the milieu where the individual Christian found himself could be interpreted in many ways. Joseph Bosse-Platière stressed re-Christianisation through personal example. By living their Christianity in their daily lives, by acting in fields,

[79] *Le Nouvelliste*, 22 March 1933.
[80] On the electoral lists of the Chambres d'Agriculture the twenty communes that sent delegates to the 1931 congress of the JAC had on average 79% of proprietors, compared to 72% in the department as a whole. *Le Nouvelliste*, 2 September 1930.

markets, festivals and syndicates as they would on Sundays, Jacistes would 'insensibly lead the masses back to the Church'.[81] The problem lay in deciding *how* a Christian should set such an example, for some were led in an apparently secular and antielitist direction. Claudius Delorme believed that the goal of re-Christianisation could be achieved by showing that there were Christian solutions to the practical problems which confronted peasants in their daily lives. He and others like him drew on the antiliberal tendencies of social Catholicism in order to give a new importance to Catholic agricultural syndicalism. For Delorme agricultural unions had degenerated into merely commercial concerns. He called for a regenerated syndicate which would take more account of peasant interests, and ultimately 'share more equitably production, consumption, labour and profit'.[82] What is more, in order to gain access to non-believers some were prepared to compromise doctrinally. For example some were willing to drop opposition to Sunday working, a traditional bone of contention in the villages. The elites of the USE were therefore suspicious of the JAC both on social and religious grounds.[83] Starting out from an integrist conception of Catholicism which attacked the separation by liberals of religion and daily life, the JAC ended up in a quasi-secular position. In this way the JAC and other social Catholic movements prepared the way for the Croix de Feu and PSF, which claimed to stand above the religious divide. Yet the secularism of the JAC had very narrow limits. The movement remained organisationally and ideologically dependent upon the Church, and was perceived to be so by its opponents. This helps to explain why the social critique of the JAC was contained within the right.

This can be illustrated by looking at a key figure in the ascent of the JAC. Jean-Marie Parrel, aged 52 in 1933, shared many of the ideas of the Jacistes, of which a group flourished in his own commune of Messimy. He possessed about 10 hectares – a considerable farm on the plateau – which he worked himself. In 1932 Parrel took over from the late Régis Rambaud, director of the *Nouvelliste*, as president of the cantonal syndicate of Vaugneray. In his inaugural speech Parrel recognised that he had neither the culture nor the notoriety of his predecessor, but felt that he had at least 'the advantage of being closer to you, of being one of you'. He immediately set about the formation of communal sections of the USE, with the aim of involving peasants more directly in syndical activities. In 1936 Parrel became a vice-president of USE.[84] Yet Parrel, was also a *conseiller général* and member of the bureau of the Fédération républicaine in the Rhône. His debt to the Catholic

---

[81] *La Croix de Rhône*, 31 March 1935.   [82] *Ibid.*, 14 February 1936.
[83] Gayet, 'L'Union du sud-est', 75–7.   [84] Pin, 'Un Notable paysan', 63–84.

and liberal values of the Progressisme of the 'bonnes familles' of the plateau is evident even in his corporatism. He saw in it a means of protecting the family, its savings, and the spirit of initiative which characterised small property, against the industrial methods of large-scale farmers.[85] Parrel remained faithful to the Fédération républicaine. Other activists were linked to Christian democracy via the weekly *La France rurale*. But in the longer term the JAC also fed into the Croix de Feu.

Conclusion

Three conclusions can be retained from this discussion of rural society. First, a crisis of notable politics was reflected in the rise of the JAC, a development which threatened both Progressistes and those more to the right. The Progressiste hegemony had depended on economic prosperity and the tacit support of the Church. Vulnerability of peasants to the market, together with the Church's renewed emphasis on social Catholicism, therefore placed the liberal elites in a difficult situation. The domination of rural society by a largely urban elite and class conflict within rural society imply rejection of Pierre Barral's argument that tensions within rural society were subordinate to rural/urban conflict.[86]

Second, the emergence of the JAC provides an example of the inseparability of religion and class conflict in interwar France. As Philippe Gratton argues, rural society was divided by class conflict. But this did not lead to clear class alliances. As a Catholic Jean-Marie Parrel was unable to see peasant socialists as allies, even though corporatism and co-operatives both represented attempts to deal with the help-lessness of the peasantry in the market. As well as emphasising the economic weakness of peasants, Parrel attributed the decline of the peasantry to the spread of lay values, associated in turn with market individualism. It was therefore natural that he should have participated in a project designed to re-Christianise rural society, partly in order to protect his material interests. Thus Parrel pursued class interests, as he perceived them, within the right. This illustrates again how difficult it was for conservatives, although conscious of the need for unity against socialism, to rise above divisive material interests and ideological references. Furthermore, the JAC shows that the Church was not simply a tool of conservatism.

Third, the crisis of notable politics in the Rhône was paralleled elsewhere in France, for the 1920s saw the beginnings of autonomous

---

[85] *L'Union républicaine*, 31 March 1935.   [86] Barral, *Les Agrariens français*, 14.

mobilisation on the part of conservative peasants in a number of areas, paralleling the discontent expressed by the SFIO in regions like the Beaujolais. The movements concerned varied widely in complexion, but all shared a mixture of antisocialism and hostility to the elites. In Brittany the Christian democrat abbé Mancel mobilised 15,000 working peasants, thus earning the hostility of the Fédération républicaine, the established agricultural syndicates and the Church. In Alsace the Bauernbund was supported by German-speaking medium peasants and was deeply antagonistic to the French-speaking elites who dominated local Comices agricoles. In 1928 Albert Debon stood as a 'peasant' candidate in Vire (Calvados), claiming that he was much better qualified than his Fédération républicaine rival, a lawyer, to represent a rural constituency. In Côte-d'Or Fleurent Agricola's Parti paysan took upon itself the mission of defending peasant society against industrial civilisation. It progressed above all in the conservative east of the department, expressing hostility to local conservative elites. Most important was Défense paysanne of Henri Dorgères. The movement resulted partly from the intrigues of Breton nobles like François d'Harcourt. But in Brittany Dorgères also drained support away from the antielitist Mancel unions. In the Rhône peasant mobilisation, for the moment, remained confined to Catholic organisations. The reasons for this were the relatively well-organised nature of agricultural syndicalism and relative isolation from price falls (except in the Beaujolais). The populism of the Fédération in the Rhône, to be examined in the following chapter, may also have helped to channel peasant grievances. But in the longer term peasants in the Rhône were to express discontent through the Croix de Feu.[87]

Taken together, this chapter and chapter three illuminate the instability of Third Republican society. There was little evidence here of a consensus around the ideas of the stalemate society. French society was characterised by a series of competing projects, each defined in material and ideological terms. Even the elites were not fully integrated into a self-conscious national ruling class. This was symbolised by the exclusion, except briefly under the Bloc, of Lyonnais politicians from Aynard to Isaac and Bonnevay from ministerial office, in spite of the respect enjoyed by all of them in Parliament and the economic and social power

---

[87] Barral, 'Les Syndicats des cultivateurs cultivants'; Goodfellow, 'Fascism in Alsace, 1918–1940' (Ph.D. dissertation, Indiana University, 1992); Jean Quellien, *Bleus blancs, rouges: politique et élections dans le Calvados* (Caen, 1986), 348; T. Hohl, 'Le Parti agraire et paysan français. Une tentative agrarienne en Côte-d'Or (1929–1939)', *Annales de Bourgogne* 59 (1988), 140–50; Pascal Ory, 'Les Syndicats bretons de cultivateurs-cultivants', *Mouvement social* 67 (1969), 147–71.

they possessed. The example of the Rhône also illustrates the extent to which these competing visions had been institutionalised in interest groups, including Chambers of Commerce and Agriculture, the CGPF and its local affiliate AICA, the USE and JAC, the veterans associations and the FNC. Increasingly these bodies were seen as undermining parliamentary sovereignty and as subverting the national interest. It was these problems which the conservative Prime Minister André Tardieu sought to address.

5   The crisis of the right I: 1928–1932

The social and ideological conflicts described in the two previous chapters had a significant impact on conservative politics in the Rhône. The heirs of Progressisme in the Fédération républicaine represented, in terms of our categories, an example of the constitutional-elitist right. Sovereignty was located in a parliamentary system designed to keep power in the hands of a small group said to be qualified by wealth and talent to know what was best for an indivisible nation. The Fédération therefore eschewed formal party organisation and relied on indifference and deference for mass support. Bodies intermediate between parliament and the individual, political parties included, had little role to play. Thus Aynard supported the Fédération but never occupied a formal position in the party, preferring to cultivate an image of independence. Yet the 1920s witnessed developments which undermined this elitism. A significant number of corporate and professional associations had developed.[1] Neocapitalists, their allies in the Alliance démocratique and Christian democrats sought to complement 'formal' political democracy with a network of professional associations, topped by an 'economic council'. At the same time the Church began to mobilise its organisational resources within the republican system. Catholics also spoke of reconciling individual and society through involvement in professional associations.

The result in the Rhône was that by 1932 the party system had undergone a significant modification. The influence of big business in local politics declined dramatically. Some, like Auguste Isaac, turned to the Alliance démocratique, which in terms of its constitutional-elitist structures and moderate republicanism doubtless reminded him of the Fédération of his youth. But within the Alliance he had to compete with diverse interests which included individuals close to the Radicals and anticlerical reformists with sympathies for neocapitalism like Weitz. From the point of view of Isaac, however, the Alliance remained much more attractive than the Fédération. Between 1928 and 1932 the latter

[1] Maier, *Recasting Bourgeois Europe*.

116

was torn apart by a struggle between two groups which owed little to the Progressiste tradition. A Catholic reformist tendency was led by the deputy François Peissel, who also enjoyed the sympathy of the Christian democratic PDP. On the other side stood Perret, who incarnated a new kind of nationalist politics which combined reactionary elitism with symbolic mobilisation of the people based on an alliance with conservative elements within the Church. By 1932 Perret had gained control over the party. But in 1932 this caused the pro-Tardieu deputies Peissel and Sallès to join Georges Pernot's (deputy of the Doubs) dissident group in the Chamber. Thus the constitutional-elitism of the old Fédération had begun to give way to movements which located sovereignty with the people. The PDP's democratic, pluralist and constitutional-popular conception of the people was radically different from Perret's, who should be situated somewhere between the constitutional-elitist, authoritarian-elitist and authoritarian-populist poles. But both movements played some part in preparing the way for the leagues of the 1930s.

The immediate background to this transformation of political structures in the Rhône was Tardieu's attempt to adapt the parliamentary system to the rise of corporate associations and class politics. By far the best analysis of this period is that of François Monnet, who argues that Tardieu failed partly because he did not break fully with an elitist liberalism – a 'libéralisme capacitaire'. However Monnet's analysis owes much to the stalemate society thesis. Tardieu and the neocapitalists are depicted as an isolated elite which was unable to overcome either the structural impasse of the economy, the preoccupation of the French with stability, or a republican tradition opposed to the 'very practice of power'.[2] In this chapter it will be suggested that there was significant support for many of the ideas of the neocapitalists. But neither the neocapitalists themselves nor Tardieu made a real effort to weld it into a coherent movement, partly because they were unable to escape the tangle of cultural and economic allegiances within French society. Politics should therefore be seen in terms of an ongoing struggle between a number of groups, defined ideologically and socio-economically, rather than as a series of fruitless attempts by minorities to breach a common culture.

André Tardieu and conservative reformism

The conservative victory in the general elections of 1928, coupled with economic expansion, created an audience for partisans of modernisation

---

[2] Monnet, *Refaire la république*, 135, 172.

in business and political spheres. Even the conservative Comité des Forges was not wholly averse to change.[3] Tardieu's service at the Ministry of Agriculture reassured the rural world. In the Rhône conservatives shared in the triumph of 1928. Candidates who were members of, or linked to, the Fédération won three out of four rural seats (Bonnevay at Tarare, Delorme at Givors and Peissel at l'Arbresle), while Antoine Sallès won the 2nd arrondissement in Lyon. Meanwhile in the 3rd arrondissement the former socialist mayor Victor Augagneur made a political come-back. He won the seat by conducting a populist and nationalist campaign against Herriot's administration of the city. In the economic sphere the only complaints were of a slight decline in exports following stabilisation of the Franc and of shortage of labour in the engineering industry.

Reform is most often identified with the Tardieu cabinets of 1929–30. In fact some of the measures adopted during his premiership had been under discussion for a number of years. Tardieu's predecessor, Poincaré, did not himself promote a distinctive strategy in domestic politics. But within his government partisans of reform and expansion nevertheless often won the struggle to influence him. His decision to stabilise the Franc in 1928 is a good example. Poincaré's economic policies, meanwhile, have been seen as proto-Keynesian.[4] Poincaré resigned as prime minister in July 1929. There was then a period of uncertainty, for although the Radicals had withdrawn from Poincaré's majority in November 1932, elements of the centre-right had not given up hope that the Union nationale, including the Radicals, could be rebuilt. The fall of Briand in October 1930 showed that this was impossible, and opened the way for a frankly right-wing majority under Tardieu, which lasted from 3 November 1929 until 4 December 1930 (with a reshuffle in February 1930). After Tardieu's fall reform continued under Pierre Laval in three ministries from January 1931 to February 1932. Tardieu himself returned to power in February, just in time to preside over the right's defeat in the general election of the following month. So it would be more exact to speak of a series of initiatives rather than a coherent programme associated with a single individual. Monnet sees Tardieu's programme itself as lacking in originality, locating it within the Colbertian tradition of the French state.[5] This may be true, but the essential point is that Tardieuism was

---

[3] AN F⁷ 13 240, reports of 3 December 1927, 17 December 1927, 16 December 1927; Martin Fine, 'Toward corporatism: the movement for capital–labour conciliation in France, 1914 to 1956' (Ph.D. thesis, Wisconsin, 1971); Jeanneney, *De Wendel*, 375–6.

[4] Jeanneney, *De Wendel*, 321–54, 380–408; P. Saly 'Poincaré keynésien', in *Le Capitalisme français (19ᵉ–20ᵉ)*, ed. P. Fridenson and A. Straus (1987), 33–45.

[5] Monnet, *Refaire la république*, 145–51, 153–61.

part of an ongoing debate about the nature of French society and the state's role in it.

Tardieu's purpose was to adapt the state to the changes brought about by the war. The parliamentary system, he argued, had been rendered impotent by the fact that the French had abandoned their 'traditional individualism'. Both parliament and executive were therefore subject to the 'direct action' of organised interests. Also concentration of capital and internationalisation of the financial system threatened further to undermine state power. The state therefore had to be sufficiently strong to aid the 'vital forces of the nation' and to arbitrate the multitude of conflicts which since the war had disrupted French society. Creation of a state which was genuinely representative of the national interest would in turn permit Tardieu to achieve his 'prosperity policy'. National unity would be cemented by shifting attention from political divisions to the economic domain, where distribution of the fruits of progress would bind all classes to the nation.[6] Tardieu failed, however, because his economic recipes were not universally approved and because he did not recognise that 'neutral' technocratic measures carried a cultural baggage which meant that they caused conflict rather than consensus.

In order to strengthen the state Tardieu reduced the number of ministers in his cabinet, refused to consult the parties on the formation of his government and promised to make frequent use of the question of confidence. Tardieu collaborated with leagues like the Croix de Feu.[7] But he had not yet become the authoritarian of the mid-1930s. His goal was still to remake the parliamentary right: 'this heterogeneous mixture of former students of the catechism, heirs of the Rights of Man and manipulators of capital which hardly deserves to be called an opposition'.[8] He spoke of a conservative party on the British model and was also influenced by American political methods – André Citroën advised him on the adaptation of advertising techniques to French politics.[9] Tardieu's emphasis on advertising suggests that he saw the people as playing a relatively passive role in politics. Indeed, he did not break entirely with the liberal conception of politics. Tardieu did not aim to create a conservative party on the model of the structured parties of the left. Rather he thought in terms 'of enlightened elites committed to the general interest, with the masses mobilised as spectators rather than actors'.[10] Tardieu made little effort therefore to create a unified party in

---

[6] A. Tardieu, *L'Epreuve du pouvoir* (1931), 52–5; Monnet, *Refaire la république*, 103–74.
[7] Monnet, *Refaire la république*, 449–69.
[8] A. Tardieu, *Sur la Pente* (1935), xxxvii–xxxviii.
[9] Monnet, *Refaire la république*, 115, 130–1.   [10] *Ibid.*, 107–8.

the country itself, concentrating instead on parliamentary alliances. Some conservative politicians did attempt to create a pro-Tardieu conservative party. The best known was the Centre de propagande des Républicains nationaux, created by Henri de Kerillis in 1927. It set out to provide common propaganda themes and to produce a core of trained activists for the right. There is however little evidence of direct support from Tardieu.

In the social sphere Tardieu was more ambitious. His ministries are regarded by one historian as 'the epitome of the neocapitalist movement for renovation'. Ernest Mercier, although Tardieu suspected him of sympathies for the left, was admitted to the inner circles of government.[11] Abolition of the right to strike for civil servants was meant to reinforce the neutrality of the state. In the private sector, on the other hand, Tardieu regretted the feebleness of both workers' and employers' unions. He envisaged formal collaboration of organised interests with the state in order to ensure general prosperity.[12] The economic cornerstone of Tardieu's policy was a 'National Retooling Plan', an ambitious programme of public works, including rural electrification, water purification, and improvements to the telephone network. The intention was to bind the clientele of the Radicals to the right, whilst providing opportunities for industry.[13] Tardieu agreed with Redressement français that overabundance of small businesses in France was an obstacle to economic progress.[14] But it was hoped that rural electrification would convince the peasantry that economic progress offered new possibilities, not decline. Wage-earners, meanwhile, would be won over by social reform. The shock-troops of anticommunism, said Tardieu, would be found in Jouhaux's CGT.[15] Tardieu presided over 'rectification' and implementation of the 1928 Social Insurance Act. In 1932 a Family Allowances Act was passed. In an effort to improve human capital, secondary education became free in 1930 to 1933. The government looked favourably upon the idea of creating a single-track secondary school system, the *école unique*. Finally, prosperity was to be underpinned by international collaboration. Briand remained Foreign Minister throughout the period. His policy of *rapprochement* with Germany was accompanied by encouragement of international

[11] Kuisel, *Mercier*, 55, 90; Gérard Brun, *Techocrates et technocratie en France (1914–1945)* (1985), 218–19.
[12] Tardieu, *L'Epreuve du pouvoir*, 55, 125 (speeches of 1 June 1930, 12 June 1930); Kuisel, *Capitalism*, 66–9, 91.
[13] M. Clague 'Vision and myopia in the new politics of André Tardieu', *French Historical Studies* 8 (1972), 105–29.
[14] Tardieu, *L'Epreuve du pouvoir*, 118–19.   [15] Monnet, *Refaire la république*, 140.

economic collaboration. His project for a European tariff union was warmly received in exporting circles.[16]

In sum, Tardieu's reforms were designed to use economic prosperity and social reform to integrate wage-earners into a broad conservative consensus led by progressive businessmen and politicians. One problem was that Tardieu's acceptance of intermediate bodies in the social sphere was accompanied by the indifference of an elitist nineteenth-century liberal to political parties. Indeed, prosperity was meant to depoliticise society. Economic interest would transcend outdated quarrels about religion; socialism would be the principal enemy, but prosperity would incorporate workers into the nation. But such were the complexities of Third Republican politics that apparently neutral technocratic measures could have unforeseen consequences. Although Tardieu spoke of consensus around material concerns, he also believed the idea of economic progress to be rooted in the ideas of 1789. The logic was that acceptance of the French Revolution was an essential component of social cohesion. This assumption excluded a major part of the Catholic right.

By 1931 the expectations of 1928 had begun to evaporate. Tardieu fell from power in December 1930. Nazi gains put paid to the hopes of Briand. It was unfortunate too that the high point of neocapitalism coincided with the first signs that the world economic crisis would not spare France. Employers rapidly lost enthusiasm for social reform. Even without these difficulties it is unlikely that Tardieu would have succeeded. He failed to persuade the Radicals to accept the position of junior partners in a right-wing coalition.[17] Among the reasons given by Herriot for refusing Tardieu's offer was that acceptance would cause the Radical electorate to turn to communism.[18] Tardieu's mistake was to assume that shared anticommunism should lead to political unity.

Perhaps more seriously, Tardieu's own coalition showed signs of breaking up. In Parliament the right wing of the Fédération had begun to destabilise the government before Tardieu took power. Open conflict erupted in the summer of 1929 over Poincaré's proposal to evacuate the Rhineland and ratify the Young Plan for war debts and reparations. In October Marin's supporters helped ensure the fall of the Briand government. The Fédération supported the very similar Tardieu government which succeeded it, but only because there was no alternative. In the regions and in the party press Fédération discontent continued to simmer. For Jean-Noël Jeanneney, Marin and his followers, unlike the

[16] Fridenson, *Histoire des Usines Renault*, 52.
[17] Berstein, *Histoire du Parti radical*, 154–69; Clague, 'Vision and myopia', 110.
[18] Monnet, *Refaire la république*, 132.

rest of the Fédération, put antiGermanism above the need to preserve the Union nationale as a bulwark of social order.[19] Irvine, on the other hand, minimises the ideological dimension, stressing instead resistance to Marin's attempts to discipline the Fédération.[20] Neither issue, though important, can be isolated from the Fédération's opposition to the government's programme as a whole.

Above all the Fédération opposed the Social Insurance Acts.[21] These laws brought together all the tensions of the Third Republic. Simplifying greatly, the government proposed a regime in which wage-earners in all industries would pay the same level of contribution. Those who opposed the law preferred a system which would be run by existing mutual aid societies. Since these bodies would be empowered to set their own levels of contribution this solution was favoured by employers with high labour costs. Hence the opposition of forgemasters like de Warren and de Wendel in the Fédération. But there were also religious reasons for the government's project opposition. The Church saw mutual aid societies as essential to its charitable functions. Cardinal Maurin in Lyon feared that control of communal insurance funds might fall into the hands of the *instituteur*. This in turn reinforced his suspicion of Catholic trade unions, for they enthusiastically supported the law.[22] In 1930 eighty Fédération deputies voted in favour of Xavier Vallat's Catholic-corporatist inspired counterproject. Thus the Social Insurance Law fused both religious and economic tensions within the right. In sum, the Fédération saw antisocialism and anticlericalism as inseparable. For Jean Le Mee the two were brought together in the person of the *instituteur*, the epitome of both socialism and anticlericalism. With such assumptions it was inconceivable that one could combat socialism by setting aside the religious question.[23]

Tardieu's reforms, again the social insurance laws in particular, were also the focus of extra-parliamentary agitation which expressed a more general hostility of sections of the rank-and-file of the right to the political class. Particularly radical was the proto-fascist Défense paysanne of Dorgères.[24] Meanwhile the Fédération des contribuables mobilised shopkeepers and small business. This movement was led by individuals with links to the extreme right, while the rank-and-file were drawn from the electorates of both Radicals and the right. In 1930 the

[19] Jeanneney, *De Wendel*, 415–35.
[20] Irvine, *French Conservatism*, 51.   [21] *La Nation*, 3 May 1930.
[22] *Semaine religieuse de Lyon*, 19 January 1929, 22 March 1929.
[23] *La Nation*, 13 December 1930; D. G. Wileman, 'L'Alliance républicaine démocratique: the dead centre of French politics, 1901–1947', (Ph.D. dissertation, York University, Canada, 1988), 184–5.
[24] *La Nation*, 16 August 1930.

Fédération des contribuables and Défense paysanne formed a common front to oppose the Social Insurance Act.[25]

Tardieu's reforms had been designed to stabilise the Republic and to create a broad conservative party. Yet the results were the opposite of those counted upon. Multiple divisions within the right were exposed well before economic crisis affected France. These were evident both in conflict among the established conservative parties and in the growth of populist movements of the right which attacked both the conservative elites and the parliamentary system. In the Rhône the liberal elites reluctantly supported some of Tardieu's measures. Others were more wholehearted, including engineering employers, the Catholic trade unions and other social Catholics, Peissel's wing of the Fédération, elements of the Alliance, and Bonnevay. Reformist ideas were not the province of a tiny elite. But the supporters of reform were divided socially and culturally, and neither Redressement nor Tardieu made a real attempt to organise a popular base. Rather more succcessful in this sphere was one of Tardieu's chief opponents, Perret, who by 1932 had transformed the Fédération into the organisational show-case of the parliamentary right in France. But neither did Perret achieve his hegemonic ambitions. Like Tardieu he sought to unite the right around economic issues, but defined this 'neutral' terrain in such a way as to exclude many conservatives.

The partial eclipse of the liberal elites

The main bastions of the Progressiste tradition in business and agriculture, the Chamber of Commerce and USE, on the face of it, demonstrated a suspicion of social reform perfectly in accord with the classic liberal view of political economy. In 1927 the Chamber of Commerce rejected the idea of compulsory paid holidays on the grounds that they would have an adverse effect on competitiveness.[26] Not surprisingly, Chamber of Commerce publications were full of criticisms of the Social Insurance Acts, seen as a reward for laziness and as unfairly penalising firms with high labour costs.[27] A spokesman for the dyeing industry argued that existing mutual aid schemes, precisely because they were mutual, kept down the sickness rate and encouraged the loyalty of workers, especially immigrants, to the enterprise.[28] The USE meanwhile

---

[25] P. Ory, 'Le Dorgèrisme'; W. Hoisington, Jr, *Taxpayer Revolt in France* (Stanford, 1973).
[26] CRCCL, 1927, 306–8.
[27] *Ibid.*, 1929, 703 and 1930, 583–4; PVCCL, 16 February 1928.
[28] CRCCL, 1928, 674.

played a leading role in a campaign to make social insurance optional in agriculture.

Yet for a number of reasons the attitude of the liberal elites toward Tardieu was equivocal. First, the Alliance démocratique, of which Tardieu was a part, occupied a key position in Parliament. It was more or less permanently in government and often controlled the Ministry of Commerce. Business, agricultural and other organisations were careful therefore to remain on good terms with Alliance politicians. This is perhaps why a number of business organisations on the national level were headed by individuals considerably more progressive than their members – the steel and coal lobbies headed by Lambert-Ribot and Peyerhimoff were good examples. In the Rhône Henry Morel-Journel had contacts which extended into the Radical Party. Félix Garcin, President of the USE, maintained good relations with Tardieu. Garcin campaigned for him in the USE bulletin, and supplied him with local political intelligence.[29] This was in spite of the fact that Garcin taught political economy at the Catholic University, and was managing director of the *Nouvelliste*, an extreme opponent of Tardieu.[30]

A second reason for flexibility was that many of the elites approved Briand's foreign policy. Thus the Chamber of Commerce appealed for implementation of the Young Plan as a means of fending off the international economic crisis.[31] This in turn implied maintaining Briand in the Cabinet, opposition to Marin's destabilisation of the government, and even a tacit acceptance of social reform. This is a reminder that some of the elites questioned aspects of liberalism. Concrete evidence can be seen in the Chamber's view that compulsory family allowances should be approved in order to avoid penalising those firms which had their own private schemes.[32] The attitude of big business was that if there had to be social reform, then it must be applied to small firms as well as large. In this the Chamber differed from medium and small business, which would, in an ideal world, have preferred no insurance system at all. Similar differences resurfaced on several occasions, particularly after the Popular Front reforms of June 1936. Finally, in line with liberal orthodoxy, the Chamber demanded that budget surpluses be used to finance tax cuts.[33] Yet it welcomed Tardieu's plan for national retooling on condition that it did not involve new taxes, and that it resulted in 'genuine' public works.[34]

The ambiguous attitude of the liberal elites to Tardieu's reforms was accompanied by growing political isolation in the Rhône. This was

[29] Gayet, 'L'Union du sud-est', 99–110.   [30] Barral, *Les Agrariens français*, 222–30.
[31] CRCCL, 1929, 601.   [32] PVCCL, 24 October, 29.
[33] CRCCL, 1929, 623.   [34] PVCCL, 2 October 1930.

illustrated by the fortunes of Auguste Isaac, who like Aynard had symbolised the interpenetration of big business and conservatism. Until 1924 Isaac was national president of the Fédération. Yet in April 1930 he resigned from the party. On the one hand Isaac was divided from Perret's wing of the Fédération by the fact that he supported Briand's policy of *rapprochement* with Germany. He called for a 'modern foreign policy', in which young people would get to know each other in order to learn to settle the economic questions which caused international conflict.[35] Isaac also attacked Marin and Perret for their willingness to tolerate the presence within the ranks of the Fédération of 'patriots of monarchical origin who sought to get themselves elected under the Republican banner with our money'.[36] On the other hand Isaac had little sympathy for the reformists in the Fédération. He denounced Fédération deputies for failing to prevent 'the pillage of public finances', for supporting veterans' pensions, salary increases for civil servants and social insurance. Isaac's combination of Republicanism and liberalism in domestic and international politics was similar to that of Julien Riboud (also of the USE), who broke with the Rhône Fédération in October 1929 after it had rejected his call for maintenance of the party in its 'centre/centre-right tradition', tax cuts, mutualisation of social insurance, and 'international pacification'.[37]

Representatives of big-business families continued to come to meetings of the Fédération throughout the 1930s. But they preferred its more eclectic rural meetings to partisan urban gatherings. Some, such as Edmund Gillet and his son-in-law François Balay (head of the Société des Colorantes de France, a Gillet subsidiary), came only as rural mayors. But after 1930 such people no longer dominated the leadership of the Fédération as they had in the days of Aynard and Isaac. Neither did they become deputies. Significantly Isaac's protégé Morel-Journal did not go on from the presidency of the Chamber of Commerce to a political career, although he regarded the step as a natural and desirable one.[38] Another index of the declining influence in local politics of the liberal elite is that there ceased to be any connection between politics and bourgeois 'cercles'.[39] In the 1930s Fédération sympathisers still preferred the Cercle de l'union to the Cercle de commerce, which was closer to the Radicals and lay centre-right.[40] But whereas before the war most leaders of the Fédération had been members of the Cercle de

---

[35] AN 317 AP 82, National Council meeting, 24 October 1925.
[36] AN 317 AP 73, Isaac to Guiter, 19 April 1930.
[37] *Ibid.*, Riboud to Guiter, 5 October 1929.
[38] *Journal d'Henry Morel-Journal*, 11 November 1932.
[39] Pinol, 'Mobilités et immobilismes', 225–64.
[40] Members of *cercles* are listed in the *Annuaire Tout-Lyon*.

l'union, by the 1930s only twelve out of 2,968 known Fédération sympathisers belonged to it. Those who did were often an older generation of business politicians. For example Morel-Journel attended a weekly 'economists' lunch' at the Cercle de l'union, where he met such figures as Auguste and Humbert Isaac, Jean Coignet (a former Fédération senator), Edmond Gillet and Oscar Cambeforte. All were of liberal-conservative convictions.[41] But none of the leading figures in the Fédération in the 1930s was a member of either *cercle*.

One area in which the liberal elite did continue to exercise influence was through party funding. Perret's correspondence with Marin shows that he regarded income from business as essential. The Fédération's accounts for the 1936 elections show that it was dependent for income upon three sources: donations by local businessmen; subsidies from the Union des intérêts économiques (UIE) (an organisation sponsored by the Comité des forges and other conservative businessmen); and thirdly money from the national organisation of the Fédération.[42] In the latter case Lyonnais banks (including Aynard's) played a significant part.[43] Moreover, the Fédération's financiers were not afraid to use their influence. In 1929 Isaac warned national secretary-general Jean Guiter that the Fédération would regret its lack of regard for the public finances when next it asked for funds.[44] Such pressure was sometimes successful. In the summer of 1935 Perret was taken to task (in private) by Isaac for an article he had written in the *Union républicaine*, in which he had detected a rather improbable conspiracy of banks, oil and insurance companies against the Fédération. Isaac demanded an explanation for sentiments more usually associated with the communists.[45] Perret was clearly worried by this threat to his funds, and assured Marin that because of his lack of financial independence he had never dared say what he really thought of the banks.[46] Whether Perret was referring to the independence of himself as an individual or of his party is hard to say. What is certain, however, is that in 1935 Perret's own firm was in financial difficulty. Overlapping personal and party networks were mobilised to help him out, and at one point Perret was reduced to the

[41] *Journal d'Henry Morel-Journel*, 16 June 1929, 2 July 1930.
[42] AN 317 AP 76, Perret to Marin, 23 October 1926. For example Perret received 25,000 francs from an unnamed donor for the Senate elections of 1926. AN 317 AP 81 contains accounts for the 1936 election.
[43] AN 317 AP 75. The national Budget Commission of the Fédération included two sons of Aynard together with Oscar Cambefort, all members of the board of the Aynard bank.
[44] AN 317 AP 73, Young Plan dossier.
[45] AN 317 AP 76, Isaac to Perret, 18 August 1935; *L'Union républicaine*, 18 August 1935.
[46] AN 317 AP 76, Perret to Marin, 22 August 1935. 'Il est certain que je n'ose pas dire ce que je pense des "banques" - car si elles m'abandonnaient à Lyon - que deviendrais-je??? [*sic*] Quel malheur de ne pas être riche et indépendant complètement.'

point of asking for a paid function in the national organisation of the Fédération. Perret candidly admitted that if he accepted financial help then political strings would be attached.[47] A party like the Fédération did not have the autonomy from the elites which would have derived from possession of a genuine mass membership.

All the same, the position of big business had changed since the days when Aynard, Isaac and Jean Coignet had combined leadership of the Chamber of Commerce with involvement in the Fédération and parliamentary careers. This, however, was only a relative set-back, for influence in political parties was not an essential condition of economic power. Big-business elites had been squeezed out of the emergent mass parties, which were marked by anticapitalism, but in rural areas of the department in particular, as well as in the 2nd arrondissement of Lyon, informal political networks remained important. Indeed, these were often the areas where the right was able to elect deputies. Furthermore many large firms had moved their headquarters to Paris, where they were better placed to build direct relations with the state, especially the Ministry of Commerce, which was usually in the hands of friendly politicians. This reminds us that the French state should not be seen as a unitary body acting consistently in the interests of one group. Nevertheless, some sections of the elites were unhappy with their exclusion from political influence. They reacted by turning to the Alliance or by flirting with the antiparliamentary right.

Support for Conservative reformism in the Rhône

In the Rhône at least there was considerable sympathy for many of the ideas with which Tardieu was associated in both professional groups and political parties, above the lay centre-right, the PDP and the left wing of the Fédération. The problem was that the centre-right of French politics was occupied by a plethora of groups which agreed on little more than the value of centrism, democracy and Republicanism. They were divided by all the usual cultural and economic conflicts. Difficulties were compounded by the fact that Tardieu himself took no action to remedy the situation, preferring to appeal directly to public opinion.

The lay centre-right

The Alliance démocratique was an archetypal constitutional-elitist party.[48] It was a purely electoral organisation whose members sat with a

[47] AN 317 AP 76, 16 July 1931.
[48] D. G. Wileman, 'P.-E. Flandin and the Alliance démocratique'; Wileman, 'L'Alliance républicaine démocratique'.

variety of parliamentary groups. In the Rhône the only available membership figures reveal that it had only eighty members in 1939.[49] Even in the 6th arrondissement of Lyon, where the Alliance was strong, it acted through an independent Union des comités républicains. The strength of the Alliance lay rather in the extent to which it won the support of parliamentarians – in the Rhône they were largely dissidents of the Fédération. Jean-Baptiste Delorme (deputy for Givors) left the Fédération in 1931 in protest against its increasingly reactionary stance. But he made no effort to set up a rival organisation in his constituency. He used the Alliance label, but relied on a handful of friends when the time for re-election came in 1932. Best known was Laurent Bonnevay, who had left the Fédération for similar reasons in 1928. He did not join the Alliance, but sat with one of its parliamentary groups, the Républicains de gauche. The Alliance also elected municipal councillors in the 2nd, 5th and 6th arrondissements, though in the 2nd councillor Jean Mercier's views were indistinguishable from those of the Fédération which dominated the arrondissement.

There were two reasons for this distrust of formal party organisation. First, Alliance members held that politics should be left to the haute bourgeoisie and that education and reason would ensure that the masses remained loyal to it.[50] Parties were seen as distorting the relationship between parliament and the sovereign people. Bonnevay defended the pluralism of the republican movement, admitting even the communists to the charmed circle in 1935. But he also saw himself as an almost mystical emanation of the republicanism of 'la France profonde', a relationship unmediated by parties or committees. One of the reasons for which he joined the Républicains de gauche was his opposition to the efforts of Perret and Marin to discipline the Fédération.[51] Here then was another example of Rosanvallon's 'libéralisme capacitaire', and even in the case of an unimpeachable republican like Bonnevay it was accompanied by ambiguity on the question of pluralism. Secondly, the Alliance was a means through which interest groups like the Chamber of Commerce, the USE and a host of others could make contact with the state. Since many of the groups which used the centre-right in this way were to its right politically, formal organisation and a programme would have been a hindrance.

The loose structures of the lay centre-right facilitated domination by a wealthy elite. With some justice the party was seen by André Siegfried as

[49] BN Papers of the Alliance démocratique, Carton 1.
[50] Wileman, 'L'Alliance républicaine démocratique', 187–8.
[51] Le Petit Montagnard de Tarare, 4 October 1931; AN 317 AP 76, manuscript of an article for La Nation.

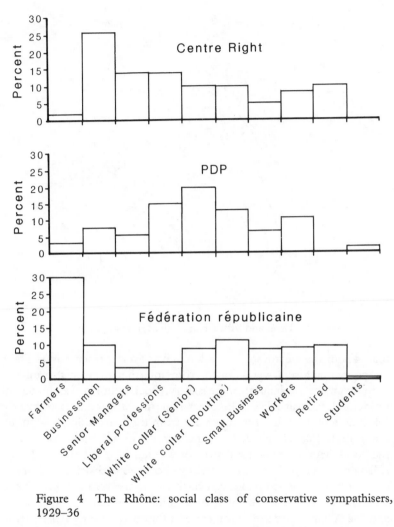

Figure 4   The Rhône: social class of conservative sympathisers, 1929–36

the expression of 'organised capitalism'[52] In the Rhône merchants and industrialists represented 26% of fifty-eight known sympathisers, and were easily the largest category. Together with senior managers and engineers they represented 40% of the total, while 54% were drawn from the ruling class in its broadest sense, including the liberal professions (see Figure 4). Since these groups amounted to no more

[52] Siegfried, *Tableaux des partis,* 179–80.

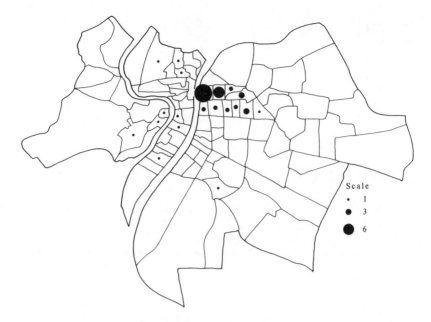

Map 11   Lyon and Villeurbanne: the centre-right, 1928–39

than 4% of the electorate this is a massive overrepresentation. The rest of the sympathisers were drawn from intermediate social groups and none from the proletariat or peasantry. Social elitism was matched by residential exclusiveness. The great majority of sympathisers lived in a select area of the 6th arrondissement from the Place Edouard-Quinet in the south to Place Puvis de Chavannes in the north and westwards along the cours Morand (polling districts 607 and 608) (Map 11). Thus the Alliance developed in the wealthy bourgeois districts of the 6th arrondissement which had given birth to Progressisme and the Fédération. There were also personal continuities between the Aynard group and the Alliance. Etienne Fougère had founded the original Fédération organisation in the 6th arrondissement in 1903, but then turned to the Alliance. Julien Riboud and Auguste Isaac, also linked to Aynard, attended the odd Alliance meeting. Further evidence of continuity comes from the fact that four centre-right leaders, including the progressive businessmen Weitz and Fougère, were members of the same club, the Cercle de commerce, previously noted for its contrast to the more conservative and Catholic Cercle de l'union. Another link was that both won support from Protestants. Protestantism in Lyon had always been on the advanced wing of bourgeois politics, feeding into Radicalism and even socialism as well as the centre-right. Three leading figures in the centre-right were Protestants: Edmond Weitz, Guy Aroud, and the Independent Radical Jean Lambert.[53]

But neither Riboud nor Aynard was able to dominate the Alliance, for it was much more disparate than Progressisme had been.[54] Some of its members were sympathetic to Redressement français. Most important was Fougère who became national vice-president of the movement. Much to the annoyance of Perret he attempted to obtain money for Redressement français in Lyon.[55] In 1928 Fougère was elected to parliament in the Loire (again to Perret's disgust), where he proved to be a firm supporter of Tardieu. This suggests that neocapitalist ideas developed partly out of the progressive business tradition of the 6th arrondissement. No other Alliance activist is known to have joined Redressement, but there was nevertheless a broader movement in favour of reform. Until 1930 Edmund Weitz was departmental president of the Alliance. He saw himself as representing the 'new industries' and was opposed to the liberal–silk elite for a mixture of cultural, political and ideological reasons, contrasting the 'feudal' *soierie* with his own 'democratic' engineering industry.[56] His enthusiasm for reform, rationalisation, expansion and collaboration with labour were all seen in the previous chapter. Speaking on behalf of the engineering industry in the Chamber of Commerce, Weitz accepted that the Social Insurance Act was not perfect, but urged that it be implemented in the 'widest and most loyal spirit'. Unlike other business leaders he did not demand a delay in its introduction.[57] In the elections of 1928, Aroud, Alliance candidate in the 7th arrondissement, called for a 'république syndicale', to be brought about by 'les jeunes equipes'.[58]

Weitz claimed that the engineering industry as a whole supported the Alliance, and there is doubtless an element of truth in this. But some engineering employers probably leaned towards the Radical Party, a fact which further undermined the coherence of the lay centre-right. Philippe Vermorel, owner of a firm making agricultural implements in Villefranche, was a Radical senator in the 1920s. François Grammont, boss of a large electrical and telephone company, was Radical candidate in the 6th arrondissement of Lyon in the elections of 1936. Particularly representative of the overlaps between Radicalism, the Alliance and engineering was the journalist Aroud, who in December 1935 wrote a

[53] *Le Nouvelliste*, 3 May 1936.
[54] Wileman, 'L'Alliance républicain démocratique', 181, 184.
[55] AN 317 AP 76, Perret to Marin, 23 October1926.
[56] *Le Nouvelliste*, 6 March 1928.
[57] CRCCL, 1929, 697.   [58] *Le Nouveau Journal*, 26 April 1928.

series of reports on the engineering industry in the pro-Radical *Lyon républicain*. He had recently left the Alliance for the Radicals.

So the liberal elites did not dominate the Alliance in the way that they had controlled the Fédération. They had to contend with representatives of new industries like the engineering industry, the sympathies of which went sometimes to the left. Furthermore, the role of big business as a whole in the centre-right declined at the beginning of the 1930s. Edmond Weitz withdrew from active politics in 1930, concentrating his efforts on the Chamber of Commerce.[59] Fougère's role in politics in Lyon was reduced after he was elected deputy of the Loire in 1928. Big businessmen remained numerous in the Alliance. But when the party was reorganised in December 1930 leadership passed to Dr Augros and Eugène Mansuy, who ran a medium-sized pottery wholesaling concern. Indeed, the centre-right included a number of businessmen who operated on the margins of the Alliance and Radicalism and who combined hostility to big business with anticlericalism. For example the anticlerical silk merchant Eugène Schulz claimed to represent a 'liberal bourgeoisie', which recognised the dependence of commerce upon the purchasing power of the masses.[60] One of his main concerns was protection of the artisanate through alliance with the Radicals. He therefore saw neocapitalism as threatening the artisanate. This shift in the Alliance from liberal big business to the anticlerical middle bourgeoisie was related to the growing ascendency within the party, particularly its local organisations, of national leader Pierre-Etienne Flandin, who coupled an organisational drive with a desire for alliance with the Radicals.[61]

Given the differences in traditions and aims of the various components of the centre-right there was much room for misunderstanding. This was illustrated in March 1928 by a quarrel at a meeting of the Comité républicaine de commerce et de l'industrie, better known as the Mascaraud Committee. Schulz urged republicans to defend the 'lay ideal' and to guard against the 'new feudalism' which was 'raising itself up on the backs of the great trusts, cartels and big banks'. This provoked an angry response from Weitz. Evoking his leadership of the Alliance, of the engineering employers and his Alsatian blood, he denied the right of a representative of the 'feudal' silk industry, which had built itself up through exploitation of subcontractors, to denounce big business. He alone was qualified by his support for reform and collaboration with

---

[59] *Journal d'Henry Morel-Journel*, 14 June 1929.
[60] *Bulletin mensuel de commerce, de l'industrie et de l'agriculture* (*BMCIA*), January–March 1928.
[61] Wileman, 'L'Alliance républicaine démocratique', 222–4.

trade unions to utter such sentiments. Weitz resigned from the Mascaraud Committee. Controversy continued in the press, where Fougère and Paul Charbin weighed in respectively as honorary and current Presidents of the SFS, asking why Weitz had to cite 'injurious and false opinions about the greatest of Lyonnais industries of which the supremacy in Lyon has always been so difficult for him to accept?' Weitz had quarrelled with Schulz whose opposition to the liberal Catholic elite he shared, and with Charbin and Fougère whose social and economic views were similar to his own.[62]

Thus the Alliance appealed to a diverse group of business interests, ranging from those loyal to the liberal Catholic tradition like Isaac, through neocapitalists like Fougère, to anticlerical proponents of industrial progress like Weitz and the anticlerical bourgeoisie made up of professionals, civil servants and smaller businessmen. As Siegfried argued, the centre-right was 'attracted simultaneously towards the anticlericalism of the left, and to the Catholicism of the ruling class and to organised capitalism'.[63] It included many who were ready to engage in reform, but it was an unpromising instrument for transformation of the French party system.

Christian democracy and Tardieu

More coherent support for conservative reformism came from the Catholic moderate right. More precisely, there was a reformist cartel consisting of the Fédération left, the PDP and the CFTC, supported by the deputy Peissel. His parliamentary colleague Bonnevay occupied an independent position intermediate between this group and the Alliance. Whereas the Alliance represented an example of constitutional-elitism, the Catholic centre-right was a constitutional popular movement. As such the latter was a product of pressure both from the conservative rank-and-file and from the efforts of sections of the elites to create a new conservative consensus.

Within the social Catholic network formed by the CFTC, *Chronique* and PDP there was a good deal of support for the main planks of Tardieu's platform. The CFTC did not explicitly endorse Tardieu. But we have seen that its dominant left wing favoured rationalisation, economic progress and social reform.[64] Above all the CFTC supported social insurance. The CFTC hoped one day that a truly corporatist system with workers' participation would be created, but condemned

---

[62] *Le Nouvelliste*, 5 March 1928; *Bulletin mensuel de commerce, de l'industrie et de l'agriculture*, January–March 1928.
[63] Siegfried, *Tableaux des partis*.   [64] *La Voix sociale*, August–September 1926.

employers' schemes for mutualisation as a cover for selfish interests. In the meantime they accepted the existing law.[65] The PDP explicitly approved the Tardieu administrations – the PDP deputy Champetier de Ribes (Basses-Pyranées) was a member of all three Tardieu cabinets and also of those of Laval. In particular the PDP emphasised foreign policy, without forgetting the relationship between international pacification and prosperity.[66] But there were a number of obstacles to the integration of the PDP into a genuine conservative party led by Tardieu. It was notables like Peissel and Bonnevay who remained in charge of reformist forces in the Rhône.

First, the PDP's conception of the party did not match Tardieu's belief in a unitary nation represented by an enlightened elite. According to the PDP deputy Marcel Prélot (Nord), his party was unique on the right in that it was characterised by 'a quasi-spontaneous growth from below, and was the truly democratic and popular work of devoted and obscure activists'.[67] In the Rhône this claim to emanate from the people was to some extent reflected in the social and political structures of the party. The party's accounts for 1929 suggest that there were perhaps 350 dues-paying members in that year. Subscriptions to *Le Petit démocrate*, the national party journal, went from between 255 in 1929 to 517 in 1932 and reached over 1,000 in 1935. The PDP had more members than the Alliance but considerably less than the Fédération.[68] The PDP may have been a small party, but Prélot was correct in his belief that its principles of organisation were unlike those of Fédération or Alliance. Its local organisations were known as 'sections', a term borrowed from the left implying both democratic discussion and submission to majority opinion.[69] This contrasted with the connotations of secretiveness and elitism in the term 'committee'. Like the left the PDP was open about differences of opinion in its meetings. This reflected its acceptance of social conflict and a desire to institutionalise it, whereas the Fédération and Alliance clung to the myth of a unique national interest.

In terms of the background of its membership too the PDP could claim to be different. The average age of its sympathisers, at 40, was considerably less than that of the Fédération (49) or the lay centre-right (47). Over half of the 128 sympathisers whose professions are known were white-collar workers, and as in the CFTC there was a bias towards

[65] *Ibid.*, 15 July 1923; December 1928; November 1929.
[66] *Le Nouveau Journal*, 9 March 1930; 31 May 1931; Delbreil, *Centrisme et démocratie chrétienne*, 195–9.
[67] *Bulletin des 'Démocrates populaires' (Région lyonnaise)*, January 1929.
[68] Delbreil, *Centrisme et démocratie chrétienne*, 76, 460–1; Passmore, 'The right and the extreme right', 141–2.
[69] *Le Nouveau Journal*, 14 April 1931.

higher-grade workers (see Figure 4). PDP white-collar workers also recruited in the same areas of the 3rd, 5th and 6th arrondissements where the CFTC left wing was strong. PDP activists were rare in the 4th, however, for the numerous Catholic white-collar workers there preferred the Fédération, Œuvre des cercles and the Corporation. PDP white-collar workers were also more likely to have been born in the Lyon conurbation than those of the Fédération, who had often migrated to the city from rural communes. So syndicalism and support for the PDP were partly a product of socialisation in city and parish. Employers too were overrepresented in the PDP, but constituted a smaller proportion than any other party of the right. Industrial workers were as rare in the PDP as in the right in general.

It is difficult to make a direct connection between the strength of the petty bourgeoisie in the PDP and the populism evident in Federal president Jacques Tourret's view that the three founding principles of the PDP were individual liberty, property and abolition of privileges.[70] This populism cannot be interpreted literally. Not all sections of the lower middle class favoured the PDP. White-collar workers in the public sector were substantially underrepresented, as were artisans and shop-keepers. Furthermore, the most overrepresented group in relation to the electorate was in fact lawyers and professors. PDP leaders were drawn almost exclusively from this class: both departmental presidents in our period, Jacques Tourret and Charles Bryon, were lawyers. Populism resides as much therefore in opposition to a 'bourgeoisie' defined in a certain way as to social origins in a strict sense. Take for example the PDP intellectual Crétinon's lament on the ties of the Church to the ruling class:

What a shame it is that the Church in France should serve nobles and the bourgeoisie and exclude the people! In supporting the Church these classes seek to bend it to their will. I have realised this for many years – I am rich, but I am able to break with class prejudice . . . Leo XIII struggled in vain to break the ties which chained the destiny of the Church to these conservative parties which fatally exploit it.[71]

In other words the popular claim of the PDP must not be interpreted in purely sociological terms, but in the context of a series of ideological, political and historical oppositions.

The Catholicism of the PDP was another obstacle to the creation of a united conservative movement behind Tardieu. The Party aimed to create a non-confessional conservative party of the centre-right, and so

---

[70] *Ibid.*, 7 January 1928, 31 May 1931.
[71] C. Ponson, 'Joseph Vialatoux, le philosophe lyonnais', in *Cent ans de Catholicisme social à Lyon et en Rhône Alpes*, ed. J.-D.Durand *et al.*, 470.

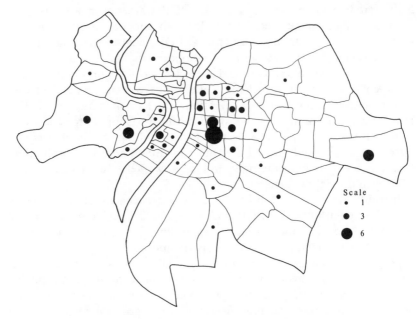

Map 12   Lyon and Villeurbanne: PDP activists, 1928–39

was careful to avoid formal links with the Church and stressed its acceptance of *laïcité*.[72] But such a party could not be brought about simply by stating a commitment to religious pacification. The PDP can be understood only in terms of its Catholicism. This was clearly evident in the geography of its support, which coincided with the presence of the Church (Map 12). True, the most important concentration of activists was in the Cité Rambaud, a Catholic housing development in the 3rd arrondissement. In the 2nd arrondissement PDP members lived close to institutions like the *Chronique* and the Catholic University. There was also a number of activists in St Just and Point du Jour (districts 510 and 505), adjacent to the Basilica of Fourvière. Outside Lyon activists were most numerous in the canton of Thizy, especially in Cours, a town marked by high religious practice and where the main political division on the right was between AF and the PDP. Not only was the PDP confined largely to areas of high religious practice, but it was deeply imbricated in the institutional life of the Church. Claudius Dériol described PDP sections as 'parish gangs'. Most priests, he said, supported the Fédération, but many *abbés* favoured the PDP. Dominicans, with their democratic

---

[72] Raymond-Laurent, *Le Parti démocrate populaire*, 76; Delbreil, *Centrisme et démocratie chrétienne*.

tradition, were prominent, as were those who had been members of the Sillon. Sympathetic clergy were often attached to the parish-based Cercles d'études sociales. Participation in these offshoots of the *Chronique sociale* frequently led to involvement in the PDP. Significantly, whereas the Fédération, as we shall see, used the parishes to mobilise a passive rank-and-file through encadrement of leisure activities, the PDP grew out of 'democratic' discussion groups. Dériol is in fact typical of the social Catholic network of which the PDP was a part. He was introduced to the Cercles d'études by a former Sillon member, François Perrier, who was also animator of the PDP's youth group. In the Cercle of St Pierre des Terreaux, Dériol, then a young bank employee, met Georges Forestier of the CFTC. Dériol went on to become editorial secretary of the CFTC journal *La Voix sociale*. He also organised a support group for the Dominican journal, *Sept*.[73] It would be tedious to enumerate the many other examples of such links.[74] Suffice it to note that Jacques Tourret, founding president of the PDP federation of the Rhône, and legal councillor to the CFTC, left the party to succeed Marius Gonin as Secretary-General of the Semaines sociales in 1938.

There was, then, a fundamental ambiguity in the PDP's conception of politics. It sought to create a non-confessional democratic centrist party stretching from the Radicals to the moderate Fédération represented by Peissel. Yet it also believed that democracy needed to be regenerated through recognition of its Christian roots. Some sought to resolve the contradiction by separating religious and political life.[75] But this option became increasingly difficult with the rise of Catholic Action, founded on the belief that re-Christianisation could be achieved by 'living' Christianity in daily life. Thus in Lyon the pro-PDP intellectual Joseph Vialatoux called for a 'moralisation' of politics, and argued that morality should 'penetrate and inform from within all human activities, in order to determine essentially and in the interior the weight to be given to each form of activity, and to integrate all of them in the unifying finality of Man'.[76] In view of these contradictions it is not surprising that, as J.-C. Delbreil shows, the PDP showed themselves unwilling in practice to collaborate with the Radical Party unless it gave up its anticlericalism. Had Tardieu achieved his goal of incorporating the Radicals into his majority he would doubtless have caused disarray in the PDP.[77]

Thus the PDP's centrist aspirations conflicted with its right-wing

[73] Interview with Dériol, 15–18 June 1987.
[74] For example Georges Forestier spoke to the 3rd section on the 'Statut légal des employés' (*Le Nouveau Journal*, 20 March 1930).
[75] Delbreil, *Centrisme et démocratie chrétienne*, 101–5.
[76] Ponson, 'Joseph Vialatoux', 471–4.
[77] Delbreil, *Centrisme et démocratie chrétienne*.

practice. Rather than to the Radicals the PDP looked to its right. In fact some key individuals within the social Catholic network were linked to the Fédération. Most important was Marius Gonin of the *Chronique*. It was perhaps because he was to the right of many activists that Gonin insisted that the *Chronique* itself remain apolitical.[78] He nevertheless subscribed to the journal of the Fédération.[79] He also played a crucial role in the conservative press, as managing director of the *Nouveau journal* and editor of *Salut public*. Both were sympathetic to the Fédération left.[80] Fédération activists and particularly local councillors were frequently seen at PDP meetings.[81]

The PDP also possessed links with the deputies of the Fédération left. Bonnevay was the son of a republican *conseiller général* of the 1870s. He had represented the Beaujolais mountains in Chamber of Deputies and Senate since 1902.[82] He resigned from the Fédération in 1927, though most of his local collaborators remained sympathetic to it. He joined no other party after his departure from the Fédération, though he sat in parliament with the more left-leaning of the Alliance's two groups, the Républicains de gauche. Bonnevay, like Isaac and the father of Julien Riboud, had been loyal to Aynard. He shared the Republicanism and Catholicism of this group, but he was further to the left on social issues. In his youth he had been associated with the Groupes d'études. Bonnevay was a firm supporter of the whole range of Tardieu's reforms. His resignation from the Fédération in 1927 had been provoked by a quarrel with Louis Marin over the Locarno treaties. He also campaigned in favour of Social Insurance and cheap housing.[83] Bonnevay argued that loose party organisation would permit him to pursue his own ideas on the social question free from the interference of reactionaries like Perret.[84]

Peissel, deputy for the Arbresle constituency (northern plateau and Lyonnais mountains), was also seen frequently at PDP meetings. When in 1932 Peissel refused to join the Fédération group in the chamber, it was to follow Georges Pernot, national leader of the pro-PDP tendency in the Fédération.[85] In his youth a Catholic trade unionist, Peissel had much in common with the PDP. He was also a firm supporter of

---

[78] Ponson, 'La Chronique sociale', 27.   [79] *Ibid.*, 30.
[80] *Archives de la Chronique sociale*, trunk 3, dossiers *Nouveau journal*, and *Salut public*, especially report and letter of 6 November 1930, signed by Gonin.
[81] *Le Nouvelliste*, 14 October 1928.
[82] Marc Du Pouget, 'Laurent Bonnevay, un notable libéral et social', in *Cent ans de catholicisme social*, ed. J.-D. Durand,. 159–69.
[83] *Le Nouvelliste*, 15 May 1926; 2 October 1928.
[84] AN 317 AP 76, Bonnevay manuscript of an article for *La Nation*, 1926.
[85] Irvine, *French Conservatism*, 13.

Tardieu. He was engaged in principle to abrogate the lay laws, but he regarded the notion of combat on that terrain as a trap set by the left.[86] Like Tardieu Peissel preferred a consensus around economic prosperity rather than religion. His ideas on social reform were very advanced for a member of the Fédération. He proposed a system of binding conciliation and arbitration in industrial disputes and collaboration with the CGT as a means of drawing it into the system.[87] Social Insurance was seen as making up for the inadequacies of mutual aid societies.[88] Peissel also favoured the 'Locarno spirit' in foreign affairs.[89] But his interventions show that much more was at stake than international relations alone. He felt the essential question to be whether the Fédération was a party of government or opposition. Electoral victory had given the right a unique chance. Freed from dependence on the Radicals it was possible to 'render healthy the state school system by introducing the national spirit into it, introduce tax cuts, pay off the national debt . . . organise defence of our frontiers, implement the social insurance law, continue to show confidence in the national destiny through a policy of interior peace, and safeguard public order against the antisocial schemes of the revolutionaries'.

Peissel's views reveal then that he perceived the right's programme as an interrelated whole. He also spoke, like Tardieu, of creating a neutral economic *terrain d'entente*. But he was no more capable of setting aside old rancours than any other conservative. Domestic order was said to be dependent on developing a 'national' spirit in the school system – that is through a purge of the anticlerical teaching profession. He opposed government proposals for free secondary education on the grounds that the present system of private scholarships was adequate.[90] Peissel's views also demonstrate that support for Tardieu's programme was not confined to a small elite. The problem was rather that Peissel did not seek to create a coherent reform movement. His contacts with the PDP remained informal. He did not participate in the reorganisation of the Fédération undertaken by Perret, and instead relied on the notables who had traditionally dominated rural constituencies.[91] Bonnevay also remained within this organisational tradition. He was backed by a small committee in Tarare to which the mayors of rural communes were invited for the purpose of unanimously endorsing candidates. Both won support through patronage and favours. Like earlier Republicans with

---

[86] *Le Nouveau Journal*, 24 May 1928.
[87] *Ibid.*, 5 March 1929. Many in the Fédération regarded the CGT as illegal.
[88] *Le Nouveau Journal*, 24 March 1929.   [89] *Ibid.*, 14 December 1929.
[90] AN 317 AP 73, Peissel to Guiter, 6 September 1929.
[91] AN F^7 13 261; *Le Nouvelliste*, 5 January 1932 on Peissel's campaigns.

their promises of railways, they offered running water and electricity to outlying regions.[92]

The reaction against conservative reformism

Nationally, the coalition which opposed Tardieu was no more coherent than that which supported him. Among Louis Marin's followers in the right wing of the Fédération were elitist business politicians of the classic type such as the forgemasters Edouard de Warren and François de Wendel. Others such as the ex-monarchist Xavier Vallat and the proto-fascist Philippe Henriot adopted a more populist style. Outside parliament mass organisations such as the Fédération des contribuables, Défense paysanne and the Parti agraire mobilised against social insurance. In the Rhône none of these organisations gained a significant foothold. This was because under the leadership of Perret the Fédération transformed itself into a structured mass party with a large membership and a discourse which combined reactionary elitism with populism.

Aged 47 in 1930, Perret was the son of a *fabricant de soieries* who had been a leading figure in the ALP. Whether Perret junior was ever a member of the ALP is unknown. But what is certain is that after serving in the artillery during the war he was attracted by the intransigent nationalism of Louis Marin. Thanks to his unceasing activism Perret rose rapidly in the party hierarchy, struggling for ascendency with Peissel, president in the Rhône from 1925.[93] On the latter's election as deputy in 1928 Perret took on the position of 'active president', and became president in his own right in December 1931. In mid-1932, after a crisis provoked by the refusal of Peissel and his ally Sallès to sit with the Fédération's group in the Chamber of Deputies, Perret's control over the Fédération became absolute. In the summer of the previous year he had become a member of the national Executive Committee. Given that he never held a significant electoral mandate, Perret's rise to such a position was remarkable in a party of *élus* like the Fédération.

Perret's dissatisfaction with conservative reformism was plain before Tardieu's accession to power. Even at this stage he recognised Tardieu as the dominant personality on the right now that Poincaré had retired. Thus at a meeting of the Fédération National Council in September 1929 Perret warned Fédération sympathisers not to surrender to the mystique of Tardieu in the way they had to that of Clemenceau and Poincaré.[94] He made clear too that in the current crisis of the Fédération

---

[92] *Le Petit Montagnard de Tarare*, 19, 27 July 1931.
[93] AN 317 AP 78, cutting from *La Nation*.
[94] AN 317 AP 73, minutes of Conseil national, 28 September 1929.

his support went to Louis Marin. He rejected demands from some within the party that the Fédération back the current Briand government. The Fédération could give no guarantee to a ministry responsible for 'financial demagogy, social insurance, a cowardly foreign policy, and reform of secondary education'. He also condemned the unhealthy influence of the party's parliamentarians and the tendentiousness of the press, which he believed to be in the pay of government and business. Foreign policy was then only part of the question. Perret went on to elaborate a strategy designed to remake the right along populist, nationalist and antisocialist lines. Populism was evident in the call for a new kind of pseudo-democratic activism against the old-style notable politics symbolised by 'certain deputies', and in the intention to renovate France with the help of 'popular elements' rather than the 'bourgeoisie en place'. The underlying assumption was of a unitary national interest incarnate in an indivisible people.

This interpretation of popular sovereignty distanced Perret from the pluralism of the PDP, while the commitment to mass mobilisation (limited as it was) divided him from the elitism of Tardieu. Perret's movement therefore represented a step towards the synthesis of authority and populism found in the far right. But in so far as Perret's Fédération resembled any other party it was the ALP, in which his father had been involved. Alexandre Bosse-Platière, Perret's ally in the Beaujolais, was another with roots in the party of De Mun. The ALP itself had survived in the Rhône until 1929.[95] It sent fifty delegates to the congress of 1928 which chose Peissel as the conservative candidate in the Arbresle constituency. But after this date it merged into the Fédération. A crucial role in bringing together the two movements was played by the short-lived Ligue des droits de la nation. This league had been formed under the patronage of the ALP in 1929, and brought together the most reactionary members of the ALP with Perret's wing of the Fédération.[96] After 1929 the ALP ceased to have an autonomous existence. The Fédération shared with the ALP its mobilisation of a popular following through an alliance with the Church, nationalism and a blend of liberalism with corporatism. Thus the ALP was instrumental in the revival in the 1930s of a much modified Legitimist strand in the right. The roots of the Fédération in this tradition illuminate the limits of Perret's populism, which meant in practice the endeavour of marginalised sections of the elites to mobilise from above a relatively passive

---

[95] *Action libéral populaire. Bulletin mensuel du comité régionale*, January 1927 to December 1929; B. F. Martin, *Count Albert de Mun: Paladin of the Republic* (Chapel Hill, NC, 1978), 161–2.

[96] *Ligue des droites de la nation*, January 1930.

body of support against the 'bourgeoisie en place' through alliance with the Church and crypto-royalist rural notables.

The activists of the Fédération

This is confirmed by a brief look at the background of Fédération sympathisers from 1928 to June 1936. Unlike its right-wing rivals the Fédération possessed activists in almost all the communes of the department and polling districts of Lyon and Villeurbanne.[97] The Fédération was more of an interclass party than was the Alliance or PDP (Map 5). Categories in which the right did badly in electoral terms were also numerous in the Fédération. Particularly striking is the large number of activists in working-class suburbs such as Vénissieux and Villeurbanne. In absolute terms peasants were the largest single group (30%). White-collar workers of all grades were also well represented (21%). The elites meanwhile were less prominent in the Fédération than the Alliance or even the PDP.[98] But if Fédération sympathisers are compared to the electorate as a whole in the agglomeration of Lyon then a different picture emerges. The most overrepresented group was businessmen. Also overrepresented, in decreasing importance, were the liberal professions, farmers (a prosperous minority in the urban electorate), senior managers, students, higher-grade white-collar workers and the retired. Small-business, manual workers and white-collar workers in public service were all underrepresented. The deeper roots of the Fédération in the bourgeois centre of the city are underlined by the higher turnover of activists in working-class suburbs.[99] In the countryside too the elites were very substantially overrepresented, the peasantry were present in a proportion about equal to their presence in the electorate, and the petty bourgeoisie and workers were all under-represented. Finally, just as the elites were overrepresented in the party as a whole, so they dominated the party leadership. Of forty-two members of the departmental bureau there were twelve businessmen, sixteen members of the liberal professions and two senior managers. In addition five retired persons were of bourgeois origin. In sum, the Fédération can be characterised as a relatively popular party led by wealthy businessmen and professionals.

But not all sections of the elites were attracted to the Fédération. We

[97] Such was the ubiquitousness of Fédération activists that mapping them reveals little. See Passmore, 'The right and the extreme right', 144–52.
[98] Business represented 10% of sympathisers, senior managers 4% and the liberal professions 5%.
[99] Passmore, 'The right and the extreme right', 151.

have already seen that Perret's rise coincided with a fall in the representation of big business within the party. It was now lawyers, doctors and medium family businessmen like Perret himself who dominated the party. It is also significant that business support for the Fédération came from traditionally conservative sectors of the economy. These included cotton manufacturers in the Beaujolais mountains.[100] Silk manufacturers were also overrepresented, especially Perret's own church ornament and gold braid sector, more reliant than any other on highly skilled artisan labour. The only other overrepresented branch was building, pushed towards the right perhaps by years of violent conflict with the activist trade unions of that industry. The engineering industry, on the other hand, was substantially underrepresented.[101] Support among the liberal professions came from lawyers, traditionally a right-wing group, and from doctors, who may have been pushed to the right in opposition to social insurance. In comparison with the Alliance the Fédération recruited relatively few senior managers or engineers. Similarly its white-collar support came from the 5th arrondissement and Croix-Rousse – home of the conservative Corporation des employés de soieries. The PDP on the other hand gained its white collar support largely from the left bank of the Rhône. In the countryside the Fédération increasingly won the support of large landowners, sometimes noble, in the mountainous west and Beaujolais. But the bulk of rural supporters were from peasant 'bonnes familles'. In sum the Fédération pulled together groups which had little to gain from the reformist and neocapitalist vogue, and which were poorly represented in business or agricultural associations. And as far as the elites were concerned, the social profile of the Fédération increasingly resembled that of the AF.

The association of the Fédération with the conservative bourgeoisie was reinforced by a geographical shift in Fédération support away from the historic centres of moderate Republicanism on the Lyonnais plateau towards areas of more recent conversion to the Republic: the Monts du Lyonnais and the Beaujolais (Maps 13–14). In Lyon Fédération support declined in the 6th arrondissement, birthplace of Progressisme, in the 3rd thanks to the rise of the PDP and in the 5th where the Fédération suffered from the rivalry of both the PDP and Alliance. The Fédération meanwhile increased its support in the 2nd and especially the 4th arrondissements, areas inhabited by the Catholic old bourgeoisie, the silk industry, and the Œuvre des cercles (Maps 15–16).[102] The social

---

[100] Textile manufacturers represented 15% of firms according to the 1931 census and 20% of Fédération business sympathisers.

[101] In the census 16%, compared to 5% of Fédération sympathisers.

[102] Passmore, 'The right and the extreme right', 108–9.

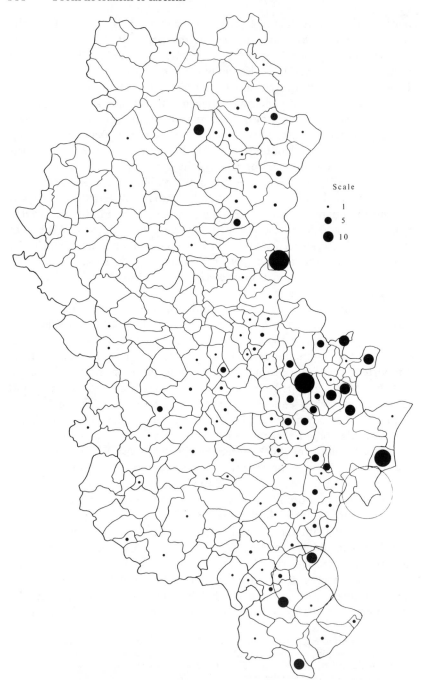

Map 13   The Rhône: Fédération républicaine activists, 1930

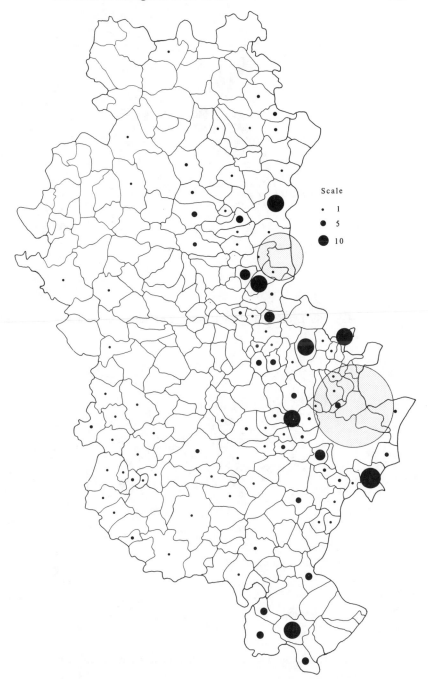

Map 14   The Rhône: Fédération républicaine, activists, 1933

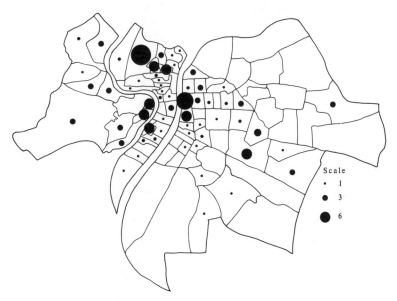

Map 15   Lyon and Villeurbanne: Fédération républicaine activists, 1930

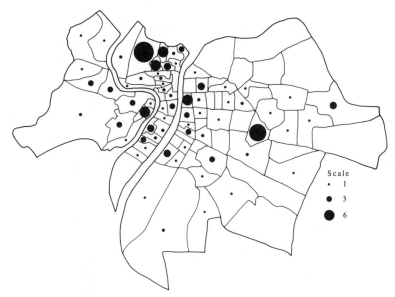

Map 16   Lyon and Villeurbanne: Fédération républicaine activists, 1933

profile of the Fédération suggests that its populism consisted less in an appeal to the popular classes in a literal sense, than to a coalition of conservative groups, which in religious and socio-economic terms defined themselves in opposition to the left, the government and the deputies of the right. Populism was as much an organisational and ideological construct as a social one.

Organisation

In the 1930s the Fédération républicaine du Rhône became, in the words of W. D. Irvine, the 'organisational showpiece of the party'.[103] Organisation was intimately related to Perret's populist drive against 'certain deputies' and the 'bourgeoisie en place'. The enemies of the Fédération were vaguely defined, but clearly Perret's view that activists should have a say in the direction of the party was far removed from the approach of Peissel or Bonnevay, let alone Isaac, whose style was likened to that of an English 'milord'.[104] Under Perret the Fédération developed a complex network of organisations. At the summit was a bureau of about twenty-five persons, elected by secret ballot from the 100-member Conseil départemental. Below this was a 500-member Comité départemental which rarely met. The base was made up of committees, theoretically present in all communes and cantons of the department and the arrondissements of Lyon. From 1928, and especially in 1930, the loose electoral committees of the various arrondissements of Lyon were brought into the Fédération fold.[105] Dependent organisations included a Comité d'ouvriers et employés, a Groupe des jeunes, several social centres, two groups dedicated to providing the children of the underprivileged with holidays,[106] a *boules* federation, Solidarité scolaire which supported private schools in the 2nd arrondissement, and two small concerns which provided cheap housing.[107] Membership, according to internal party documents, reached about 3,000 in 1933 – roughly one third of the entire national membership.[108]

Impressive as this structure was, it was nevertheless incomplete. The party claimed in 1929 to have committees in all thirty-three cantons in

[103] Irvine, *French Conservatism*, 39–41.
[104] *La Nation*, 5, October 1929; *L'Union républicaine*, 11 September 1932, 7 January 1934, 12 May 1935; Gric, *Les Courantes politiques*, 60.
[105] *Le Nouveau journal*, 2 December 1930 on the creation of the Fédération in the 7th.
[106] The Tutélaire du premier arrondissement, and the Œuvre des enfants à la montagne in the 2nd arrondissement.
[107] The Cités jardins de la Fédération républicaine in the 5th arrondissement; the Société coopérative de construction in Villeurbanne.
[108] AN 317 AP 80, Guiter to Marin, 11 January 1933.

the department, as well as in 150 of its 269 communes.[109] Yet the press mentions the existence of no more than thirty-six committees outside the commune of Lyon from 1928 to May 1936, of which five were cantonal committees. Of these only a handful were active on a continuous basis: those in Lyon itself, the working-class suburbs of the west and south and the cantonal committees of Condrieu, Neuville sur Saône, Villefranche and Givors. In reality the Fédération represented a compromise between notable and party politics. Even in the 2nd arrondissement of Lyon a modified form of notable politics survived. Here the Union des comités républicains remained independent of the Fédération throughout the period, even though it was dominated by sympathisers of Perret, and did not differ from him on most issues. Antoine Sallès, deputy for the arrondissement, endeavoured to maintain an above-party image, and, given Perret's reputation for extremism, sought to avoid too close an identification with the Fédération. For the same reason Sallès refused to join the Fédération's parliamentary group in 1932.

In rural areas of the department the organised Fédération struggled to gain a foothold. In many areas of the plateau Peissel remained influential. In the Monts du Beaujolais, Bonnevay's fief, the Fédération made no attempt to organise until 1936. In more traditionally con-servative parts of the countryside – the Lyonnais mountains and the Beaujolais – Perret's wing of the Fédération was dominant. But this often amounted to little more than a formalisation of the power of notables who did not depend wholly on allegiance to the party. In the Monts du Lyonnais the family of the Marquis de Gayardon de Fenoyl, for example, had occupied the mayoralty of St Foy l'Argentière for much of the nineteenth and twentieth centuries. The Comte de Lescure, *conseiller général* for the canton of St Laurent de Chamousset, was personally affronted when a Radical list defeated him in municipal elections in Chambost-Longessaigne in 1935.[110] In the Beaujolais too nobles often joined the Fédération. In Corcelles Guy de Saint-Laumer operated a *Clochemerle*-style alliance with the clergy. For contact with the peasantry conservative notables relied on informal contacts through institutions like the Comices agricoles, agricultural syndicates and Office agricole du Rhône. These distributed prizes to the prosperous 'bonnes familles' which formed the backbone of the Fédération. Indeed, four of the twenty-one farmers who won prizes from Office agricole in 1926 were known Fédération sympathisers.[111] The Fédération also relied on

[109] *La Nation*, 19 January 1929; *Le Nouvelliste*, 19 March 1929.
[110] ADR 4m, *Conseils municipaux*, dossier St Laurent de Chamousset.
[111] Guicherd et Ponsart, *L'Agriculture du Rhône*, 396–401.

prosperous peasant mayors for their influence upon the wider electorate. A campaign meeting for the 1928 election at St Symphorian market was described by the press as 'a veritable plenary assembly of mayors'.[112]

We have seen, however, that there was a long-term crisis of notable politics. Deference to the 'traditional authorities' could not be counted upon anywhere. This was true whatever the political nuance of the notable. Julien Riboud's investiture by eight of the canton of Monsols's eleven mayors was insufficient to prevent ignominious defeat in the *cantonales* of 1934. Perret failed to build a position in the commune of St Bonnet le Troncy, even though he owned a summer residence there and was an employer of local weavers. Yet in the general elections of 1936 Perret stood against the seemingly impregnable Bonnevay and won 40% of his 1932 vote, though not enough to win the seat. Perret's reorganisation of the Fédération must be seen in the context of this crisis. The willingness of nobles such as Saint-Laumer and De Lescure to attach themselves to the Fédération was part of an attempt to contain a nascent rural mobilisation. A good example is the commune of Montromand in the Monts du Lyonnais. It had for many years been administered by the local priest – he had once threatened to close cafés which opened during mass – who occupied the position of secretary to absentee mayor Alexandre La Batie.[113] But in the late 1920s La Batie (also active in the Fédération's committee in the 6th arrondissement of Lyon) set up a Fédération committee in the canton, which was dominated by notables. At one Fédération meeting the *curé* of St Laurent sat on the platform alongside La Batie and all of the canton's mayors.[114] La Batie was to find, however, that in the local elections of 1937 his position in the canton had been undermined by the PSF.

The Church

So Perret's wing of the Fédération consisted of a cartel of rural notables and urban activists drawn from groups opposed to Tardieu. A closer look at the Fédération's urban committees reveals, moreover, that even here it only partially resembled a genuine mass party. It did not imitate the left by taking its message to the streets and cafés. It was timidly suggested that 'aperitifs dominicaux' should be organised on Sunday mornings, at a time when bourgeois men were in the habit of lazing in

---

[112] *Le Nouveau Journal*, 15 April 1932.
[113] ADR 4m, *Conseils municipaux*, dossier St Laurent de Chamousset, report of 9 May 1941. *L'Union républicaine*, 30 April 1933. See also ADR 4m, *Conseils municipaux*, dossier St Symphorian sur Coise, report of November 1940 on Duerne.
[114] *L'Union républicaine*, 30 April 1933.

cafés while their wives prepared dinner, but little came of this.[115] Rather Perret attempted to create an organised party through links with the Church.

Cardinal Maurin advised Catholics to vote for those who were prepared to help the Church reconquer its lost rights, which could only have meant the Fédération.[116] Many of the senior laity probably shared Maurin's crypto-royalist outlook, and few were involved in the Fédération.[117] But the organisations they had created increasingly played an important, if indirect, role in conservative politics. At the lower level there were many personal ties between Fédération activists and the Church. Perret's brother was an *abbé* in the parish of St François de Sales; another activist in the seventh arrondissement, Louis Chassagnon, was brother of the bishop of Autun.[118] On the wall of the headquarters of the 4th arrondissement Fédération committee were portraits of Marin and Perret either side of a crucifix. Most important was that the Fédération drew on the parish-based 'groupes d'hommes' for its mass support.[119] Relations between party and these parish *cercles* were especially close in the 4th arrondissement, where Perret himself was vice-president of the Cercle paroissiale of St Bruno – the president was a cousin of his. In the 2nd arrondissement Fédération municipal councillors such as Charles Bennier and Paul Montrochet patronised the *cercles*. For the average *cercle* member, the main points of contact with the Fédération were *belotte* and *boules* tournaments organised by the latter.[120]

These contacts reveal much about the changing nature of the Fédération. The circles were the descendants of De Mun's Œuvre des cercles ouvriers, founded in 1871. In 1908, in recognition of a limited proletarian participation, the reference to workers was quietly dropped.[121] After the war the movement experienced substantial growth, perhaps because of increased opportunity for leisure resulting from the Eight Hour Law. In 1933 it claimed 5,000–6,000 members in forty-two groups.[122] In the 1930s the Œuvre des cercles was still marked

---

[115] *Ibid.*, 10 July 1932, 3 July 1932.   [116] *Le Nouvelliste*, 25 January 1932.

[117] One exception was the Comte de la Sparre, a Beaujolais winegrower and doyen of the Faculté catholique.

[118] Victor Bérard and M. Plasson, both of the 7th arrondissement, received respectively the Order of St Gregory the Great and the *Croix pro ecclesia et pontiface*.

[119] Variously known as *cercles d'hommes*, *groupes d'hommes* or *cercles paroissales*. Interview with Dériol, 16 August 1987.

[120] *L'Union républicaine*, 9 February 1936.

[121] Ponson, *Les Catholiques lyonnaises*, 42–5.

[122] *Le Nouvelliste*, 6 May 1933; 6,000 in fifty-two groups were claimed in *Le Nouveau journal*, 6 March 1937.

by the integrism of its founders. Its diocesan bureau included four nobles and three prominent members of Action française.[123] The president until 1929, Joseph Lucien-Brun, was an ex-Legitimist who had been a leading member of ALP before 1914. He remained mayor of Curis au Mont d'Or.[124]

A major reason for the spread into the political sphere of the Œuvre des cercles was the formation of the FNC in 1924 and condemnation of Action française in 1926. We saw in chapter two that from the mid-1920s the Church began to use its organisational resources within the Republic. In the Rhône a Ligue de défense catholique (LDC) had been set up with Maurin's help in 1917. It affiliated to the FNC on its foundation. By 1933 the LDC claimed 24,000 members in 145 sections, of which fifty functioned 'normally'.[125] In spite of the condemnation of Action française the Church's new strategy gave hitherto marginalised sections of the elites a new field of action, for it refused to recognise political divisions as far as matters of faith were concerned. Many examples could be given of the opportunities this opened up. The former Legitimist Charles Jacquier, the first President of the LDC and FNC, has already been mentioned; his successor was another royalist, Gabriel Perrin. Such figures did not become involved in the Fédération. But there was a tacit alliance. FNC meetings, like those of the Œuvre des cercles, were attended by members of the Fédération, from Peissel to Perret.[126] With the defeat of the Cartel and the return of religious peace the FNC moved away from centre stage, both locally and nationally. But some of its spokesmen, like Philippe Henriot, Xavier Vallat and Victor Perret, turned to the Fédération as an alternative field of activity. They were able to benefit from the overlap in membership between the Œuvre des cercles, the LDC and the Fédération.[127] Thus in recruiting from the Cercles d'hommes the Fédération tapped into a (much modified) Legitimist and militantly Catholic tradition which had reached it via the ALP and even the Action française. Opposition to Tardieu was therefore defined religiously as much as it was economically. Alliance between the Fédération and the Church, however, had the side effect of importing conflicts within the parishes between conservatives and Christian democrats into the Fédération.

---

[123] Count Louis de Longevialle, president of the AF group in Villefranche, Colonel Delorme, and Henry de Moinecourt, a royalist journalist.
[124] *Le Nouvelliste*, 19 March 1928.
[125] *Ibid.*, 29 May 1930, 20 November 1933.   [126] *Ibid.*, 9 February 1936.
[127] *Le Nouveau Journal*, 23 March 1925.

The extreme right

The Fédération also used the Jeunesses patriotes (JP) to mobilise support. On one occasion the JP journal referred to league and Fédération as 'sister organisations, pursuing the same goals'.[128] Perret sometimes joined JP leader Taittinger on the platform at meetings.[129] For the Fédération the most significant result of collaboration was the creation of a youth group, which emerged in 1929 out of a group of Etudiants républicains nationaux (ERN), with links to both Fédération and JP.[130] The ERN played an important part in Perret's reorganisation of the party, obtaining a sizable membership, and preparing the way for new sections of the party proper. It shared Perret's goal of remaking the bourgeoisie in an 'activist image'.[131] Its leader Roger Fulchiron disclaimed any intention to create a new league. Rather 'his movement would second the action of older activists'.[132] Perret's influence over the Groupe des jeunes and the JP was doubtless favoured by common recruitment in the parish network.[133]

Links between the Fédération, the youth group and the JP were, however, problematic. Perret was distrustful of all leagues, seeing them as draining money and troops from the Fédération.[134] He had a particular reason for distrusting the JP. Taking account of the relative stability after the fall of the Cartel, Taittinger had decided that parliamentary action was the only way forward. He therefore ordered JP militants to support the policies of Tardieu and to collaborate with the Centre de propagande of Henri de Kerillis in its efforts to create a united conservative party behind Tardieu.[135] Perret ridiculed Kerillis's obsession with the 'British model', pointing out that the Labour Party was currently in power in Britain. In Perret's view the Fédération was perfectly suited to the task of organising the right.[136] Perret took little heart from the fact that not all JP activists in Lyon were enamoured of either Kerillis, Tardieu or even Taittinger: for Etienne de Raulin, Kerillis's methods were more suited to the launching of a new brand of chocolate than to politics.[137] Those JP, like de Raulin, who were closest politically to Perret were adepts of a violent street politics which Perret

---

[128] *L'Alerte*, August 1929.
[129] AN F[7] 13 235, report of 18 January 1929; *Le Nouvelliste*, 22 November 1932.
[130] Interview with Me Roger Fulchiron, 11 February 1987.
[131] *Le Nouvelliste*, 17 May, 1931.   [132] *Le Nouveau Journal*, 17 September 1930.
[133] See chapter nine.   [134] AN 317 AP 76, 9 July 1930, Perret to Buré.
[135] Soucy, *French Fascism: The First Wave*, chapter 8.
[136] AN 317 AP 76, Perret to Paul Gand, 22 April 1930.
[137] *L'Union française*, July 1930. On Kérillis and the Lyon JP see AN F[7] 13 235, 24 January 1928, 18 January 1929.

feared would get out of hand.[138] Furthermore, all within the JP saw the league as uniting and by implication leading the right.[139] Indeed, Perret's critique of the individualism and selfishness of conservative leaders was echoed by the leagues and could potentially be turned against him. Perret was constrained by his goal of mobilising the 'popular classes' against the establishment, just as he was by his links with the Church.

Politics, Catholic nationalism and economics

In an interview marking his accession to the Presidency of the Fédération in the Rhône in 1931 Perret stated that 'twelve years of experience have shown me that it is possible to attract many sympathisers and hesitants if we endeavour to move away, little by little, from pure politics towards the economic terrain by means of a study of the organisation of work, production and the corporation'.[140] The problem was that the idea of fighting on a 'neutral' economic ground was shared by factions of the right which interpreted the economic very differently. Perret's arch-rival Fougère, for example, echoed Redressement français in calling for the primacy of the economic over the political and for a patronal voice in government.[141] Perret's own economic ideas were moreover inseparable from his populist antipathy to sections of the conservative establishment. He sought to mobilise the people from above by alliance with notables and conservative Catholic organisations. Thus Perret's conception of neutrality was loaded with political, economic and ideological baggage.

Perret placed the centre of gravity of conservatism in the Fédération. He was contemptuous of those who disguised themselves as leftists in a vain attempt to win Radical sympathies.[142] As Bosse-Platière put it, the Radicals had simply to understand that the only meaningful conflict was between the Fédération and the SFIO.[143] The assumption was that peasants and small businessmen voted for the Radicals only because they had been duped and that the right merely had to lay before them the economic verities. Perret assumed, moreover, that his own view of political economy was identical to the national interest. The economic truth according to Perret owed something to liberalism. He was often presented as an heroic individual struggling against adversity in both

---

[138] AN 317 AP 7, Perret to Taittinger, 19 April 1929.
[139] *L'Union française*, 9 March 1929. *Le Nouveau Journal*, 4 April 1930.
[140] *Le Nouvelliste*, 23 December 1931; cutting from *Gringoire*, undated, in AN 317 AP 77/8.
[141] *Le Nouveau Journal*, 23 February 1926.   [142] *Réveil du Beaujolais*, 24 March 1931.
[143] *L'Union républicaine*, 19 June 1932.

economic and political life. It was said that as a young man he had been sent to work as a weaver because of the collapse of the family firm, but that through hard work he had been able to rebuild his patrimony.[144] The first issue of *L'Union républicaine*, the mouthpiece of Perret's wing of the Fédération, added an 'absolute respect for property', and liberty of conscience, teaching, press and association. Government interference in the economy, high taxes and unbalanced budgets were anathema to Perret. Neither did he consider that economic or technological progress could be halted.[145] Yet Perret's economic views were ambiguous. The influence of the Legitimist tradition and of the social Catholicism of the ALP can be seen in an article setting out his basic philosophy in 1932:

As long as the world has existed true happiness has been impossible without education within the family, schooling also directed by the family, conscientious work, respect for one's elders, for hierarchy, tradition and discipline, the corporatist organisation of the profession, contentment with one's lot – free from envy or unmeasured ambition, the aspiration towards gradual and deserved success, generosity towards the less fortunate, love of one's home, the Motherland and the [religious] faith which conditions everything.[146]

In spite of the emphasis on hard work and individual effort this was very different from Edouard Aynard's view of an elite constantly renewed by social mobility. For Perret there was a natural social order ordained by God and transmitted in the form of tradition to each generation. Respect for its values was learned in the family, the basic unit in a hierarchy which also comprised profession, generation and, at the summit, the nation. Within this hierarchy individual ambition should be restrained and limited.

Central to Perret's economic ideas was the corporation. He called for mixed employer–worker syndicates and for the representation of social forces in parliament. His particular concern was that large factories would undermine the supply of skilled labour and destroy the family workshop. He called for artisans to be reserved a proportion of apprenticeships. He also saw the Chambers of Trades, set up in 1925, as a first step in the protection of apprenticeship and skilled labour, and hoped that eventually they would lead to a return of corporations. This would ultimately lead to collaboration of a working-class elite with capitalists. [147] Clearly these preoccupations owed much to conditions in his own branch of the silk industry. He pursued the same goals in the Chambre des métiers de la soie, of which he was director. Thus when he

[144] Cutting from *Gringoire*, AN 317 AP 77/8.
[145] *L'Union républicaine*, 18 March 1934.   [146] *Ibid.*, 24 July 1932.
[147] *La Nation*, 5 and 12 January 1929; *Le Nouvelliste*, 12 January 1929; *L'Union républicaine*, 17 April 1931.

called for the return of women to the home he did not have in mind the bourgeois ideal of the non-working woman. On the contrary, return to the family workshop would permit the wife to work alongside husband and children, thereby reconciling family and professional duties.[148] All in all the Fédération's corporatism was fairly limited. It amounted to little more than paternalist control of labour and protection of endangered crafts. Nonetheless, its incompatibility with the expansionist ideas lauded by Tardieu is plain, especially as Perret spoke of a return to artisan production, at least for those industries where mass production was not essential.[149] Perret's conception of 'objective' economic interests turned out to consist in a desire to remake France in the image of the silk braid industry.

His view of the economy was also shaped by his religion. True, Perret called for pacification of the religious struggle, and in order to spare Radical sensibilities stressed the republicanism of the Fédération.[150] Yet Perret's idea of religion was no more neutral than his view of the economy. This became clear when in July 1930 Tardieu accepted a Radical amendment to a motion on the fiftieth anniversary of the Ferry education laws which spoke of 'liberty and neutrality of education'. As a result of the outrage of many in the Fédération, Tardieu failed to carry the amendment. For Perret this affair represented a return to the days of Emile Combes. Like Tardieu he argued that the religious quarrel had been transcended by the sacrifices of Catholics during the war. But in Perret's view the 'neutrality' of the state system would be a sham so long as mayors could not rid themselves of *instituteurs* who insulted motherland, family and religion and constituted the backbone of the CGT. Worse still the government was seeking to strangle private-sector education by means of free secondary schooling.[151] Doubtless Perret also shared Cardinal Maurin's view that the Social Insurance Acts represented a means for socialist school teachers to subvert Catholic charity.[152] For Perret the precondition of religious pacification was a purge of the teaching profession. Tardieu and Perret were therefore unable to recognise each other as allies, even though both called for religious peace in order to defend 'objective' economic interests. Indeed, Perret felt that by making concessions on the schools issue Tardieu actually endangered social peace. Thus Perret's aim to shift political debate onto neutral territory contained in practice a divisive set of economic and Catholic references. This was not surprising given the

---

[148] *L'Union républicaine*, 9 October 1932, 17 July 1932, 8 December 1935.
[149] AN 317 AP 82/3.
[150] *L'Union républicaine*, 1 May 1932.   [151] *La Nation*, 12 July 1930.
[152] *Semaine religieuse*, 22 March 1929.

Fédération's dependence on notables and the Church for influence over the masses.

Nevertheless, Perret's populism provided a space within which more advanced opponents of the status quo could operate. Perret's nationalist antiGermanism was viewed favourably by the royalist press. For Perret, like the equally antiGerman *Nouvelliste*, it did not matter what regime was in power in Germany, its essential bellicosity remained constant.[153] Both condemned the Young Plan, opposed early evacuation of the Rhineland and execrated Briand (the *Nouvelliste*'s obituary of Briand was so venomous that it reputedly earned a rebuke from Cardinal Maurin).[154] It is probable that Perret supported the *Nouvelliste*'s opposition to Briand's plan for European unity (an idea supported by some in Redressement français) on the grounds that it would harm trade with the Empire, Britain and the USA.[155] This points to the connection between international and domestic politics. There was nothing original in the fact that Fédération nationalism was also meant to integrate French society. For Perret the nation was the supreme focus of loyalty beyond family and profession. Bosse-Platière's definition of the nation as an intangible link between individuals and classes had been one of the commonplaces of the right since the turn of the century.[156] But Perret's nationalism also possessed an oppositional character. It is evident in his view of foreign policy. Commenting on the arrival in power of Hitler, Perret asked whether our 'ostriches' in Parliament would finally comprehend? He went on to quote Kipling: 'my sons are dead because our leaders lied'.[157] Thus he contested the legitimacy of those who believed that it was in the national interest to demand *rapprochement* with Germany. He called for a new national movement like that of the Great War under the banner of the Fédération and which would assert the spirit of the nation over the parties. Perret therefore had as much right to a voice in party affairs as an *élu* because he had proved his commitment to the nation in the trenches (an idea later to be taken further by the Croix de Feu). The radicalism of Perret's nationalism, at least in this period, should not be exaggerated. He spoke of partnership between deputies and activists mandated by war service. He did not seek to eliminate or absorb other conservative parties, speaking instead of an alliance stretching from moderate Radicals to the Fédération.[158] Nevertheless, Perret's views proved attractive to elements of the far right, especially in the JP; his committees were penetrated by

---

[153] *Ibid.*, 24 April 1931; *L'Union républicaine*, 26 March 1933.
[154] *Le Nouvelliste*, 9 March 1932.
[155] *Ibid.*, 17 July and 13 September 1929.   [156] *L'Union républicaine*, 14 April 1935.
[157] *Ibid.*, 21 May 1933.   [158] *La Nation*, 12 April 1929; 5 October 1929.

extremists.[159] Under the impact of the crisis of the mid-1930s Perret's own discourse became more radical. For the time being, however, the populism of the Fédération neutralised the far right. This is perhaps why neither the Fédération des contribuables nor Défense paysanne was able to establish itself in the Rhône in this period.

Perret' s victory

At first, Perret's views had only a limited resonance outside of the circles already referred to. Hostility to Marin reached a peak after he had participated in the overthrow of Briand in October 1929. Perret defended Marin in public debates with Peissel, and in the press lauded his 'clairvoyance'.[160] But in private even he was doubtful. Perret informed Marin that 'hundreds' of subscriptions to La Nation had been cancelled. Marin's partisans in Lyon dared not utter his name. The great majority of naïve activists, said Perret, took the word of those whose election they had made possible. Perret advised Marin to make a tactical withdrawal. Otherwise, if Marin lost the presidency, Perret himself would have to submit to the will of the majority in Lyon.[161] The weakness of Perret's position was shown by the fact that in January 1930 he pledged his support for the new Tardieu cabinet, even though Briand remained a member of it.[162] Some months later, to Perret's horror, deputy Jean-Baptiste Delorme resigned from the Fédération. Yet in mid-1931 local sections began to vote motions in support of Marin.[163] In December Peissel gave up the Presidency of the Rhône Fédération to Perret, ostensibly because of pressure of work.[164] The new balance of forces is illustrated by three disputes which occurred in 1931 and 1932.

The first related to control of the press. Thanks to the acquired position of the Nouvelliste it had always been difficult for moderates to get their views across. In the period in question the Nouvelliste remained as committed as ever to the re-Christianisation of France and retained its classical liberal opposition to social reform.[165] Several attempts to set up a rival had failed. The most recent was the creation in 1924 of the Nouveau journal. According to managing director Marius Gonin, it was 'the only [Lyonnais] newspaper which frankly follows the line of the

---

[159] For example the JP member and future Croix de Feu leader Louis Marchal was able to replace a Fédération member as candidate in the 7th arrondissement in the 1928 general election.

[160] Le Nouveau Journal, 14 December 1929; La Nation, 15 March 1930.

[161] AN 317 AP 73, Perret to Marin, 23 December 1929.

[162] Le Nouvelliste, 18 January 1930.   [163] Ibid., 27 June 1931; July 1931.

[164] Le Nouveau Journal, 20 December 1931.

[165] Le Nouvelliste, 1 January 1928; Demaison, 'Visites à la presse'.

Tardieu government'.[166] Although Perret was a member, the board was heavily weighted towards the left Fédération and centre-right: Peissel and Fougère were both members.[167] In spite of the backing of several wealthy industrialists the *Nouveau journal*'s circulation of 40,000 was 30% too low to cover its costs.[168] By the spring of 1931, with the arrival of the economic crisis, the situation of the *Nouveau journal* was critical.[169] Negotiations with press magnates Pierre Laval and Raymond Patenôtre took place, but the outcome was that the *Nouvelliste* took over the paper in December.[170] The *Nouveau journal* became in effect the *Nouvelliste* with a different editorial. A few months before a general election the *Nouvelliste* was 'more than ever master of the political battle field'.[171] From the point of view of the moderate right the timing could not have been worse, for in November 1931 Laval sold *Lyon républicain* to the Radical Patenôtre. The paper then ceased to insert conservative communiqués.[172] Moderates, to the disgust of Peissel, Cozon and Gonin, were left only with the uninspiring evening paper *Salut public*. In a time of economic hardship *Salut public*'s bourgeois clientele, seeing it as a luxury, tended to stop buying it.[173] To compound the difficulties of the moderates the Fédération began to publish *L'Union républicaine* in April 1932. It was personally owned by Perret. It did not open up its columns to his rivals.

The second conflict took place in the Beaujolais, part of a long struggle between the business notables of Villefranche and the rural militants represented by Alexandre Bosse-Platière. In 1931 the former had been able to sabotage the creation of a Fédération youth group in Villefranche. Bosse-Platière meanwhile was evicted from his post as political editor of the local newspaper, the *Réveil du Beaujolais*.[174] Surprisingly, in 1932 Bosse-Platière was selected by the Union des républicains, an independent body, to carry the flag of the right in the elections of 1932. Yet he found himself faced by a dissident candidate, the Villefranche businessman Ernest Planche, loyal to the centre-right

---

[166] Fonds Gonin, Gonin report, 6 November 1930.   [167] *Ibid.*, 19 December 1925.
[168] *Ibid.*, November 1929. On one occasion Charles Gillet donated 400,000 francs to bail out the paper.
[169] *Ibid.*, Gonin report, 13 April 1931.
[170] *Ibid.*, Falaize to Gonin, 7 December 1931; Cozon to Gonin, 8 April 1932 and 19 March 1932.
[171] *Ibid.*, Falaize to Gonin, 7 December 1931.
[172] *Ibid.*, Cozon report, 19 March 1932; Fred Kupferman, *Laval, 1883–1945* (1987), 65–9.
[173] Fonds Gonin, Gonin report, ?1931; Cozon to Gonin, 6 January 1932; H. Isaac to Cozon, 7 February 1932.
[174] ADR Cour de Justice de Lyon, report of 1945.

and moderate Fédération.[175] In the course of the campaign even Bosse-Platière's own committee turned against him and resigned. Planche outdistanced Bosse-Platière on the first ballot, forcing the latter's withdrawal. Yet soon after the election Bosse-Platière was able to create a section of the Fédération in the constituency. In September 1933 the old Union des républicains dissolved itself and ceded its property to the Fédération.[176]

The third conflict resulted from the decision of Peissel and Sallès to join Georges Pernot's dissident parliamentary group in 1932. Their action was the logical outcome of the conflicts which had divided the Lyonnais right since 1928 and represented rather more than an act of nihilistic individualism portrayed by Irvine.[177] For Perret this was a betrayal of the Fédération and its activists.[178] Peissel's defence of the autonomy of deputies was insufficient to prevent the Comité directeur, presided by Perret himself, from banning all assistance to Sallès and Peissel as long as they remained in the dissident group.[179] The Fédération stopped short of expulsion.[180] At least two Committee members supported Sallès and Peissel, criticising the rightwards turn of the Fédération.[181] These sanctions had no practical effect. They were not announced to the public. Both deputies continued to attend Fédération meetings.[182] Nevertheless, Perret's enhanced influence in the Fédération was unmistakable, especially since after 1932 Peissel shifted rapidly towards his position. Sallès had in any case been close to Perret, supporting Peissel only for tactical reasons.

The reasons for Perret's victory are those evoked at the beginning of the chapter to account for the disappointments of Tardieu: economic crisis and the resurgence of international tension. In 1931 even Edmund Weitz called for a halt to reform.[183] The victory of the Cartel in 1932 also contributed to the shift to the right. There were also local factors to be taken into account. The leading business supporters of neocapitalism, Fougère and Weitz, played little active role in Lyonnais politics after 1930. On the political side the reformist deputies Peissel and Delorme were in a weak position, representing rural constituencies which gained

---

[175] *Réveil du Beaujolais*, 16 March 1932; *L'Union républicaine*, 26 June 1932.
[176] *L'Union républicaine*, 20 November 1932, 11 September 1932, 10 September 1933.
[177] Irvine, *French Conservatism*, 58–62.
[178] *L'Union républicaine*, 26 June 1932.
[179] *Ibid.*, 17 July 1932; AN 317 AP 73, Perret to Marin, 10 June 1932.
[180] AN 317 AP 73, Damaz to Guiter, 22 June 1932.
[181] AN 317 AP 73, Charbin to Guiter, 25 June 1932.
[182] AN 317 AP 80, Perret to Marin, 10 June 1932.
[183] CRCCL, 1930, 624 (published in 1931).

little from reform. The *rapprochement* of Perret and Peissel after 1932 is evidence of Perret's growing influence. Yet the security of Perret's position should not be exaggerated. His success was incomplete. Notables remained influential within the Fédération and in the right in general. Tightening of party structures had contributed to intensification of conflict with rival strands in the right. In spite of the temporary rediscovery of conservative unity after the elections of 1932, conflict was soon to resurface, and was no longer contained within the parliamentary right. Moreover, Perret's establishment of control over the Fédération may have contributed to Radical gains in the elections of 1932. The example of the Rhône shows a shift away from the constitutional-elitist politics favoured by Aynard and Isaac towards more popular or populist parties like the PDP and Perret's Fédération. This was reflected in the partial withdrawal of the liberal elites from local politics. Big business shifted the locus of its activity to Paris, from where it was possible to lobby the state directly. The emergence of mass parties was in the case of the PDP part of a shift towards organisation of interests and collaboration between capital and labour; in the case of Perret's Fédération it represented a reaction against such tendencies. In both cases the Church's new emphasis on mass mobilisation played a significant part.

Tardieu's reform project must be seen in the context of the same developments. He endeavoured to resolve a perceived crisis of the parliamentary state by incorporating organised interests into the system. But he sought to achieve this within the framework of an elitist liberalism. Interests would be bought off by economic prosperity. And as Monnet argues, Tardieu remained an archetypal Third Republican political fixer. Like the prewar Italian politician Giolitti, he sought to integrate 'new forces' into society by means of parliamentary deals. Although he spoke of a disciplined conservative party, it was conceived in parliamentary terms, not as a structured mass party. As a result he failed to capitalise on support for many of his ideas. Tardieu, then, broke only partly with the tradition of 'libéralisme capacitaire'. He remained convinced that an enlightened elite was best qualified to represent a nation conceived in unitary terms.

The fact that Tardieu belonged to a recognisably Orleanist tradition provides some support for Rémond's view that the French right was defined by the perennity of certain mentalities. There is also an element of truth in his view that Tardieu merely added the cult of economic expansion to Guizot's liberalism. Nevertheless, Rémond's categories do not do full justice to the complexities of a liberalism torn between a more traditional 'libéralisme capacitaire' based on individual liberty and a left liberal emphasis on association and economic democracy. Similarly, we have seen that Perret's Fédération owed much to a conjunctural revival of counterrevolutionary traditionalism. But this tradition too had been substantially modified by the ALP's Catholic populism and by the Church's new strategy of parish mobilisation. Moreover, Perret accepted many aspects of liberalism. Finally, the PDP cannot be fitted into any of Rémond's categories, marrying as it did left liberal pluralism and Catholic integrism. Traditions should, then, be seen not as strait-jackets, but as resources used by political movements in function of ideological preconceptions and material interests. Individual movements were promiscuous in the traditions upon which they drew. This emphasis on diversity also casts doubt on the Marxist view that there was an underlying unity of the right in defence of capitalism. Tardieu owed his failure partly to the fact that he made the same assumption. In reality mere commitment to a 'neutral' economic interest was insufficient to create practical unity, given the interweaving of ideological and material interest within the right.

Finally, this chapter suggests some preliminary conclusions about the nature of Third Republican society. Tardieu did not, as Monnet suggests, represent an enlightened minority frustrated by the 'republican synthesis'. The issues which inspired neocapitalists were debated throughout society. Tardieu's views on the need to strengthen the state were shared by almost all on the right (with exceptions such as Bonnevay in the Rhône). There was also much support for social insurance and international co-operation. Reformists nevertheless met considerable opposition from those concerned to defend quality production and skilled labour, while both camps were cross-cut by the clerical/anti-clerical conflict.

Tardieu's reforms, moreover, had a negative impact on the stability of the right and of French society. C. S. Maier argues that in interwar France there was no development of corporatist structures to match those which emerged in Germany in the 1920s. The middle classes were not therefore caught between organised capital and labour and did not turn to fascism.[184] Maier, however, halts his analysis in 1926. After that date France developed a social insurance system which became a bone of contention in the 1930s crisis, as sections of the right began to link attacks on welfare benefits and antiparliamentarianism. Already in the Tardieu period, the Social Insurance Acts had created a populist mobilisation against them which sometimes took on an

[184] Maier, *Recasting Bourgeois Europe*, 579–94.

antiparliamentary tone, though we have seen that this populism cannot be linked to the middle class alone. In the Rhône the fragmentation of the right, coupled with the development of populist discourses, prepared the way for the emergence of the leagues in the 1930s.

6   The impact of the economic crisis

For Pierre Milza one of the principal reasons for the failure of fascism in France was the lesser gravity of the economic crisis compared to Italy and Germany. There was therefore no mobilisation of the 'most stable elements' of society, no feeling of 'uncertainty' sufficient to lead to a demand for power on the part of extremist movements, and no failure of the ruling elites. The middle classes remained faithful to republican values and institutions. Even partisans of authority like La Rocque were ultimately committed to the Republic. This argument shares with the 'stalemate society' thesis the assumption of a powerful common culture, and indeed the view that the Croix de Feu represented merely a Catholic and authoritarian version of the Radical Party, equally committed to maintaining the status quo.[1] This interpretation confuses the conditions which lead to the emergence of a fascist *movement* with those which produce a fascist *regime*. It also assumes that a fascist regime can emerge from only one set of conditions, a view which rules out the possibility of an unsuccessful fascist movement.[2] In fact a social crisis may produce several varieties of right-wing authoritarianism. In Germany crisis gave birth to the Stahlhelm, the Strassers, Hitler and von Papen, and led the Catholic Centre Party to salute 'führer Brüning'. In France the crisis brought about a movement for reform of the state within the parliamentary right, accentuated the populism of some in the Fédération républicaine and produced the Croix de Feu, PSF and PPF, and even caused some parts of the right to turn to the Popular Front. It may well be that the hold of republicanism over wide sections of opinion helped prevent the leagues from expanding sufficiently to win power. In that sense the crisis probably was 'less serious' in France. But that could not prevent the emergence of a fascist movement from a crisis of the right.

The purpose of this chapter is to show that the mid-1930s witnessed a deep social crisis, due to the impact of economic depression on an

---

[1] Milza, *Fascisme français*, 137, 223–5.
[2] Dobry, 'Février 1934 et la découverte de l'allergie de la société française au fascisme', *Revue française de sociologie* 30 (1989), 511–33.

already divided society, which produced a diffuse authoritarian mood. In the following chapters we shall see that this made possible the emergence of authoritarian, populist and sometimes fascist movements of the extreme right. It should be borne in mind that the conflicts which will be described in this chapter were only in appearance exclusively economic. The question of social insurance, for example, involved a complex of material and ideological issues. Furthermore, the sense of crisis in the mid-1930s derived as much from fear of the left and of a new war as it did from the depression.

In the Rhône, although Redressement français had gone into decline, the concerns of neocapitalists continued to disrupt conservative politics in the depression. A Malthusian response was far from universal. Although few showed a positive interest in social reform, many large firms persisted with the investment and rationalisation strategies which seemed to threaten a system of production based on quality and flexibility. Indeed, enthusiasm for mass production spread more widely among big firms in the silk industry. This exacerbated the crisis of the liberal elite, for small and medium firms were increasingly suspicious of big business. Shopkeepers meanwhile mobilised behind movements which combined anticapitalism and hostility to the Chamber of Commerce with right-wing populist overtones. This was paralleled in the countryside by the crisis of another bastion of the liberal elite, the USE, which was troubled by financial difficulties, the rise of specialist associations and the further progress of the JAC. Tensions within the right-wing constituency were enhanced by the attraction of some white-collar workers and even businessmen to the programme of the Popular Front, especially the forty-hour week. Finally, these relatively straight-forward conflicts were complicated by the activation of an enormous number of pressure groups, which made it difficult to form any permanent alliance or political strategy. The desperate defence of sectional interests produced a feeling of social disintegration.

In order to reconcile special interests and public good many conservatives demanded restoration of state authority. They agreed that this meant disciplining of the trade unions, especially those of civil servants. Most also agreed that the grip of the Radicals and Socialists on the machinery of state should be loosened, along with that of the petty bourgeois and trade union interests they supposedly represented. But Michel Margairez is only partly right to argue that the movement for reform of the state reflected the efforts of monopoly capital to eliminate the influence of workers and the petty bourgeoisie in parliament.[3]

---

[3] Margairaz, 'La Droite et l'état'.

Although some capitalists thought in this way – in particular there was hostility to the social insurance laws – conflicting interests within the right prevented the development of a coherent strategy. The question of corporatism was particularly illustrative of such difficulties. Whilst corporatists shared a common desire to discipline the CGT, the doctrine remained a contested one, entangled with a multitude of economic and ideal interests. We shall see that the conflicting demands of both interest groups and politicians for reform of the state and corporatism placed impossible demands on the parliament. Many were to conclude that salvation could come only from outside the system.

The economic crisis

The contrasting experiences of Germany, Britain and the USA show the difficulty of establishing a direct relationship between fascism and the 'seriousness' of an economic crisis. In Germany industrial production fell at its worst to 58% of its 1928 level in 1932. In France the bottom of the slump came in 1935 when industrial production fell to 75% of what it had been in 1928. This is a significant though not enormous difference which is perhaps compensated by the greater length of the French crisis. Whereas German industrial production recovered its 1928 level in 1936, French output remained below that level on the outbreak of war. The agricultural crisis in France was perhaps both longer lasting and more severe than in Germany.

At least as significant as these international comparisons was the differential impact of the depression within France. Shopkeepers, artisans, peasants and small and medium business suffered the greatest proportionate losses of income. These categories often supported the Radicals, but also provided many troops for the right. The impact of the depression on the elites was more variable. The better fortunes of big capital were reflected in the relative health of incomes from industrial and commercial stocks. The belief of small businessmen that a 'sheltered sector' had escaped the depression therefore had some basis in reality.[4] The liberal professions improved their position, as did those drawing income from property or pensions. The most important point, however, is that at the same time as the depression adversely affected large sections of the conservative electorate, the working class got off relatively lightly in terms of both real wages and job losses.[5] Although official figures substantially underestimate the level of unemployment in

---

[4] Kolboom, *La Revanche des patrons*, 48–9.
[5] A. Sauvy, *Histoire économique de la France entre les deux guerres*, 4 vols. (1965–75), 137. Berstein, *Histoire du Parti radical*, 220–30.

France, it still did not reach German levels. In fact, from the point of view of the right, this only aggravated the sense of crisis. Far from being crippled by mass unemployment, the French working-class movement was homogenised and stabilised by the elimination of its most marginal elements.[6] France therefore experienced political polarisation at a time when the left was well placed to use the strike weapon, and where the clientele of the right and Radicals bore much of the burden of the slump. In Germany on the other hand the advance of communism was accompanied by extreme weakness of the labour movement.

At the end of 1930 Albert Cotte, president of the Union des marchands de soie, was still able to attribute the lesser gravity of the crisis in France to 'natural prudence and national savings'.[7] Yet in 1931 a crisis developed from which the *fabrique* never truly recovered.[8] Prices fell owing to massive overproduction of raw and spun silk in Japan and of woven cloth in the USA and expansion in the use of rayon.[9] By 1935 French silk exports had plunged to 10% of their 1928 value. Turnover fell by 80%. Membership of the Syndicat des fabricants fell from 725 in 1929 to 300 in 1937.[10] In the dyeing sector the number of firms in the arrondissement of Lyon fell from 119 to 69.[11] Unemployment may have reached 35% in silk weaving in 1934.[12] The number of workers employed in the dyeing industry was reduced by no less than 55% between 1928 and 1934. Those who remained were on short time.[13]

In the metallurgical industries turnover fell from 2.2 billion francs in 1930 to less than one billion in 1934.[14] The number of workers employed fell by 43%. German competition and the end of rural electrification were the most often cited causes. Worst hit of all were those making machinery for the silk and dyeing industries.[15] A notable victim of the crisis was Edmond Weitz, obliged to sell his heavy machinery concern to the Barras group in 1936.[16] Best able to cope with the crisis were highly capitalised firms in the electricity industry. But even here experience was variable.[17] In the shoe industry the workforce fell from 5,000 in 1930 to 2,000 in 1935.[18] The building industry lost

[6] Noiriel, *Les Ouvriers dans la société françaises xixᵉ–xxᵉ siècles* (1986), 171–84.
[7] CRCCL, 1930, report of Cotte.
[8] CRCCL, 1931, 527–52; AN F[7] 13 040, 3 December 1931.
[9] Laferrère, *Lyon, ville industrielle*, 217–18; CRCCL, 1930, 567, 644; CRCCL, 1931, 557.
[10] CRCSF, 1928 and 1937.   [11] CRCCL, 1937, 415–17.
[12] *Lyon républicain*, 26 September 1934. Geni, 'L'Organisation professionelle', 112.
[13] CRCCL, 1934, 378.
[14] CRCCL, 1933, 390–8; *Lyon républicain*, 15 December 1935.
[15] *Lyon républicain*, 15 and 29 December 1935.
[16] Laferrère, *Lyon, ville industrielle*, 300; CRCCL, *Lyon républicain*, 15 and 29 December 1935.
[17] *Lyon républicain*, 29 December 1935.   [18] CRCCL, 616–20.

about 4,000 of the 10,000 workers it had employed in 1930. Rather than multiply endlessly such examples, suffice it to say that only printing, gas and electricity supply passed through the crisis without difficulty.

The effect of the crisis on non-business conservative supporters is harder to measure. But there is considerable evidence of white-collar unemployment. In 1933, not the worst year of the crisis, it was reported that in a sample of twenty-eight Lyon firms the number of office workers had fallen by 28% between 1929 and 1932. White-collar workers did not perhaps suffer unemployment to the same extent as the unskilled. The most significant effect was perhaps to decrease opportunities for promotion. There is also evidence to suggest that engineers had been affected by unemployment.[19]

In the countryside too the turning point was in 1931, when the prices of wine, grain, milk and fruit all collapsed; indebtedness spread. To some extent the possibility of retreating into subsistence farming blunted the effect of the crisis. Furthermore, the Rhône peasantry benefited from relatively high wheat prices because the region was not self-sufficient in grain.[20] Worst affected were those most dependent on the national and international market. Wine prices collapsed as a result of the poor quality harvest of 1931 at the same time as growers were obliged to face competition from French North Africa. Large growers had to cope with rising labour costs and the need to offer more attractive contracts to ever scarcer sharecroppers. For small and medium proprietors income from wine sales ceased to cover production costs.[21] The delayed impact of the crisis outside the Beaujolais helps to explain why economic crisis led at first to the radicalisation of the peasantry only in the latter area, where it was the socialists who benefited. Peasants in the rest of the department began to turn to the Croix de Feu only in late 1935.

From liberalism to corporatism

The depression may not have been as serious in France as it was in Germany. But its material effects must be seen in the context of a society already riven by chronic divisions. Indeed, social stability had depended less upon a common culture or hegemony than on the political weakness of subordinate groups and on rising real income for the majority of

---

[19] PVCCL, 29 June 1933; *Chronique sociale*, March 1934, 219–20.

[20] Barral, *Les Agrariens français*, 218–21; Garrier, *Paysans du Lyonnais*, 596–8, 602–5. Burel, 'La Vignoble beaujolais', 52; *Le Nouvelliste*, 14 March 1931; 19 July 1934; 22 August 1935; Garrier, *Paysans du Lyonnais*, 612–14.

[21] Garrier, *Paysans du Lyonnais*, 596–8, 602–5. Burel, 'La Vignoble beaujolais', 52.

social groups, however unfairly distributed. But in the depression the cake began to shrink, particularly for some sections of the bourgeoisie and lower middle class. Rewards could now be preserved only by transfer of resources between groups; by means of wage cuts, reform of social insurance and deflation. Conservatives sought to achieve this through a mixture of repression and ideological strategies. A reformed state would establish harmony among the special interests which had mushroomed during the depression and in particular would discipline the CGT, perceived as a major obstacle to deflation. At this belated stage ideology too gained in importance, as conservatives sought to convince subordinated groups that the national interest demanded equal sacrifice by all. Corporatism too was important, for it was meant to control the CGT, harmonise conflicting interests within the ruling class and promote an ideology of class collaboration. In sum, whereas expanding capitalism had no interest in encouraging class comparison, since workers and peasants gained relatively less than the elites, capitalism in crisis had every reason to convince the masses that burdens should be shared equally by all. This was particularly true in 1930s France, where in relative terms some sections of the ruling class suffered disproportionately from the depression.[22]

Ideology, then, took on a new importance in the depression. But the various elements of the conservative constituency sought to integrate France in their own images, thereby increasing conflict. Projects for constitutional reform were advanced from a variety of perspectives and connected to diverse views of French society. Corporatism was an equally contested ideology. At a minimum, 'corporatism' refers to a system of legally backed professional associations with powers over production, marketing and perhaps industrial relations. Corporatism is therefore distinguished from liberalism with its belief either in individual liberty or in *voluntary* association. Beyond this there was little agreement, as reflected in the variety of terms used to distinguish the 'organised profession', 'ententes' or the 'directed economy'. But there were three main issues at stake. First, big firms argued that corporate bodies, in which membership would be optional, should be directed by existing employers' associations. This would permit them to fix prices and to contain and neutralise the discontent of smaller firms. Compulsory membership, on the other hand, was more often favoured by medium and small firms and by representatives of peasant proprietors as a means of ensuring that their interests were taken into account. Secondly, historians have generally seen corporatism as a means of limiting

---

[22] Parkin, *Marxism and Class Theory*, 82–4.

economic progress'.[23] In reality it was difficult to classify in traditional/ modern terms. Conflicts between large, medium and small business conceptions of corporatism were entangled with debates over the nature of industrialisation, and with the struggles of conservative peasants and white-collar workers. Finally, there was the question of the compatibility of corporatism with democracy. 'Corporatism' is sometimes used to designate the institutionalised bargaining of social democracy. But in the 1930s, thanks to the circumstances in which corporatism arose, and because of the suspicion of pluralism of some conservatives, it was often a step towards authoritarianism. We shall see that there were important continuities from one type of corporatism to the other.

Business, rationalisation and corporatism

In the previous chapters we saw that the elites had been divided economically into three groups: reformist engineering firms represented by Weitz; weavers such as Fougère and Charbin who hesitantly supported aspects of neocapitalism; and those such as Morel-Journel who were faithful to the liberal tradition, but whose commitment to rationalisation and big business contained a potential for conflict. From 1931 there was a *rapprochement* of all three groups, with only a few (such as the Isaacs) remaining within the liberal tradition. On the one hand engineers moved away from the advanced reformism of the 1920s now that wage cuts had become a priority. In December 1933 they unilaterally denounced the collective contract of 1928, citing the economic crisis as justification.[24] On the other hand large firms in both metallurgy and weaving responded to the crisis with a drive to invest in new more productive machinery and to rationalise work practices, especially through round-the-clock working.[25] This brought them into conflict with the proponents of a more 'flexible' productive system and with small and medium firms. The conflicts this engendered were particularly clear in silk weaving. Here large employers saw falling prices, which they blamed on the 'unfair' competition of home weaving, as the main obstacle to their investment strategy.[26] Thus Vautheret, President of the Syndicat des fabricants, argued that since family workshops now produced the same articles as factory producers, it was unfair that they should enjoy exemption from the turnover tax, pay income tax at a lower rate, avoid the jurisdiction of the labour

---

[23] J. Jackson, *The Politics of Depression in France 1932–1936* (Cambridge, 1985), 95–6; Sauvy, *Histoire économique de la France*, 371–2.
[24] *La Voix sociale*, December 1933 and February 1934.
[25] CRCCL, 1932, 285–91; PVCCL, 22 March 1932.   [26] CRCCL, 1930, 552–3.

inspectorate, and not be obliged to pay social insurance contributions.[27] Large weavers argued that a state sanctioned 'entente' would permit big business to limit competition. Such a body, financed by a tax on raw materials used by weavers, would destroy looms offered for sale, regulate work practices in small workshops and impose minimum prices.[28]

We are less well informed about other sectors, but there is evidence of similar concerns in the engineering industry. Engineers, understandably in the circumstances, were pessimistic about the economic situation. But this was not incompatible with commitment to technical innovation. *Lyon républicain*'s enquiry into the engineering industry in 1935 found that employers unanimously rejected the notion that the crisis was due to production having outstripped a 'natural' level of consumption. They dismissed the idea of restrictions on the output of machines (demanded by some Radicals). One employer protested 'what madness to want to halt technical progress. Technical innovation creates new needs . . . On the contrary, we must create ceaselessly.' In the engineering industry too intervention to halt the fall in prices was seen as the precondition of recovery.[29] In the Chamber of Commerce Weitz was a strong supporter of ententes, which he too took to mean state backing for the decisions of his own big-business-dominated trade association.[30]

Indeed, most sections of big business favoured this form of corporatism.[31] This was revealed by wide enthusiasm for the abortive Marchandeau Bill of January 1935, which envisaged legal enforceability of industrial cartels, should a majority of firms demand it. Indeed, the project originated in the request of the Syndicat des fabricants, channelled through the CGPF, that the government take measures to protect the silk industry. The Marchandeau project was well suited to big business because it gave a central role to employers' associations, and avoided compulsory corporatism.[32] At first all the major economic interests in the Rhône supported the bill (including the USE).[33] But in parliament it was substantially amended by the left, so employers were doubtless relieved when it became lost in the intricacies of the Senate.[34] Nevertheless, in October 1935 the Laval government issued a decree

---

[27] AJG, Vautheret to Godart, 5 November 1934.
[28] AJG, Daniel Isaac to Minister of Commerce, 13 October 1935; PVCCL, 24 January 1935; *La Chronique sociale*, July 1936, 543–56.
[29] *Lyon républicain*, 15 and 29 December 1935; PVCCL, 25 October 1934.
[30] *Lyon républicain*, 29 December 1935. Georges Villiers called frankly for 'l'économie dirigée'.
[31] PVCCL, 14 February 1935.
[32] PVCCL, 25 October 1934; *Lyon républicain*, 27 October 1935.
[33] *L'Union républicaine*, 17 February 1936; *Lyon républicain*, 22 February 1935.
[34] Passmore, 'Business, corporatism and the crisis of the French Third Republic'; Massoubre, *Les Ententes industrielles*; Geni, 'L'Organisation professionelle', 112–41.

providing for a compulsory entente in the silk industry alone. In a referendum *marchands de soie* and *gros façonniers* voted in favour of the entente. But the accord narrowly failed to gain the assent of the necessary three-quarters of *fabricant-usiniers*.

The entente's opponents portrayed it as a means for big business to restrict industrial progress through state-backed cartelisation.[35] Certainly there is evidence to support this point of view – even Weitz was worried about the silk industry's intention to destroy excess capacity. Yet there were significant continuities with neocapitalism, for the aim of big business was to end state protection of small firms. Furthermore, just as big business had shown a pragmatic attitude to Tardieu's reforms, so the proponents of ententes showed themselves ready, albeit reluctantly, to accept representatives of the state and the CGT in the entente.[36] In fact, the categories of traditional and modern are of little use, for both the 'mass' and 'flexible' production systems could reasonably be seen as modern. And whether willingness to collaborate with trade unions is seen as traditional or modern depends on choice of the 1960s or 1980s as a vantage point.

Whatever the case, the corporatist projects of big business created considerable opposition. Smaller factory owners ensured the failure of the silk entente: those *fabricants-usiniers* who voted for the accord had an average of 223 looms as opposed to 139 for those who opposed it.[37] *Fabricants non-usiniers* also opposed the entente, though since they owned no looms they could not participate in the referendum.[38] Their chief spokesman, Victor Perret, believed that the Marchandeau law, would make 'small family-based concerns disappear in order to serve the needs of the trusts and cartels'.[39] Similar views were expressed in other sectors. A representative of the clothing industry argued that if an entente imposed limits on production, then small firms would be forced out of business.[40] That a new founders' section of the engineering employer's association was formed in 1934 suggests discontent within this group of small and medium employers.[41] Small and medium business opposed the Marchandeau and silk industry projects from diverse standpoints. Daniel Isaac, fittingly for a son of Auguste Isaac, invoked the liberal tradition. In contrast, a minority of pro-Radical *fabricants*, such as Joseph Fructus, believed that a minimum wage set by the state would solve the problem of falling

---

[35] Kuisel, *Capitalism and the State*, 95.
[36] AJG, Eymard to Van Gelder, 4 November 1935.
[37] CRCCL, 1935, 148.   [38] *Le Nouvelliste*, 5 December 1935.
[39] *L'Union républicaine*, 17 February 1935; AJG, Fructus to Godart, 28 and 30 September 1935, for a defence of 'flexible production'.
[40] PVCCL, 14 February 1935.   [41] *Le Nouvelliste*, 13 June 1934.

prices without letting the industry fall into the hands of 'reactionary' Catholics like Perret or big business.[42] Others did not oppose corporatism in principle. Victor Perret dismissed the Marchandeau and silk ententes only because he insisted on compulsory membership as a counterweight to big business influence.[43]

The fragmentation of small and medium business was underlined by the fact that one such group, the *gros façonniers*, actually supported the entente. They believed it would enable them to eliminate competition from home weavers and secure a minimum price (*tarif*) from *fabricants non-usiniers*.[44] *Gros façonniers* took the most advanced view of corporatism. Jean Monomy claimed that the entente was inspired by papal encyclicals on the social question, and his association signed a wide-ranging agreement with the CFTC.[45] After the failure of the entente the *gros façonniers*, to the horror of big business, rallied to the demands of the CGT and CFTC for a forty-hour week, abolition of shift working and a minimum wage. It was hoped that such measures would restrict the competition of both big business and artisans.[46] Thus medium firms were divided ideologically and economically. We shall see that their discontent was expressed largely in the political sphere, in parties ranging from the Radicals (Fructus) and PDP (*gros façonniers* like Monomy) to the Fédération républicaine (Perret). Later the Croix de Feu/PSF was to win the sympathy of such firms. All, however, broke in some measure with liberalism.

The liberal tradition was indeed in crisis. Even those who protested allegiance to it had moved some way from the liberalism of Aynard. Daniel Isaac attributed the longevity of the crisis to the unwillingness of employers to regulate production in accordance with possibilities for sales, and condemned certain *gros façonniers* who added to overproduction by producing cloth on their own account.[47] Such a view was hardly reconcilable with the principle of free enterprise. Meanwhile the Chamber of Commerce, once the bastion of liberalism, had been weakened. It appeared to many to be a mere extension of the silk lobby. Demands of other industries for protection against imports were rejected by the Chamber in the name of liberalism, while the silk industry was permitted defence against Japanese 'dumping'.[48] In the controversy over the compulsory entente in the silk industry the Chamber officially

[42] AJG, Fructus to Godart, 28 and 30 September, 26 October and 16 December 1935.
[43] *L'Union républicaine*, 24 November 1935.
[44] *Le Nouveau Journal*, 1 November 1931; *Le Nouvelliste*, 26 and 29 November 1931; *La Voix sociale*, July 1932.
[45] *La Voix sociale*, July 1932; November 1935.   [46] *Bulletin des soies*, 25 April 1936.
[47] AJG, rapport Isaac, 13 October 1935.
[48] PVCCL, 16 February 1933.

adopted an attitude of neutrality.[49] Yet President Morel-Journel agitated for the entente's extension to rayon production, and headed a pro-entente delegation to the Mayor of Lyon. It was alleged that his aim was to force Courtaulds, newly established at Calais, to join the French artificial textile cartel. In 1936 Morel-Journel resigned as Chamber President in mysterious circumstances.[50] Thus the Chamber's position as arbiter of the general commercial interest was increasingly contested by small and medium business.[51] This was typical of the way in which acute interest group competition undermined the autonomy of representative bodies.

Small business and shopkeepers

The best organised of the opponents of the liberal elite were small-business groups, especially shopkeepers. Little attention has so far been paid to this group in this book because the bulk of small business preferred to act through the Radical Party, and was relatively inactive in business organisations. But from 1933 small business began to play an autonomous role. From our point of view this is important for two reasons. First, it acted as a pole of opposition to the Chamber of Commerce. Second, it was tempted by the extreme right.

In the early 1930s shopkeepers became increasingly concerned with sectional interests. Consumers accused them of profiteering. Shop-keepers themselves railed against factory purchasing co-operatives, 'prix uniques', the high wages reputedly paid to civil servants, and the turnover tax, which they sought to replace with a production tax – an idea to which industrialists were naturally opposed.[52] Delzeux, the small-business representative in the Chamber of Commerce, redoubled his efforts to push the demands of small business but gained little more than positive noises.[53] Discontent of shopkeepers was doubtless one reason for Radical gains in the elections of 1932. Yet once in power the Radicals did little to satisfy this part of their constituency. Partly this was because the required tax cuts would have been achieved principally by reducing the salaries of civil servants – another element of the Radical electorate.[54]

---

[49] AJG, Eymard to Van Gelder, 4 November 1935; PVCCL, 17 October 1935.
[50] AJG, Eymard to Van Gelder, 4 November 1935, and report on Morel-Journel of group 3 (Haute nouveauté) of the SFS; PVCCL, 30 October and 14 November 1935; *Lyon républicain*, 10 November 1935.
[51] PVCCL, 22 April and 8 February 1934.
[52] ADR 4m 235: the Prefect's monthly reports routinely mention dislike of profiteering shopkeepers. PVCCL, 12 April 1934; *Journal de Villefranche*, 9 January 1932.
[53] CRCCL, 1934, 271–2; PVCCL, 8 February 1934, 30 April 1931, 14 February 1935.
[54] AN F[7] 13 040, 3 November 1932; Berstein, *Histoire du Parti radical*, II, 230–6.

Small-business protest began in the winter of 1931–2. The running was made by a new organisation, the Union fédérale des commerçants, artisans et petits industriels de la Croix-Rousse (UF), which by the end of 1935 claimed 6,000 members. Already during the electoral campaign of 1932 the UF was suspicious of parliamentarians.[55] In September 1932 the UF took the lead in formation of a Front unique, which grouped associations in several parts of the conurbation. In the following winter, against the background of governmental paralysis over the financial question, protest moved onto the streets.[56] Early in March a joint appeal by the Front unique and the more conservative Fédération des commerçants détaillants for a half-day closure of shops met with an unexpected success. This *journée* inaugurated a series of demonstrations which coincided with a national campaign by small business.[57] In the Rhône the movement was patronised not only by the Front unique, but by the pro-Radical Fédération d'alimentation, the ACS, the UCS, AICA and even the USE. Only the Chamber of Commerce stood aside, having been warned by the government to do so.[58] Soon, however, a gap appeared between the Front unique and its moderate allies. The latter refused to participate in a national day of action on 28 May 1933, arguing that further demonstrations on the streets would compromise the cause. The Front unique went ahead on its own and claimed 1,000 demonstrators in the morning, and another 3,000 in the evening. The call for shop closures in the afternoon also appears to have been fairly well supported.[59]

Once the budget had been voted, agitation died down. It resumed only briefly during the financial crisis which provoked the fall of the Flandin government in May 1935. The Front unique broke up. But the UF turned to electoral politics. In May it stood in the municipal elections, obtaining respectable scores in the 1st and 4th arrondissements. Then in November 1935 it put forward candidates for the two seats in the retail section of the Chamber of Commerce. For the UF Marcel Perdriel accused the UCS and ACS of seeking to monopolise the elections on behalf of big business, while the ACS condemned Perdriel's 'demagogy'. On the first ballot the UF was a mere 111 votes behind the sitting members, but was beaten on the second round.[60] This relative

[55]   *Le Nouvelliste*, 26 February 1932, 26 March 1932, 2 February 1932.
[56]   *Ibid.*, 16 September 1932, 30 January 1933.
[57]   Hoisington, *Taxpayer Protest*; Jackson, *Politics of Depression*, 65–6.
[58]   PVCCL, 30 March 1933.
[59]   AN F⁷ 13 040, 1 June 1933; *Le Nouveau Journal*, 16 February 1933; *Le Nouvelliste*, 29 May 1933.
[60]   ADR 10m 103 and 105; *Lyon républicain*, 24 November 1935; *Le Nouveau Journal*, 12 December 1935, 16 December 1935, 21 December 1935, 7 December 1935.

success was crowned in the 1936 general elections, when the UF's candidate in the Croix-Rousse, Alfred Elmigar, gained a creditable 18% of the vote and fourth place on the first round. But to general astonishment Elmigar won on the second ballot. The Fédération républicaine candidate had withdrawn in Elmigar's favour, while the left vote was split between Radicals and SFIO.

Elmigar's victory may have been something of a freak, but it dramatised the importance of the shopkeeper movement. It shows first the extent to which politics had degenerated into a struggle between sectional interests. The propaganda of the UF contained little besides narrow economic demands. Only antiparliamentarianism and a hint of corporatism gave the movement a wider appeal.[61] Second, developments in the Rhône parallel W. D. Hoisington's claim (not in his case backed by evidence) that the national small-business movement, represented by the Fédération des contribuables, brought a section of the Radical electorate together with the far right.[62] There is substantial evidence in Lyon for the Radical origins of rank-and-file UF supporters. In June 1936 the Radicals lost more votes in the Croix-Rousse, where Elmigar presented himself, than anywhere else in the agglomeration, and his best scores were in the lower-middle-class central districts of the area.[63] The police noted the presence among the leaders of the Front unique of a number of Action française activists.[64] Of greater long-term significance was Perdriel, President of the UF, who moved from royalism to become a prominent activist in the Croix de Feu. The extent of far-right influence should not be exaggerated. The UF was characterised by political eclecticism. In the 1935 municipal elections the UF list fused with that of the SFIO on the second ballot. Elmigar had at one time been a member of the Fédération and in Parliament sat with the centre-right. Nevertheless, the potential attraction of shopkeepers to the far right was dangerous for the regime, and demonstrated the extent to which traditional allegiances were called into question. The Republican tradition did not automatically function as a barrier to fascism. Once out of power in 1934 Radical deputies and local councillors took an interest in the UF and may have helped bring their supporters back into the republican fold.[65]

---

[61] *Le Nouvelliste*, 16 September 1932.   [62] Hoisington, *Taxpayer Protest*.

[63] This is confirmed by the pattern of shop closures on days of action and by voting returns for the 1935 Chamber of Commerce elections (*Le Nouvelliste*, 29 May 1933; ADR 8 Mp 103).

[64] AN F^7 13 040, 1 June 1933. AN F^7 13 205, 17 November 1928; ADR 4m 244, June 1936.

[65] *Lyon républicain*, 14 May 1934.

Landowners, peasants and corporatism

Just as the position of the Chamber of Commerce was undermined during the depression, so to was that of the USE. At its origins the USE had subscribed to a paternalist version of corporatism founded on natural hierarchy. But as the USE in the 1920s became a pressure group operating within the Republic, it turned to liberalism. In 1934 it turned again to corporatism. It adhered to the new Union nationale des syndicats agricoles (UNSA), which had been formed out of the venerable Union central des syndicats agricoles by a new generation of corporatist big farmers and academics, such as Le Roy Ladurie and Salleron.[66] For USE president Garcin, a liberal who taught political economy at the Faculté catholique and managed the *Nouvelliste*, conversion to corporatism was dictated by a number of considerations.[67]

One was that as part of the national trend towards sectional organisation, the USE faced the rivalry of specialist organisations, representing, for example, wheat, wine and milk producers. The USE was able to ensure that its representatives sat in some of these bodies, but they nevertheless constituted a threat to its claim to represent a unitary rural world. Furthermore, in the 1920s the only real contact of the USE with its peasant base had been through commercial activities.[68] But co-operative selling was compromised by the depression.[69] Corporatism therefore represented a means for the USE to reassert its monopoly of rural representation and to reaffirm its links with the peasantry.

Corporatism was also meant to neutralise conflicts over prices between large and small producers. In the grain market the familiar problem was that small producers were obliged to sell immediately after harvest, when prices were at their lowest, whereas large producers could wait for prices to improve. In 1933 the Radical government introduced a minimum price for grain, which although widely avoided was nevertheless bitterly resented by large growers. There was a parallel discontent among large winegrowers. After the war many large growers had replanted their vineyards with hybrid varieties, which were more productive but inferior in quality. They hoped to overcome the depression by increasing production and adding alcohol to wine, but nonetheless profiting from the renown of Beaujolais wines.[70] They were

[66] Cleary, *Peasants, Politicians and Producers*, 73; Barral, *Les Agrariens français*, 233.
[67] Gayet, *L'Union du sud-est*, 92–5, 118–19. Berger, *Peasants against Politics*, 120–9.
[68] Cleary, *Peasants, Politicians and Producers*, 48–51; Berger, *Peasants against Politics*, 84; Pin, 'Un Notable paysan', 71.
[69] Cleary, *Peasants, Politicians and Producers*, 72–4; Pin, 'Un Notable paysan', 71.
[70] *Le Nouvelliste*, 11 December 1934.

therefore hostile to the Statut viticole voted by a conservative government in 1931, for it included restrictions on the sugaring of wine, limits
on new plantations and taxes on high producers. Legislation was later
modified to include further advantages for small growers.[71] Large
growers also resented a new tax on production.[72] Both grain and wine
producers therefore called for a return to the free market.[73] But in the
longer term the USE saw corporatism as a means to establish control of
the 'profession' over pricing.[74] For these reasons it approved the first
big-business-inspired version of the Marchandeau law.[75] The interests
of large growers are evident in Saint-Olive's definition of corporatism as
voluntary adhesion to the syndicate, but the legal right of the syndicate
to impose prices on all.[76]

Small peasants and *viticulteurs*, however, saw things differently. Small
growers in the Beaujolais, not satisfied with the Statut Viticole,
demanded ripping up of hybrids.[77] But since the discontent of small
winegrowers was expressed through the SFIO, it is of less interest to us
than the views of those who claimed to represent small peasants
elsewhere in the department. Discontent surfaced in December 1934
when the Flandin government abolished the minimum grain price. Jean-
Marie Parrel, a sympathiser of the JAC and token peasant in the upper
reaches of the USE, demanded a gradual rather than immediate phasing
out of price controls. In the short term he was prepared to accept the
'économie dirigée'.[78] In 1935 Parrel condemned the industrial methods
of large farmers, which he felt would destroy savings, the family, and the
initiative which characterised small property. His views were not
'Malthusian' in a simple sense, however, for like many in the JAC he saw
co-operation as a means of allowing small farmers to compete with large.
Like the leaders of the USE he favoured organisation of the profession,
but envisaged it in broader terms. Parrel had organised communal
sections of the USE, which he regarded as a step towards a genuine
organisation of small producers.[79] It is not clear whether Parrel believed

[71] Barral, *Les Agrariens français.*   [72] *Le Nouvelliste*, 7 February 1931.
[73] *Ibid.*, 30 July 1930, 11 December 1934. *L'Union républicaine*, 15 September 1935.
[74] *L'Union républicaine*, 17 February 1935. *L'Agriculteur du sud-est*, 24 December 1934;
  Berger, *Peasants against Politics*, 120–9. Winegrowers were perhaps less enthusiastic
  about corporatism.
[75] *L'Union républicaine*, 17 February 1936; *Lyon républicain*, 22 February 1935.
[76] *Le Nouvelliste*, 25 December 1935 and 6 April 1936; See also editorials of 21 June 1930
  and 28 June 1935.
[77] *Le Nouvelliste*, 13 December 1934.
[78] *L'Agriculteur du sud-est*, 24 December 1934; *L'Union républicaine*, December 1934, 31
  March 1935.
[79] *L'Union républicaine*, 31 March 1935.

in compulsory syndicalisation, but it is certain that his ideas represented a challenge to the establishment.

Thus the corporatist turn of the USE in 1934 was designed to reassert its position *vis-à-vis* specialist associations, establish the control of large producers over pricing, and respond to the pressure of the JAC. The leaders of the USE, like those of UNSA on the national level, were still mainly large landowners, but they were prepared to see greater involvement of the base. Garcin spoke of the need to 'make sap rise from the roots to nourish the leaves'.[80] The USE therefore co-opted JAC activists like Claudius Delorme as 'auditors' of its *conseil d'administration*, while, thanks to the patronage of Julien Riboud, Parrel rose to the highest levels of agricultural syndicalism.[81] It is possible that these tactics may have helped prevent the much more radical Défence paysanne from developing in the Rhône. But encouragement of the JAC also helped create a space for peasant activists. At the end of 1935 the latter began to turn to the Croix de Feu. Doubtless the failure of the USE to turn itself into a genuine corporatist body, its financial weakness and lack of political influence in a period when the left was on the rise, together with the failure of the parliamentary right to take account of the concerns of peasants, encouraged the recourse to the far right.

Catholic trade unions and the slump

Between 1932 and 1936 the CFTC's relationship to the right became ever more complex. On the one hand the new hostility of the right to social reform, its commitment to deflation and the attractiveness of the social programme of the Popular Front widened the gulf between Catholic trade unionists and conservative elites. On the other, the connection of material interest with Catholic values ensured that the CFTC remained within the right.

During the recession, like so many other groups, the CFTC intensified its efforts to protect the material interests of its members. Every edition of *La Voix sociale* reported violations of the Eight Hour Law and Social Insurance Acts. The CFTC demanded that police and labour inspectorate be given greater power to enforce industrial legislation, and that workers' delegates watch over conditions in their own factories.[82] Above all the CFTC demanded the forty-hour week without loss of pay as a means of combating unemployment. The CFTC was also pushed to the left by the fact that once the right had returned to

[80] Pin, 'Un Notable paysan', 73.
[81] Gayet, *L'Union du sud-est*, 70ff. Pin, 'Un Notable paysan'.
[82] *La Voix sociale*, November 1934.

power in February 1934 it seconded the efforts of some employers to roll back social insurance legislation. Thus in June 1935 the CFTC attacked a plan to divert social insurance monies into national retooling.[83] There was, then, a significant degree of convergence between the CFTC and the demands of the left as far as practical issues were concerned, coupled with a feeling of non-representation in the right.

The CFTC also participated in a moderate improvement in the fortunes of trade unions in general from 1934. From 1931 until late 1934 employers faced little resistance as they cut wages and rationalised work practices.[84] Catholic trade unions shared the general crisis of trade unionism and in the Prud'homme elections of 1932 lost most of the gains of 1929.[85] But in 1934 and 1935 there was a small increase in strike activity and in the first five months of 1936 alone there were thirteen stoppages. Furthermore, some of these were notable for the scale of the enterprises concerned (Gillet, Aciéries de Longwy, Berliet, SASE artificial fibres), for the degree of support among the workforce and for the advanced nature of the demands of the strikers.[86] In the same period CFTC activists began to report success in recruiting new members. In the Prud'homme elections of December 1935, the CFTC lost one of its seats, but gained votes as participation levels increased.[87] The CFTC was also radicalised by the new climate in the factories. In a dispute in the Cours blanket industry in 1931 the CFTC engaged in an orgy of anticommunism and organised a 'professional' union.[88] Yet four years later the CFTC joined with the CGTU in the strike committee at Gillet, merely adding the demand for a joint commission of workers and bosses. Similarly, whereas at the time of the Doumergue deflation in March 1934 the CFTC had shown little sympathy for the protestations of *fonctionnaires*,[89] by the time of Laval's measures the CFTC declared its solidarity with civil servants and railwaymen.[90] Further evidence of radicalisation can be seen in the fact that even the leader of the conservative wing of the CFTC, Auguste Gruffaz, added an anti-capitalist note to his discourse. It was, he said, those employers who had overinvested during the 1920s who were now cutting wages.[91] He even attacked the *fabricants non-usiniers*, with whom he had traditionally

---

[83] *Ibid.*, June 1935.
[84] Gric, *Les Courantes politiques*, 206–7; *La Voix sociale*, March, April, May 1931.
[85] *La Voix sociale*, November 1932.
[86] AN BB[18] 3010, various reports of the Procureur-général, March and April 1936. *Lyon républicain*, 23 March 1935; Saint-Loup, *Marius Berliet*, 205–14.
[87] *La Voix sociale*, October and December 1935.   [88] *Ibid.*, March, April, May 1931.
[89] *Ibid.*, April 1934.   [90] *Ibid.*, September 1935.
[91] *Ibid.*, December 1930, February 1931.

enjoyed good relations, for their exploitation of *façonniers* and opposition to the silk industry entente project.[92]

Yet if the CFTC endorsed the material programme of the Popular Front it never approved its political platform. The CFTC's position within the conservative bloc was never in doubt. The principal reason was that CFTC material interests only superficially conflicted with its right-wing politico-religious allegiance. The structures of social Catholicism in the parishes permitted the articulation of its material concerns and gave meaning to them. Above all, the interests of CFTC white-collar workers had always seen promotion prospects as part of their material interests, and this brought into play the Catholic values on which success was believed to depend. So as promotion became more difficult during the depression, the CFTC stressed even more the fitness for advance of those marked by Catholic values.[93] Thus one of the chief demands of white-collar workers during the depression was for a 'statut des employés', which would have given white-collar workers the right to a say in recruitment and to exclude women from the job market. The same Catholic values were reinforced by the political overtones of the strikes of this period. The Gillet strike of 1935 in particular was directed against deflation and 'fascism', as well as employers.[94] Furthermore, antifascists identified the leagues with the Republic's hereditary enemies, including the Church.[95] Even Catholic gymnastic associations were attacked as appendages of the leagues.[96] Relations were most problematic in the building trade, where the main trade union was marked by revolutionary syndicalism and a ferocious anticlericalism.

Like other groups the CFTC sought to resolve the contradictions of its position through corporatism. Like the JAC, the CFTC's view of corporatism was more advanced than that of the elites. The Marchandeau and silk proposals were seen as a chance to introduce collective contracts, an unemployment fund, and bargaining between employers and workers.[97] CFTC corporatism can be distinguished from authoritarian versions by the acceptance of the primacy of parliament and of the principle of free choice of syndicate.[98] This project was nevertheless designed to discipline the CGT, control access to white-collar status and regulate female employment.[99] In a more general sense the function of CFTC corporatism was to reconcile a society divided between capital

---

[92] *Ibid.*, September and December 1933; December 1935.
[93] *Ibid.*, July–August 1933; December 1934; May 1935.
[94] *Ibid.*, June 1935; February 1934.   [95] *La Flèche*, 1 December 1934.
[96] ADR 4m 236, 3 July 1934.
[97] AJG, CFTC to Minister of Commerce, 15 October 1935. *La Voix sociale*, February 1935.
[98] Launay, 'Le Syndicalisme chrétien', 306–13.   [99] *La Voix sociale*, June 1935.

and labour. To this end it contained both a moral appeal for class collaboration and an element of coercion, for membership of a syndicate was to be compulsory.[100] CFTC leaders avoided the question of what they would do were the CGT or government to refuse to accept Catholic unions as legitimate representatives of the workers. In spite of Maurice Thorez's 'outstretched hand' to Catholics during the election campaign of 1936, there is little evidence that CGT activists were willing to moderate their anticlericalism. It is therefore understandable that some white-collar workers felt that they could best protect job status and promotion prospects through a more vigorously anticommunist version of corporatism. Some saw the Croix de Feu as an alternative means of reconciling the anticommunism anticapitalism, and status concerns of white-collar workers, especially as the parliamentary right was increasingly resistant to social reform.

Conclusion: corporatism, authoritarianism and the crisis of the Third Republic

There was in the Rhône little evidence of wide adherence to the values of the 'stalemate society', or of agreement between capitalists and small producers or between agrarian and industrial classes. Even some small shopkeepers, pillars of the republican system, had been detached from traditional leaders. On the contrary, the economic crisis exacerbated an ongoing conflict conditioned by a web of ideological and socio-economic perspectives as various groups sought to defend threatened advantages through incompatible ideological strategies. Particular emphasis has been given to the further erosion of the liberal/big-business tradition of the Lyonnais right by complex divisions within the elites and by a mobilisation of subordinate groups. Yet these relatively straightforward conflicts were only part of an intense struggle of competing interests. From 1931 newspapers were filled with press releases from a multitude of special interests, rendered all the more confusing because there were Catholic and republican responses to every problem.[101] It would be tedious to enumerate the multiple conflicts between, for example, veterans and the government, landlords and shopkeepers, shopkeepers and consumer groups. Suffice it to say that stable alliances were disrupted by the sheer diversity of economic interests expressed and by the intersection of economic and ideological concerns.

Two examples illustrate the point. First, we have seen a convergence

---

[100] *La Voix sociale*, January 1933.   [101] PVCCL, 13 October 1932.

around the idea of corporatism on the part of big-business elites and the USE. Yet corporatism could not form the basis of a new alliance, for the same groups were simultaneously driven apart by other issues, of which protection was the most important. Within the Chamber the protectionist Weitz repeatedly clashed with the free traders of the silk industry (even though the latter demanded measures against Japanese 'dumping').[102] Yet all sections of industry denounced excessive agricultural protectionism, thus arousing the hostility of the USE.[103] Second, there is little evidence of convergence of peasants, white-collar workers and shopkeepers into a 'middle-class' movement, though the term was beginning to appear in political discourse. The CFTC denounced shopkeepers for breaching the Eight Hour Law and opening on Sundays.[104] All three groups demanded cuts in the number and/or wages of civil servants. Many contemporaries believed that they were caught up in a war of all against all. Jean Monomy spoke of a 'terrible vicious circle', Edmund Weitz of 'primo vivere!'[105]

The same struggles were reproduced across France. Berstein shows that the Radical governments of 1932–3, although in principle agreed on a deflation, had been unable to implement it because of the conflicting demands of the civil servants, peasants and small-business interests in their electorate.[106] When the right returned to power in 1934 it naïvely believed that by elevating government authority above the special interests represented by the Radicals, socialists and civil servants, it would succeed where the Radicals had failed.[107] For example Morel-Journel denounced the influence of the artisan lobby, and by implication the Radicals, in parliament.[108] There is then some truth in the view that the movement for reform of the state was part of an effort by monopoly capitalists to eliminate the representatives of workers and the petty bourgeoisie from parliament.[109] But the right was too divided to implement such a programme, and indeed the left could not be attacked without dividing the elites. Morel-Journel's attacks on the artisanate, for example, were inseparable from a rationalisation project possibly to be carried out through the *loi Marchandeau* and alliance with the labour movement. In contrast Perret, a defender of quality production based on artisans, viewed the *loi Marchandeau* as evidence of the interference of

---

[102] *Ibid.*, 3 July and 13 November 1930, 14 November 1935; CRCCL, 1931, 562–3.
[103] *Le Nouvelliste*, 19 April 1934, 25 September 1934; PVCCL, 13 November 1930; CRCCL, 1930, 568. *L'Agriculteur du sud-est*, 19 September 1934, 2 May 1935.
[104] *La Voix sociale*, March and December 1933, March 1934.
[105] CRCCL, 1931, 597.   [106] Berstein, *Histoire du Parti radical*, 221–36.
[107] Monnet, *Refaire la République*, 355–6.
[108] PVCCL, 30 April 1936; CRCCL, 1935, 69–73.
[109] Margairaz, 'La Droite et l'état'.

the 'trusts' in parliament.[110] Thus the elites were divided over the nature of the capitalism they wished to defend and whether defence could be achieved best by alliance with workers or small producers. And since the right included elements whose material interests overlapped with those of supporters of the left, deflation alienated conservative white-collar workers, while the Flandin government's ending of price support in the grain market in 1935 stirred up discontent among right-wing peasants.

The contradictions of right-wing responses to the depression were especially clear in the case of deflation. On the one hand the right was conscious that threatened advantages could be protected only by transfer of resources from subordinate groups. To this end it promoted the view that deflation was in the national interest. Yet the various elements of the right simultaneously requested subsidies for themselves. Textile manufacturers in the Nord demanded contracts for military uniforms.[111] Veterans denounced the inability of Parliament to confront CGT opposition to deflation, but demanded that old soldiers should be the last to suffer from spending cuts. Louis Renault bombarded Laval with suggestions for cuts in public spending, but also wanted tax incentives to encourage road use.[112] It is therefore unsurprising that conservative governments did not pursue deflation with the single-mindedness attributed to them by the left. Flandin ruled out further cuts because everyone also wanted increased services.[113] His successor Laval decreed a 10% cut in government expenditure in the summer of 1935. Yet this was combined with measures to support prices in the shoe, silk, wheat, wine and sugar markets and the creation of 3,000 new government jobs.[114]

Thus the pursuit of incompatible sectional interests led to a cycle of expectation and disappointment which ultimately compromised the parliamentary system. As early as September 1932 the Prefect of the Allier reported to the government that

The public is well aware that there is only one solution to current problems – reduction in government expenditure. But it is also aware that no-one is willing to assume the role of scapegoat, and that parliamentarians, out of private interest, will find it a moral impossibility to approve the necessary measures. It is therefore expected that successive ministries will fall until we reach the point where the situation is much aggravated.[115]

[110] *L'Union républicaine*, 17 February 1935; *Lyon républicain* 19 September 1934; *L'Agriculteur du sud-est*, 2 May 1935; PVCCL, 14 November 1935.
[111] P. Punelle, 'Etude d'une mentalité patronale: le Nord industriel de 1930 à 1935', *Revue du Nord* 51 (1969), 641–50.
[112] Fridenson, 'L'Idéologie des grands constructeurs'.
[113] Wileman, 'L'Alliance républicain démocratique', 258–9.
[114] Jackson, *The Politics of Depression*, 105–11.
[115] Quoted in Howlett, 'La Rocque', chapter 1; AN F[7] 13 038, Commissaire spécial de Lorient, 3 March and 2 December 1933.

Similar sentiments were evident in the Lyon Chamber of Commerce. Its members admitted their inability to produce a detailed motion on the subject of deflation, given the depth of divergence on concrete issues. Their solution was to demand that the government resume its role as sovereign arbitrator in order to put an end to 'the politics of perpetual concession which sacrifice the general interest to the disorderly crush of selfish appetites'.[116] A strong state would reassert the primacy of the 'national interest'.

Thus there was a feeling that authority and coercion were needed both to restore national unity and to protect individual interests. The coercive dimension of projects for reform of the state was reinforced by the fact that the assumption of a pre-existing state of harmony was illusory, for pluralism and conflict characterise 'stable' societies. Rather crisis had rendered discord unacceptable. The elites responded to the threat to their privileges by seeking to convince the masses that the 'national interest' demanded wage and public-spending cuts. This ideological offensive drew upon the assumption of a unitary national interest, shared, furthermore, by those raised in both the liberal and the Catholic traditions. On the one hand we have seen that many liberals remained within the tradition of 'libéralisme capacitaire', in which an enlightened elite alone was qualified to discern the interests of the nation. On the other the Catholic tradition assumed a hierarchy of family, profession and nation, all greater than the sum of individuals who comprised them. The belief in the unitary nation was also associated with the conviction that disorder was due to the presence in the economic sphere of 'alien elements', ranging from 'cowboy businessmen', through civil servants and trade unionists to foreign artisans. As we have seen, both Morel-Journel and Perret denounced the influence of mysterious powers within parliament. The fact that these occult influences were defined as antinational legitimated the use of coercion against them.

The vogue for corporatism also contributed to the authoritarian mood. R. F. Kuisel argues that businessmen were opposed to corporatism because they viewed it as a cover for state intervention and restrictions on free enterprise.[117] Corporatism was just that. But from the point of view of contemporaries, its beauty was that it seemed to conjure away the contradiction between pursuit of individual interest and the conviction that restraint was needed. Corporatism was based on the assumption of a single professional and national interest. Yet individuals assumed that this higher good was identical to their own concerns. Again both liberal and Catholic traditions encouraged such beliefs. The former held that

---

[116] PVCCL, 19 January 1933.   [117] Kuisel, *Capitalism and the State*, 102–4.

pursuit of enlightened self-interest benefited the collectivity; the latter assumed that if the individual was suffused with the national spirit, then his/her interests would harmonise with those of the group. These considerations explain the willingness of so many, at a time of acute sensitivity to sectional interests, to sacrifice their autonomy to a professional body, or even to a strong leader. Indeed, many of the projects discussed in this chapter involved compulsion on the part of the state. Big business and the USE demanded legal enforceability of the decisions of employers' organisations, justifying this by means of obscure distinctions between 'state regulation' and 'state direction'.[118] Perret assumed a legal obligation to join ententes, as did many on the Christian democrat wing of social Catholicism. Some demanded 'depoliticisation' of trade unions as a precondition of corporatism. The CFTC defended free choice of union, but left open what would happen if the CGT refused to play by the rules, speaking only of the need for a preliminary moral transformation. The authoritarian potential of corporatism is underlined by a striking similarity between the Marchandeau project and Mussolini's law of 16 June 1932, which permitted firms controlling 70% of production in a given sector of the economy to ask for a compulsory cartel. To be sure, there was nothing intrinsically fascist about this scheme. But many nevertheless contrasted the weakness of France with the supposed vitality of the 'young' fascist state. Johannès Dupraz, deputy director of the local affiliate of the national employers' association, visited Italy in 1935. On his return he published an enthusiastic account of the regime's corporatist policies.[119] Dupraz went on to write for the journal of the PSF.

Thus authoritarianism derived from the drive to obtain sacrifices from the subordinate classes, coupled with the need to unify the ruling elites and the assumption of a unitary national interest. By 1934 special powers became essential to government. The arguments put forward in this chapter would doubtless not satisfy Pierre Milza. He could still object that this crisis was 'less serious' than in Germany or Italy. In a certain sense he would be right to do so. The point, however, is that a given set of circumstances will produce a variety of responses, not all of them on the right, but possibly including authoritarian and/or populist solutions. Authoritarianism, even when coloured by sympathy for Mussolini, could lead in many directions, for there is no automatic link between a particular type of crisis and the kinds of political movement it generates, let alone the chances of a particular movement winning power. We must therefore turn our attention to the responses of political parties to the depression.

[118] *Lyon républicain*, 15 December 1935, for an example of definitional confusion.
[119] J. Dupraz, *Regards sur le fascisme* (Lyon, 1935).

7   The crisis of the right II: 1932–June 1936

In the general elections of 1 and 8 May 1932 the left returned to power with 335 deputies against only 230 for the right.[1] In the Rhône the writing had been on the wall since the previous year when the Radicals had won back the 3rd arrondissement constituency in a by-election following the death of the nationalist, Victor Augagnaur. In the general election Peissel, Bonnevay and Sallès all retained their seats, but Delorme was defeated. Nationally, however, the right had some cause for hope, for the Radicals and the SFIO had allied only for electoral purposes. Herriot, more concerned to reassure the banks than he had been in 1924, had rejected socialist proposals for a minimum programme. So he became prime minister at the head of a 'concentration' ministry of Radicals and centre-right with SFIO support. Herriot's moderation did not equip him to cope with growing domestic and international crises. Already in 1932 Weimar politicians had been demanding the right to re-arm. In October 1933 Hitler withdrew from the League of Nations. The fact that reparations had ended in 1932 in turn hindered elaboration of an effective response to the economic crisis. The Radicals, like the right, believed a balanced budget to be the precondition of economic recovery. Deflation provoked opposition from those who bore its brunt, such as civil servants, while others felt that cuts did not go far enough. Herriot fell in December. He was succeeded by ineffectual governments under Paul-Boncour (December 1932 to January 1933) and Daladier. On Daladier's fall in October 1933 the situation became critical. Governments under Sarraut and Chautemps came and went before Daladier returned to power on 30 October 1933. Daladier's aim was to enlarge the government by including members of the Alliance démocratique. At the same time Daladier sought to reassure the left by dismissing Prefect of Police Jean Chiappe, notorious for his

---

[1] The following paragraphs are based on reports in all the Lyonnais dailies; Herriot, *Jadis*; Berstein, *Édouard Herriot*; Berstein, *Histoire du Parti radical*; Gric, *Les Courantes politiques*; M. Moissonnier, 'Front populaire et identité communiste à Villeurbanne (1933–1936)', *Cahiers d'histoire de l'institut de recherches marxistes* 24 (1986), 56–67.

nationalist sympathies. This served only to enrage a far right already engaged in a hysterical campaign against the implication of a number of Radical politicians in a financial scandal perpetrated by a disreputable bond dealer, Sacha Stavisky. On the evening of 6 February 1934 various leagues and veterans' groups demonstrated on the Place de la Concorde. Their target was Daladier's new government, at that moment presenting itself to parliament. Some demonstrators attempted to force their way across the Seine into the Chamber. The police opened fire and sixteen were killed. The next day Daladier, in spite of having won a confidence vote, resigned. Ex-president Gaston Doumergue was called out of retirement to head a government of 'Union nationale', which included Tardieu and Herriot as a symbol of a 'truce' between parties.

Outside parliament the left–right division became more meaningful than ever. In response to the riots of 6 February antifascist committees were formed across France, including socialists, Radicals, and in Saint-Denis even communists. On 12 February the communist controlled CGTU joined a general strike called by the CGT in protest against the events of 6 February. In the following months the Communist International urged the PCF to begin unity of action talks with the SFIO. On 27 July 1934 the two parties formed the Front commun. Convinced that fascism could be defeated by depriving it of petty bourgeois troops, the communists urged the Radicals to join the antifascist movement. Conclusion of a Franco-Soviet mutual assistance pact in May 1935, and the consequent support of the PCF for French national defence, enabled the Radicals to respond positively. Daladier joined with Blum and Thorez in sealing formation of the Popular Front at a great demonstration held on 14 July 1935 in Paris. At the end of the year Daladier succeeded Herriot as president of the Radical Party. The theme of republican defence benefited above all the communists, who made gains in the municipal elections of May 1935, foreshadowing their breakthrough in the general election of 1936.

Polarisation was especially marked in the Rhône because of the erosion of Herriot's position. At first local Radicals had rushed to join antifascist committees. But by April they had largely been eliminated because of Herriot's participation in the Doumergue government and in particular his support for deflation, an issue which had become inseparable in the eyes of the left from antifascism. Relations between Herriot and the SFIO, never good, declined further. In the local elections of October 1934 the Radicals had to suspend meetings because of attacks by socialists and communists. The Radical party itself became hopelessly split. Herriot's determination to steer a middle way between left and right was sapped by a pro-Popular Front faction led by the deputy Maurice Rolland and the municipal councillor Henri Collomb, and a pro-right group led by deputies Paul Richard and Paul Massimi. Herriot stubbornly pursued a middle way. Hence his support for the Flandin government of November 1935, based on a 'third party' alliance of Radicals and Alliance démocratique. This strategy was tested in the municipal elections of 1935. The Radicals won an absolute majority on the Lyon city council. But this victory owed much to socialist and communist support on the second ballot – even Herriot himself needed left-wing votes. Socialists challenged Radicals in Lyon, while communists captured the town halls of working-class communes like Villeurbanne and Vénissieux. Repeated across France, the revelation of the extent of Radical electoral dependence on the socialists and communists ensured the failure of the 'third party' and contributed to the fall of Flandin on 30 May 1935. Herriot participated in the more right-wing Laval government which succeeded Flandin. But his position became ever more anomalous as the Radical Party moved closer to the Popular Front. In June 1935 he suffered the indignity of expulsion from the Ligue des droits de l'homme for his role in 'antirepublican governments'. On 14 July 1935 Herriot attempted to organise a Radical event separate from the Popular Front demonstration, but found that many activists participated in the latter. Eventually, on 18 December, Herriot resigned as national president of the Radical Party. For Serge Berstein Herriot's subsequent withdrawal from the political limelight represented the end of a certain liberal republicanism, which had shown its inability to deal with economic and political crisis, and which had been eclipsed by the rise of Marxism and the nationalist right.[2]

This polarisation raised new problems for conservatives. The right had traditionally aimed its propaganda at the Radicals, hoping to detach them from the SFIO. Socialists, communists and the needs of their working-class supporters had been more or less ignored. But with the rise of the communists many were attracted by the Croix de Feu's endeavour to mobilise the working class in a new national community. It is difficult to exaggerate the intensity of anticommunism, for it involved the conviction that the party aimed to provoke war against Hitler in order to seize power in France. With the benefit of hindsight such fears can be seen to be exaggerated (historians have not detected a genuine revolutionary danger even in Italy or still less Germany, where fascism did come to power). But given the proximity of the carnage of World War One and the Russian Revolution, the feebleness of democracy in interwar Europe and France's own turbulent past, contemporary right-

---

[2] Berstein, *La République en personne*, 239–40.

wingers may be forgiven for fearing that communist electoral gains, coupled with more or less continuous demonstrations in the streets, meant that the French Republic too must eventually fall either to left or right. Such fears were to fuel the 'palingenetic' rhetoric of the Croix de Feu. Anticommunism was also connected to immediate interests, given that the privileges of the dominant class could be defended only by transfer of resources away from subordinate groups. Yet however widespread was hatred of communism, it could not create conservative unity. Indeed, its very depth increased the intensity with which incompatible projects were pursued.

At first it had seemed that victory of the Cartel would reunite conservatives around reform of the state, deflation and antisocialism. Yet the limits of unanimity had been evident as early as 1932. Tardieu's bid to become a British-style 'leader of the opposition' failed on 7 June when only 115 conservative deputies supported his interpellation of the new Herriot government. Refusal of the followers of Flandin to support him reflected their desire to draw the Radicals into a centre alliance. In disgust at Flandin's behaviour, Tardieu withdrew from the Républicains de gauche, and with Paul Reynaud set up his own group, the Centre démocratique, designed to form the core of a Union nationale majority. But his efforts to build bridges to the right came up against the inability of many in the Fédération républicaine to forget his reforming policies of 1930.[3]

The hopes of conservatives were raised once again by the arrival in power of Doumergue in February 1934. But by the end of the year the right was once again in turmoil. Doumergue had failed either to resolve the economic crisis or to reform the state, and on 8 November he resigned. The immediate cause was the departure of Herriot from the cabinet. But divisions within the right also played a part. On the one hand Tardieu and the Fédération right linked reform of the state to deflation, disciplining of the CGT and a drive against social insurance.[4] Few in the Alliance, on the other hand, were fully committed to such a programme. Flandin sought instead to build a 'third party' alliance with the Radicals, and this had made possible Herriot's desertion of the Doumergue government. To cement this alliance Flandin jettisoned constitutional reform and deflation once he became prime minister. We saw in the previous chapter that the bitter antagonism of interest groups also took its toll on the governments of Doumergue, Flandin and Laval, and that many of the conservative rank-and-file were alienated by deflation and the increasingly reactionary tone of the parliamentary

[3] Monnet, *Refaire la république*, 237–47, 255–61.
[4] M. Perrot, *La Monnaie et l'opinion publique* (1955), 231.

right. Some were even attracted to the programme of the Popular Front, a fact which underlines the problematic nature of the left/right boundary, and that conservative movements were obliged to guard their frontiers against an enemy partly internal to itself. The result of these tensions was that parties oscillated between echoing the special concerns of interest groups, enunciation of broad principles and/or authoritarianism.

The Rhône provides a good example of the crisis of the right. Tensions were especially acute because of the growth of communism in the Lyonnais *banlieue*, the erosion of Herriot's position and the polarisation of conservatives between Perret's nationalism and Bonnevay's mystical attachment to the republicanism of 'la France profonde'. Some conservative leaders began to collaborate with the leagues. Many of the rank-and-file of the right turned to the Croix de Feu. Authoritarianism, moreover, tempted conservatives from a variety of right-wing traditions. It was not the result of a mysterious reactivation of a Bonapartist tradition.

The Alliance démocratique

Efforts to reorganise the Alliance in 1930–1, following the withdrawal of Weitz and Fougère, soon fizzled out, and in 1932–3 little was heard from the party. The accession of Flandin, long a partisan of better organisation, to the national leadership late in 1932 (officially in March 1933) had some repercussions in the Rhône. A youth group appeared in January 1933. In 1934 sections were set up in the arrondissements of Lyon for the first time. The most important, inevitably, was in the 6th arrondissement. There were also groups in the 5th and 2nd, though the latter was rather weak. From then until 1939 the Alliance had a more or less continuous organisational presence in the Rhône. But the party remained riven by factions.[5] Partly this was a reflection of the national rivalry between the partisans of Flandin and Tardieu, supporters respectively of concentration and Union nationale. On the one hand the views of Jean Mercier, municipal councillor in the 2nd arrondissement, were almost indistinguishable from those of the Fédération. On the other Bonnevay followed Flandin and, although not an Alliance member, received money from government funds when Flandin was prime minister in 1935.[6] But the issues ran much deeper than a quarrel over tactics. The growing ascendency of the antiFédération strand of the Alliance coincided with a further shift away from big business, already evident in previous years, towards an anticlerical bourgeoisie typified by

[5] Gric, *Les Courantes politiques*, 251.
[6] Wileman, 'L'Alliance républicaine démocratique', 240–1.

Dr Augros and Eugène Mansuy. This reflected both the decline of big-business influence in a district once the home of Progressisme and the growing sectionalism of French politics. Indeed, consisting of a cluster of parties, committees, interest groups and individuals united only by their central position in politics, the lay centre-right was more vulnerable to sectionalism and polarisation than any other movement.

Some in the Alliance were tempted by authoritarianism. Indeed, it was possible to turn aspects of the party's ideology to the far right, once, of course, it was detached from democracy. As Wileman argues, the Alliance saw itself as an enlightened elite identified absolutely with the national interest, and had some difficulty in seeing left-wing governments as legitimate.[7] We have seen that Tardieu sought to exclude the left permanently from power.[8] In the Rhône these ambiguities were evident in the ephemeral Alliance youth group formed in 1933. One of its co-founders, René Bouteille, had previously been a member of the Jeunesses patriotes. For Bouteille the Alliance should reconcile Frenchmen over the heads of the old parties, said to have broken apart under the force of new ideas. This would create a strong France able to stand up to Germany.[9] There was nothing inherently antidemocratic about this. But it perhaps explains why neither Reynaud nor Flandin was willing to patronise the new group.[10] And this kind of thinking might have smoothed the passage to the far right of men like Emile Roux. Roux, a manager in a silk firm, was a municipal councillor in the 6th arrondissement and president of the Lyon section of the conservative veterans' organisation, the UNC. In the 1936 election he and a group of veterans stood as 'old soldiers without links to the Croix de Feu'. Roux himself stood against Peissel. In 1937 Roux joined Doriot's PPF and as president of the Légion played a significant part in the Vichy regime.[11] Another example was Ernest Planche in the Beaujolais, who had stood in the 1932 general election on a joint Fédération/Alliance platform, but in 1936 as a 'républicain antiparlementaire'.

Such an itinerary, however significant, was not, however, typical of centre-right activists. Increasingly the party came into conflict with the increasingly reactionary Fédération. In the general election of 1932 Mansuy had represented both Alliance and Fédération in the 6th arrondissement on a common platform.[12] But as Perret became more extreme relations declined. Perret charged Mansuy with opposition to

---

[7] *Ibid.*, 248.   [8] Monnet, *Refaire la république.*
[9] *Le Sud-est républicain,* October and November 1933.
[10] Papers of Paul Reynaud – thanks to Julian Jackson for this information.
[11] Cour de Justice, 1989, dossier Roux; ADR, élections législatives 1936.
[12] *Le Nouveau Journal,* 25 April 1932.

the inclusion of Marin in the government, and with support for the legacy of Briand, which, Perret argued, had produced Hitler. The centre-right had failed to agree to punishment of all the swindlers of the Stavisky affair and had opposed the deflation and tax reductions required by industry and agriculture.[13] In other words, the Alliance refused to participate in Perret's twin offensive against parliament and social reforms. Indeed, some in the Alliance saw the Marchandeau Bill on compulsory ententes as the first step in a post-liberal organisation of the economy in which state and private industry would be partners, and in which all 'interests' would be represented.[14] This was the kind of thinking which had raised the fears of many opponents of ententes. Bonnevay, the effective leader of the centre-right in the Rhône now that Peissel had moved towards the right, showed the same commitment to social reform. In his Monts du Beaujolais constituency he joined PDP and CFTC in condemning wage cuts.[15] Such policies did not endear him to local employers. All but one of the numerous industrialists on Bonnevay's committee deserted to Perret's new Fédération committee in 1935.[16]

Thus the economic conflicts which had divided the right in the late 1920s remained alive, thanks to the Fédération's efforts to roll back the Tardieu reforms. Yet in general the polemics between Fédération and Alliance did not focus on such issues. Rather Bonnevay spoke of material issues to his constituents but of defence of the Republic in his polemics with Perret. He defended *scrutin d'arrondissement* in particular. Partly this was because supporters of reform linked it to social reaction. Also, proportional representation in the regional framework would have deprived Bonnevay of the ability to distribute patronage in his constituency. Generally, however, Bonnevay preferred to speak in terms of abstract principles. In 1935 he declared that the *conseil général* was the expression of a profoundly Republican people, which held itself ready to break any attempt to impose 'personal power': 'Lyonnais and Beaujolais republicans are divided in discussion, but united in action.'[17] Political divisions were therefore superficial. Just as Perret, confronted by political conflict and class struggle, was to fall back on a Catholic morality, so Bonnevay resuscitated the language of Waldeck-Rousseau. In 1935 there was even a revival of the quarrel over *laïcité*, as Eugène Mansuy, to Perret's annoyance, asserted that there had been no popular

---

[13] *L'Union républicaine*, 5 May 1935.   [14] *Le Nouvelliste*, 22 March 1935.
[15] *Le Petit Montagnard de Tarare*, 9 September 1934.
[16] *Ibid.*, 23 December 1934, 13 January 1935.
[17] Bonnevay, *Histoire du conseil général*, 79.

education before Jules Ferry.[18] Unable to contend with a deep crisis, both Fédération and Alliance sought harmony and stability in the rhetoric of the epoch in which they had emerged.

The liberal side of this legacy was, however, capable of radically different interpretations and contributed in some cases to the development of authoritarianism. Even Bonnevay's republicanism assumed a unitary national interest and was suspicious of parties. This authoritarian potential need not be realised, and no-one would seriously accuse Bonnevay of proto-authoritarianism. But his dogmatic insistence that the parliamentary system contained within itself the means to resolve all problems hardened political divisions and exacerbated conflict. Most significantly, for Bonnevay anyone who suggested constitutional reform placed themselves outside the democratic fold. Hence Bonnevay's own campaign against the leagues, and his description of Perret as 'chef des politiciens fascistes du Rhône'.[19]

Christian democracy

The PDP too experienced crisis in this period. The party had to deal with two fundamental problems, both aggravated by the political polarisation and sectionalisation of politics. First, like the CFTC, the party was pushed to the left by the material grievances of its largely white-collar rank and file, while its integration into the social Catholic network, which permitted articulation of and shaped those grievances in the first place, tied the party to the right. On the national level the trade union wing of the party, represented by figures such as Maurice Guérin, was critical of the party's support for the Doumergue and especially Laval deflations. But most in the party remained deeply hostile to the left. This was revealed by the refusal of the PDP to participate in Sarraut's concentration administration (24 January 1936), even though in theory the party was committed to this form of government.[20] Conflict was magnified in the Rhône thanks to the strong presence of white-collar workers in the local party. The second problem was common to many movements claiming to represent the lower middle class in a period of social polarisation. Themes such as popular democracy, 'les classes moyennes', and the dual opposition to big capital and Marxism, were features which drew the PDP towards the Radicals. But with the exception of democracy these ideas were also shared by the extreme right. We saw in the case of small business that Radical ideology might provide, in certain circumstances, a bridge

[18] *L'Union républicaine*, 3 November 1935.   [19] *Le Nouvelliste*, 27 October 1935.
[20] Delbreil, *Centrisme et démocratie chrétienne*, 286, 289, 290–1.

to the far right. The same applied to the PDP. This does not mean that the PDP was proto-fascist, any more than the liberal tradition was. The point is rather that *depending on context* a wide variety of ideologies can provide material for fascists. Furthermore, Delbreil demonstrates the attraction of many PDP activists to the Croix de Feu, in spite of the very different attitudes of the two movements towards democracy and authority.

There was some sympathy for authoritarianism within the *Chronique*. One member of the editorial board, Henri Franchet, had been leader of Rhône ALP and had played a significant part in the Ligue des droits de la nation, which in 1930 had campaigned for reform of the state. Franchet, as editorialist in the *Nouveau Journal* was to show a strong sympathy for the Croix de Feu and PSF. Furthermore, the events of 6 February 1934 caused divergences of opinion within the *Chronique*.[21] In April Colonel Roullet wrote in *La Chronique sociale* of the impatience displayed by 'some of our friends' at our 'peaceful methods'. Even he celebrated the riots of 6 February as a manifestation of the 'French spirit', but nevertheless felt that the recourse to the gendarme was a lazy solution.[22] One PDP activist who launched frankly into authoritarianism was Maurice Vicaire, municipal councillor in the 6th arrondissement and secretary-general of the Cartel des combattants.[23] In his involvement in the veterans' movement he was typical of those in the PDP who turned to authoritarianism.[24] In 1936 Vicaire stood as a veterans' candidate in order to protest against the theft of the victory of 6 February. He denounced 'the political spirit which poisons our town', and called for budgetary deflation, reform of the state, corporatism as a means of protecting small property against capitalism, and national unity in the face of the revival of Germany. He gained 15% of the vote – perhaps from the same constituency which had supported Elmigar in the Croix-Rousse.[25]

A more typical response of PDP activists to polarisation of 1934–6 was uncertainty. One example was Jules Maire, editor of the *Petit Montagnard de Tarare*. A member also of the Fédération until late 1935, Maire was on the right of Christian democracy. In the month before the collapse of the Cartel, he had been calling for 'pitiless cuts' in government spending, and for assertion of the authority of the state against 'feudalisms large and small'. He approved of the riots of 6

[21] Ponson, 'La Chronique sociale de Lyon en 1940', 28.
[22] *La Chronique sociale*, April 1934, 251–4.
[23] The Cartel de Combattants linked the two main national veterans' associations, the UNC and the Union fédérale.
[24] Delbreil, *Centrisme et démocratie chrétienne*, 295–6.
[25] *Le Nouvelliste*, 12, 15, 16, 18 and 22 April 1936.

February, seeing them as the work not of fascists, but of the 'people'.[26] Maire also called for a 'government of Public Safety'. Yet its members were to be Doumergue, Flandin, Herriot and his own patron Bonnevay. Furthermore, Maire approved of the antifascist strike of 12 February as useful warning to those extremists who had attempted to exploit the events of 6 February.[27] Over the next months Maire's views emerged from this flux. He backed Bonnevay, although at times somewhat reluctantly, in his struggle against Perret. But it is possible nevertheless to see that centrism could, in some circumstances, lead on to hostility to 'politicians' who divided France between right and left.

Just as some sections of the PDP were pulled to the right, so the left of the PDP progressed. In Cours the PDP joined with the CFTC in opposing wage cuts in the blanket industry, thereby earning the distrust of local employers. This campaign contributed to the election of the PDP leader Dr Lheritier to represent Thizy in the *conseil général* in October 1934, and the capture of the *mairie* of Cours from the left.[28] In Lyon members of the party's youth groups were reported to have been seen at Popular Front meetings.[29] In the city the left of the PDP was led by the *lycée* professor, Jacques Bonnet, secretary-general of the Rhône federation. Bonnet's programme matched the democratic corporatism of the CFTC. He regarded corporatism as the necessary complement of reform of the state. Typically, Bonnet explained that he was in accord with the Popular Front on the main elements of its programme – international peace, social reform and defence of the Republic against the leagues.[30] He did not join the Popular Front because it was an electoral manœuvre which masked communist plans for class struggle and revolution.[31] Yet the PDP had fewer qualms about engaging in polemics with Perret and the Fédération, regarded as antirepublican and fascist representatives of the 'two hundred families' committed to stirring up civil war.[32]

Victor Perret: 'chef des politiciens fascistes du Rhône'?

From 1932 Perret consolidated his position within the Fédération. Peissel and Sallès moved closer to his right-wing nationalism. The sanctions taken against the two deputies for their refusal to sit with the Fédération's parliamentary group remained a dead letter. Both continued to attend Fédération meetings. The activities of Sallès in

---

[26] *Le Petit Montagnard de Tarare*, 3 December 1933, 14 January and 11 February 1934.
[27] *Le Petit Montagnard de Tarare*, 11 and 18 February 1934.
[28] *Ibid.*, 9 September 1934, 1 and 13 January 1935.
[29] *Le Nouveau Journal*, 14 July 1935.   [30] *Trait d'Union*, April 1936.
[31] *Ibid.*   [32] *Trait d'Union*, April 1936.

particular were reported in *Union républicaine*. The two deputies still refused to return to the fold in the 1936 legislature, but their conservative credentials were underlined by joining an intergroup professing support for the PSF. This *rapprochement* may seem surprising given that Perret had shifted so far to the right that for *Lyon républicain* he was 'duce authentique de la Fédération républicaine à Lyon'.[33] His populist nationalism was indeed radicalised in three stages, but he stopped some way short of fascism.

In the first period, from the victory of the Cartel in 1932 until mid-1934, Perret's basic strategy was familiar. He sought to create a broad conservative alliance by placing economics and hence the national interest above party politics. The national interest now required far-reaching cuts in government expenditure. But this was part of a wider programme, for the new conjuncture appeared to offer the opportunity to undo the reforms of the Tardieu years and to put into practice some of the long-nurtured projects of the Fédération right. This in turn implied reform of the state. One goal was revision of the Social Insurance Laws along mutualist lines.[34] The great mistake was that they had been 'transported onto the field of pure politics, and with the stimulus of demagogy, they were voted in the greatest of disorder, without listening to the qualified people who would have to implement them'.[35] Another concern was deflation, to which the principal obstacle again was parliament and the influence in it of civil servants. If the latter resisted deflation, then their 'revolutionary' unions must be repressed.[36] Thus it was assumed that in order to enforce the 'general interest' then state authority must be raised above political and economic interests.[37]

From 1933 the Fédération demonstrated a growing interest in constitutional reform. Fédération propagandists protested that revision of the constitution was a means of saving the Republic by eliminating abuses. So it is worth looking briefly at exactly what reform entailed. The Fédération's views were set out by Charles Gautheron, president of the party's Villeurbanne committee. The central purpose was to free the state from the 'dictatorship of parliament', where sectional interests such as the CGT, civil service unions and corrupt deputies reigned supreme. Not only therefore would parliament be downgraded, but civil service trade unions, the backbone of the CGT, would be abolished. Parliament would be weakened by losing the power to initiate financial measures, and perhaps any legislation at all. The lynchpin of the new constitution would be a strengthened presidency, which would have the right of

[33] *Lyon républicain*, 9 October 1935.   [34] *Le Nouveau Journal*, 6 April 1932.
[35] *L'Union républicaine*, 27 May 1934.   [36] *Ibid.*, 30 October 1932.
[37] *Ibid.*, 19 February 1933.

dissolution and to call referenda, and perhaps the sole right to propose laws. The president would be elected by a college of 1,000 consisting of parliamentarians (reduced in number) sitting together with representatives of 'the competences', i.e. Chambers of Commerce, agricultural organisations, the universities, and the 'working class' (the CGT would by this time have been greatly weakened). Finally, Gautheron detailed a series of narrowly constitutional measures such as female suffrage, proportional representation, family suffrage, obligatory voting and reduction in the numbers of deputies, all of which, it was assumed, would permanently exclude the left from power.[38] Clearly Gautheron's programme did not break entirely with the elective principle. Measures like proportional representation were on the face of it democratic. But their impact was limited by making the president the real focus of power, by the mode of election of the president, and by the downgrading of parliament and the attack on the cadres of the left by means of the 'statut des fonctionnaires'. Furthermore, Gautheron's claim that this was a Republican programme rests on an unspoken divorce of Republic and democracy. The Fédération protested its loyalty to the Republic, but it never mounted a defence of democracy. This mystification is one which is encountered in all the constitutional projects of the far right. In sum, the Fédération's project was similar to that of Tardieu in its aim of permanently excluding the left from power and its denial of pluralism.[39]

At this stage, however, the Fédération still believed that its ideas could be implemented by winning a majority in Parliament. Perret appealed to the precedent of the collapse of the Cartel and the return of Poincaré in 1926.[40] This was not, however, incompatible with exploitation of the Stavisky scandal, or with predictions of a 'confrontation' between public opinion and the Cartel. The riots of 6 February were for Perret 'the expression of popular anger', and evidence that 'no-one wants the "comrades" republic', or the combinations, swindles and cover-ups of the government of parties'.[41] The arrival in power of Doumergue seemed to offer the chance to implement the Fédération's programme, for the notion of a link between deflation and reform of the state was widely accepted on the right, and was also the object of a campaign on the part of business interests.[42] In the Rhône the tone of Chamber of Commerce motions became openly political.[43] AICA too questioned the parliamentary regime, hoping that moral force would be sufficient to

---

[38] *Ibid.*, 23 and 30 April and 20 August 1933, 11 February 1934.
[39] Monnet, *Refaire la république*, 300–5.
[40] *L'Union républicaine*, 22 October 1933.   [41] *Ibid.*, 11 February 1934.
[42] Jackson, *The Politics of Depression*, 88–92. Margairaz, 'La Droite et l'état'; *Le Nouvelliste*, 23 April 1934.
[43] PVCCL, 8 February 1934.

bring about the necessary reforms.[44] The Fédération insisted that the inquiry into the Stavisky affair be widened into a veritable purge. He personally urged Tardieu 'above all don't let go of these rogues, for . . . if they were in your place they wouldn't let you go. Confidence will not return until justice, complete justice, is done.'[45] The notion of 'Staviskites' was wide enough to include those guilty of the murder of patriots on 6 February, revolutionary teachers and civil service unions. The 'cleansing' would also include a 'definitive break with the SFIO'.[46] Nevertheless, Perret still believed that the purge could be carried out by the Union nationale coalition of conservatives and Radicals.[47]

But by the summer of 1934 the Fédération was tiring of constitutional methods. In the *Réveil du Beaujolais* Bosse-Platière wrote that Tardieu had been duped into joining the government, thereby earning an angry rebuke from Tardieu himself.[48] In August 1934 Perret denounced those who continued to believe in the myth of a 'national truce'. The reasons for this disillusion were not specific to the Rhône. In Perret's mind the aggravation of the economic crisis in spite of the Doumergue deflation and Radical opposition to Doumergue's weak programme of constitutional reform were linked. Perret felt that Doumergue's fundamental mistake had been to include the Radicals in the government, but did not explain how a government could be formed without them.[49] He stated merely that had the programme of purges outlined above been carried out, then the Cartel would have disappeared definitively.[50] On the fall of Doumergue Perret warned the Radicals: 'treason of this sort will not remain unpunished'.[51]

Another reason for Perret's disillusion with the Union nationale was the *rapprochement* of socialists and communists and the formation of the Front commun in July 1934. The communists also made gains in the *cantonales* of October 1934. Furthermore, the left engaged in a systematic campaign of disruption of meetings of the leagues, which occasionally spilled over into attacks on the parliamentary right. The most serious was at a gathering held jointly by the Fédération and Alliance for the local elections of October 1934 at a café in the 6th arrondissement. About 100 left-wingers invaded the café. The meeting

[44] J. Dupraz in *Bulletins et documents l'AICA*, November 1934, reprinted in *La République lyonnaise*, 6 January 1934.
[45] AN 324 AP 13, Perret to Tardieu, 19 and 24 July 1934.
[46] *L'Union républicaine*, 26 August 1934.   [47] *Ibid.*, 25 March 1934.
[48] *Réveil du Beaujolais*, 25 July 1935, 1 August 1934. AN 324 AP 13, Tardieu to Perret, 18 August 1934.
[49] Jeanneney, *De Wendel*, 483. Similarly for de Peyerhimoff of the coal industry the alternatives were 'either inflation or dictatorship'. De Wendel agreed: 'C'est la conclusion à laquelle je suis arrivé depuis un bon moment déjà.'
[50] *L'Union républicaine*, 26 August 1934.   [51] *Ibid.*, 18 November 1934.

was abandoned as chairs were thrown and windows smashed. Shots were fired. There were a number of injuries.[52] In July Perret had already denounced the government for permitting such a campaign. Were this to continue, Perret warned, conservatives would take the law into their own hands:

We will not let that happen. We are conscious of our duty to enlighten the masses and to tell them the truth – the whole truth. And if [the government] persists in its present attitude we will organise ourselves in order to ensure the defence of our liberties, for we can no longer accept the almost daily physical attacks on men, young men, whose only crime was to make use of their rights as citizens.[53]

Perret was to repeat such apocalyptic threats on several occasions during the next eighteen months.[54] The prospect of a reunified CGT provoked him to write that 'the hour is approaching when all the guilty will have to account for their criminal actions. The high court, prison and civic destitution are legal and democratic punishments.'[55] Perret's belief in the revolutionary threat was reinforced by the international situation. At first Perret and his allies had urged a strong line against Hitler, seeing him as just another aggressive German statesman. But PCF endorsement of the Franco-Soviet pact in May 1935 led to a fundamental change of perspective. This became clear in Perret's attitude to the crisis caused by Italian designs on Ethiopia. He praised Mussolini for having restored the soul of the Italian nation, and charged the Popular Front with seeking war in order to foment revolution in France and to gain revenge for the Duce's suppression of freemasonry. By the time of Hitler's re-occupation of the Rhineland in March 1936 Perret's foreign policy consisted merely in denouncing communism and those like Briand, Herriot and the British, whose misguided policies had so weakened France.

It is then understandable that Bonnevay should have referred to Perret as 'chef des politiciens fascistes du Rhône'. As evidence for such a charge one could point to sympathy for Mussolini, authoritarianism, the appeal to violence, anticommunism, and an undercurrent of xenophobia and even antisemitism.[56] There was also an antielitist and anticapitalist element in Fédération propaganda. The social and political establishment was held responsible for failure to deal with the economic crisis, constitutional reform, the threat from the left and the revived German menace. Perret spoke of the 'total lack of initiative and enterprise among

[52] AN F[2] 2667, report of 1 October 1934; *Lyon républicain*, 2 and 3 October 1934; *L'Union républicaine*, 7 October 1934; *Le Nouvelliste*, 5 October 1934.
[53] *L'Union républicaine*, 15 July 1934.   [54] *Ibid.*, 15 July 1934, 15 September 1935.
[55] *Ibid.*, 6 October 1935.   [56] *Ibid.*, 14 April 1935.

our statesmen'. He had little faith in the Doumergue government, and less in those of Flandin or Laval.[57] Big business was denounced for favouring dubious political combinations for short-term gain, while the Fédération's own programme had been frustrated by a conspiracy of oil companies, banks and insurance companies.[58] Perret, as our discussion of the entente in the silk industry showed, had good reason for disliking the 'puissances d'argent'. And he was in personal difficulties with the banks. Antielitism implied populism, which was in turn connected to authoritarianism. Thus Alexandre La Batie held that the hierarchical organisation of the army was analogous to the democracy from which it emanated. The army was an interclass organisation which attenuated the social inequalities of a regime which 'claims to be founded on equality of rights and duties'. What La Batie meant by equality was common submission to discipline, which provided the unity once derived from the monarchy.[59] This kind of populism went far beyond that of 1930, when Perret had merely spoken of a partnership between activists (standing for the people) and deputies.

But for three reasons Perret remained closer to the authoritarian-elitist than the authoritarian-populist, let alone fascist, right. First the Fédération was hardly suited to be either the vehicle for a popular mobilisation or the instrument of a fascist dictatorship. The existence of such a party is essential to fascism, for it provides the means by which a new national elite will take power from the discredited establishment. Perret's Fédération was a revamped notable party, dependent on the Church for its links with the masses. It was a part of the ruling class, albeit a marginal one. Gautheron's ideas on constitutional reform suggest that the authoritarian remaking of France would be carried out through existing institutions, not a new mass movement.

Second, Perret distrusted the street politics of the leagues. Certainly the violence of his language sanctioned their activity. There were some contacts between Fédération and leagues. The party's Villeurbanne committee claimed in March 1934 to be taking the lead in the formation of a 'Front national'.[60] Perret's followers precipitated a crisis in the Fédération by their refusal to vote a Conseil général motion for disarmament of the leagues on the grounds that it failed to condemn simultaneously the arming of the left. Yet collaboration between Fédération and leagues was surprisingly limited between 1932 and 1936. Fédération attendance at meetings of the Jeunesses patriotes was

[57] *Ibid.*, 15 July 1934, 24 February and 18 August 1935.
[58] *Ibid.*, 26 August 1934, 18 August 1935.   [59] *Ibid.*, 29 July 1934.
[60] ADR 4m 235, Prefect, 31 March 1934; *L'Union républicaine*, 26 August 1934.

less common than in previous years.[61] One reason might be that in 1935 the Jeunesses patriotes were denouncing the *modérés*, and calling for the arming of the people and for a 'national revolution'. Also the Jeunesses patriotes was now outclassed in terms of membership by the Croix de Feu. There was some contact with the latter. There was some overlap in membership, the most notorious example being Pierre Burgeot, who benefited from the secret support of the league in his election campaign in 1936.[62] A few Croix de Feu activists also appear on Fédération lists in the municipal elections of 1935, admittedly in areas where the right had no chance of victory, and without any reference to their affiliation to the league.[63] Such contacts were less extensive than with other leagues, and in any case hidden from the public.

As to Perret's private attitude to the leagues, we can only guess. Given his reservations before 1932, his polemics with the PSF from 1936, and the absence of close collaboration with the leagues in the period between, there is little to suggest that Perret saw anything more than a subordinate role for them.[64] The only league which was explicitly condemned was the Défense paysanne of Dorgères, which was seen as encroaching on the terrain of the parties, and as engaging in demagogic opposition to the decree laws of Laval.[65] Since the Défense paysanne was not established in the Rhône the Fédération had no need to fear the repercussions of such an attack. So perhaps this was a coded warning to all the leagues. It is most likely that Perret saw the leagues as a means of combat against the left, and was prepared to use them to call to order the feeble conservative establishment. Irvine is probably correct to argue that the Fédération tolerated the leagues as long as they did not encroach on its own terrain.

A third reason why the Fédération cannot be seen as fascist is that it never ceased to speak for a narrow section of the ruling class. Certainly Perret's appeal was greater than in the Tardieu period. But the essential problem was that like other organisations the Fédération found it difficult to balance and reconcile the contradictory demands of its supporters. This was especially difficult in a party where a narrow group of notables was responsible for policy. As a result the Fédération tended to oscillate between pleas for respect of the general interest and special pleading for the merchant-manufacturing branch of the silk industry. From time to time the silk industry, unlike any other branch of the

[61] For examples see *Le Nouvelliste*, 9 April 1934, 9 February 1935.
[62] AN 317 AP 88, Burgeot to President of PSF in the 6th arrondissement, 12 May 1938; Burgeot to Marin, 13 May 1938.
[63] Notably the engineer Pierre Combes in the 3rd arrondissement.
[64] *La République lyonnaise*, 1932.
[65] *L'Union républicaine*, 3 and 17 November 1935.

Lyonnais economy, was the subject of Perret's weekly editorial in
L'Union républicaine.[66] Perret also called for a general return to the
family workshop.[67] This had been one of his reasons for opposition to
the Marchandeau bill, another question on which Perret's views
diverged from the majority of businessmen. He called for a programme
of public works, which would include the restoration of national
monuments and the tapestries they contained. This would give work to
weavers of embroidered silks such as those Perret himself produced.[68]
To finance this project Perret favoured a large national loan. Although
he argued that public works would eventually profit the nation, there
was no disguising the incompatibility of this measure with deflation.[69]
This simultaneous pressure for deflation and subsidy is typical of the
kind of pressure faced by the government, and was a major cause of the
crisis of parliament. Elitism was also evident in Gautheron's constitutional schemes. The President would be chosen neither by parliament
nor by universal suffrage, but by the professional associations of the
ruling class, who would also have a say in the formulation of legislation.
Just as interest groups appealed simultaneously to general and sectional
interests, so too did the Fédération. Trades unions would be suppressed
and Chambers of Commerce given a role in government, all in the
interest of restoring state 'neutrality'.

Perret had little to offer the increasingly strident popular constituency
of the right. The party's only social policy was mutualisation of social
insurance. The forty-hour week was rejected on the grounds that it
would cause big business to increase productivity through 'machinism',
thereby endangering the artisanate.[70] Price support measures demanded
by the peasantry were rejected on the grounds that 'heaven helps those
who help themselves'. The Fédération took the side of large landowners
against the government's wine laws. Shopkeepers were accused of
profiteering by the Fédération-sponsored Ligue de défence des con-
sommateurs, and Perret envisaged transformation of shopkeepers into
agents of big companies.[71] There can be little doubt that the groups
concerned, given the heightened sensitivity to professional interests in
this period, were aware of the Fédération's views. It is not surprising that
the popular constituency of the right should feel neglected by its leaders.

So the conservatism of Perret cannot be described as fascist. Rather, it
represented the authoritarianism of a narrow section of the Lyonnais
elite, which attempted to mobilise 'the people' in symbolic terms from

[66] Ibid., 18 March 1934, 24 November 1935, 29 January 1939.
[67] Ibid., 18 March 1934.   [68] Ibid., 9 October 1932.
[69] Ibid., 3 and 17 March 1935.   [70] Ibid., 28 January 1934.
[71] Ibid., 16 October 1932.

outside in order to remake the ruling class. Perret distrusted the genuine mobilisation of the leagues. Consequently he was unable to produce the platform of a genuine 'national opposition'. It is perhaps surprising that Perret did not, to this end, exploit his own long-standing commitment to corporatism and the wide popularity of that doctrine in conservative circles. Corporatism continued to form a part of Perret's discourse.[72] He approved in principle the idea of corporative organisation of the silk industry. He was also aware of the doctrine's integrative potential. It is worth quoting at length his views on the subject for they demonstrate perfectly the function and appeal of corporatism:

It will be necessary, as soon as possible, to bring about a *rapprochement* between industrial and agricultural producers; for too long they have been set against each other for reasons upon which it is useless to insist.

There are no founders, weavers, metallurgists, chemists, electricians, farmers, winegrowers, big sharecroppers and small peasants. There are only Frenchmen who work and produce, and their interests are identical.

So we are convinced that a *rapprochement* of all organisations of producers is possible. We have Chambers of Commerce and Chambers of Agriculture that are perfectly able to undertake this great national work with its enormous economic importance.

It would, moreover, be an excellent means to limit somewhat, whilst awaiting a total transformation, the grip of politicians on all the institutions of the life of our country.

In this quotation we see the assertion of a mythical national interest and the ascription of division in the nation to outside agents. Typically, however, the national and professional interest would have to be enforced by compulsory membership of the syndicate and the disciplining of 'commerçants marrons'. Yet for all this, corporatism was never more than a sub-theme of Fédération propaganda. Apart from Perret, few writers in *L'Union républicaine* showed much interest in it. Corporatist ideas appear in only two or three of the dozens of electoral addresses produced by the Fédération. More common were defences of liberalism. Even Perret re-asserted on several occasions his allegiance to the liberal tradition.[73] One explanation for this paradox is that Perret's corporatism was aimed at the protection of the merchant-manufacturing mode of production. Yet we have seen that those most loudly demanding corporatist measures at this time had little interest in the artisanate. Indeed, many of them saw corporatism as a means of developing mass production. This might well have discouraged Perret from pressing to hard his own version of corporatism.

---

[72] *Ibid.*, 16 October 1932.
[73] See for example his advice to farmers on page 202.

Furthermore, liberalism was still influential in the Fédération, reinforced by the fact that most activists read the *Nouvelliste*. We have seen that some in the silk industry remained faithful to liberalism. This had been the predominant motif in the campaign against the entente project. The chief opponents of the entente were precisely those medium factory producers and *non-usiniers* who were also found supporting Perret's wing of the Fédération. It is significant that Perret was much more outspoken on the subject of corporatism when speaking to the Fédération's national congress than he was in Lyon.[74] There was in any case no necessary connection between a desire to preserve luxury industry and corporatism. Perret regarded corporatism as a means of protecting skilled labour. But another activist argued that the laws of supply and demand, based on individual initiative and private property, were ideally suited to a nation of small business, diverse tastes and quality production.[75]

What Perret did share with liberals of this type was a suspicion of big business and mass production. He therefore tended to fall back on their peculiar brand of liberalism, with its assumption of a natural level of demand which could be ignored only at great risk. This enabled him to attribute the crisis to a moral imbalance. For Perret, 'one could not with impunity violate the laws of morality or of nature, especially as these laws, together with tradition, have for too long been replaced by speculation in all its forms, illegitimate profits, immorality in business, the theory of least effort, and the immoderate thirst for gain and pleasure'.[76] This was a definition of liberalism which excluded big business and optimistic Progressiste liberalism. But it included those who defined themselves in terms of a set of austere Catholic and liberal values. Another advantage of this moral discourse was that there was no need to discuss concrete issues. In December 1934 Perret stated that he could not pronounce on wine and wheat prices because he lacked appropriate qualifications – a disability which had not excluded him from membership of the Comice agricole of Lamure. The Fédération's manifesto for the senatorial elections of 1935 put forward no agricultural programme at all, even though a large proportion of delegates represented rural communes. It was simply asserted that town and country had a common interest.[77]

The disadvantage of such a strategy was that it did not have the wide appeal of corporatist doctrine, with its ability to proclaim the primacy of profession and nation, whilst simultaneously permitting the illusion that

---

[74] AN 317 AP 82/3, manuscript of Perret speech.
[75] *L'Union républicaine*, 11 November 1934.   [76] *Ibid.*, 17 February 1935.
[77] *Ibid.*, 4 December 1932, 13 October 1935.

individual interests too would be satisfied. In the eyes of many on the right the Fédération remained elitist and egotistical. The collaboration of the Fédération with the leagues was not, however, as close as many imagined. Indeed, the leagues increasingly tended to criticise the Fédération in the same terms as the PDP, seeing it as an emanation of big capital and a failed political class. Perret had played the role of sorcerer's apprentice.

The divisions of the Parliamentary Right

Until late 1934 relations between conservative parties in the Rhône had been fairly good. The crisis in the Fédération in 1929 and 1930 did not prevent the right and centre-right from putting forward single candidates in all constituencies but the Beaujolais in the general elections of 1932, even though some in the PDP felt that too many concessions had been made to the right.[78] All the same, Perret's establishment of control over the Fédération had begun to change things. Already in the 6th arrondissement the setting up of a separate Fédération committee in 1931 had led to difficulties. In the *cantonales* of that year the Alliance and Fédération were unable to agree upon a single candidate. Mansuy withdrew on the second ballot without advising a vote for the Fédération, and openly voted for the Radicals.[79] The turning point came in the late summer of 1934, coinciding with Perret's change of tack and the emergence of the Croix de Feu. The issue which precipitated conflict was Laurent Bonnevay's role as President of the Parliamentary Commission of Inquiry into the events of 6 February. After the Commission reported in December Perret launched an attack on Bonnevay, whose view that 6 February had represented a fascist plot was soon to be put forward in a book. From this point on Perret, Bonnevay and others were engaged in continuous polemic.

The conflict had repercussions on the Conseil général. In October 1934 the right gained a majority in this body. Bonnevay became President, at the head of a Union nationale majority. But in August 1935 the right split over the question of the leagues. Perret was scandalised that only five Fédération councillors had voted against a motion which condemned 'factious leagues', but said nothing of the communists. Three conservatives even voted in favour.[80] In October

---

[78] *Bulletin des 'Démocrates populaires'*, January 1929.
[79] *Le Nouvelliste*, 12 September 1931; *L'Union républicaine*, 3 November 1935.
[80] Against: Bosse-Platière, Sallès, Parrel, Burgeot and Sabarly (all Fédération). Abstained: Anier, De Lescure, Nicolas (Fédération); Augros, Mercier (Alliance), Maire (Fédération/PDP). For: Lheritier (PDP), Delorme, Mansuy (Alliance).

Bonnevay put up a centre-right list against that of the Fédération in the Senate elections. A month later the breach in the conservative majority on the *conseil général* was confirmed, as the Fédération's representatives were evicted from its bureau. A new centre majority supported by the SFIO elected a bureau of Alliance and Radical supporters. Bonnevay retained the Presidency.[81]

Not surprisingly the right fought the general election of 1936 in the greatest of confusion. Candidates were chosen only after an unprecedented degree of faction fighting. Bonnevay was behind manœuvres to present a centre right candidate against Peissel, and was conspiring with Herriot to present an antiPopular Front Radical in the 2nd arrondissement. Neither of these efforts bore fruit.[82] Bonnevay himself faced a challenge in his own constituency from Perret, who mounted what he called 'a punitive expedition'. Bonnevay was viewed sympathetically by the communists, while Action Française aided Perret. There were incidents at many election meetings.[83] The situation was most confused in the 6th arrondissement. Here the Fédération chose Pierre Burgeot only because it could find no-one better. Also competing for the right-wing vote were an Independent Radical and an ex-PDP veterans' candidate. The Alliance, egged on by Bonnevay, put forward no candidate at all, its aim being to present Mansuy on the second ballot. This plan, however, backfired. With the conservative vote split, Burgeot was far enough ahead of his conservative rivals on the first ballot to make his withdrawal impossible. So unedifying was the confusion in the 6th arrondissement that there were rumours that business was ready to put forward a 'non-political', 'economic' candidate.[84] But in fact the influence of big business in an arrondissement which had once provided the backbone of Aynard's support had greatly declined. Whereas the right had presented a single candidate in thirteen out of fourteen Rhône constituencies in 1928 and 1932, there were competing conservative candidates in six constituencies in 1936.

Thus on the eve of the arrival in power of the Popular Front, the right in the Rhône was in a deep crisis. Long-term conflicts became acute during the economic crisis and were particularly evident in debates over the *loi Marchandeau*. The rise of the Popular Front was insufficient to create unity. The right was divided by political tactics and buffeted by intense

[81] Bonnevay, *Histoire politique*, 76–8.
[82] ADR, élections législatives, 1936, 14 November 1935, 18 March 1936.
[83] *Le Nouvelliste*, 14 April 1936; ADR, élections législatives, 1936, Lheritier to Prefect.
[84] ADR, élections législatives, 1936, 5 December 1935, 22 February and 1 March 1936; *La République lyonnaise*, 1 February and 18 April 1936.

interest-group conflict. At times parties seemed to have fallen into the hands of narrow interest groups such as the Catholic merchant-manufacturers who dominated the Fédération, the anticlerical bourgeoisie in the Alliance or the reformist white-collar workers of the PDP. At other times parties took refuge in the outdated ideological references of the period which had spawned them. As Antonio Gramsci put it in 1933, 'French parties are . . . mummified and anachronistic historico-political documents of the various phases of past French history, whose outdated terminology they continue to repeat.' He warned ominously, 'their crisis could become as catastrophic as that of the German parties'.[85] Gramsci was unduly pessimistic. But demands for authority and 'restoration' of national unity were present in all parts of the political spectrum. Many rank-and-file conservatives, moreover, were to turn to the leagues. Big-business elites were increasingly excluded from local political influence; some saw the Croix de Feu as a means of restoring their influence.

We have also seen that authoritarianism developed out of *all* the conservative traditions in the Rhône. Morel-Journel's suspicion of the 'law of number' and universal suffrage derived from an Orleanist distrust of democracy.[86] Perret's authoritarianism stemmed from his roots in right-wing social Catholicism. Some in the PDP and Alliance were attracted to authority by the search for a 'third way'. So Rémond's contention that each of the strands of the French right was intrinsically opposed to fascism must be qualified. This is all the more necessary given that in recent years a reassessment of the nature of liberal-democratic culture in France has taken place, which shows a certain unease with the notion of 'alternance' or even pluralism.[87] This does not, however, mean that French traditions should be seen as universally corrupted by 'proto-fascism'. That elements of so many traditions could be turned to account by fascists renders the concept of 'proto-fascism' too general to be of use. It is better to regard the various traditions considered as harbouring authoritarian potentials which could in particular circumstances be realised. Such conditions existed in the 1930s, and help to explain the emergence of the Croix de Feu.

[85] Antonio Gramsci, *Selections from the Prison Notebooks of Antonio Gramsci*, ed. Q. Hoare and G. Nowell Smith (1971), 210–23.
[86] Morel-Journel, *Journal*, 30 April 1936; PVCCL, 13 February and 13 April 1936.
[87] Odile Rudelle, *La République absolue* (1986).

8   The Croix de Feu

As René Rémond recognised, the Croix de Feu is the key to the problem of fascism in France. For over two years the league was at the centre of political debate, providing the justification for the formation of the antifascist Popular Front. It was incontestably a mass movement, with somewhere between 300,000 and 400,000 members by the time of its dissolution in June 1936. So if the Croix de Feu was fascist, then no longer can fascism be seen as the concern of marginal intellectuals or a product of Nazi occupation. Broadly speaking the league has been seen in three ways.

K.-J. Müller hesitates between seeing the Croix de Feu as an example of 'circumstantial fascism' or Bonapartism, but is ultimately less concerned with classification than with explaining its origins in a crisis specific to France.[1] In his view the league was a response to demands for representation on the part of emergent groups such as modern business and white-collar workers. Once the Radicals had met these claims in 1937–8 by shifting to the right, the Croix de Feu/PSF declined. Müller's approach has the advantage of placing the leagues in their socio-economic context. But problems arise from his reliance on concepts derived from functionalist sociology. Social conflict is seen as an adjustment of the system to changed circumstances, so the extent to which the leagues sought actively and self-consciously to transform French society is obscured. Furthermore, although we shall see that in the Rhône the Croix de Feu recruited from 'emergent' groups, it did not 'represent' them unproblematically. Also, the question of classification *is* important if we are to illuminate differences between the many anti-democratic movements of this period, and if comparisons are to be made between right-wing extremism in France and Germany or Italy.

Comparison is all the more important given that Rémond's case that the Croix de Feu were not fascist rests on an assumption of the uniqueness of French traditions. For Rémond the league represented a

---

[1] Müller, 'French fascism and modernisation', 75–100.

variety of Bonapartism – a form of conservatism particular to France, which synthesises democracy and authority.[2] This means a strong executive, weak parliament and a plebiscitary link between leader and masses, but respect for universal suffrage. Bonapartism comes in left or right varieties according to whether it emphasises democracy or authority. Left Bonapartism is close to fascism, lacking only a mass party. But historically, it has been the socially conservative and authoritarian version of Bonapartism which has been preponderant, and it is into this category that the Croix de Feu must be placed. Philippe Burrin makes a similar distinction within Bonapartism between a conservative 'national-caesarism' and more radical 'national populism', and agrees that the Croix de Feu was an example of the former.[3] The chief problem with this view is that the league can be shown to have been a populist and antiestablishment mass movement. This raises the question of whether, in spite of the views of Rémond and Burrin, the Croix de Feu could usefully be seen as 'left Bonapartist' or 'national-populist'. For Burrin national-populism involves a plebeian or déclassé rank and file and leadership, a rhetoric of denunciation, decadence, xenophobia and perhaps antisemitism. But national-populism is said to differ from fascism in that it is respectful of popular sovereignty and is not totalitarian. There are difficulties with Burrin's definition of the concept, which include the assumption of a necessary relationship between social composition and political complexion, and the unfalsifiable view that leaders are either plebeian or déclassé. Burrin's definition of totalitarianism – the will to achieve 'total' transformation of society – is so exacting that no movement could be fascist. It is easy to demonstrate that the Nazis saw some parts of German society as more in need of transformation than others. Nevertheless, national-populism is a potentially useful category because it rightly distinguishes fascist from non-fascist movements of (in our terms) the authoritarian-populist right.

Another possibility is that the Croix de Feu was, as Robert Soucy and William Irvine argue, fascist.[4] For these authors fascism is the pursuit of social and economic conservatism by violent and authoritarian means, so, as with Rémond and Burrin, the populism of the Croix de Feu is neglected. For Soucy the ruling class responds to economic crisis and a socialist threat by abandoning parliamentarianism for authoritarianism.

[2] Rémond, *Les Droites*, 204–5.
[3] Burrin, 'Le Fascisme', 634. Similarly Milza (*Fascisme français*, 137) sees the Croix de Feu as a variety of authoritarian, paternalist and traditionalist conservatism, resembling the Catholic social regime of Dollfus in Austria.
[4] Soucy, 'The Croix de Feu'; Soucy, *French Fascism: The Second Wave*; Irvine, 'Fascism in France'. Irvine places more emphasis on the antibourgeois *rhetoric* and popular *style* of the movement.

The fascist movement therefore opposes both socialism and liberalism. One problem is that liberalism and authoritarianism are seen merely as alternative political methods; the right is assumed to be able to switch between them without compromising a more fundamental social conservatism. We have seen that in the Rhône liberalism was tied up with complex material and ideal interests, so antiliberalism necessarily involved opposition to sections of the ruling elite. The approach of Soucy and Irvine has something in common with the Marxist view in which monopoly capital uses the fascist party to mobilise the petty bourgeoisie against parliament and the labour movement in order to secure undisputed control over the state.[5] Certainly big business showed interest in the Croix de Feu, and some sought to use it to curb the powers of parliament and undermine welfare legislation. But there was rather more to the movement than this.

In this chapter it will be argued that the Croix de Feu was fascist. But whereas, with the exception of Müller, historians agree that the Croix de Feu was conservative and elitist, the league's populism will be emphasised. Moreover, fascism should be seen as a sub-species of the authoritarian-populist right. Such movements (fascist or not) claim that only the people can restore national unity, deal with the left, and defend the state against foreign enemies. They are therefore both reactionary in their hostility to the left and radical in their opposition to the old right and to the state elites. To emphasise the populism of the Croix de Feu does not mean that it was in any sense left-wing. On the contrary, the Croix de Feu was *more* hostile to the left than the parliamentary right, for it wished to destroy the pluralism that permitted communist parties and trade unions to operate. Also, opposition to the elites was partial. In effect they were condemned for failure to carry out conservative tasks. For this reason the populist far right attacks only 'Jewish' or 'international capitalism'. The Croix de Feu's view of the 'people', furthermore, was shaped by reactionary class and gender biases. But its radicalism must be taken seriously, for the reverse is also true: Croix de Feu solutions to the problem of the working class and women were, as we shall see, marked by a search for populist mass mobilisation which differentiated it from the traditional right, whether authoritarian-elitist or constitutional-elitist. Also, we shall see that the radicalism of the league was nourished by all the tensions that had marked the right wing in France, and which can be analysed in terms of 'dual closure'.[6]

Fascist movements share all the general features of authoritarian-

[5] Maurice Thorez, *Œuvres Choisis*, I, 136–89.
[6] Even where the Croix de Feu or PSF showed sympathy for Popular Front reforms such as the 40-hour week or compulsory arbitration in labour disputes, this does not mean

populism, but, as Burrin argues, they are less respectful of democracy and pluralism. They seek to impose an historically conditioned world-view by means of mass mobilisation expressed above all in a para-militarism which differentiates such movements from the non-fascist populist far right. Fascism is most likely to arise in circumstances of extreme tension, marked by the feeling that the nation is in the grip of a life or death crisis out of which final defeat or renewal will emerge. The fascist movement sees itself as the vehicle of national regeneration. As Roger Griffin argues, it represents a 'palingenetic ultra-nationalism' dedicated to rebirth of the nation. Thus a fascist movement is characterised by a synthesis of radicalism and reaction expressed in extreme nationalism, antifeminism, antisocialism, hostility to minorities such as Jews or Freemasons, antiparliamentarianism, antiliberalism and a populist opposition to the social and political elites.

This definition, however, means little outside of an historical context. Given that a fascist regime did not emerge in France, it is particularly necessary to distinguish the conditions which permit the emergence of a fascist *movement* (along with other kinds of authoritarianism) from those which allow it to win *power*. Preceding chapters have focussed on the chronic divisions of French society and of the conservative elites. On the one hand this divisiveness was important in that fascism was a reaction against it, and on the other the same divisions made possible the detachment, in conditions of crisis, of the conservative rank-and-file from traditional allegiances. Linz's concept of 'political space' throws additional light on why a fascist movement was able to develop among the right-wing rank-and-file.[7] In most of France the parliamentary right remained in the hands of notables. In the Rhône the Fédération was better structured, but the rank-and-file still played little part in the life of the party. The PDP was a mass party in terms of structure and ideology, but was small – Christian democracy depended more on the support of notables like Bonnevay and Peissel. There was no equivalent in France of the Centre Party which did much to inhibit the development of Nazism in Catholic areas of Germany. Another condition which favoured the emergence of the fascist movement was the sense of national disintegration during the economic crisis, coupled to fear of war and revolution described in the previous chapter. This was sufficient to promote in some circles a 'palingenetic myth'. Finally, a tradition of right-wing extremism favoured the emergence of the Croix de Feu. But this factor should not be overestimated. Fascism in both Germany and

---

that they had left-wing or socialist sympathies. Such measures are not intrinsically left-wing, and have often been favoured by conservative movements.

[7] Linz, 'Some notes toward a comparative study of fascism'.

Italy was very much a new synthesis of old ideas. In France aspects of both liberalism and Christian democracy were also grist to the fascist mill.

The conditions which permit a fascist movement to gain power are different. The notion of political space is again useful, for, as Rémond and others have argued, the hold of Radicalism over large sections of the petty bourgeoisie was an important obstacle to fascism in France. It is true that the Radical Party was often as poorly structured as the right. And we have seen that in the Rhône shopkeepers had became detached from Radical politicians, demonstrating that the Republican tradition was not necessarily an obstacle to right-wing extremism. But the active manipulation of the Republican tradition by the Popular Front ensured that Radical supporters remained within the Republican fold. One further point can be emphasised. The victory of fascism in both Italy and Germany owed much to an alliance with conservatives (usually of the authoritarian-elitist type such as von Papen).[8] Such contacts were not merely tactical, but intrinsic to the combination of radicalism and reaction which characterises fascism. In France conservatives in business and parliament showed goodwill towards the leagues, and often joined the movement itself. In so doing they did much to destabilise the Republic. But the leagues were never invited to join the government. More attractive options always remained available. The purpose of this chapter is then to understand the nature of the Croix de Feu, especially its populism, to relate the emergence of the league to the general crisis of the French right, and to elucidate some of the reasons for the league's failure. First, however, it is necessary to examine the nature of the far right in the Rhône before the rise of the Croix de Feu.

The extreme right before the Croix de Feu

Until 1934 the far right in the Rhône was dominated by Action française. In 1928 it still possessed 1,100 members in the agglomeration of Lyon, and probably as many in the rest of the department.[9] The movement had a wide influence outside its own ranks, attracting 3,000 to hear Maurras in February 1928, in spite of appeals by Cardinal Maurin for Catholics to stay away.[10] In 1925 a rival to Action française appeared in the form of the Jeunesses patriotes, and at its peak in 1929–30 it may have had somewhere between 500 and 800 members in the Rhône. A brief account of the two movements will illuminate the continuities and discontinuities between La Rocque's league and its precursors.

[8] Blinkhorn, 'Fascists and conservatives'.   [9] AN F⁷ 13 205, 17 November 1928.
[10] AN F⁷ 13 040, 4 July 1933; AN F⁷ 13 205, 27 February 1928, 20 January 1929.

Action française had much in common with Victor Perret's wing of the Fédération. Indeed royalists often expressed approval of Perret's 'national' politics.[11] Like Fédération sympathisers, royalists lived mainly in the old centre of the city, the 1st, 2nd and 4th arrondissements, and were less strong in the 3rd and 6th. It recruited from the Catholic elites, including landowners in the Beaujolais and Lyonnais mountains.[12] Wealthy business families such as the Cabauds and Berliets (although the latter were Legitimists) also favoured the league.[13] Also prominent were merchant-manufacturers in the silk industry – Louis Jasseron, leader of the south-east region throughout the period, was from a family of manufacturers of embroidered silks. Leaders were largely ex-officers, lawyers and medium businessmen – the same more modest sections of the elites which supported the Fédération. Perhaps typical was 36-year-old Emile Brun, owner of a blanket factory in Cours, president of the Roannais federation from 1928. Mass support came from students and the middle and lower middle class, especially white-collar workers, and included a certain working-class presence. The main difference between Action française and the Fédération was that the royalists had little peasant support.

Royalism also shared with the Fédération a dependence on the parish-based Œuvre des cercles and Catholic student organisations. Therefore condemnation of Action française by the pope in 1926 was a considerable blow. Action française could no longer use the organisational networks of the parishes, while the refusal of the *Nouvelliste* to print its communiqués cut it off from the wider Catholic audience.[14] Royalist elites withdrew into the world of salons, politicised *soirées mondaines* and public lectures which formed part of the social circuit of 'Tout Lyon'. The league's arrondissement-based sections had a difficult life after 1928, and all attempts to revivify them, including efforts to emulate the Croix de Feu by turning party offices into social centres, came to nothing.[15] In these difficult circumstances Action française managed to keep together a core of Commissaires and Camelots by placing them in firms owned by sympathetic employers, such as Berliet, and Descours and Cabaud. They were guaranteed free medical treatment, one month's

[11] *La République lyonnaise*, 4 April and 28 March 1931.
[12] AN F⁷ 13 205, 4 December 1928; for maps see Passmore, 'The right and the extreme right'.
[13] Bruno Flachère de Roustan, who had succeeded his father as representative of the Duc de Guise in the south-east, was a member of the board of directors of Descours and Cabaud.
[14] AN F⁷ 13 205, 17 November 1928.
[15] ADR 4m 637 (associations), 13 October 1932, 5 March 1936; AN F⁷ 13 205, 18 October 1932.

wages in case of sacking, and permission to leave work whenever called upon by Action française.[16] As we have seen, the Fédération was the main beneficiary of the exclusion of royalists from the parishes, while the Jeunesses patriotes penetrated Catholic student organisations.[17] The emergence of the Jeunesses patriotes therefore did little to change the character of the far right. Rather it split the royalist elites from the student wing of the movement, which was increasingly attracted to the Jeunesses patriotes. Many of the latter were from families which had in the past supported Action française. Indeed, if anything the republican Jeunesses patriotes were less popular in their recruitment than Action française, for the former lacked the ability to constitute factory cells.[18]

The same elitism was evident in royalist and Jeunesse patriotes discourse. *La République lyonnaise* stated that the cadres of the restored monarchy would be provided by the aristocracy, 'in which a special aptitude for diplomatic and military careers, thanks to education and blood, still survives', together with businessmen, fathers of families, practitioners of charity, elements of the intelligentsia and the artisanate. But Action française cannot be seen simply as a movement of the authoritarian-elitist right, for there was also a populist side to its discourse. The monarch was presented in terms similar to those used by republican defenders of the strong state, as a leader independent of the sectional interests, and representative of the 'pays réel' rather than the 'pays légal'.[19] This reminds us that the Catholic elites, especially those brought up in the integrist schools favoured by royalists, occupied an equivocal position within the republican system. They were excluded from many areas of state employment, let alone government, even though they possessed considerable economic power. And, of course, the royalist elites supported a movement committed in principle to the violent overthrow of the Republic. At a meeting in 1926 it was emphasised that Action française would not flinch from direct action, for the Republic still had many defenders who would not give up without a fight.[20] Thus, if Action française were ultimately closer to the authoritarian-elitist than to the authoritarian-populist right, it nevertheless contained a populist potential which helped prepare the way for the Croix de Feu.

Much the same can be said of the Jeunesses patriotes. We have seen

[16] F[7] 13 205, 17 November 1928.
[17] *La République lyonnaise*, 25 June 1927. AN F[7] 13 205, 27 December 1928; AN F[7] 13 234, 14 May 1927.
[18] The movement was, however, financed by big business, perhaps including Gillet, and Taittinger himself (AN F[7] 13 235, 11 January 1930).
[19] *La République lyonnaise*, 5 March 1932.
[20] AN F[7] 13 200, 11 March 1926; F[7] 13 205, 13 October 1928.

that in 1928, under the leadership of Marcel Didier, the Jeunesses patriotes turned away from antiparliamentarianism and collaborated with Kerillis's pro-Tardieu Républicains nationaux. The new moderate line was, however, contested by a radical tendency led by a 27-year-old who rejoiced in the name of Etienne de Raulin de Cuelteville de Réal Camp. He was notorious for once having faked an armed attack on himself in Rennes. In Lyon he advocated collaboration with Action française and prepared for combat in the street.[21] De Raulin was forced out of the Jeunesses patriotes after his arrest on a fraud charge. But with some success he kept up his agitation for a united front of all nationalist groups. By the end of 1930 de Raulin seemed to have won out, as the Jeunesses patriotes voted a motion critical of Taittinger. Preparations for the organisation of an armed 'groupe de fer' began. The result was Didier's resignation from the presidency of the Lyon section in November 1930 – soon after he became director of the Républicains nationaux.[22] De Raulin represented a Maurrassian tendency within the Jeunesses patriotes. His view was that France should be governed by a trained élite, leaving everyone else to get on with work and family life. But there was an implicit populism in his emphasis on street action and anticapitalism.[23]

Thus the Jeunesses patriotes and Action française functioned as a pool of organisational, financial, ideological and human resources on which the Croix de Feu was able to draw. This raises the wider question of whether or not fascism was alien to French traditions. There is no need to rehearse here the debate over Zeev Sternhell's work, for the intellectual origins of French fascism have been well researched and are not the main concern of this book. Suffice it to say that although many aspects of Sternhell's work are debatable, few would now disagree that there were proto-fascist elements in the thought and practice of Déroulède, Barrès and even Maurras. Three further points can be added. First, there is no straightforward relationship between the existence of a proto-fascist tradition and the emergence of a fascist movement. Indeed, it is arguable that the kind of street-fighting nationalism which prefigured fascism was much more evident in pre-1914 France than in Germany or Italy.[24] The

---

[21] L'Union française, 7 April 1929.

[22] AN F^7 13 235, 19 April 1929. The police reported on 27 February 1930 that a Jeunesses patriote member had said 'qu'il y avait assez de victimes et que, au revolver il fallait répondre par le revolver, à la matraque par la matraque'. L'Union française, 5 May 1929; Le Nouvelliste, 25 February 1930.

[23] L'Union française, September 1928.

[24] R. Chickering, We Men Who Feel Most German: A Cultural Study of the Pan-German League (Boston, 1984); A. de Grand, The Italian Nationalist Association and the Rise of Fascism in Italy (Lincoln, 1978).

precursors of the Nazis were much more conservative and elitist than, say, the Ligue des patriotes. In both Germany and Italy the emergence of mass fascist movements was largely unprecedented. It resulted from the meeting of a number of traditions in a specific conjuncture. Second, one cannot speak of a French radical right (or Bonapartist) tradition hermetically sealed from general European developments. On the one hand the idea of a plebiscitary relationship between leader and people was integral to Nazism.[25] On the other the French leagues drew on the Italian and German experience. In private La Rocque discussed the future of the Croix de Feu in the light of German and Italian examples. Such influences were not merely tagged on to a French essence.[26] Thirdly, we saw in the previous chapter that authoritarianism developed out of all of the major traditions of the French right, and sometimes this could lead to fascism. Indeed, even left-wing ideologies could be turned to the far right. That this did not happen on a mass scale in France in this period was a result of historical circumstances, not anything intrinsic to socialist thought. These considerations throw into doubt the whole concept of proto-fascism. It is impossible to identify particular traditions which lead ineluctably to fascism. Rather fascism as a potential exists in many ideologies. But it is equally true to say that there is a proto-democratic potential within fascism, as the evolution of the PSF towards republican conservatism was to demonstrate. In both cases the interaction between traditions and context is crucial. Thus in France the radical right underwent a transformation following the 'fascist riots' of 6 February 1934.

The 6 February 1934 in the Rhône

Neither the Jeunesses patriotes nor the royalists benefited from hostility to the Cartel in 1932–3. The Jeunesses patriotes newspaper disappeared in December 1932. It proved difficult to replace Didier as president, and in January 1933 the Phalange universitaire had to be dissolved. Action française was less a reaction to crisis than the expression of long-term hostility to the regime. So it was relatively immune to conjunctural problems. But already in March 1929 Action française found it difficult to find people willing to sell L'Action française in the street.[27] One index of the weakness of the far right was the rarity of violent incidents. In October 1928, Action française activists, led by Emile Brun, invaded a sitting of the municipal council.[28] Apart from a number of clashes with

[25] A. Hitler, Mein Kampf, translated by W. Mannheim (1969), 347–9.
[26] Quoted in Howlett, 'La Rocque', 171–78.   [27] AN F⁷ 13 200, 15 March 1929.
[28] AN F⁷ 13 205, 4 December and 31 October 1928.

Communist Party newspaper sellers outside the offices of *Le Progrès* in early 1930, and violence between communists and Camelots in Vaise in June 1931, this was the last disturbance of any importance before February 1934.[29]

Paris was not the only city in France to experience disturbances in that month. In Lyon the first demonstrations were the work of nationalist students who on 11 January staged a mock funeral of the Republic. The coffin was followed by several hundred people.[30] *L'Action française*, which contained the most lurid accounts of the Stavisky scandal, sold unusually well.[31] On 6 February the five o'clock edition of *Salut public* contained a call from the Jeunesses patriotes for the population to assemble at six. At 6.30 the Jeunesses patriotes themselves arrived and began to distribute tracts. They were soon joined by a group of Camelots and Croix de Feu. Within a short time a crowd estimated by the police at several thousand had gathered. News from Paris of shootings raised the temperature. Amidst cries of 'Ca ira, les députés, on les pendra', demonstrators attacked trams and formed columns. But although the police, on their own admission, were overrun, attempts by demonstrators to force their way up the rue République to the Hôtel de Ville were not well coordinated. Communists meanwhile fought with police on the Place Terreaux in front of the Town Hall. From about 9.00 until 10.00 pm there was a lull. Then there was a second, lesser demonstration. There were further demonstrations on the two following nights, now met by CGT counter-demonstrations. The two sides insulted each other with cries of 'Vive le roi!' and 'les Soviets partout!'' Café chairs and revolvers were used as weapons. There were eighty arrests.[32]

Clearly the riots in Lyon were less serious than those in Paris. There was no attempt to invade the Hôtel de Ville. Had this been a priority of the leagues then they could have assembled on the Place Terreaux, instead of half a mile away at Place Bellecour. Partly this was because of the symbolic significance of Bellecour to the extreme right. This enormous square, once known as the Place Louis-le-Grand, on which stood a large equestrian bronze of Louis XIV, was the traditional starting

---

[29] *Le Nouvelliste*, 17 and 25 February 1930; F[7] 13 205, 10 June 1931. These incidents owed more to the violent turn of the Communist Party in this period than to a revival of the far right. See S. Audoin, 'Le Parti communiste français et la violence, 1929–1931', *Revue historique* 269 (1983), 689–712.

[30] AN F[7] 13 040, 3 February 1934: the police estimated 4,000 per day from the 5 December 1934.

[31] AN F[7] 13 040, 3 February 1934.

[32] This account is compiled from daily press in Lyon, and from AN F[7] 13 040, 3 February and 3 March 1934.

point of the right's demonstrations. It is, however, too easy to use the obviously mythical status of the 'fascist coup' to discount the riots of 6 February. The leagues in this period enjoyed a level of sympathy which the Prefect believed was unprecedented in Lyon.[33] Secondly, we have seen that few conservatives were ready to condemn the riots. Even the national UNC vice-president, the Lyonnais Humbert Isaac, a reputedly unimpeachable Republican, wrote that without the demonstrations 'la République aurait vécu'.[34] Thirdly, the riots happened at a time when, as we have seen, antiparliamentarianism affected even the shopkeeper constituency of the Radicals. The small business movement in Paris, the Fédération des contribuables, actually participated in the riots of 6 February.[35] Putting these developments together, the Lyonnais example suggests the beginnings of a serious crisis of the regime. The argument must not, however, be overstated. In early 1934 the extreme right remained weak and dispersed. The bulk of active leaguers were probably students.[36]

The events of 6 February nevertheless had a significant impact on the extreme right, not only causing growth of the leagues, but accentuating their populism. This was evident in a tract distributed by the Jeunesses patriotes on 6 February in Lyon:

APPEAL to the PEOPLE of Lyon
Enough scandal, enough thievery, enough politicians, official protectors of the swindlers. A majority which covers up for the robbers of savings is their accomplice. We are not casting suspicion on the innocent, but we demand an inexorable justice against the guilty, however highly placed they are. Authority in France will be respected the day it is respectable. Parliament must cleanse itself, or the people will take the task upon themselves.

This tract is not as radical as that distributed by the Jeunesses patriotes on the Place de la Concorde.[37] It leaves open the door to an alliance of leagues and conservatives by implying that not all parliamentarians were guilty. Indeed, some Jeunesses patriotes continued to collaborate with the Républicains nationaux.[38] But the threat of popular action against parliament accentuated the populist tone of the radical wing of the Jeunesses patriotes. Indeed, when its press reappeared in late 1933 it supported Taittinger's call for a 'national revolution' – a slogan which looks forward to Vichy, but which was inspired by Hitler and Mussolini.

[33] AN F[7] 13 040, 3 March 1934. See also AN F[7] 13 040, 3 February 1934.
[34] Quoted in Prost, *Les Anciens Combattants*, I, 164.
[35] W. A. Hoisington Jr, 'Toward the sixth of February: taxpayer protest in France, 1928–1934', *Historical Reflections* 3 (1976), 49–67.
[36] AN F[2] 2667, 9 February 1934. The one participant whose occupation is known was a student at the medical faculty.
[37] Reprinted in Bonnevay, *Le Six février*.   [38] *L'Alerte*, November 1933.

J.-H. de la Barrière declared in October 1933 that 'the humanitarian, democratic and internationalist' phase of the postwar period was now outdated. The only alternatives were either 'social revolution' or a 'national recovery by means of authority and order'.[39] On the evening of 7 February de la Barrière was arrested at Place Bellecour. Subsequently the tone of the radical wing of the Jeunesses patriotes became ever more violent.[40] Charles Favre-Gilly warned that 'on future occasions the nationalists would go into the streets armed and well armed, in order to be able to resist the police on equal terms, should they be tempted to repeat their glorious deeds'.[41] In 1934 a number of Jeunesses patriotes members, among them Favre-Gilly, figured in the ranks of the Croix de Feu.

The Croix de Feu

After 6 February 1934 the Jeunesses patriotes and Action française shared in the general expansion of the leagues. A measure of their success is that they were able to muster respectively 200 and 900 marchers for the 1934 Joan of Arc parade, whereas in the two previous years they managed only small delegations. Their showing in 1935 was also respectable, at 500 and 210 respectively. But by this time both movements had been eclipsed by the Croix de Feu, which counted 2,500 marchers in 1935 and 4,000 in 1936.[42] The first thirty-four Croix de Feu members had met in Lyon on 8 December 1929. By 1932 there were 300 members.[43] Communiqués from the league began to appear regularly in the conservative press in 1933. Prefectoral reports first mentioned the Croix de Feu three days before the riots of 6 February.[44] In 1934 and especially 1935 the Croix de Feu grew rapidly.[45] If it is assumed that the league was able to mobilise two thirds of its members for the 1936 Joan of Arc parade then it is possible to guess at a total membership of 6,000 on the eve of dissolution. By 1936 the Croix de Feu was already the largest far-right organisation hitherto seen in the department.

A number of difficulties confront the historian of the Lyonnais Croix de Feu. Few police reports survive. Unusually for a movement of its importance, the Croix de Feu did not regularly publish a journal. Only five numbers of *Le Flambeau du sud-est* appeared from January 1934 to April 1936, of which only three survive. Few communiqués were

---

[39] *Ibid.*, October 1933.   [40] *Ibid.*, April 1934.
[41] *Ibid.*, 14 February 1934, May 1934.
[42] Figures from ADR 1m 172 and from the antifascist journal *La Flèche*. The Croix de Feu claimed 15,430 in 1936 (*Le Nouvelliste*, 11 May 1936).
[43] *La Relève*, 11 November 1930, December 1930, April 1931, January 1932.
[44] ADR 4m 236, 3 February 1934.   [45] *Le Nouvelliste*, 8 July 1934.

released to the press. Nevertheless, this elusiveness, even semi-clandestinity, is revealing. The Croix de Feu deliberately set out to create a *national* image, above parties and factions, and made little effort to tailor propaganda to the localities – *Le Flambeau du sud-est* consisted largely of extracts from La Rocque's speeches. So the local historian is obliged to draw on the league's national journal *Le Flambeau*, for this journal provided doctrine and guidance for activists in a way that the Fédération's *La Nation*, for example, did not. Furthermore, the public image of the league was not constructed by a detailed programme set out in the press, but by means of tracts, posters and terse press communiqués, and above all through the league's paramilitary demonstrations. If we look at the Croix de Feu in this way it is possible see the combination of extreme hostility to the left, of a radical drive against the establishment and paramilitarism which is typical of fascism.

A further general consideration is that in the period between the summers of 1933 and 1934 the Croix de Feu underwent a process of radicalisation. Hitherto it had been a sort of national-military lobby, pressing the government on the state of the armed forces, veterans' pensions and foreign policy.[46] Until 6 February the league remained sufficiently 'apolitical' for the military governor of Lyon and Cardinal Maurin to patronise it. Paul Chopine, national leader of the paramilitary wing of the movement until March 1934, attributed radicalisation to La Rocque's overweening ambition, developed in the course of 1933.[47] Whatever the case a significant step was taken with the setting up of the Volontaires nationaux (VN) in December 1933, which became the most dynamic wing of the movement, and claimed 600 members in Lyon and 1,500 in the region in mid-1934.[48] The expansion of the league after the riots of 6 February 1934 provoked further change, but perhaps the greatest stimulus was the failure of the Doumergue government and the simultaneous emergence of the Front commun in the late summer of 1934. We have seen that Victor Perret at this time predicted that 'men of order' would soon take matters into their own hands. It was in this period that the Croix de Feu first took to the streets in the Rhône.

A 'ferocious independence'

The refusal of the league to elaborate a programme was a part of this transformation. It also reveals the simultaneously radical and reactionary

---

[46] *Ibid.*, 13 January 1932. La Rocque's editorial in *Le Flambeau* on 1 January 1934 had been on the army.
[47] Paul Chopine, *Six ans chez les Croix de Feu* (1935), 95.
[48] *Le Nouvelliste*, 8 July 1934.

nature of the movement. One of the central concerns of the league was to present itself as independent in political and social terms.[49] In this respect the Croix de Feu was well placed simply by virtue of being a new movement, untainted by the compromises forced upon Action française and Jeunesses patriotes. But the image was also deliberately created, as the following tract distributed by the VN reveals:

> Les Volontaires Nationaux
>   sont
> Farouchement indépendants
> Solidement organisés
> Leur programme est simple
> Servir la France

This image was reinforced by independence from rival movements of the extreme right. At first the Croix de Feu had drawn some of its cadres from the Jeunesses patriotes. President of the Rhône section Louis Marchal, a medium businessman, had been a leading figure in Antoine Rédier's Légion in the mid-1920s and later the Jeunesses patriotes.[50] Colonel Chêne and Charles Favre-Gilly, both of whom had been presidents of the Jeunesses patriotes, also occupied positions in the Croix de Feu. But by mid-1934 such overlaps were much less common and in the spring of 1935 a new leadership was put in place. The new president was Maurice Freynet, who had no known political past. Concern for independence had been one reason for La Rocque's refusal to participate in the riots of 6 February. Even this was turned to advantage. One of Chopine's grievances against la Rocque was that he had managed to appropriate the glory of 6 February without having done anything on that day, cultivating the image that the Croix de Feu somehow held the fate of the nation in its hands.[51] Neither did the league adhere to the Front national, formed in June 1934 by the Jeunesses patriotes and Solidarité française, with the informal support of Action française.[52] In 1936 the Croix de Feu did not even participate in the committee which had traditionally organised the Joan of Arc parade.[53]

Pierre Milza sees the absence of contact between the Croix de Feu and the extreme right as evidence that the former was not fascist. He also makes much of links to Tardieu in 1931–2 and to the possibility that La Rocque might have saved the Laval ministry in December 1935.[54] History is of course littered with alliances between fascists and

---

[49] AN 451 AP 81, Louis Gros to President of La Tribune du Rhône.
[50] Soucy, *French Fascism*, 27–38.   [51] Paul Chopine, *Six ans.*
[52] AN F^7 13 028, 16 June 1934.   [53] ADR 1m, dossier Jeanne d'Arc, 1936.
[54] Milza, *Fascisme français*, 137.

the parliamentary right. What is more important is that, typically of fascist movements, the Croix de Feu combined collaboration with the right with denunciation. In 1934 and 1935 la Rocque's league was keen to dissociate itself from the parliamentary right. It distanced itself from the Doumergue government more rapidly than any of its rivals: la Rocque's description of it as 'a temporary dressing on the gangrene' was widely publicised in the Rhône. To be sure the dressing should not be ripped off, but the Croix de Feu should hold itself ready to clean out the wound.[55] During the election campaign of 1936 the disappointments of parliamentary 'national union governments' were contrasted with the 'real people's truce which the Croix de Feu was calling for'.[56] For La Rocque, the modéré, likened to the shirker of the War, had succeeded only in playing the game of the communists. Once the final reckoning came then at the head of the list of guilty would be the 'negligent guardians', whose 'failures and turpitude would be proclaimed and punished'.[57] Not surprisingly the Croix de Feu had fewer contacts with the Federation than the Jeunesses patriotes or even Action française.

The image of independence was further reinforced by the league's profession of neutrality towards religious faiths. In this respect the Croix de Feu represented a new departure, for hitherto any movement of the right or extreme right desirous of mobilising a popular constituency had been dependent upon the parishes. Again, 1934 was the turning point, for before then a number of clerics had been members of the league, while Cardinal Maurin himself usually attended the league's annual mass.[58] Each year on the 11 November the Croix de Feu held services in Catholic and Protestant churches and even in a synagogue. Colonel Morin-Pons, a member of the Comité directeur, was a Protestant. We shall see that the league may have won some support among anticlericals. Whether or not this was the case, it remains significant that in the mid-1930s Catholics felt the need to join 'neutral' organisations.

Rather than from the parishes, the Croix de Feu developed out of the veterans' movement. The league had originally been formed as an elite among veterans, open only to those with a distinguished war record – Marchal had been cited in the Journal officiel in 1915, and was also leader of the DRAC, an organisation which lobbied for the interests of mobilised clergy.[59] Antoine Prost rightly argues that the mass of veterans

---

[55] Le Nouvelliste, 10 February 1934.   [56] Ibid., 27 March 1936.
[57] Le Flambeau, 1 January, 6 April and 12 October 1935.
[58] Le Nouvelliste, 12 November 1933. Clerical members included the chaplain of the garrison of Lyon.
[59] La Relève, 7 December 1930.

were reluctant to follow those who attempted to use the movement for political purposes.[60] All the same, the conservative UNC in particular was essential to the growth of the Croix de Feu. Humbert Isaac, departmental president of the UNC, was personally hostile to the Croix de Feu, but was unable to prevent a fellow member of the Rhône UNC leadership using the movement to set up a Croix de Feu organisation in the Ardèche.[61] The league participated in all the events of the *ancien combattant* calendar, with the express intention of winning members.[62] Members were urged to pay special attention to the small world of regimental associations, 'where everyone knows each other and where those in search of reflected glory find it hard to bring to fruition their "personal combinations"'.[63] In the countryside some Croix de Feu groups were constituted by veterans' groups.[64] Undoubtedly this propaganda effort was successful, for with an average age of 40 in 1932, the league recruited heavily among the war generation: 31% of sympathisers were drawn from those aged 36 to 39 in 1934 who had borne the brunt of the fighting. With a departmental membership of nearly 30,000 in 1935, the veterans' groups represented an organisational resource able to rival the Church. Indeed, the Croix de Feu followed the veterans' associations in setting up bars and games rooms in its sector headquarters – an implicit threat to Church organisations.[65] Association with the veterans' movement allowed the Croix de Feu to appropriate the image, in conservative eyes, of the *génération de feu* as the incarnation of the national interest, fraternity and class collaboration. The reference to the veterans' movement also connected with the league's populism. Service in the trenches implied both submission to hierarchy and a sense of equality under fire, making the Croix de Feu both an elite defined by service to the nation and a product of the people.

Preoccupation with independence and the refusal to draw up a conventional programme revealed both a desire to overcome social and political conflict and a populist hostility to the establishment. The integrative function of Croix de Feu ideology was particularly evident in its attitude to foreign policy. La Rocque's views on the international situation were in many respects similar to those of Perret. He opposed the Russian alliance and was convinced that the 'bloody cabal' he feared so much was seeking revolution through war. Unlike Perret he left open

---

[60] Prost, *Les Ancien Combattants*, I, 193; R. Soucy, 'France: veteran politics between the wars', in *The War Generation: Veterans of the World War*, ed. S. Ward (New York, 1975), 59–99.
[61] Prost, *Les Anciens Combattants*, 165, letter of 9 June 1934.
[62] *La Relève*, November 1930, January 1931.   [63] *Ibid.*, November 1930.
[64] *Le Nouvelliste*, 9 July 1933 and 3 November 1934.
[65] ADR 4m 637, 5 March 1936; *Le Flambeau*, 3 August 1935.

the possibility of talks with Hitler once France had recovered its strength. Generally, however, the league had few positive ideas on foreign policy. Nothing at all could be done until the patriotic consciousness of the nation had been raised through reform of army and schools. The Croix de Feu was the sole alternative to communist bellicism.[66]

Populism was also present in the view that the elites were too decadent to resist Hitler.[67] Hence La Rocque's desire to appeal to the nation as a whole. He stated that 'we were endeavouring to address ourselves to all Frenchmen, without particularly distinguishing any category of citizens, motivated by the simple desire to go directly to the people, the great source of generosity, power and life'.[68] For the colonel national unity could be durable only if it brought together the people themselves rather than just political parties.[69] This implied a populist hostility to the political establishment. La Rocque claimed that Croix de Feu was superior to the old right because it valued 'action' over debate. The old right, he said, was led by individuals who were isolated from the people and unable to enthuse a crowd.[70] The 'modéré saw the "men of action" as a reproachful reflection of their own guilt and regret'.[71] Thus, taken together with the stress on action, the 'vagueness' of the Croix de Feu's programme reinforced a populist and even subversive image which implicitly set the league against the parliamentary right.

Furthermore, the stress on action over programme would seem to be one of the defining characteristics of fascism.[72] Recent work on Germany has shown that the radical momentum of Nazism came from a combination of radical activism, mobilising myth, tactical flux and leadership based on charismatic authority.[73] The Croix de Feu was of the same species. La Rocque's authority was based on his perceived special characteristics, chiefly his war record. This had supposedly given him the capacity for the long and silent reflection which would enable him to deal with the unforeseen events which were bound to confront a leader.[74] Members were bound to him by personal loyalty – Marchal

---

[66] *Le Flambeau*, 18 May, 12 October and 30 November 1935, 2 May 1936.

[67] *Ibid.*, 2 May 1936.   [68] *Ibid.*, 7 September 1935.

[69] AN 451 AP 81, Circular of 22 May 1933.   [70] *Le Flambeau*, 1 January 1935.

[71] *Ibid.*, 1 January and 12 October 1935.

[72] Mussolini stated in September 1922: 'They ask us for programmes, but there are already too many. It is not programmes that are wanting for the salvation of Italy, but men and will power.' Quoted in Mark Robson, *Italy: Liberalism and Fascism, 1870–1945*, (1992), 53.

[73] Ian Kershaw, '"Working towards the Führer". Reflections on the nature of the Hitler dictatorship', *Contemporary European History* 2 (1993), 103–18; P. Melograni, 'The myth of the Duce in fascist Italy', *Journal of Contemporary History* 12 (1976), 221–37.

[74] La Rocque, *Service Public*, 96–7.

pledged to follow la Rocque 'to the end'.[75] Accounts of his speeches emphasise the 'enthusiasm' of audience reaction to him as a person rather than the details of his political position. For example, reports in *Le Flambeau* of a rally commemorating the battle of the Marne in September 1935 speak of the order and discipline of the audience, but also record that at the end of La Rocque's speech 'a human tidal wave pushed towards the leader, in order to cry out to him their faith, their tenderness, their devotion'. As far as content was concerned, *Le Flambeau* emphasised La Rocque's belief in the ultimate victory of a movement based on the war generation.[76] Participants in the Parisian 11 November parade of 1935 were said to feel that they were 'working for a destiny which was beyond their individual understanding; that a great effort was demanded of them, that they were, as our leader has often repeated, the "executors of the lamentations of our dead" '.[77] This emphasis on emotional commitment was also connected to a palingenetic myth. La Rocque hammered home the message that France had entered upon a decisive moment in its history. In October 1935 he explained that an alliance of Freemasons and communists aimed to destroy the Croix de Feu and ultimately western civilisation by provoking violence on the streets and by using the Italian invasion of Ethiopia to foment international war. His article ended on an apocalyptic note:

In our own time, not Moscow's, we will rise up as one. What came from darkness will be returned to darkness. The blood and the suffering of our comrades will be the only justification we need. Those who seek power through civil war and European war will soon be deserted by all honest men and left only with barbarians in the pay of foreigners. Our discipline and coolness will ensure the precision and the efficacy of our acts.
We will have them![78]

Thus the Croix de Feu saw themselves as heroic individuals engaged in a struggle against decadence, working for an ill-defined national regeneration, guided by a charismatic leader and deriving legitimacy from the fallen of the Great War.

Of course, caution must be exercised in making comparisons between the Croix de Feu and fascist movements in Germany and Italy. The mobilising myths propagated by La Rocque and his acolytes were less dissolvant of the existing order. La Rocque did not share Hitler's international expansionism. Nor was his opposition to the established political order as systematic as that of Hitler. But it is in the context of

---

[75] *Le Nouvelliste*, 21 October 1933, 23 January 1934; Chopine, *Six ans*, 89–91, 143.
[76] *Le Flambeau*, 5 October and 16 November 1935.   [77] *Ibid.*, 16 November 1935.
[78] *Ibid.*, 12 October 1935.

such beliefs, together with the paramilitary organisation of the league, that the specific constitutional projects of the league must be analysed.

The Croix de Feu and the Republic

One of the crucial questions concerning the Croix de Feu is whether it was respectful of democracy and pluralism. If it was, then the movement could be placed in Burrin's national-populist category. If not then this would be additional, though not conclusive, evidence for the fascism of the league. Certainly La Rocque denied that he was a fascist, protested his loyalty to the Republic and claimed that he only wished to see parliament infused with the spirit of 'public service'.[79] Two preliminary comments can be made. First, Mussolini made a decisive break with the old order only after painful struggle between radicals and moderates. The attitude of fascists to the liberal state is therefore complex, and it is in the very nature of fascism both to oppose and to overlap with conventional right-wing movements. Second, the protestation of loyalty to the Republic cannot be taken at face value, for by the 1930s the idea of the Republic was deeply contested. It had been appropriated by movements like the Jeunesses patriotes in order to distinguish themselves from the royalist Action française. And since the days of Déroulède republicanism had expressed the populist claims of radical right. Thus the demonstrators of 6 February had sung the *Marseillaise* as they attempted to break into the Chamber of Deputies.

The Croix de Feu's constitutional proposals were set out in *Le Flambeau du sud-est* by VN leader André Rossignol.[80] The lynchpin was a strong presidency, whose mode of election was never mentioned. The president's function would be to arbitrate conflicting interests expressed through a corporative system. Parliament would occupy only a secondary role. Corporations would be based on 'depoliticised' syndicates, which would be forbidden to organise on the national level. Also included were measures such as proportional representation, reduction in the number of deputies, extra votes for fathers of families and votes for women. There is nothing intrinsically fascist about these proposals. The league's constitutional projects were similar to those of Tardieu and the Fédération, though it should be remembered that those schemes were based on a desire to exclude permanently the left from power. But almost identical constitutional schemes were elaborated by movements generally seen as fascist, such as Solidarité française and the supposedly

---

[79] La Rocque, *Service Public*, 254–8; *Le Flambeau*, 1 January 1935.
[80] *Le Flambeau du sud-est*, 15 October 1934; *Le Flambeau*, 1 October 1933; La Rocque, *Service Public*, 196–216.

fascist dissidents who left the 'too conservative' Croix de Feu in the autumn of 1935.[81] And a harder edge was added by the declared intention to outlaw the 'generators of disorder' (the communists and probably the socialists).[82] In view of such ambiguities, the constitutional schemes of the Croix de Feu must be looked at in the context of the league's wider discourse. In fact, compared to supposedly fascist groups like Solidarité française the Croix de Feu devoted relatively little attention to constitutional projects. La Rocque argued that because the parliamentary right was 'too feeble to breathe a new spirit into the young generation, it confined itself to drawing up procedures and constitutions as detailed as they are inapplicable'.[83] Thus the Croix de Feu sought to present itself as a movement which acted rather than talked and thereby to distinguish itself from the old right.

Also, the language of the Croix de Feu blurred the distinction between hostility to the system as it functioned and the principle of democracy. In his *Service public* La Rocque drew upon a long-standing conservative critique of democracy. Electoralism, he said, led to the triumph of short-termism, demagogy and materialism over the interests of the nation. One should therefore reform the Republic. But he also denounced 'the disgrace of our institutions, political corruption and the waste since 1918 of so much generosity'.[84] This ambiguity was reflected in the propaganda of the league in the Rhône, where Rossignol asked 'do you really believe in the luxury of our present parliamentary system, which has resolved none of the problems of the day, problems which will become the anguishing realities of tomorrow?'[85] In the light of pronouncements it *could* be argued that the Croix de Feu opposed not the Republic but those who ran it. Doubtless the Croix de Feu told themselves this, for otherwise they risked assimilation to the royalists. The problem was that Republican institutions were made up of people, so the terms in which its personnel were denounced spilled over into hostility to the regime. For example, an activist in Lyon announced that 'this movement has decided to cleanse the country of the troublesome elements which are stirring it up in order to ensure for France a life of order and honour: freemasonry is the principle agent of the disarray in our country'.[86] This parallels La Rocque's belief in a 'bloody cabal' of Marxists, capitalists and Freemasons, dedicated to the destruction of western civilisation.[87] In effect the political class was identified with a group of antinational conspirators.

---

[81] *Solidarité française du sud-est*, 7 February and 12 March 1934.
[82] *Le Flambeau*, 25 November 1935.   [83] *Ibid.*, 1 January 1935.
[84] La Rocque, *Service Public*, 78–92.   [85] *Le Flambeau du sud-est*, October 1934.
[86] *Le Nouvelliste*, 19 June 1935.   [87] *Le Flambeau*, 1 February 1935.

From here it was a short step to the belief that the established authorities were illegitimate. This assumption was evident in La Rocque's contrast between the 'popularity' expressed behind the curtain of the polling booth and that of a 'great mass movement' which was the product of a 'mandate which could not be resold in Parliament or in the profitable enterprises of spa towns (for example)'.[88] In March 1934 he told his followers in Lyon that 'the Palais Bourbon might be an episode [in a career], but it could never be worth a war record'.[89] Thus the veterans and the Croix de Feu were placed on a higher plane where they alone were the guardians of morality and the national interest. One activist could therefore describe himself as an old soldier returning to service to save France for a second time: 'to remake France as pure as it was for four and a half years'.[90] This puts the league's commitment to 'legal' action in a different light. Thus La Rocque had followed many others on the extreme right in portraying the riots of 6 February as a response to an attempted coup on the part of Daladier. Rioting therefore became a 'legal' means of overthrowing a cabinet.[91] He also threatened that patriots might once again take upon themselves tasks more usually reserved to the state.[92] Thus there was within Croix de Feu discourse a quasi-insurrectionary current, clearly expressed in Louis Marchal's contention that honest men were not obliged to follow those with dirty hands.[93]

This raises the question of how the Croix de Feu envisaged the conquest of power. The notion that renovation could come from within the system was rejected. The Croix de Feu expected little from the parties of the right. The league itself could not have won power by constitutional means, for it refused to participate in elections. During the campaign for the 1936 elections *Le Flambeau du sud-est* declared that it did not expect renovation to come from a failed electoral system, but that the league would nonetheless attempt to ensure that good candidates were put forward.[94] La Rocque was in the difficult position of having to defend legality from outside the system. He therefore hoped that the government would be brought to its knees by its inability to cope with growing disorder. But it would not fall of its own accord. The Croix de Feu had to display an image of collective and disciplined strength, through its paramilitary demonstrations, and the 'idol with feet of clay' would collapse and the league would be called into government.[95] In this way La Rocque sought to reconcile concern for order

[88] *Ibid.*, 11 November 1935.   [89] *Le Nouvelliste*, 21 March 1934.
[90] *Ibid.*, 4 October 1935.   [91] La Rocque, *Service public*, 260.
[92] *Le Flambeau*, 10 December 1935.   [93] *Le Nouvelliste*, 23 January 1934.
[94] *Le Flambeau du sud-est*, April 1936.
[95] *Ibid.*, 1 January 1935 (La Rocque's editorial and an interview reprinted from *Candide*); *Le Flambeau*, 16 March 1935.

and legality with the expression of popular hostility to the status quo. Transformation of the political system would, nevertheless, be achieved outside of the normal electoral process and by the implicit threat of physical force. Stronger measures were not, however, entirely ruled out. This was implicit in Louis Marchal's defence of the Croix de Feu's 'passivity' on 6 February: '[our calm] conforms to the orders of the Croix de Feu, which is "not to become involved in any agitation unless it is a strong action which will succeed"'.[96]

Whether, as some historians have maintained, La Rocque himself lacked the nerve to take power is impossible to say, even with the benefit of hindsight. But what is certain is that La Rocque's own discourse was deeply ambiguous. On the one hand he multiplied endlessly his strictures against premature action. On the other he sought to mobilise his supporters through a rhetoric of H-Hour and constant 'states of alert' and mobilisations. At the Marne demonstration of September 1935 La Rocque urged his troops to hold themselves ready for all eventualities: 'I am certain that the coming winter will be decisive both for the world and for France. I am convinced too that France will be saved.'[97] The hour of decision would come during the Croix de Feu's next campaign of paramilitary mobilisations, not during the general elections of April–May 1936. Here again we see one of the defining characteristics of fascism – in Roger Griffin's terms the sense of living through a decisive turning point in human history, out of which national regeneration would emerge.

Paramilitarism

Far from representing a superficial borrowing from foreign movements, paramilitarism was an essential part of La Rocque's strategy for power in that it was meant to demonstrate the movement's fitness to govern.[98] Members of the paramilitary organisation doubtless also expected to play a significant role in the new France, especially as La Rocque was committed to 'depoliticisation' of the CGT and purge of the administration. La Rocque's view, nevertheless, was a cautious one. In order to create an image of discipline he opposed 'premature' actions, which he claimed would cause the league to fall into a Popular Front trap.[99] As Irvine and Soucy have argued, La Rocque was conscious of the relative weakness of the far right in France. A further reason for restraint was

[96] *Le Nouvelliste*, 15 February 1934.
[97] Extract from *Le Figaro*, reprinted in *Le Flambeau*, 5 October 1935.
[98] Rémond, *Les Droites*, 290; Milza, *Fascisme français*, 135-6.
[99] *Service public*, 9–13, 261; *Le Flambeau*, 18 July, 1835.

that he aimed not just to overawe communist supporters but also to win their hearts and minds. The league could not therefore 'attack the prodigal sons of the motherland'.[100] But in practice La Rocque's desire to keep tight control over his movement proved difficult.

The tactic of paramilitary mobilisation was perfected in the late summer and autumn of 1934. Part of the impetus was provided by changing fortunes in the struggle for the streets. The experience of Lyon would seem to be paradigmatic. During the 6 February crisis an Action française activist had been able to boast that 'the streets belong to us'.[101] The following period was marked by a series of demonstrations and often violent clashes between left and right. In the summer the police warned the Interior Ministry of 'a certain anxiety' amongst the population caused by the extent of agitation, disorder and violence.[102] In 1934 and 1935 firearms were used on at least nine occasions, there were two deaths, and a number of serious injuries. It is striking that the leagues quickly lost the initiative to the left. There were many complaints of disruption of meetings of the right and far right by antifascists, 'in circumstances which turn each demonstration into a bloody riot'.[103] In March Action française cancelled a meeting in the 6th arrondissement after receiving threats from the left. Several activists turned up anyway and one royalist was injured by a bullet in the shoulder.[104] At about this time the Jeunesses patriotes and Action française were reportedly holding talks with the Croix de Feu and certain veterans' groups with a view to organising protection for their meetings.[105] The most spectacular confirmation of the new balance of forces came on 20 June 1934 when antifascists mounted a large and violent demonstration against a meeting held jointly by the Jeunesses patriotes, Solidarité française and Action française. The star speaker, Jean Renaud of Solidarité française, was outraged that only 200 had turned out to hear him, but he thanked those who had not been 'too frightened' to come.[106] This fiasco marked the effective end of the influence of the participant movements in Lyon. After this date Action française carried on a private, and sometimes deadly, war against Gaston Bergery's Front social.[107] But neither

[100] Interview with La Rocque in *Candide*, reprinted in *Le Flambeau*, 1 January 1935; La Rocque, *Service public*, 88; *Le Flambeau*, 2 November and 1 February 1935.
[101] *La République lyonnaise*, 20 Jan. 1934.
[102] AN F[7] 13 028, 3 July 1934; *Le Nouvelliste*, 3 October 1934.
[103] *La République lyonnaise*, 14 July 1934; *L'Alerte*, September 1934.
[104] *Lyon républicain*, 8 March 1934; *La République lyonnaise*, 10 March 1934.
[105] AN F[7] 13 238, 13 April 1934.
[106] *Ibid.*, 19 March, 5 April and 18, 22 and 25 June 1934. One person died in the demonstration.
[107] AN F[7] 13 028, 30 June 1934; *Le Nouvelliste*, 28 June 1934. See *Le Nouvelliste*, 15 March 1935 for a royalist attack on a Marc Sangnier meeting.

movement, engaging as they did in dispersed and ill-disciplined street action, was a credible anticommunist force. These developments coincided with growing disillusion with the Doumergue government, which amongst other things was held to be unable to keep order.[108]

Croix de Feu meetings too were subject to disruption all over France, though in Lyon the league made little public showing in the first half of 1934.[109] It was against this background that on 7 July 1934 La Rocque instructed that meetings would henceforth be organised without prior public notice, as they had been in Paris and Marseille in the previous June. He stressed the need for surprise in choice of date and place – more important even than the attraction of a large audience. Meetings would be precisely and discreetly organised, unexpected and frequent. Police reports indicate that in the same period La Rocque ordered that in case of 'serious events' in any part of the country local leaders were to convoke all members. They were to assemble on the outskirts of the town, where drivers would receive sealed envelopes containing their destination, which were to be opened in the course of the journey. The eventual destination would be unknown even to the regional leaders. Further circulars indicated that La Rocque himself would in future arrive unannounced at meetings, and gave precise details for the preparation of such occasions.[110] In October the police in Lyon reported that regional leaders had sworn to obey 'without understanding and without discussion the orders of Paris'.[111]

It is well known that the Croix de Feu was organised in a paramilitary fashion. In early 1931 the main affiliates of the league, the Croix de Feu et Briscards and the Fils et filles des Croix de Feu set up paramilitary organisations known as 'Disponibles', or 'Dispos' for short. Then in December 1933 the VN were formed as a sort of volunteer corps linked to the Dispos.[112] Equivalent groups in other organisations sold newspapers and provided security at meetings – as in the case of the Camelots du Roi and Commissaires de l'Action française. But the Dispos were also a sort of citizens militia, ready to act in the event of grave danger. Elaborate plans were laid for such an eventuality. The Dispos themselves

[108] *L'Union républicaine*, 15 July 1934.
[109] At Asnières (AN F⁷ 13 028, report of 7 July 1934); Livry-Gargan (AN F⁷ 12 968, report of 12 May 1934).
[110] AN 451 AP 81, circulars of 18 July 1934 and 4 September 1935; AN 451 AP 85, minutes of the Grasse sub-section, 3 May 1934, 1 June 1934 for the organisation of meetings; AN F⁷ 13 028, 27 October 1934. See also Weng Ting Lung, 'L'Historique et la doctrine des Croix de Feu et du Parti Social Français', (thèse de droit, Nice, 1970), 48–51.
[111] AN F⁷ 13 028, 27 October 1934.
[112] In January 1934 the VN absorbed the Fils et Filles des Croix de Feu and the Regroupement national autour des Croix de Feu.

were periodically put on states of alert, during which they were obliged to attend local offices. The Dispos were organised into 'hands' of five men, and into groups of three hands. The Croix de Feu and VN themselves were often organised in the same way.[113]

Many of the league's mobilisations conformed to the pattern desired by La Rocque. These included major nationwide events such as the annual commemorating of the battle of the Marne. In September 1935 5,000 Croix de Feu from all over the south-east assembled at Grand-Lemps (Isère). Pierre-Joseph Arminjon, a *Nouvelliste* journalist who accompanied the column from Lyon, described enthusiastically how the manœuvre had been organised in scrupulous secrecy at twenty-four hours notice.[114] The whole thing went off in perfect order. Yet the significance of this kind of manœuvre should not be underestimated. In 1937 Arminjon was to describe with the same boyish enthusiasm his participation in a squad which helped break a strike of farm workers in the department of the Marne. He described the following exchange when he reported for duty:

– Are you afraid of a fight?
– I am a former . . . well . . . 'dissolved' if you like.
– Good, good; but be careful: no politics. You are here only to save the harvest.[115]

The Marne mobilisation was more than a mere picnic. Whatever La Rocque's intention, it is hardly credible that such manœuvres were not seen by participants as preparation for future action. This was the view of Paul Chopine who left the league partly, he said, because La Rocque was leading the movement towards civil war and fascism.[116]

Neither should the significance of the second type of Croix de Feu mobilisation be underestimated – the large-scale set-piece parade in the centre of the city. The order of march for the Joan of Arc Parade of May 1936 was extremely detailed. At the head of the column were six cars, followed by twelve cyclists and twenty-four Dispos in two ranks of twelve. The body of the parade was protected by files of Dispos on each side of the street. Marchers were to wear a jacket, medals, arm-bands and insignia.[117] The military tone was emphasised by the fact that the Croix de Feu column directly followed that of the army. The standard of Croix de Feu became visible in the Avénue Maréchal-Foch just as that of the 9th regiment of *cuirassiers* disappeared.[118] The purpose of such

[113] AN BB[18] 3048[2], report of 31 June 1936; Chopine, *Six ans*, 130, 149–50.
[114] *Le Nouvelliste*, 23 September 1935.   [115] *Ibid.*, 28 July 1937.
[116] Chopine, *Six ans*, 161–5.
[117] ADR 1m 172, 16 May and 11 November 1935, May 1936.
[118] *Le Nouvelliste*, 11 May 1936.

demonstrations was first to impose 'respect on those who might be tempted to cause trouble. The events we are experiencing oblige us to show our cohesion and discipline.'[119] Secondly, such parades were an implicit reply to those of the Popular Front. The point was taken by the *Nouvelliste*, which described the 1936 Joan of Arc parade thus:

Those who had witnessed the passage of the communist hordes on Mayday were profoundly impressed by the contrast. Whereas the Muscovites had paraded in indescribable disorder, behind their red flags and hate-filled banners, screaming the 'Internationale', and hurling insults at a whole section of the population, the Croix de Feu marched in an order and silence which made a profound impression on the crowd.[120]

The parade was an allegory of a society in which hierarchy and military discipline would be applied to civil society. The distinctively fascist character emerges from the implication that such reforms would be brought about through mass mobilisation in a paramilitary formation.

A second category of demonstrations involved the unannounced appearance of a paramilitary formation in the centre of Lyon. Since the supposedly secret instructions for the first such rally fell into the hands of an antifascist newspaper we are well informed about it. The plan was for two days of events, to be camouflaged behind a fund-raising sale and a musical evening. On the morning of Saturday 22 December la Rocque was to arrive unannounced by plane. Dispos were to assemble at Place Tolozan (overlooking the town hall), from where they would depart for a rally at Bourgoin in Isère. They would keep badges and arm-bands in their pockets until the order to don them came from section leaders. Members were warned to take 'no personal initiative'.[121] In the event things did not go as planned. On Saturday morning *Lyon républicain* appealed for a 'riposte ouvrière et démocratique' at Place Tolozan.[122] At the last moment the organisers changed the assembly point, but a number of Croix de Feu went to Place Tolozan where they were met by a hostile crowd. The demonstration was not, however, a complete fiasco, for 200 Dispos were able to set off from the alternative destination. On the following day 3,000 people heard la Rocque speak at a cinema in Lyon.[123] A circular from Marchal announced that the affair had proved that the Croix de Feu were a force against which attempts at revolution would be broken.[124]

Other mobilisations, perhaps the most notorious, took the form of sorties into working-class suburbs, probably organised on departmental initiative. As the orders for one motorcade put it, 'the greatest secrecy

[119] ADR 1m 172, 11 November 1935.   [120] *Le Nouvelliste* 11 May 1936.
[121] *La Flèche*, 29 December 1934.   [122] *Lyon républicain*, 22 December 1934.
[123] ADR 4m 236, 26 December 1934.   [124] *La Flèche*, 19 January 1935.

must be maintained in order to retain the advantage of surprise'.[125] In 1935 there were a series of expeditions to such destinations as St Etienne, Villefranche, Vienne and Givors. The St Etienne motorcade, in which 500 Dispos travelled in a convoy of 104 cars, was probably the most impressive after the Marne commemoration.[126] In late August 1935 a caravan of Dispos arrived in the industrial commune of Décines, a few kilometres to the west of Lyon in Isère. They proceeded to fill the town and according to the mayor to annoy the inhabitants. A counter-demonstration was rapidly organised. As the Dispos emerged from a meeting projectiles were thrown and revolver shots exchanged. A number of Croix de Feu were injured and their cars damaged.[127] It is difficult not to see an intimidatory purpose in such activities. The unexpected arrival of a motorised and highly organised convoy of Dispos in an overwhelmingly working-class area, in a period when cars were still a rare sight outside of affluent city centres, cannot be interpreted in any other way. When the extreme social and political segregation of the Lyonnais agglomeration is taken into account, along with the concentra-tion of Croix de Feu membership in the bourgeois centre of the city, then motorcades take on the character almost of an invasion of a foreign country. They were also a riposte to increasingly frequent left-wing demonstrations in the centre of the city. Burrin's distinction between the Croix de Feu's desire merely to intimidate the left, and the deliberate provocation of disorder on the part of the Nazis, is meaningless. The league could and did provoke disorder.[128] Indeed, the image of disciplined strength desired by La Rocque was undermined by the league's populist claim to carry out tasks of which the government was believed to be incapable, and by definition of the league's enemies as antinational criminals. Also, in order to constitute itself as a national movement it had through its mobilisations to demonstrate its ability to bring the *banlieue rouge* back into the nation. The problem was that it came up against an equally problematic claim on the part of the communists to hegemony over the same areas. Disorder was the inevitable result.

Sometimes La Rocque found it difficult to keep his movement under control. Its members were, like those of rival movements, engaged in 'routine' conflicts such as those between paper sellers in the rue République. Chance meetings of leaguers and antifascists sometimes got

---

[125]   *Ibid.*, 26 January 1935; PV Conseil municipale Décines, 27 January 1936.
[126]   ADR 4m 235, June 1935.
[127]   PV Conseil municipale Décines, 27 January 1936 (thanks to Annie Grange for this information). *Lyon républicain*, 21 September 1935.
[128]   Burrin, *La Dérive fasciste*, 191–2.

out of hand. In Villefranche in the summer of 1934, a young metal worker who was a member of both the VN and Action française shot a member of the SFIO youth group.[129] In November 1935 four Dispos returning from a demonstration got out of their car to rip down antifascist posters in Villeurbanne, whereupon they were shot at by a procommunist café owner. One of the Dispos was seriously injured in the face.[130] In general, however, La Rocque's strictures against individual action seem to have restrained his followers.

Dissidence was expressed rather through calls for La Rocque to commit the movement as a whole to action. Police reports nationally throughout 1935 speak of a broad opposition to the 'inaction' of La Rocque which had the support even of his right-hand man, Ottavi.[131] In September Pierre Pucheu, Bertrand de Maudhuy and their followers quit the VN.[132] In Lyon too there were many reports of conflict among the Croix de Feu, and of opposition to Marchal and his right-hand man, Morin-Pons. In March 1935 Le Flambeau announced that Marchal had been promoted to regional leader, leaving Morin-Pons in charge in the Rhône. But the next issue stated that this had been a secretarial error, and that the changes had merely been proposed by Marchal to the national Administrative Council. At the end of the following month Marchal and Morin-Pons were sacked. Eugène Rouillon took over the region and Maurice Freynet the Rhône. The issues involved are unclear.[133]

Dissent within the Croix de Feu resurfaced during its paramilitary campaign of November and December 1935, described above. There is indirect evidence to suggest that mobilisations were being organised on local initiative. In Le Flambeau La Rocque repeated endlessly his strictures against premature action. He ordered that all meetings should henceforth be notified to headquarters in Paris, ostensibly so that La Rocque himself would have the opportunity to make a surprise visit, and forbade sorties outside section territory.[134] The culmination of the crisis came on 3 December 1935, when, in the Chamber of Deputies, the Croix de Feu deputy Jean Ybarnégaray agreed with Blum that both sides would disarm their followers. La Rocque subsequently toured the

---

[129] ADR 4m 269, report of the Sub-Prefect of Villefranche; La République lyonnaise, 21 July 1934.
[130] Lyon républicain, Le Nouvelliste, 28 and 29 November 1935.
[131] AN F⁷ 13 241, reports of 13 June, 11 July and 30 November 1935; Fonds La Rocque, AN 451 AP 85, minutes of the meetings of the sub-section of Grasse.
[132] Howlett, 'La Rocque', 157–62. For the manifesto of the dissidents, La République, 29 September 1935.
[133] Le Flambeau, 23 and 30 March 1935; Le Nouvelliste, 28 April 1935; Lyon républicain, 30 March 1935.
[134] AN 451 AP 81, circulars of 30 September and 19 October 1935.

country in order to reinforce central direction. On 19 December he stated in Lyon that 'if by any chance anyone has infiltrated our ranks in order to search for an adventure or in the hope of violent acts on our part, then they can quit the movement'.[135] At the same time a poster proclaimed that 'the Croix de Feu does not generate disorder. It does not wish to provoke anyone.'[136] La Rocque's strategy had backfired. Rather than appearing to middle opinion as a force for order, the Croix de Feu seemed to be a subversive movement. Paramilitary mobilisations were temporarily suspended until the summer of 1936.

The place occupied by violence in the Croix de Feu was complex. It owed something to both the Italian fascists and the Nazis. The idea of mass mobilisations was borrowed from Mussolini, but whereas the Squadristi were prepared to evict left-wing municipalities, the Croix de Feu stopped short of investing town halls. Like those of the Nazis, Croix de Feu demonstrations were designed rather to overawe opponents and to win converts by presenting the league as the only force capable of defeating the left.[137] In this respect Croix de Feu tactics also owed something to the Faisceau of Georges Valois, which also used mass meetings and H-hour rhetoric.[138] The Croix de Feu differed from the Nazis in degree, for it was clearly less violent. But just as the Nazis found that SA violence sometimes became counter-productive, so La Rocque faced problems. Again the most important point of comparison, however, is that there was something particularly fascist about Croix de Feu paramilitarism. It can be seen in the peculiar combination of reaction, evident in the fact that mobilisations were clearly directed against the left, with the populist claim that they represented a movement of the people. This in turn was coupled to a drive to impose its ill-defined world-view through mass mobilisation. The same features can be seen in the league's social programme.

The social programme of the Croix de Feu

The Croix de Feu sought to create a new national community through mass mobilisation in a militarised movement. A populist programme of this nature necessarily had repercussions beyond the political sphere, for it is impossible to separate the people/state opposition from other sources of contradiction such as class, gender or religion. We must

---

[135] *Le Nouvelliste* and *Le Nouveau Journal*, 20 December 1935.
[136] *Le Nouveau Journal*, 3 December 1935.
[137] R. Bessel, *Political Violence and the Rise of Nazism* (1984).
[138] A. Douglas, 'Fascist violence in France. The case of the Faisceau', *Journal of Contemporary History* 19 (1984), 689–712.

therefore turn our attention to the social programme of the Croix de Feu. In order to avoid anticipating the argument of the following chapter, two issues will be dealt with here: Milza's contention that the Croix de Feu's ideas represented a traditional Catholic paternalism and the role of the state in Croix de Feu discourse, for Milza also argues that the hostility of the Croix de Feu to state intervention in the economy disqualified it from being fascist.[139]

Croix de Feu discourse was suffused with anticapitalism. La Rocque held that international capitalism, behind which could be found the City of London, was part of a conspiracy which also included Freemasons and the Third International. This unholy alliance sought European war, civil war in France and ultimately the collapse of western civilisation.[140] In the Rhône the message that the Croix de Feu were 'free from the influence of parties and politicians and against high international finance' was hammered home in countless tracts.[141] Of course, anticapitalism had its limits and was as contradictory as any other aspect of the league. In effect big capitalists were being blamed, like politicians, for the emergence of a threat to privilege and property. Yet Croix de Feu anticapitalism was connected with real sources of tension within the right.

For this reason the Croix de Feu social programme cannot be seen as a traditional social Catholic paternalism. It is true that La Rocque drew on ideas long familiar to the right. He spoke favourably of the need to rebuild a sense of tradition, referred to the French nation as an 'organism' and wanted to revive such *ancien régime* curiosities as the right of 'remonstrance'.[142] Yet on closer inspection La Rocque's social ideas turn out to have been as paradoxical as other aspects of the league. There was little explicit mention of religion in *Service public*, and still less in the party press. This stemmed from the desire to present the league as a truly national movement. All the same it is evident that La Rocque was influenced by ideas current in social Catholic circles. But the weakness of the Milza thesis is that by the 1930s the social Catholic tradition itself had become subdivided to include elements which opposed traditional paternalism. Indeed, we have seen that some varieties of social Catholicism combined populism and anticommunism in such a way as to create affinities with the radical right.

The ambiguity of the social Catholic heritage can be seen in La Rocque's views on social hierarchy. He spoke in terms which superficially resembled the Legitimists. Excessive ambition combined with unemployment had created an anarchic battle for material existence

[139] Milza, *Fascisme français*, 137.   [140] *Le Flambeau*, 13 April and 21 September 1935.
[141] ADR 4m 236, tract of December 1935. *Le Nouvelliste*, 4 October 1935.
[142] La Rocque, *Service public*, 129, 208–10,

which fomented class struggle and damaged the health of the social organism. But the Legitimists had used organicism to underpin a world-view in which the well-being of society depended on constituent elements sticking to their allotted spheres.[143] La Rocque on the contrary saw the social organism as naturally unstable, resembling a mixture of liquids of different densities and agitated by contradictory currents in which some elements were rising and others falling. The task of the state was to keep this struggle for existence from damaging the nation. Furthermore, differences in rank could be justified only by services rendered to the collectivity. A position based on inheritance, speculation or unproductiveness was illegitimate.[144] In other words, La Rocque's ideas emerged from a flux of traditionalist ideas about order and hierarchy, and liberal and social Darwinist ideas of competition and struggle. The result was a synthesis which reinforced the paradoxical nature of the movement. In the following chapter we shall see that the movement's ideas about corporatism were constructed partly out of traditionalist materials, but that like the Croix de Feu the PSF quoted with approval the socialist revisionist Henri De Man.[145]

The Croix de Feu's view of the state was equally ambiguous. Milza identifies fascism with a maximalist view of state power implicitly based on the totalitarian theory. In fact the question of state intervention was a matter of controversy among fascists in Germany and Italy.[146] La Rocque's view was nuanced. He distinguished between the need for a strong state able to keep order and prepare the nation for war, but called for self-government by the professions in the economic sphere, the economic 'organism' being refractory to regulation.[147] But even La Rocque rejected liberal doctrines as permitting the development of an irresponsible and parasitic capitalism. He called for the state to take upon itself the task of arbitration, inspection and punishment.[148] Another writer defined his opposition to 'étatisme' still more paradoxi-cally as the subjection of the state to private interests, permitted by manipulation of the masses through 'electoralism'. Defined thus 'étatism' meant *weakening* of the state. So to fight 'étatism' it would be necessary to restore the primacy of the state over individual interests![149]

[143] R. R. Locke, *French Legitimists and the Politics of Moral Order* (Princeton, 1974), 154–69.
[144] La Rocque, *Service public*, 117–22, 124–8.
[145] *Le Flambeau*, 2 March and 13 April 1935.
[146] D. Roberts, *Italian Fascism and the Syndicalist Tradition*, 304–5; J. Noakes and G. Pridham, *Nazism 1919–1945* I: *The Rise to Power 1919–1934* (Exeter, 1983), 66–7.
[147] La Rocque, *Service public*, 139, 197–8.
[148] La Rocque, *Service public*, 139–40, 148; *Le Flambeau*, 1 January 1935.
[149] *Le Flambeau*, 2 March 1935.

In the Rhône André Rossignol called for 'a strong state, free from the dictatorship of money, free from the occult dictatorship of the lodges which today govern us and which pursue mysterious international goals' – in other words a state with increased power to regulate the economy.[150] Furthermore, in the context of the intense interest-group conflict of the mid-1930s corporatism too contained a potential for authoritarianism. La Rocque held interest groups responsible for the failure of a parliament to resolve the economic crisis.[151] He sought through corporatism and restored state authority to reconcile them with the general interest, and permit them to play the determining role in regenerating deficient institutions.[152]

It is not therefore surprising that the Croix de Feu programme of 1936 recognised that the state would have initially to take a leading, if indirect, role in the establishment of the *profession organisée*. La Rocque took care to stress that even when fully established the organised profession would not have a direct legislative role, for this would permit special interests to carve out a sphere of influence.[153] The state would always in the last resort decide contentious issues. The league also envisaged state control over the Bank of France and measures to reduce the influence of financial institutions over private enterprise. The most important point, however, is that the Croix de Feu envisaged a decisive break with the institutions of the liberal parliamentary system. Again the fascism of the Croix de Feu can be seen in the combination of reaction in the call for depoliticisation of trade unions with radicalism in the form of mass mobilisation through corporatism. Hence the Croix de Feu's belief that the Croix de Feu must 'encadre' new rural corporatist bodies. All of this implied intervention in the economic and social spheres on the part of a state that was truly independent and representative of the people.

The activists of the Croix de Feu

Of course, the state could never have been genuinely independent. Rather we are dealing with what historically situated individuals *thought* a neutral state would look like. This means that the Croix de Feu demands for a new relationship between state and people must be seen in the light of the concerns of party activists and sympathisers. There is relatively little information on the types of people who joined the Croix de Feu. Nevertheless, it is possible to derive some tentative conclusions

[150] *Le Flambeau du sud-est*, 15 October 1934.
[151] Passmore, 'The French Third Republic', 427–33.
[152] La Rocque, *Service public*, 81–3.   [153] *Ibid.*, 211–12.

by comparing a small (unrandom) sample of Croix de Feu activists with the wealth of detail available on the PSF.

The Croix de Feu was an overwhelmingly bourgeois and petty bourgeois movement. No less than 59% of those resident in the conurbation lived in wealthy areas as defined by Jean-Luc Pinol. Most members were drawn from the ruling class, the urban lower middle class and from 1935 the peasantry. There is no evidence of substantial working-class support. At the other end of the social scale there is little evidence of open support from the Lyonnais big-business elite. Morin-Pons was a member of a well-known banking family. But he was excluded from the movement in April 1935. Indeed, in the course of 1934 and 1935 the Croix de Feu nationally distanced itself from too visible representatives of big capital such as Ernest Mercier and François de Wendel.[154] Whether big business financed the league in the Rhône is impossible to say, but since every other right-wing political movement received such money, it would be surprising if it had not got its share. In sum, a few Lyonnais big businessmen turned to the Croix de Feu, perhaps seeing it as a means of restoring lost influence in local politics. But they were not able to dominate it.

Given that the Croix de Feu recruited relatively few big businessmen or industrial workers, it would be tempting to see it as an expression of lower-middle-class hostility to both capital and labour. Populism must however be understood in relation to all of the conflicts of the right, so the Croix de Feu was able to draw upon a broad coalition of groups which opposed both the communists and the political establishment. Such conflicts were sometimes personal, and usually beyond the reach of the historian. A rare insight comes from the case of Jacques Morel-Journel, who in 1935 led the Croix de Feu in the Beaujolais. He was the brother of the Chamber of Commerce president, but lived as a bourgeois landowner in a commune near Villefranche and was reputed to have resented his exclusion from the family business.[155]

There is also some evidence to confirm Müller's identification of the Croix de Feu with the demands for representation on the part of emergent social groups.[156] Senior managers and salaried engineers, for example, were important within the Croix de Feu. A particularly revealing example, for it brings together personal antipathies with wider concerns, is that of Marcel Canat de Chizy, company secretary at the

---

[154] Philippe Mâchefer, 'Les Croix de Feu' confirms that in the course of 1935 La Rocque attempted to secure the independence of the Croix de Feu from financiers like Pierre Pucheu and Ernest Mercier.
[155] *Journal d'Henry Morel-Journel*, 21 November 1929.
[156] Müller, 'French fascism', 89ff.

Société lyonnaise du textil. Canat did not get on with Henry Morel-Journel, one of the chief shareholders in the firm.[157] He defended the abortive entente project in the silk industry on the grounds that it gave engineers like himself a greater say in business matters. Canat's suspicion of the business elite was shaped too by his role as president of the Catholic engineers association, USIC, an organisation which was to play a significant role in the 'cadres' movement after 1936. The Croix de Feu also won the support of bosses of medium to large family firms. Some belonged to sectors which had been favourable to the Tardieu reforms. Two were bosses of medium engineering firms, a sector which had traditionally supported the anticlerical moderate right and which was to be substantially overrepresented in the PSF.

But the Croix de Feu's recruitment was eclectic. It also included businessmen from older branches of the economy, including one representative of the luxury branch of the silk industry. In fact the league drew upon medium firms in general, reflecting the growing hostility to large firms evident since the onset of the depression. We have seen that medium firms had good reason to feel unrepresented either by the Chamber of Commerce or by established political parties. There were, of course, important conflicts of interest among medium business. But in the Croix de Feu they were obscured by corporatism, refusal to pronounce on detailed policy issues, and paramilitary activism. We shall see that as the PSF turned into a conventional political party, conflicts between business interests began to emerge as the leadership opted for the concerns of the progressive wing of the bourgeoisie. Such a development might have already been underway in the days of the Croix de Feu. Activists lived most often in the areas of the old bourgeoisie in the 2nd arrondissement rather than in the progressive 6th. But qualitative evidence suggests that by 1935 the 6th arrondissement was beginning to outstrip the 2nd, as it did in the PSF.[158]

The Croix de Feu must also be placed in the context of the mobilisation of subordinate sections of the right. In the countryside from late 1935 the league began to profit from the breakdown of notable politics. We have already seen that the veterans' movement played a part in this process, illustrating its importance in the development of peasant sociability. In the mountain commune of St Martin en Haut the Croix de Feu was set up by the president and vice president of the communal

---

[157] *Journal d'Henry Morel-Journel*, 29 November 1935.

[158] Map 9 in Passmore, 'The right and the extreme right', suggests overrepresentation of central areas. But *Le Flambeau du sud-est*, April 1936, suggests rapid growth in the 3rd and 6th arrondissements.

veterans organisation.[159] The Croix de Feu also drew on social Catholicism. A letter of Abbé Marteau, chaplain of the JAC in the Rhône, to Félix Garcin, reveals a 'growing confusion between this group [the Croix de Feu] and Action catholique'.[160] The Croix de Feu, then, fastened onto the discontent of young conservative peasant proprietors. Given the youth of JAC activists it is unlikely that they were the sole source of peasant support for the Croix de Feu. But the JAC was one part of a wider social Catholic movement.

The influence of the Croix de Feu in social Catholic circles extended well beyond the JAC. Abbé Marteau spoke of links between the Croix de Feu and Catholic Action *in general*, mentioning the largely middle-class ACJF in particular. He drew attention to 'the place occupied in our organisations by certain propagandists [of the Croix de Feu] and the patronage they accord to them', and to 'the indiscreet propaganda of this group towards our activists'.[161] The precise details of such links are a matter for further research. Suffice it to recall that Canat de Chizy was a former president of USIC, and that the pro-Croix de Feu journalist Henri Franchet was on the administrative council of the *Chronique*.[162] There is no direct evidence of Croix de Feu penetration of the CFTC. All that can be said is that Croix de Feu white-collar workers lived in those parts of the city from which the CFTC recruited its members.

There were a number of reasons for the connection between social Catholicism and the Croix de Feu. First, many social Catholic activists sought to collaborate with non-Catholic organisations in order to demonstrate the relevance of Christian solutions to social problems, and ultimately therefore to achieve re-Christianisation. The Croix de Feu seemed to fit the bill because it was both eclectic in its appeal, and committed to establishment of a new morality which owed something to social Catholic doctrine. Second, both shared a belief in the need for a new elite recruited from the people. Third, the corporatism of the social Catholic movements had been designed to assert the material interests of groups such as white-collar workers and peasants against the elites, but also to combat the left. In the context of 1935 the authoritarian and anticapitalist corporatism of the Croix de Feu doubtless seemed a more effective way of achieving these ends, now that neither employers nor workers seemed to be interested in class collaboration. Of course, the convergence of social Catholicism with the Croix de Feu was not automatic. Abbé Marteau saw the goals of the two movements as antipathetic, and feared that the elites of Catholic Action would be lost

---

[159] *Le Nouvelliste*, 3 November 1934, 9 July 1933.
[160] Michoud to Garcin, 30 March 1936, quoted in Gayet, 'L'Union du sud-est', 73–4.
[161] Gayet, 'L'Union du sud-est', 73–4.   [162] Interview with Jacques Darodes.

in the ideologically eclectic Croix de Feu.[163] Furthermore, Marteau's letter implies that the Church feared the rivalry of the Croix de Feu in the social field.[164]

The major conclusion of this chapter is that the Croix de Feu was fascist – however moderate the movement's constitutional programme might seem at first glance, and however cautious La Rocque undoubtedly was. The Croix de Feu's project was inseparable from the radical activism of a mass movement which regarded itself as a new elite drawn from the people, mandated by the fallen of the Great War, invested with the task of national regeneration and guided by a leader with heroic qualities. Croix de Feu members were convinced that the existing system was anti-national, and that the agents of corruption were communists, politicians and Freemasons all united in a conspiracy against France. The league expected to win power by semi-legal means in circumstances of extreme crisis and knew that its first task would be a purge of administration and trade unions and suppression of the Communist Party. Crucially, members would have expected this repression to be carried out not simply by the agencies of the state, but by their own movement, and must have believed that this was what they had been training for in their paramilitary mobilisations. Once these preliminary tasks had been achieved the league would set about the task of reforming the constitution. Above all it would establish a corporate system in which antagonistic interests would be subordinated to the needs of the nation. In Griffin's terms it is possible to see in the Croix de Feu a populist palingenetic ultra-nationalism, engaged in a crusade to regenerate a decadent nation. It is in this combination of radical populism with reaction and the use of force by a mass movement that fascism is to be detected.

To argue that the Croix de Feu was fascist, however, does not mean that it stood any chance of coming to power. Rémond suggests that fascism could not implant itself in France because of the strength of a democratic tradition, embodied in the lower-middle-class supporters of Radicalism. The right too is seen as impermeable to fascism, for it was divided between a traditionalist wing which looked to the *ancien régime* rather than forwards to fascist revolution, and a liberal-Orleanist wing which had long since accepted democracy.[165] These arguments must be qualified. We have seen that corporatism and authoritarianism emerged from all the strands of the right and that sometimes this led to fascism.

---

[163] Gayet, 'L'Union du sud-est', 73–4.
[164] AN 451 AP 172, Bruyas to Madame de Préval, 4 February 1939; Howlett, 'La Rocque', 218.
[165] Rémond, *Les Droites*, 222–3.

We have also seen that some pro-Radical small businessmen were turning towards antiparliamentarianism and even the Croix de Feu. Neverthless, Rémond's argument contains a good deal of truth. The existence of the Republican tradition (together with the foreign policy needs of the Soviet Union) explains why in France the reaction of the left to the threat of fascism was fundamentally different from that of its counterparts in Germany and Italy. The Popular Front, unlike the left in Germany, paid close attention to the material interests of workers, peasants and the lower middle class. By combining this with attacks on the Croix de Feu in the language of traditional Republican hostility to personal power and 'feudalism', groups such as shopkeepers were drawn back into the republican fold. The '200 families' slogan could even attract quite substantial businessmen, given the extent of anticapitalism within the right. Finally, the Croix de Feu were confronted on the streets by a mobilisation of Republicans. During the Croix de Feu's campaign of December 1935 Rhône antifascists declared a 'levée en masse'. Mayors warned of an imminent coup. In Tarare preparations were made to block communications between Lyon and Paris. The town hall of Villeurbanne was protected by the hoses of the municipal fire brigade. One rural commune was reported to have blocked its main street with a cart.[166] The result was that the Croix de Feu, far from establishing its own credibility as a force for order, found itself facing accusations of subversion and provocation.

Another reason for the failure of the Croix de Feu was that the elites were never tempted to bring the movement into government. Nationally important businessmen like de Wendel and Mercier were interested by the league, but were worried by its radicalism. They saw La Rocque only as a last resort.[167] Similarly the leaders of the right in parliament never felt obliged to bring the Croix de Feu into government. Bearing in mind the lessons of 1924–6 and 1932–4, they remained convinced that the Radicals could be detached from the socialist alliance. Even if this could not be done, right-wing Radicals in Chamber and Senate could be relied upon to exercise a moderating influence, especially in the field of economic policy. Here then is a major differences between Germany and France. In Weimar Germany the centre had crumbled away, so conservatives could find mass support only on the far right. Even if elements in the French elites had wanted to do a deal with the Croix de Feu, they were less well placed to do so than their German counterparts, for they were unable to make and break governments in the way that von Papen and Hugenberg could. In the Rhône business leaders like Morel-

[166] *Lyon républicain*, 1–4 December 1935.
[167] AN F[7] 13 241, 20 July 1935; Jeanneny, *De Wendel*, 705, AN F[7] 12 900, 4 July 1935.

Journel were certainly disenchanted with parliamentary democracy. Big business as a whole in the Rhône had become somewhat detached from political parties in the early 1930s. Deputies like Peissel and Sallès had shifted closer to the nationalism of Perret. Sallès was among five Fédération *conseillers généraux* who voted against a motion condemning the leagues. But their support remained heavily qualified, and at no time did a campaign to include the league in the government develop. On the contrary, in spite of his antiparliamentarianism, Morel-Journel retained links with centre and even centre-left politicians like Herriot. Thus in France, although a very serious political and social crisis did develop, the unity of the left together with the republicanism of the police and the fact that the elites possessed alternative options, made a break with the existing regime a risky proposition.

Neverthless, the Croix de Feu was part of a crisis of the right, for many rank-and-filers were rather less confident that the system could heal itself. The league represented a coalition of discontented right-wingers, including white-collar workers, peasants, medium and small business. Most were Catholics, but a few anticlericals were probably also attracted. These groups shared anticommunism and a hostility to the political and social 'establishment'. As such, they can be understood in terms of dual closure. Family businessmen appealed to the people in order to pursue a struggle against big business. White-collar workers and peasants used mass mobilisation in order to defend their position in the labour or agricultural markets, against both the left and capitalists. These subordinate groups remained within the right because their struggles crystallised around aspects of one of the 'dominant ideologies', Catholicism in particular. It was because Catholicism was intertwined with economic power that subordinate groups were able to use it to gain advantages over non-Catholics. But they were nevertheless on the watch for signs that the elites were lukewarm in defence of these values.

The Croix de Feu succeeded better than the parliamentary right in synthesising its diverse constituency into a 'national' movement, inde-pendent from sectional interests. Where the Federation addressed its audience as property owners, and often openly defended the interests of a section of the ruling class, the Croix de Feu spoke only of Frenchmen, ignored the quarrel over religion, and avoided issues of economic policy. The limits of this 'consensus' should, however, be stressed. The Croix de Feu was not really independent. It conformed in reality to the idea of the national interest held by certain members of the right. Furthermore, this coalition was held together in large measure by authority and paramili-tarism. As the PSF became a more conventional political party all the old conflicts of the Lyonnais right were to resurface within it.

9 The right and the Popular Front

The general election of 26 April and 2 May 1936 produced an overall majority for the Popular Front of 378 seats. The discipline of the left benefited above all the PCF, which increased its seats from eleven to seventy-two, while the SFIO moved from 131 to 147 seats and therefore became the strongest party in the coalition. The main losers were the Radicals, who fell from 157 to 106 seats. The right gained only 220 seats. Political polarisation was reflected in an increase in the numbers of Fédération républicaine deputies and a decline of the centre-right. In the Rhône the election campaign had been characterised by unprecedented faction fighting on the right, exacerbated by the efforts of business organisations, veterans and the Croix de Feu amongst others to arbitrate in the 'national interest'. This did not prevent the right from increasing its share of the registered electorate from 22% to 26%, and its deputies from three to five. Sallès and Peissel easily retained their seats. At Tarare Bonnevay obtained an absolute majority on the first round. Elmigar and Burgeot won the Croix-Rousse and Brotteaux respectively from the Radicals. Apart from the abnormal result of 1919, this was the best conservative result in the Rhône since 1871.

But the relative success of the right was a consequence of political polarisation. Even Bonnevay had lost 40% of his 1932 supporters to the nationalist Perret and had won only because the Radicals had not stood against him. The centre ground melted away as the Radical vote fell from 28% in 1932 to 16%, with the loss of five out of eight seats. In two cases it was the right which benefited: the Fédération républicaine's Burgeot in the 6th arrondissement and Elmigar in the 4th. Elmigar's win owed much to a shift to the right of the Radical shopkeeping constituency, a development which prefigured the emergence of a rightist 'neo-Radicalism' in the course of 1936–7. The same pattern was evident in the 7th arrondissement (north), where a conservative withdrawal enabled the Radical Paul Richard to retain his seat. The Radicals also suffered from the advance of the left. Herriot faced a *ballotage*. His pride was deeply wounded, and it took much persuasion on the part of his allies to prevent him from withdrawing from politics. In this case the socialists and communists, the former after much discussion, overcame their dislike of Herriot and withdrew in his favour. But in five of the other nine constituencies where a second ballot was required, Popular Front discipline functioned badly. In the 3rd arrondissement (east), for example, the SFIO candidate André Philip refused to withdraw in favour of a better-placed Radical, citing the latter's support for deflation, and won on the second ballot. The socialists also won Givors from the Radicals, while the communists took the 7th arrondissement (south) from the SFIO. The communists added this seat to Villeurbanne/ Vénissieux, gained from the socialists. Thus the PCF began its fifty-year domination of the semi-skilled working-class districts of the east and south of the Lyonnais agglomeration. The socialists remained strong in urban areas such as Vaise where factory workers and public-service employees lived side-by-side, but matched the national trend in that their position in the small towns of the plateau and the villages of the Beaujolais was strengthened at the expense of representation in proletarian areas.

The right was perhaps reassured by the fact that the communists refused to join the new Blum administration, preferring to support the government from the benches of the Chamber of Deputies. Also, Léon Blum's new government, composed of eighteen socialists, four independent socialists and thirteen Radicals, strictly adhered to constitutional practice and did not take office until 6 June, leaving the country in the hands of a caretaker government under Sarraut. Yet by then France was in the grip of a massive wave of factory occupations which had begun in Paris on 2 June, which quickly spread to the provinces and which led to the concessions of frightened employers' leaders at the Hôtel Matignon during the night of 7 and 8 June.[1] In the following days legislation granting paid holidays, the forty-hour week and collective contracts was enacted. In September a further wave of panic was caused by the devaluation of the Franc. In the Rhône strikes began in earnest only after Matignon.[2] Although an agreement based on Matignon was signed by employers and unions in the presence of the Prefect on 10 June, this did not prevent strikes from affecting the whole of the department and most sectors, from silk weaving and metallurgy to large cafés and department stores, for the rest of the month. Some 70,851 workers had been involved in strikes in Lyon and the suburbs by 13 July – perhaps half of the workforce. Membership of the CGT, which had

[1] J. Jackson, *The Popular Front in France* (Cambridge, 1988); J. Kergoat, *La France du Front populaire* (1986).
[2] AN BB[18] 3010, various reports of Procureur de la République.

fused with the procommunist CGTU earlier in the year, grew rapidly, to the point that the Rhône department became the most 'unionised' in France.[3]

Whether France really was on the brink of revolution in June 1936 is a matter for debate. Many right wingers certainly believed that it was. The *Nouvelliste* felt that France had embarked upon a 'fully collectivist experiment' and saw no solution other than to hope that the movement would fall apart of its own accord. The chief concern of the Chamber of Commerce, aware that it had lost control over events, was to secure from the government a statement of support for private property. Perret wrote to Marin of a 'truly revolutionary situation' and asked whether Blum would await the inevitable riots before taking action.[4] Obsessed with the Bolshevik model, conservatives saw revolution as the work of ruthless minorities. So the fact that the workers themselves did not directly challenge state power was irrelevant. Furthermore, the terrible precedent of Russia in 1917 was combined with memories of Jacobinism and the Commune to produce the conviction that war and revolution were intimately connected. During the run up to the election Hitler had reoccupied the Rhineland. A few weeks after the elections Franco's military rising against the Spanish Popular Front brought together in conservative minds fear of civil and international war in defence of democracy. Apprehension had been growing since the PCF had declared its support for the Franco-Soviet Pact in May 1935, and was increased by the left's demands for sanctions against the Italian invasion of Ethiopia. The expectation of an imminent seizure of power by the PCF gradually subsided after June 1936. Politicians prepared tactics for the coming parliament while employers worked to limit and even undo the damage of June. Nevertheless, fear of war and revolution remained the essential background to right-wing politics throughout the period. In particular, shrinkage of the middle ground meant that the right could no longer hope to secure its wider aims simply by winning over conservative Radicals. It was no longer possible to ignore the working-class parties.

Polarisation, coupled to the discredit of existing parties, led to a major upheaval on the right. In the Rhône, although Bonnevay and Elmigar continued to sit with the Républicains de gauche and Indépendants de gauche in the Chamber, the moderate right represented by the Alliance démocratique and the PDP collapsed. The elections favoured the

---

[3] AN BB[18] 3010, 31 July 1937; A. Prost, *La CGT à l'époque du Front populaire* (Paris, 1964), 212, 219.

[4] PVCCL, 11 June 1936; *Le Nouvelliste*, 21 June 1936; AN 317 AP 72, Perret to Marin, 17 June 1936; R. Vinen, *The Politics of French Business, 1936–1945* (Cambridge, 1991), 33.

Fédération républicaine, especially Perret's nationalist wing. Burgeot was the first real 'party man' to be elected, and sat with the party group in the Chamber of Deputies. Perret himself had done better than expected in the Beaujolais. Peissel and Sallès, although they still refused to join the Fédération's parliamentary group, moved further to the right. Elmigar had once been an FR member. In spite of this success the Fédération was shortly to lose many of its supporters to the far right. Action française had been dissolved by the government in February 1936. On 18 June, in the midst of the strike wave, it was the turn of the Francistes, Jeunesses patriotes, Solidarité française and Croix de Feu, to be dissolved. Two cases of reconstitution of a dissolved organisation were sent to the parquet, but neither led to prosecution. The only public action of the Croix de Feu during the strikes was to off-load stocks of their newspaper and to advise members to display tricolours.[5] Defiance was limited to the wearing of ten centime pieces in buttonholes: 'dix sous' (*dissous* – dissolved). All the leagues reappeared under other names. Only the PSF, the reincarnation of the Croix de Feu, was of real significance. It claimed to be on the way to 40,000 members in mid-1938, but 13,000 to 20,000 was a more likely maximum. A figure in the upper part of the range is suggested by the mobilisation, according to the police, of 15,000 supporters for the parade of 11 November 1938.[6] Whatever the real figure, there can be no doubt that the PSF was the largest political movement ever seen in the Rhône. Furthermore, in September 1936 it showed that it was an electoral force by winning a local by-election in the 2nd arrondissement. In terms of members the PSF was considerably larger than any of the left-wing parties. Beside the PSF, the other new movement, the Parti populaire français (PPF) of the ex-communist Jacques Doriot, counted for little. As early as the summer of 1937 police reports stressed its difficulty in recruiting members. It had almost ceased to exist by the end of 1938.[7]

The general picture is one of extensive politicisation coupled to social polarisation. Indeed, the coincidence of international crisis with mass strikes, communist electoral gains and a Popular Front government led by the socialists suggests, from the right-wing point of view, problems as serious as any experienced in Germany or Italy during the years preceding the collapse of democracy there. In view of the arguments advanced in previous chapters it might seem that conditions more than

---

[5] ADR 4m 236, 22 June 1936.
[6] J. Prévosto, 'La Fédération du nord du Parti social français' (mémoire de maîtrise, Paris, 1971), 41, shows that PSF claims in this department to have over 50,000 members were probably correct.
[7] Passmore, 'The Right and the extreme right', 310–11.

ever favoured fascism in France. This, however, raises a problem as far as the PSF is concerned, for in transforming the Croix de Feu into a political party La Rocque stated his intention to work within the republican system. Why then should crisis on the scale described above have led to an outbreak of relative moderation on the part of the PSF? Historians have resolved this paradox in contrasting ways. Soucy and Irvine minimise the differences between league and party, arguing that out of fear of dissolution La Rocque merely feigned commitment to the Republic. His real sympathies re-emerged with his enthusiastic support for Pétain.[8] It is true that La Rocque's change of tactics was forced upon him by the circumstances of June. The problem is that the commitment of a party to a particular set of principles is always conditional and dependent on historical context. So it is arbitrary to view the policies adopted in one conjuncture as reflecting the 'real' nature of a movement. Had France not been defeated in 1940, the PSF might easily have become a conventional conservative party. An alternative view, that of Pierre Milza, is that the PSF represented 'the first great formation of the modern French right'; a mass 'interclass party, resolutely conservative and electoralist' on the model of the British conservative party. It sought to gain a parliamentary majority by winning over the clientele of the Radicals, and moderated its programme in accordance with their sensibilities. There is some truth in this interpretation, but it must be qualified. There was no reason why a desire to win the Radical electorate should have led to parliamentarianism, for in different ways every political party in France coveted that party's voters. In fact the PSF approached the Radicals by divorcing the Republican tradition from democracy. In spite of the very real changes in La Rocque's movement in the summer of 1936, the PSF very slowly shook off its fascist past. Only in 1938–9, with the decline of the Popular Front, can we say that the PSF was on the way towards the constitutional right.[9]

The answer to the problem of the PSF lies in the contradictory pressures to which conservative politics were subject in this period. In Germany and Italy fascism had developed *after* the mobilisation of the left, and then attacked and destroyed socialist organisations as they weakened. In France, in contrast, the rise of fascism *pre-dated* the mobilisation of the left. Since the Croix de Feu had failed to prevent the crisis of June 1936, some concluded that the very tactics of the league had made the Popular Front possible.[10] Formation of the PSF can

---

[8] Soucy, 'The Croix de Feu', 168, 171; Irvine, 'Fascism in France', 211; Goodfellow 'Fascism in Alsace'.

[9] Milza, *Fascisme français*, 138–42. *Bulletin d'information du PSF*, 8 September 1937.

[10] Jacques Débu-Bridel in *L'Union républicaine*, 18 June 1936; Chopine, *Six ans*, 169–70.

therefore be seen as a recognition of the defeat of fascism in interwar France. La Rocque himself argued that, given the strength of the left in June 1936, resistance to dissolution would be futile.[11] Thus, paradoxically, the PSF gradually abandoned paramilitarism in spite of growing social, political and international tension. The growing moderation of the PSF was reinforced by the gradual dislocation of the Popular Front. In February Blum announced a 'pause' in its reform programme. On 21 June Blum resigned following the Senate's refusal to grant him decree powers to deal with a financial crisis. Two Radical-dominated administrations under Chautemps lasted until March 1938, and followed a much more conservative financial policy. Blum was to return briefly to office in March and April 1938, but the initiative now lay with opponents of the Popular Front. Daladier's arrival in power in April 1938 was welcomed by many conservatives, although he continued to rely on a Popular Front majority until November 1938.

Subject to these contradictory pressures, the PSF retained the Croix de Feu's authoritarianism and its populist hostility both to the left and to the establishment. It can therefore be categorised as a movement of the authoritarian-populist right. But it was not fascist. Although the league's commitment to mass mobilisation remained, the party no longer sought to impose its world-view by means of mass mobilisation in a paramilitary formation. It now placed more emphasis upon the ideological strategies necessary to win elections. Yet by developing a conventional political programme the PSF lost the illusion of independence. This meant that the PSF could neither win Radical support nor match the Croix de Feu's capacity to win sympathy within the old right, especially as PSF and Fédération now competed electorally. Also, latent conflicts within the PSF's own constituency began to surface. Instead of transcending the divisions of the right by means of authoritarianism, corporatism and paramilitary activism, the PSF came increasingly to reflect the concerns of certain social Catholics and economic modernisers. It could be said that the PSF collapsed into the religious and economic divisions of French society. Moreover, the 1936 crisis exacerbated these divisions at a time when the desire to unite in opposition to communism was more powerful than ever – indeed this is why conflict within the right became so bitter. To understand the conflicts within and between right-wing parties it is necessary first to look at the effects of June 1936 on the wider constituency of the right.

[11] *Le Volontaire '36*, 15 August 1936.

Interest-group politics and the Popular Front

The events of June 1936 led to the eclipse of the Chamber of Commerce, the last bastion of the liberal tradition. The new structure of labour relations had led to fundamental changes in the function of employers' associations.[12] During the strikes employers were forced to negotiate with workers' delegates, then obliged by law to discuss and enforce collective contracts, and from December 1936 to participate in a system of compulsory arbitration.[13] The Chamber, essentially a lobby operating within the parliamentary system, was ill suited for this role. It was therefore AICA, the Lyonnais branch of the CGPF (the national employers' association), which took the lead. AICA was dominated by engineering employers such as Weitz and by the minority of progressive *fabricants*. In an attempt to preserve its position the Chamber adhered to a Comité d'entente de commerce et de l'industrie, created on the initiative of the Paris Chamber of Commerce.[14] This committee grouped all the major economic interests of the region and was chaired by Paul Charbin of the Chamber. But the Comité d'entente achieved little. The CGPF and AICA used it only as cover for their own discredit for having signed the Matignon agreements. By the end of the year the CGPF, thanks to its strong opposition to Blum's suggestion of a 'second Matignon', had recovered its credibility. AICA could now afford to ignore the Comité d'entente.[15] In January 1937 Morel-Journel was obliged to admit that the Chamber had lost its primacy.[16] In the summer of 1938 the new balance of forces was confirmed by the announcement of a plan to reduce the representation of the silk industry in the Chamber, to the benefit of industrial and commercial employers.[17]

These developments further weakened the liberal–silk interest, which had already suffered from the shift of major firms to Paris, the loss of political influence to lesser figures like Perret and Peissel of the Fédération and Freynet of the Croix de Feu, sectoral diversification, and the devastating impact of the economic crisis on the *fabrique*. The silk interest had not been eliminated but it was obliged to operate within a wider industrial interest led by AICA. This new alignment was increasingly, moreover, marked by *rapprochement* of the hitherto opposed metallurgical and silk employers. Corporatism was generally accepted by big business; now that the largest silk firms approved a

---

[12] Kolboom, *La Revanche des patrons*; Vinen, *Politics of French Business*; A. Rossiter 'Corporatist experiments in Republican France, 1916–1939' (D.Phil. thesis, Oxford, 1986).
[13] PVCCL, 22 June 1936.   [14] PVCCL, 9 July 1936.
[15] PVCCL, 26 November 1936.   [16] PVCCL, 28 January 1937.
[17] PVCCL, 6 October 1938.

measure of protectionism, that issue had ceased to divide the business elites. Finally, there was a cultural convergence. A key event was the resignation of Weitz, discredited by the events of June, from the engineering employers association. The new leader was Georges Villiers, better known as postwar leader of the national employers' movement. Whereas Weitz was a Protestant, Villiers was from a well-known Catholic family. He was involved in Action catholique industrielle, dedicated to the re-Christianisation of the upper bourgeoisie.[18] That a militant Catholic should have assumed the leadership of the CSIM is evidence of developments seen before in French history. On the one hand June 1936 had led many anticlericals (as in 1848 and 1871) to recognise a social value in the Church. On the other it is possible, although evidence is lacking, that the second generation of engineering employers, having attended private schools, were less systematically hostile to the Church than their parents.

The increasing unity of big business contrasted with the emergence of a movement purporting to represent the hostility of small and medium firms to the large concerns which dominated the CGPF and which were seen as responsible for the Matignon accords. Richard Vinen sees this mobilisation as an illusion created by big business for its own ends, and denies that small and medium firms had special reasons for hostility to Matignon.[19] It is true that smaller firms, except in the building trades, had often escaped industrial action.[20] Nevertheless, there was real cause for discontent, for they could not avoid wage rises, the forty-hour week or unionisation. Furthermore, large firms were far from systematic in their hostility to the reforms of the Popular Front. On the one hand AICA and the Chamber organised mass meetings of employers against the forty-hour week and did all they could to undermine the CGT.[21] On the other hand the same big firms sought to adapt to the new situation. The question of collective contracts is a good example. Until 1936 the Chamber had opposed collective bargaining. But from 1936 big business saw compulsory contracts as a means of ensuring that small firms did not gain an advantage by avoiding wage rises and the forty-hour week (a reflection of a long-held fear that small business would gain a cost advantage in this way). Paul Charbin even complained of the 'weakness of the CGT in some areas'. The belief of smaller firms that a 'sheltered

[18] G. Villiers, *Témoignages* (1978); Pierre Trimouille, 'La Bourgeoisie chrétienne du Nord (1930–1950)', *Revue du Nord* 73 (1991), 417–27.

[19] Vinen, *Politics of French Business*, 51–2.

[20] AN BB[18] 3010: firms which experienced occupation employed an average of 141 workers.

[21] *Le Nouvelliste*, 14 May and 25 November 1937.

sector' had avoided the consequences of Matignon therefore had some basis in reality.[22]

The host of organisations representing smaller employers in branches as diverse as engineering and the drinks trade therefore had real grievances. The real interpretative problem lies elsewhere, for these movements showed scarcely any sign of activity independent from big business. There was no equivalent of the autonomous shopkeeper protests of 1934 and 1935 – indeed, immediately after the strikes of June, the UF joined with AICA and the Chamber of Commerce in a united front, the Cartel du Commerce.[23] What is more, big business soon found that it could ignore small-business demands.[24] In spite of this small business also took its place in the mass meetings organised by the CGPF. The reason was quite prosaic. Small business accepted that since CGT organisation was based in large factories, big business must take the lead in fighting against it. Thus at one of AICA's meetings Perroud of the UF, the leading opponent of big business in 1933–5, admitted that many might be astonished to see his organisation united with the 'grand patronat', but in present circumstances there was no choice.[25] AICA and the Chamber exploited this weakness by stressing the 'unity of employers', which made it possible to present attacks on big business as part of a Marxist conspiracy to divide employers.[26] But the weakness of small and medium business in the sphere of interest-group politics did not mean that their grievances were neutralised. Rather they were expressed through political parties, including the Radicals, the Fédération and most importantly the PSF.

Thirdly, the events of June 1936 had a profound impact on the CFTC. Membership increased to between 15,000 and 20,000 in forty-eight unions, not including sections of national organisations.[27] This expansion took place both in the centre of the city where the CFTC had traditionally benefited from the presence of large numbers of white-collar workers and a high religious practice, and in the industrial *banlieue* in factories such as Rhône-Poulenc. In such areas expansion was often the work of the Jeunesse ouvrière chrétienne (JOC).[28] This organisation was not left-wing, but on practical issues was often prepared to

---

[22] PVCCL, 1 January and 25 February 1937; 24 February 1938 for the guarded welcome of employers to the Statut moderne du travail.
[23] PVCCL, 25 June 1936.
[24] PVCCL, 25 June and 1 October 1936, 15 April 1937.
[25] *Le Nouvelliste*, 14 May 1937; PVCCL, 22 June 1936.
[26] *Le Nouvelliste*, 8 December 1937; CRCCL, 25 July 1938; Kolboom, *La Revanche des patrons*, 263–88.
[27] Launay, *La CFTC*, 401–2; *La Voix sociale*, 16 April 1938.
[28] *La Voix sociale*, 11 December 1937.

collaborate with the CGT.[29] So this development reinforced the more progressive side of the CFTC. This shift to the left was confirmed by the death of Auguste Gruffaz in 1937. His place as regional leader was taken by the metallurgist Raoul Duclos, while Gruffaz's own Corporation was taken over by the PDP activist Pierre Tolon. The new leader of the departmental union was the Jeune république sympathiser, Louis Naillod. The CFTC endorsed all of the reforms of the Popular Front.[30] Yet the contradictions of the CFTC position remained as strong as ever. In subsequent months, in spite of its support for the material reforms of the Popular Front, the CFTC, and still more its rank-and-file, was pushed to the right. It proved vulnerable to the offensives of both employers and Church against the Popular Front.

Many new members of the CFTC, although Catholic, knew little of the Church's social doctrine.[31] Indeed, many had joined the CFTC out of hostility to the CGT and were often isolated in a sea of CGT members – especially in proletarian suburbs.[32] The CGT did nothing to calm such fears. On the contrary, it regarded the CFTC as a boss's union. It frequently dealt out to CFTC activists the same rough treatment it gave to those of the PSF trade unions, the Syndicats professionels français (SPF).[33] The CGT was also opposed to CFTC involvement in negotiations with employers. In such circumstances the CFTC ideal of free negotiation between employers' and workers' unions was hardly realisable. It became obvious that if the CFTC was to play a part in the new system of collective bargaining then the CGT would first have to be disciplined.[34] The result was a tacit alliance between the CFTC and employers. In any case the CFTC had always regarded the strike as a last resort. It had also always been a nationalist organisation, and so was sensitive to the charge that the CGT was disrupting war production.

The CFTC was equally vulnerable to a nationwide reaction against progressive Catholicism.[35] We have seen that for Catholic trade unionists material demands were connected to concerns about status and therefore Catholic identity. The strikes of June brought material rewards. But they also contained a levelling potential, and indeed were sometimes directed against the minor supervisory personnel often found in the CFTC. This explains the popularity in this period of the

---

[29] Launay, La CFTC, 315–17, 333.   [30] Le Nouveau Journal, 19 June 1936.
[31] Ibid., 26 February 1937.   [32] Launay, La CFTC, 327–35.
[33] Le Nouveau Journal, 16 February 1937; Le Nouvelliste, 17 September 1936.
[34] La Voix sociale, 1 December 1936, 25 December 1937; Le Nouveau Journal, 10 November 1936.
[35] R. Rémond, Catholiques et communistes dans les années trente (1966), 244–51. P. Christophe, 1936: Les Catholiques et le Front populaire (1980), 103–4.

term 'collaborateur' to designate white-collar workers in general, for it set employees off from the proletariat. Concern about status also encouraged many white-collar workers to emphasise the Catholic values which supposedly justified their relatively elevated position. This coincided with the Church's own efforts to limit the influence of the CFTC left by stressing its religious purpose. Cardinal Maurin attempted to undermine the CFTC by implying in a pastoral letter that Catholics could if they wished join the SPF.[36] Maurin's successor Cardinal Gerlier, appointed in 1938, was more favourable to the CFTC. But he too was opposed to any suspicion of deconfessionalisation. He presided personally over the silver jubilee of Catholic white-collar unions in Lyon in November 1937, turning it into a celebration of the Catholicism of the CFTC.[37] Both the *Chronique* and the Cercles d'études took on an increasingly conservative tone in this period. The *Chronique*'s annual programme for 1937 and 1938 was entitled 'Marxist communism, Catholics and the middle classes'.[38] One important figure was Henry Franchet, member of the board of the *Chronique* and PSF sympathiser. Franchet began a front-page column for the *Nouveau Journal* in 1936, which he sometimes used to influence the CFTC, stressing, for example, the moral role of the JOC.[39] The JOC was open to such pressure because it too saw material reward and status as inseparable, demanding vigorous suppression of all 'fauteurs de brimades' and measures such as separation of the sexes in factories. And one of their principal concerns was to create an elite of militantly Catholic workers.[40] Thus there was a reassertion of a parish-based Catholic trade unionism against the (seemingly) more secular and procommunist unionism which flourished briefly in 1936.

One measure of the growing gap between CFTC leaders and members lay in the fact that its expansion had coincided with collapse of the PDP, once the political expression of democratic and reformist Catholicism. Meanwhile since 1935 the Croix de Feu had penetrated the social Catholic network. The changing attitude of the CFTC to industrial disputes is also informative. In June 1936 the CFTC had often participated in joint delegations to employers, usually merely seconding CGT demands. Then in 1937 the Catholic unions took a critical line on a bitter dispute at the Gillet factory, and expanded rapidly after the defeat of the strike. Finally, in 1938 the CFTC still supported the forty-

---

[36] *Chronique sociale*, 1936, 563–5; *Le Nouvelliste*, 18 and 30 June 1936.
[37] *Chronique sociale de la France*, December 1937, 397–401, 748–9.
[38] *Programme annuel pour les cercles d'études* (Lyon, 1938).
[39] *Le Nouveau Journal*, 24 July 1938; Launay, *La CFTC*, 373.
[40] *Le Nouvelliste*, 30 November 1936 for the demands of the JOC.

hour week, but opposed the general strike of 30 November, called to defend it.[41] The CFTC even organised mass crossings of picket lines.[42] This underlines the deep contradictions of Catholic trade unions, simultaneously attracted towards the material reforms of the Popular Front, but pushed to the right by the inseparability of those same demands from concern with status and Catholicism. Like small and medium business organisations, the CFTC was propelled, in spite of itself, into an alliance with big business. Many workers, white-collar workers or manual, sought to resolve this contradiction in the political sphere, particularly by turning to the PSF. It seemed to combine Catholic morality with vigorous anticommunism, yet also offered, through corporatism, a means to protect material interests against big business.

The Popular Front aggravated similar conflicts in rural society. Like white-collar workers, peasants were attracted by some of the measures of the Popular Front. Even the *Nouvelliste* was obliged to admit that the Office du blé, a means of fixing wheat prices, was popular among the peasantry and that it had contributed to a rise in income. Jean-Marie Parrel, spokesman for the peasantry in the leadership of the USE, was appointed, probably against the wishes of Félix Garcin, to the National Council of this body, where he distanced himself from the intransigent opponents of the Office du blé amongst large growers. JAC activists meanwhile came into conflict with the USE leadership because of their defence of the right of agricultural labourers to form separate unions – another example of the way in which the Popular Front pulled the right apart. These developments were, however, not incompatible with political hostility to the Popular Front. Peasants suffered directly from transport strikes, whilst the rising cost of industrial goods, seen as a consequence of Popular Front reforms, moved the terms of trade against farmers. Peasants were therefore open to propaganda which depicted the Popular Front as an urban phenomenon, especially as it was portrayed as hostile to the Catholic values to which peasant 'bonnes familles' attributed their status and relative material wealth. These developments took place against a background of continuing problems in the markets for dairy products and fruit in particular. Popular Front proposals to create a system of collective contracts for these products came to nothing. Thus in the countryside too the constituency of the right was simultaneously attracted and repelled by the Popular Front. Here too corporatism served as a means of resolving the contradiction, permitting peasant leaders to pursue both anticommunism and their own material/

---

[41] *Le Nouvelliste*, 25 November 1938; Pin, 'Un notable paysan', 90.
[42] *La Voix sociale*, 26 November and 10 December 1938.

status interests. Corporatism was also attractive to those higher up the social scale. For the latter it was both a weapon against the Popular Front and also a means of containing conflict within the right by defining its boundaries in authoritarian terms.

In all the cases we have considered there was a similar pattern. Peasants, white-collar workers and small and medium business were forced, willy-nilly, to follow the lead of the social elites. Yet at the same time there was some sympathy for the reforms of the Popular Front and considerable hostility to big business. These tensions were often expressed through the PSF, which seemed to provide a means of pursuing special interests without endangering national unity. In fact, the party's ability to synthesise contradictory interests had been reduced. Conflict within the party was further exacerbated by the fact that June 1936 was experienced as much more than a threat to property, or even to cultural capital. In fact it was perceived as an assault on the bourgeois society in its broadest sense. It saw the mobilisation of groups which had until then played a passive role within the right, such as engineers, managers and supervisory personnel. Also called into question were all of the 'codes of closure' on which the power of the ruling class was based. Hence a new sensitivity to issues as diverse as urban space and male power. In other words the Popular Front provoked a reaction from the right-wing constituency in all its diversity at the same time as there was a unanimous hostility to communism. These contradictory pressures provided the context within which the PSF operated.

From paramilitarism to electoralism?

PSF supporters demanded three things of the party. First it was to take the lead in an anticommunist struggle. Second, it was to express hostility to big business and the political establishment, seen as partially responsible for and profiting from the reforms of the Popular Front. Third, the constituent parts of the right demanded protection of material interests, which sometimes led to acceptance of measures introduced by the Popular Front. The Croix de Feu had reconciled these contradictory pressures through the illusory means of corporatism, paramilitarism, the leader cult and authoritarianism. But although the PSF remained an authoritarian-populist movement, it nevertheless attenuated the paramilitarism and the apocalyptic rhetoric of the Croix de Feu and instead elaborated a detailed programme. Meanwhile La Rocque's status as leader was damaged by Tardieu's accusations against him in mid-1937. The result was that divisions surfaced within the party, while its authoritarianism, also somewhat attenuated, was placed at the service of special interests. The populism of the PSF therefore consisted less in the radical drive against the left and the political establishment typical of a fascist movement than in the specific grievances of sections of the conservative rank and file.

Like the Croix de Feu the PSF presented itself as above social and political conflict. The key word was 'reconciliation'. Whereas the Fédération had aimed merely to lure the Radicals into an alliance of property owners, and the Alliance démocratique had aimed to create a centrist alliance based on republicanism, the PSF interpreted reconciliation as bringing together the people as a whole. As André Gautier-Brisson, director of the Rhône political bureau, put it, the goal was to bridge the gap between Radical Lyon and communist Villeurbanne and to unite the 'generous and social right' with those who mistakenly believed that only the left could bring social justice.[43] For Johannès Dupraz the PSF would achieve reconciliation because it alone was independent of the sectional interests which had distorted the efforts of the old right.[44] Hence the PSF's denunciation of the 'trusts', which had profited from the free-for-all of liberal capitalism in order to enslave France. It followed from this that the PSF alone represented the nation. Rival parties had 'emasculated the term by giving it a partisan significance'.[45] Thus the notion of 'reconciliation' involved anti-liberalism, anticapitalism, antisocialism, antielitism and the claim to represent the people.

The PSF also remained authoritarian in terms of its structures. Although it claimed to have modelled itself on the SFIO, power flowed downwards, ultimately from La Rocque himself, said to possess a unique ability to gain acceptance as 'le chef'.[46] The elective principle was not applied to the party itself. Leaders were said to have arisen by a process of 'natural selection'.[47] Former members reveal that the party retained the hierarchical system of the Croix de Feu, with 'mains', 'dizaines' and 'chefs de dizaines'.[48] Through the confidential *Bulletin d'information du PSF* and a plethora of circulars, local leaders were bombarded with instructions on every subject.[49] The local press was forbidden to improvise.[50] Local organisations were given some freedom in the choice of candidates for cantonal elections, but in national elections Paris had the last word.

Furthermore, the PSF remained ambiguous in its attitude to

---

[43] *Le Volontaire '36*, 19 February 1937.   [44] *Ibid.*, 28 April 1938.
[45] *Ibid.*, 10 August 1937.   [46] *Ibid.*, 19 February 1937.
[47] *Ibid.*, 15 December 1936.
[48] Interview with M. Marcel Brunet, 1987. ADR 4m 244, 23 September 1936.
[49] *Bulletin d'information du PSF*.   [50] *Ibid.*, 27 August 1937.

democracy. Its constitutional projects closely resembled those of the Croix de Feu, and indeed those of all other movements of the right and extreme right, including the PPF.[51] Suffice it to say that constitutional reform was seen as a step towards a corporate state, and was designed to exclude the left permanently from power. Authoritarianism was exacerbated by the international situation, for it was held that France could stand up to Germany only once the state had been strengthened. In the meantime peace should be preserved at all costs. Otherwise the communists would exploit war in order to foment revolution: one writer held that the solution to all foreign policy difficulties was to suppress the PCF.[52] In 1938, as fear of war compounded hostility to Popular Front labour legislation, the PSF demanded a 'government of public safety', made up of 'independent men' and 'designated for a limited and precise task'.[53] The PSF also found much to admire in foreign fascist regimes. Even Nazism was to be praised for its restoration of the supremacy of the ideal over sordid materialism, its nationalism, its devotion to order, promotion of class collaboration, and 'the austere and dangerous life of Nazi activists'.[54] PSF writers were, however, divided on whether a deal should be done with Hitler. On the one hand Johannès Dupraz argued that Germany should be allowed to expand eastwards. Eventually Nazism would be undermined by the need to control an expanded population of Catholics, and France would have gained time for recovery.[55] On the other F. Rollet felt that France should resist Hitler through alliance with Britain.[56] Both agreed that alliance with the USSR was unwise.

But if the PSF was populist and authoritarian, and displayed a certain sympathy for fascism in Germany and Italy, it was not the Croix de Feu. There is no reason to doubt that the PSF's goal was the legal conquest of power.[57] With time, as police reports emphasised, party propaganda became less combative, partly because of the gradual dislocation of the Popular Front.[58] In the second half of 1937 the PSF devoted most of its energy to preparation for the local elections of October which it fought as part of a broad right-wing coalition. The disappointing results of those elections only caused the party to redouble its preparations for the

[51] *Que veut le Parti social français?* (1937), 12.
[52] *Le Volontaire '36*, 1 December 1936, 19 March, 7 July and 27 September 1937.
[53] *Ibid.*, 8 April 1938; P. Machefer, 'Le Parti social français', in *La France et les Français*, ed. R. Rémond and J. Bourdin (1978), 307–27.
[54] *Le Volontaire '36*, 15 August 1936, 19 November 1937, 17 June and 11 and 18 November 1938.
[55] *Ibid.*, 25 March 1938.   [56] *Ibid.*, 6 May 1938.
[57] *Ibid.*, 8 December 1937.
[58] ADR 4m 236, 22 January and 22 February 1938.

general elections which were due to be held in 1940.[59] Another sign of growing moderation was its changing attitude to the PCF. After the Clichy riots in March 1937 the PSF campaigned noisily for its dissolution.[60] But in late 1938 the PSF did not join a noisy campaign for dissolution of the Communist party led by the Fédération and PPF.

The PSF's attitude to the Daladier government of 1938–40 is also revealing. Although the notion of a Union nationale government had long been denounced by the PSF as a 'swindle', Daladier's new administration had at first been cautiously welcomed as a sign of the death of the Popular Front.[61] Increasingly, however, the PSF feared that the popularity of Daladier would destroy its own chances of entering the government. So the Union nationale was denounced, in terms that recalled the Croix de Feu, as a 'a plaster on an infected wound'. This permitted a revival of antiparliamentarianism. Daladier was said to be menaced by the divisive and destructive impulses of Parliament and ought therefore to carry out a 'national revolution'.[62] When in July 1939 Daladier postponed for two years the elections due in 1940, the PSF was outraged. For Johannès Dupraz this was not because 'the French have a great love of voting. They have an increasing disgust for elections.' The people simply did not want to see the life of the Chamber prolonged.[63] Yet unlike the Croix de Feu, the PSF did not ask its members to prepare to 'cleanse the wound'. Rather the party campaigned for dissolution and early elections. Dupraz's incendiary language was unusual. In sum, the PSF combined residual, though often virulent, antiparliamentarianism with a practical acceptance of legal methods. It must therefore be seen as a movement of the non-fascist authoritarian-populist right, which was also increasingly constitutional. Because this evolution was partial, and because of the contradictions inherent in a populist movement, the PSF could therefore have developed in several directions, depending on circumstances. Only with hindsight can the proto-Vichy language of Dupraz be emphasised, and indeed he was to gain a position of responsibility in that regime.

Paramilitarism

The declining significance of paramilitarism within the PSF confirmed its growing moderation. The Dispos were replaced by a new organisation, the EVP, which sold newspapers and provided security at meetings.

[59] *Le Volontaire '36*, 11 and 25 March and 1 June 1938, 12 January 1939.
[60] *Ibid.*, 18 March and 7 May 1937.
[61] *Ibid.*, 22 October 1937; 28 January, 24 February, 10 and 24 March and 15 April, 1938.
[62] *Ibid.*, 12 May 1939.   [63] *Ibid.*, 2 June 1939.

There was some continuity of personnel – the Vaise pharmacist Jean Knersynski was a notorious member of both organisations. The EVP were sometimes armed.[64] The PSF also mounted set-piece demonstrations which dwarfed those of the Croix de Feu. The first was the departmental congress of February 1937, the avowed purpose of which was to overawe opponents. It unmistakably owed something to fascist rallies. A massive security operation was mounted by the party. Photographs in *Le Volontaire '36* show delegates saluting in the fascist style. Reports of La Rocque's closing speech stressed the ardour of the audience reaction rather than its content.[65] Of a rather different nature was the celebration of the twentieth anniversary of the armistice on 11 November 1938. This was the largest demonstration of the far right ever seen in the Rhône. According to the police there were no less than 15,000 marchers, including 2,000 children and 3,000 women.[66] The parade took place in the period of extreme social tension which preceded the General Strike of 30 November 1930, and must be seen as a part of the tense climate that also brought 18,000 to a CGT rally on the following day.[67] The less successful but still impressive commemoration of Joan of Arc on 12 May 1939 (4,500 marchers) was similar in style. As *Le Volontaire '36* put it, 'you will come to this demonstration with the freely accepted discipline on which our strength depends'.[68]

The PSF also engaged in less disciplined actions which led often to confrontation on the streets. During the June strikes the priority of the right was to assert its existence and to define its territory. On 22 and 23 June, at the peak of the strike movement, members of all the dissolved leagues confronted a Popular Front demonstration, which had marched through much of bourgeois Lyon, on the Place Bellecour. Both demonstrations were comparatively small – no more than 300 leaguers were involved. The police had no trouble in keeping the demonstrators apart.[69] More significantly, during the summer working-class Vaise was the scene of a series of clashes between the PSF and the left.[70] In September the PSF resumed its motorised sorties.[71] The first was to

---

[64] See page 265; J. Mazas, interviewed in 1987, informed me that the EVP were often armed with bull whips to protect them from the communists.

[65] *Le Volontaire '36*, 19 February 1936; ADR 4m 236, 22 February 1937.

[66] ADR 1m 172, 11 November 1938. The party claimed 20,000 marchers.

[67] ADR 4m 236, November 1938.

[68] *Le Volontaire '36*, 5 and 12 May 1939.

[69] *Le Nouvelliste, Lyon républicain*, 24 and 25 June 1936.

[70] *Lyon républicain*, 5 July 1936; *Le Nouvelliste*, 15 July 1936. *La République lyonnaise*, 11 July 1936.

[71] ADR 4m 236, 22 September 1936; AN BB[18] 3048[2], report of 9 October 1936 on the Nord, and BB[18] 3048[3], report of 20 January 1937 on Seine-et-Oise; F[7] 14 817, reports of May 1937 on the Cher.

Irigny, a largely working-class commune, on 11 September. After the meeting there was the usual confrontation with counterdemonstrators during which the cars of the PSF were stoned.[72] Two days later several thousand activists were transported to rural Brindas to celebrate the Battle of the Marne.[73] The most serious incidents of all were on 15 September, when the PSF held three large private meetings. Those in the 2nd and 6th arrondissements passed off without incident, but a counterdemonstration was organised against a meeting in the Salle François Coppé in the proletarian 7th. In the ensuing disturbances bullets were fired through the windows of the hall (from which side was not clear) and petrol bombs were thrown by the demonstrators.[74] These incidents did not prevent the PSF from winning a by-election in the bourgeois 2nd arrondissement in October. Rémond's view that the PSF's spectacular success was due to its having embraced constitutionalism must be questioned.[75]

For all this, paramilitarism was less important than in the past. Where the Croix de Feu had seen itself as taking over from the state, the party would go into the streets only to assist police and army. Elaborate plans were laid for such an eventuality.[76] The paramilitary mobilisations of 1936–7 did not take place against the background of the apocalyptic rhetoric which had characterised the Croix de Feu. Not surprisingly police enquiries found no evidence that the PSF in the Rhône or anywhere else planned to seize power in the summer of 1936.[77] The EVP was a much smaller organisation than the Dispos, and there was no equivalent of the VN, which had formed a sort of reserve militia. The departmental congress of the PSF certainly owed something to the style of a fascist rally. But the congress also went to great lengths to show that it was seriously preparing policies for government. Finally it is instructive to compare the 1936 Joan of Arc parade to that of 1939, for it reveals the PSF to be a party in transition. Whereas in 1936 the order of march had been kept secret, in 1939 it was published in Le Volontaire '36, though the EVP was warned to accept separate convocations. The orders were also far less detailed in 1939.

Organisationally too the movement had changed. No longer was Lyon divided into military style 'sectors'. Instead the unit of organisation was the 'section', which matched Republican administrative boundaries. The section was also more defensive in tone, designed to protect

[72] Le Nouvelliste, 12 September 1936.   [73] Ibid., 14 September 1936.
[74] Ibid., 12 September 1936; Lyon républicain, 16 and 17 September 1936.
[75] Rémond, Les Droites, 215.
[76] Howlett, 'La Rocque', 205; AN BB[18] 30 482; Le Volontaire '36, 16 July 1937.
[77] ADR 4m 244, reports of 19, 21, 23 and 24 September 1936.

Map 17   Lyon and Villeurbanne: PSF activists, 1936–9

bourgeois society against the Popular Front. This can be seen first in the
extreme density of PSF implantation in bourgeois areas of the city (Map
17). In April 1937 the police reported that up to 600 people were
attending sector meetings in central Lyon.[78] The real density of PSF
members was higher still. For example section 67, which covered the
first three polling districts of the 6th, claimed 587 members in June
1938.[79] Membership of the PSF was therefore equivalent to 12% of the
electorate, and 37% of conservative voters, although perhaps 10% of
PSF members were female. This reflects the fact that the strikes had
crystallised latent fears of invasion of bourgeois space by the 'barbarians'
of the suburbs. Apprehension was magnified by the perceived passivity
of the police and by the dissolution of the leagues.[80] One of the first
reactions of the right to the strikes had therefore been a campaign to
reassert control over bourgeois space by displaying tricolours in
apartment windows. The PSF meanwhile became a sort of state within a
state. Sections organised theatricals, musical soirées and dances. At
work members could join the SPF. The *Almanach PSF* listed approved

[78] ADR 4m 236, 24 April 1937.
[79] *Le Volontaire '36*, 1 June 1938.   [80] *Le Nouvelliste*, 6 and 24 June 1936.

shops. PSF functions represented a world free from class and political conflict and where happiness and security were once again possible.[81] The reverse side of the coin was the extreme difficulty faced by the right in penetrating proletarian suburbs, where communist hegemony had been immeasurably strengthened. Thus the PSF represented a reaction against the Popular Front which involved politicisation of whole tracts of bourgeois society. But the tone was nevertheless more defensive than it had been in the militarised Croix de Feu.

Political violence remained a feature of the PSF throughout its existence, but it was steadily marginalised. As political tension was reduced by the decline of the Popular Front, the leadership's efforts to enforce the new line bore fruit. Mass sorties into communist heartlands were rare after the spring of 1937, and indeed were banned by the national leadership.[82] Paradoxically, however, the PSF was more likely than the Croix de Feu to become involved in 'dispersed' violence now that the energies of activists were no longer channelled into the collective discipline of paramilitary manœuvres. Violence of this type was made more likely by the involvement of the PSF in conventional propaganda meetings, especially at election time. It also began to send squads to ask questions at the 'réunions publiques et contradictoires' of its opponents. Violence was frequently the result, for example at l'Arbresle in July 1938, when a PSF meeting was broken up by communists.[83] The most serious such incident occurred during the *cantonales* of October 1937 at a PSF meeting in St Fons. Trouble began as PSF members left the hall, taunted by counterdemonstrators. The police concluded that two volleys of shots were then fired by the EVP, causing the death of a 19-year-old chemical worker and serious injuries to a PSF member.[84] A few days later, presumably in revenge, the PSF candidate for the Villeurbanne constituency was shot in the leg outside his home.[85]

Thus the PSF moved from collective mobilisations to a more traditional pattern of confrontation within political meetings. But in one important respect the PSF differed from its precursors on the far right, for it also broke up the meetings of its enemies on the right. Since May 1937 there were complaints of disruption of Federation meetings by the PSF.[86]

[81] *Le Volontaire '36*, 16 April 1937.
[82] *Bulletin d'information du PSF*, 21 October 1937, February 1938.
[83] *Le Nouvelliste*, 18 July 1939. For other examples see *Le Nouvelliste*, 6 July 1937, *Le Volontaire '36*, 9 July 1937; ADR élections cantonales de 1937, 7 and 9 October 1937.
[84] ADR élections cantonales de 1937, 7, 8 and 9 October 1937. *Lyon républicain* and *Le Nouvelliste*, 10, 11 and 12 October 1937.
[85] ADR élections cantonales de 1937, 15 October 1937.
[86] *Le Nouvelliste*, 9 May and 22 June 1937; *L'Union républicaine*, 13 March 1938 (incidents at Tarare, Mornant, Anse).

The most notorious incident occurred in February 1938, at a time when relations between the PSF the and Fédération were particularly poor. In February 1938 the Fédération deputy Philippe Henriot, one of the fiercest critics of the PSF, was invited to speak at the Etoile Cinéma in the 2nd arrondissement. When he began to speak PSF members unleashed a barrage of whistles and jeers. Stink bombs and flour bags were thrown. Fighting broke out all over the cinema, mainly between PSF members and the PPF squad supposed to have provided security for the meeting. Henriot was obliged to give his talk in a nearby café. In the following weeks abuse was heaped upon the PSF by all parties from the Federation to the royalists, accusing them of adopting the methods of the communists. *Le Volontaire '36* was unrepentant, speaking of 'a severe but deserved lesson'.[87] This incident, moreover, was part of a national campaign of direct action against conservative critics of the PSF.[88]

To sum up, violence and paramilitarism were less central in the PSF than in the Croix de Feu. The St Fons incident at the end of that year was the last serious clash with the communists. No longer did the movement use paramilitary mobilisations implicitly to substitute itself for the government, to establish its fitness to rule or to embody a drive of the people against the left and the establishment. The PSF was not therefore fascist. But the party remained part of the authoritarian and populist right. The PSF may have been moving in the direction of the constitutional right. But this caused the PSF to become riven by the socio-economic and religious divisions of French society.

The new Jacobins and the Catholic Church

La Rocque placed 14 July on the same level as the fête Jeanne d'Arc.[89] The Revolution was even more essential to the PSF in Lyon, perhaps because of the strength of Radicalism there, and because of Herriot's cult of the Girondins. Opposition to Herriot may also explain why, unlike La Rocque, the Lyonnais PSF identified with the Jacobins rather than 1789. The revolutionary tradition was evoked in the title of the party journal, *Le Volontaire '36*, with its evocation of the Volunteers of 1792 and the Jacobins. The link was reinforced by the motto of the journal: 'comme celui de Valmy *Le Volontaire '36* lutte contre la tyrannie des agents de l'étranger pour la liberté et la nouvelle France'. The title

[87] *L'Union républicaine*, 27 February 1938; *L'Attaque*, 26 February 1938; *Le Volontaire '36*, 4 March 1938; ADR 4m 236, 22 February 1938.
[88] AN F[7] 14 817, 4 May 1938; *Le Nouvelliste*, 5 March 1938.
[89] For La Rocque's view see *Le Petit Journal*, 14 July 1939.

also expressed continuity with the recently dissolved Volontaires nationaux. Next to the title were the features of a National Volunteer drawn on the background of a tricolour flag. At the head of the editorial column was a *sans culotte* leaning on a pen instead of a pike. The Revolutionary heritage was appropriated in order to win over not just the Radicals, but also the socialists and communists. This was to be achieved by divorcing the Revolution from democracy, and substituting for the latter an authoritarian-populist appeal to the people.

The PSF refused to associate Jacobinism with a mission to bring democracy to the world. Like the rest of the French right the PSF refused to envisage war in defence of an abstract notion such as democracy. France should fight only if its interests were directly threatened. The idea that France had a mission to save the world for liberty was merely a device of the communists, who aimed to use the cry of 'La patrie en danger!' to imprison and shoot their enemies, and to provoke war and revolution. It followed that the communist claim to represent the nation was false. Their leaders, it was said, acted only on the orders of Stalin, assimilated to the Revolution's greatest foreign enemy, the Tsar.[90] Class conflict was therefore stirred up by foreign powers, so the PCF's linkage of Jacobin patriotism with class struggle must also be false. The Popular Front had stolen the *fête nationale* in order to divide the nation.[91] Thus in the hands of the PSF Jacobin universalism was transformed into xenophobia. The true intentions of the crowd on 14 July had been to 'boot foreigners out of France'.[92]

Thus the Jacobin heritage was used as a means of promoting class collaboration and national unity, and of undermining the Popular Front. But it must also be interpreted in the context of the PSF's radicalism. The PSF believed the Revolution to be incomplete. Politically this meant identification of parliamentarians as a feudal caste. When in July 1939 Daladier prorogued Parliament, *Le Volontaire '36* portrayed deputies as entirely free from the control of electors, who were 'taillable et corvéable à merci'.[93] The PSF also agreed with the communists on the need for an 'economic '89', on condition that it was a national movement directed against 'international finance'.[94] In fact this meant identification with 1793 rather than 1789, for the target was 'economic liberalism', a doctrine dear to the Radicals and the old right, both products of 'the bourgeois and non-social revolution of 1789', which had permitted, thanks to excessive individualism, the domination of the 'trusts'.[95]

---

[90] *Le Volontaire '36*, 25 March 1937.   [91] *Ibid.*, 14 July 1939.
[92] *Ibid.*, 9 May 1937.   [93] *Ibid.*, 4 August 1939.   [94] *Ibid.*, 14 July 1939.
[95] *Ibid.*, 14 July 1939.

The PSF's populism was also evident in the self-image of a battle-hardened elite drawn from the people and resembling the soldiers of the Year II. Thus the Convention had not saved France with an improvised army, motivated solely by revolutionary *élan*. Rather, 'political' generals had been replaced with true soldiers like Hoche and Bonaparte. Volunteers were disciplined by veterans in the *demi-brigades*, resulting in a synthesis of discipline and action: 'fearless, blameless and disinterested heroes, distrustful of financial reward which they judged unworthy of themselves, the soldiers of the Year II were disciplined to the extent that they were able to endure the most cruel suffering'.[96] The Jacobin reference was particularly marked in the EVP, whose insignia was a reproduction of Rude's *Marseillaise*. On one occasion the EVP of the 3rd arrondissement presented a tableau, in which they dressed up as *sans culottes*.[97] Fédération activists were sensitive to the Jacobin claims of the PSF. Bosse-Platière protested that in the Federation 'we have no uniforms or arm-bands, we have never marched, we are not *sans culottes*, we are without shirts of any colour'.[98]

One function of the PSF's use of the Jacobin tradition was to win support from the left by differentiating itself from conservatives like Bosse-Platière. Portrayal of Hoche as a defender of *la patrie* rather than as the 'butcher of the Vendée' is illustrative of this desire. Like the Croix de Feu, the PSF declared itself ready to respect all beliefs, including atheism, on condition that they were not exploited for political purposes. Canat de Chizy displayed an instrumental attitude towards the Catholic Church. It buttressed a necessarily inegalitarian social order, because of its 'terrible punishment for those who offend against its laws'.[99] But Catholicism alone was insufficient to hold society together. Only the 'mystique Croix de Feu', born in the trenches, could bind together rich and poor.[100] In the late 1930s the prospects for a *rapprochement* of Catholics and anticlericals did indeed seem to be good. The attempts of the Communists to reach out to Catholics, and Blum's attempted dialogue with the papacy, attracted a minority of Catholics.[101] More significantly for conservative politics, June 1936 caused some Radicals to discover the value of Catholicism as a prop of the social order. The most spectacular demonstration of this 'new spirit' came in parliament in 1939, when a number of Radicals signed a PSF motion calling for revision of the Lay Laws.[102] Herriot meanwhile made a celebrated trip to the Holy land.

---

[96] *Ibid.*, 14 July 1939.   [97] *Ibid.*, 13 January 1938.
[98] *Ibid.*, 8 December 1937.   [99] *Ibid.*, 14 May 1937.   [100] *Ibid.*, 14 May 1937.
[101] Christophe, *1936*, 180–1; Rémond, *Les Catholiques, le communisme et les crises*, 213–51.
[102] Berstein, *Histoire du Parti radical*, II, 484–6.

But in fact religion had not lost its capacity to divide French society or the right. There is little evidence that the PSF's attempts to place itself above the religious quarrel won many left-wing votes. Indeed, the Radical federation of the Rhône voted a motion condemning those who had called for revision of the Lay Laws.[103] The Instituteurs laïque du Rhône called for a renewal of anticlericalism in a much publicised conference at Belleville. This was followed by a polemic on the religious issue between the Radicals and the PSF.[104] The chances of a *rapprochement* were further undermined by the very strength of the identity between the right and Catholicism in this period. Indeed, the attempt of the left to win over the faithful had provoked a reaction on the part of conservative Catholics. It was reinforced by the Spanish Civil War, for Franco's cause was seen by many conservatives as a holy one. Of great significance locally was the murder of a young boy by a gang of children in the Croix-Rousse in April 1937. Just as it exploited the Spanish Civil War, the *Nouvelliste* stirred up public opinion. It reported that the victim, a member of a well-known Catholic family, had been returning home after purchasing a lottery ticket in aid of Catholic education.[105]

In such a climate it was difficult for the PSF to maintain its neutral attitude to religion, for Catholicism and anticommunism appeared more and more to be two sides of the same coin. At first the PSF rarely mentioned Catholicism in connection with the Spanish Civil War, preferring to base support for Franco on anticommunism and the need for allies in the Mediterranean.[106] Yet by mid-1937 the PSF was denouncing the materialist socialism, Radical Freemasonry and godless communism which had devastated the churches and convents of Spain. Neither could the PSF stand aside from the hysteria surrounding the Croix-Rousse murder, especially as the boy's father was a party member. *Le Volontaire '36* reported that, like a biblical character, the victim 'had been stoned by the enemies of religion'.[107] During the affair the PSF was obliged to restate its own support for Catholicism, and indeed to produce a special edition of *Le Volontaire '36* on this subject.

Thus the PSF's attempts to appeal to the Radical electorate by placing itself above the clerical/anticlerical divide were compromised by the increasingly absolute identification of militant Catholicism with the struggle against the Popular Front. It might, however, have had more success in overcoming clerical/anticlerical tensions within the right. After June 1936 there was no recurrence of the polemics among conservative

---

[103] *Ibid.*, 486.
[104] *L'Union républicaine*, 30 April 1939; *Le Volontaire '36*, 16 June 1939.
[105] *Le Nouvelliste*, 24 April 1937 and following issues.
[106] *Le Volontaire '36*, 24 February 1939.   [107] *Ibid.*, 30 April 1937.

parties about lay education of 1935. The Alliance démocratique, bastion of conservative anticlericalism, had fallen victim to the polarisation of June 1936. The presence of a number of engineering employers, a group at one time committed to the Alliance démocratique, in the PSF suggests that the attitudes of this group at least had changed. These were developments of great significance. But equally important was that the closer identity of right with Catholicism meant that, more than ever, conflicts *among* Catholics were imported into the right. The PSF functioned as the vehicle which brought social Catholicism into the conservative mainstream. Activists like Jacques Darodes and Philippe Andriot had been involved in the *Chronique*. Canat de Chizy, once President of USIC, claimed that papal encyclicals were the foundation of the PSF's corporatist ideas.[108] On many occasions *Le Volontaire '36* argued that Catholic Action pursued the same ends as the PSF.[109] Examples of this type could be multiplied. The main point, however, is that as the PSF perfected its electoral programme the social Catholics who had always figured prominently in La Rocque's movement were given more opportunity to develop their views. The result was that the meaning of Catholicism became a bone of contention within the right. In the polarised atmosphere of the Popular Front years social Catholics turned to the right, but their opposition to the Catholic establishment was not reduced. Thus Canat claimed that it was the PSF, not the socially conservative Victor Perret, which best reflected the Church's social teachings.[110] So far from transcending the clerical/anticlerical division, the PSF was increasingly dominated by one section of the Catholic constituency. Furthermore, the terms of Canat's attack on Perret remind us that religious conflict cannot be treated in isolation from socio-economic issues (or vice versa).

L'Etat social PSF

We have seen that after June 1936, out of fear of communism, conservative groups which had long endeavoured to define themselves in opposition to the 'establishment' – small and medium employers, peasants, white-collar workers and even manual workers – were pushed into a tacit alliance with big business. Similarly engineers, an emergent group, attempted to define a role separate from that of big capital whilst fighting off the communist threat to their authority. A similar process was visible in the Church, where the advanced wing of social Catholicism increasingly aligned itself with the drive against the Popular Front.

[108] *Ibid.*, 11 March 1938.   [109] *Ibid.*, 30 July 1937.
[110] *Ibid.*, 26 November 1937.

Yet the antagonism of these groups to big business had not diminished. The PSF provided a solution to this contradiction through its populist synthesis of radicalism and reaction. In particular the PSF fastened onto the popularity after June 1936 of the idea of the 'classes moyennes', which it connected to corporatism. Both seemed to offer a means of reconciling anticommunism and antielitism with defence of special interests. But in fact such hopes were vain. The fundamental problem was that no society could 'cohere' in the way that the PSF wanted it to. Furthermore, as it moved away from fascism the PSF was unable even to create the illusory image of a 'national' party achieved by the Croix de Feu.

The notion of the *classes moyennes*, as employed by the PSF, captures perfectly the nature of the PSF's populism.[111] A central theme of party propaganda was that the liberal economy born in 1789 had unleashed a blind struggle of selfish individuals. Because of inequality of capacities this had led to the emergence of 'economic feudalisms'. Motivated by the same greed, the workers in June 1936 had also made a series of gains, which only the 'trusts' could afford to pay for. Thus there was a tacit alliance of trusts, CGT and the state which would eventually lead to the elimination of the *classes moyennes*.[112] The implications of this discourse were simultaneously radical and reactionary.

Conservatism emerges from the belief of Johannès Dupraz, who combined a weekly column in *Le Volontaire '36* with the deputy directorship of AICA, that the rapaciousness of big business was limited by 'a certain humanism' and by its respect for the currency as a 'national reality' superior to itself.[113] Indeed, the PSF's hostility to Popular Front labour legislation matched that of employers. The radical potential of *classes moyennes* discourse was also restricted by defining the term broadly enough to include almost the whole nation. André Dominique defined the *classes moyennes* as being intermediate between the 'grand patronat' and the proletariat.[114] They therefore included artisans, managers, technicians, hairdressers, pork butchers, engineers and all the 'disinherited of the Popular Front'.[115] Since Dominique identified the 'patronat' exclusively with those at the head of medium and small enterprises and distinguished it from the 'trusts' it was possible to include the major part of the capitalist class.[116] Dupraz went further still, defining the 'trusts' in moral terms: the intervention of big business in

[111] My argument here owes a debt to Boltanski, *The Making of a Class*, chapter 1.
[112] *Le Volontaire '36*, 15 August 1936, 6 April and 31 December 1937, 12 January 1938.
[113] *Le Volontaire '36*, 28 April 1938.
[114] *Ibid.*, 26 November 1937.
[115] *Ibid.*, 26 November 1937.   [116] *Ibid.*, 12 January 1938.

politics was to be criticised only where it was 'powerful, anonymous and occult'.[117] At the other end of the social scale, some foresaw the incorporation of workers into the *classes moyennes* by various devices to be considered below. As Luc Boltanski argues, the broad definition of the *classes moyennes* made it possible to reduce the bourgeoisie to an anonymous clique and to ignore differences in wealth and power.[118] By linking the *classes moyennes* to intermediacy it was also possible to allow their representatives (i.e. the PSF) to speak in the general interest.

This in turn points to the radical implications of *classes moyennes* discourse, for sovereignty was located with the people rather than the elites. And there was no guarantee that the followers of the PSF would treat anticapitalism metaphorically. The party was indeed conscious that the idea of the *classes moyennes* was based partly on the grievances of self-conscious social groups. Writers in *Le Volontaire '36* routinely referred to the problems involved in uniting the *classes moyennes*. La Rocque told an audience in Lyon that the PSF would 'stand above' the potential discord within the *classes moyennes*.[119] Yet it is to be doubted whether the PSF in Lyon succeeded in remaining neutral, for there were fundamental divergences within the party over the definition of the middle class.

On the one hand, for Jacques Picquery the *classes moyennes* were defined by possession of a 'patrimony', which they had earned through their own labour, unlike the parasites of anonymous finance capital. This allowed capitalists who 'worked' to be distinguished from financiers. It also meant that the problem of the working class would be solved through acquisition of individual property, and would ultimately mean the 'regulated' disappearance of 'unproductive large fortunes'.[120] On the other hand Canat saw the large enterprise and the working class as permanent. He preferred therefore to place the 'cadres' at the centre of the *classes moyennes*, and to make 'competence' their essential characteristic. Again big business was implicitly excluded for its lack of expertise, as were the workers. The term 'cadre' had the additional advantage of implying leadership and status not only within the enterprise and society but of engineers (such as Canat, a graduate of the Ecole centrale in Paris) within the PSF.[121] With time it was Canat's views which won out. Picquery ceased to write for *Le Volontaire '36* in the spring of 1937.

The conflict between Canat and Picquery can be explained partly in terms of the classic dichotomy between new and old sections of the

---

[117] *Ibid.*, 28 April 1938.   [118] Boltanski, *The Making of a Class*, 56–7.
[119] *Le Volontaire '36*, 19 March 1937.
[120] *Ibid.*, 5 and 12 March and 19 February 1937.
[121] *Ibid.*, 24 February and 30 June 1939.

middle class. Since Picquery was legal consultant to an association of small silk weavers, and Canat was an engineer in an artificial fibre concern, one could therefore identify 'patrimony' with small business and 'competence' with technocratic engineers. Yet the relationship was not automatic. In other contexts engineers defined their qualifications as a form of patrimony. Similarly Canat attempted to extend the notion of cadre to include 'healthy' elements of the working class, the best small businessmen and shopkeepers, and even the most productive peasants, all of whom could be seen as possessing a level of 'competence'.[122] In this struggle to define and delimit the boundaries and nature of social groups, material issues were inseparable from ideological conflicts. From our point of view the most important practical consequence was that Canat's use of the idea of competence, and emphasis on the importance of the intermediate elite were derived from his experience of social Catholicism. He was therefore best equipped to reach social groups in which these ideas had some resonance. This is why the PSF appealed to those engineers, white-collar workers, small and medium businessmen and peasants who were sensitive either to social Catholicism or to progressive ideas of business organisation.[123] Thus as the La Rocque's movement became a party and developed its ideas on political economy its appeal was narrowed in ideological and social terms.[124]

The same applies to the PSF's use of corporatism. We have seen that corporatism arose from a crisis of the state and civil society, in which an extreme struggle between interests groups compromised the ability of bodies from the Chamber of Commerce to Parliament to mediate the general interest.[125] It was assumed that divisions were the work of outside agents such as civil servants or communists. There was said to be a single professional and general interest which could be reasserted were the professions to govern themselves. Like *classes moyennes* discourse, corporatism provided an illusory means to integrate the right and French society behind the leadership of the PSF. But as the PSF went beyond the generalities of the Croix de Feu its conception of corporatism became ever more narrow.

There is no need to linger on the role of the state in PSF corporatism, for it had not changed fundamentally since the time of the Croix de Feu. The party presented corporatism as an alternative to state intervention. Canat de Chizy preferred the Salazar regime in Portugal to the

---

[122] *Ibid.*, 19 and 26 February 1937, 14 January 1938.
[123] The only exceptions were the traditionally anticlerical engineering employers. But had they been influenced by Action catholique industrielle?
[124] This is to disagree with Boltanski, *The Making of a Class*, 62–74, who argues that a united middle-class movement was formed in this period.
[125] *Le Volontaire '36*, 1 December 1936.

'deformed' corporations of Austria and Germany.[126] Yet Canat condemned liberalism in all its forms and argued not only that agreements on pricing should be compulsory when desired by the majority in the profession, but that individuals would be obliged to join an elaborate system of regional corporations which would regulate supply and demand, labour relations and working practices, and would perhaps even manage joint enterprises. This implied the setting up of a permanent bureaucracy with legally sanctioned authority, especially as interprofessional questions would be dealt with by 'experts'.[127] The importance of the state also emerged from the fact that the highest corporate body would have no power to legislate, but would merely express its views to the political power (i.e. the presidency), which in the end would have the power to decide. In this way the 'autonomy' of the state, already freed from parliamentary control, would be restored.[128] As Canat put it, the state would 'oblige citizens to remain within the limits of the general interest, even at the expense of their particular interests'.[129] But as the PSF refined its conception of the *profession organisée* it appeared increasingly ready to place its coercive potential at the service of the relatively narrow group of interests. This argument can be elucidated by looking at the characteristics of the PSF's activists.

The activists of the PSF

There can be little doubt that the overwhelming majority of PSF activists, sympathisers and voters was drawn from the constituency of the right. Relatively few deserters from the parliamentary right played a visible role in the PSF, as keen as ever to retain its image of novelty and independence. But Octave Lavalette admitted losses from Fédération ranks at the January 1937 departmental congress.[130] And the PSF's victory in a local by-election in the 2nd arrondissement depended wholly on Fédération votes. In the local elections of October 1937 the PSF showed that it was less likely than the Fédération to win Radical votes in second ballots.[131] The PSF was also relatively bourgeois (Figure 5). If the class breakdown of the PSF is compared to the electorate in the agglomeration, then the PSF turns out to have been substantially the most bourgeois of the three major right-wing parties in this period.[132] PSF activists were heavily concentrated in bourgeois areas of the city

126 *Ibid.*, 11 and 25 March 1938.
127 *Ibid.*, 7 May, 20 August, 1 October and 31 December 1937.
128 *Ibid.*, 14 January 1938 and 25 February 1938.   129 *Ibid.*, 1 October 1937.
130 AN 317 AP 79, report of January 1937.
131 Passmore, 'The right and the extreme right', 312–14.
132 *Ibid.*: Fédération: 15% workers, 21% peasants; PSF: 12% workers, 10% peasants.

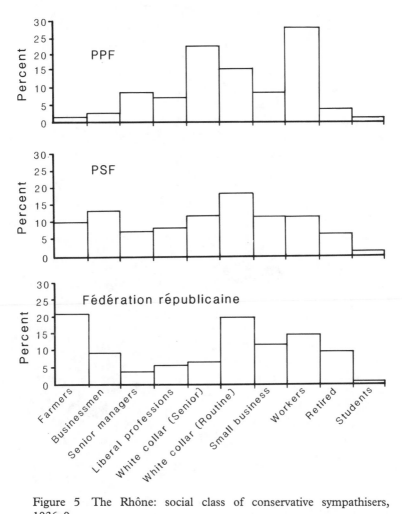

Figure 5   The Rhône: social class of conservative sympathisers, 1936–9

(Map 17).[133] The Federation, in contrast, retained its implantation in proletarian suburbs, although its committees were less active than in the past because all the parties of the right after June 1936 found it hard to engage in public activity in left-wing areas. There is then little to support Milza's contention that the PSF was an 'interclass' party. Indeed, the Fédération had a greater claim to this title.

[133] 47% of PSF activists lived in such areas, as defined by Pinol, *Espace sociale*.

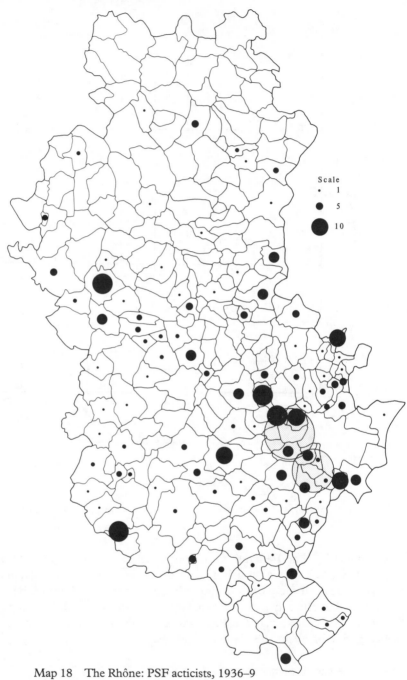

Map 18   The Rhône: PSF acticists, 1936–9

Of more interest is the question of *which* part of the conservative constituency was won by the PSF. It gathered together a coalition of groups which had long defined themselves in opposition to the conservative establishment. This was reflected in the geographical implantation of the PSF (Maps 17–18). It was particularly well implanted in the Brotteaux, where it took over the heritage of the 'progressive' bourgeoisie which had once been loyal to Aynard. It drew as much on the constituency which had supported the Alliance démocratique and PDP as it did on that of the Fédération. In the countryside the PSF did better than the Fédération on the plateau and in small towns where Aynard had done well. But it was also, as we shall see, able to benefit from a crisis of notable politics in the mountains.

These features of the PSF are emphasised by comparison with the Fédération. Under Perret the Fédération had rallied groups opposed to big business. After 1936 this was more true than ever. In the countryside it was best established in areas of traditional conservatism: the Beaujolais and the mountains, especially the canton of Belleville where large vineyards were numerous. In the city, the Fédération retreated into the 2nd and 4th arrondissements, areas dominated by merchant-manufacturing, the Œuvre des cercles and even the aristocracy – there was a new concentration of activists in the noble *quartier* between Bellecour and Ainay. Not surprisingly Perret moved politically ever closer to the successors of Action française. Meanwhile the Fédération lost support in proletarian suburbs, thanks largely to the difficulties experienced by all parties in organising in left-wing areas after June 1936. But where social tension was less (the 4th and the north-western part of the 7th), it was still able to use links to the Church to mobilise a wide following. The Federation too defined itself in opposition to the big-business elites of Lyon, and there was a populist element in its discourse. But it remained more conservative and elitist than the PSF. The contrasts were further emphasised by the fact that the PSF elaboration of a conventional political programme narrowed its appeal.

Business

The PSF included among its sympathisers a number of elite businessmen, including Henry Morel-Journal and two members of the Aynard family.[134] It is also evident from surviving party archives that the PSF was engaged in a constant search for contributions from business.[135]

[134] AN 451 AP 172, Bruyas to de Préval 15 August 1938; *Journal d'Henry Morel-Journal*, 2 May 1938.
[135] AN 451 AP 172, Frandaz to de Préval, 22 October 1937.

But too much cannot be read into this, for the PSF received funds from businessmen of diverse opinions, from the metal-trading company Descours and Cabaud, which had in the past subsidised Action française, to the republican engineering employers' association.[136] Moreover, business support for the PSF remained private and conditional. Morel-Journel was dubious about the ability of the PSF to win mass support because it was widely seen as fascist. His sympathy for La Rocque's party did not prevent him from attending meetings of the centrist Mascaraud Committee, or from welcoming the Daladier Government in 1938. Indeed, Morel-Journel was an acquaintance of Daladier's finance minister Marchandeau, with whom he claimed to have collaborated in his work of national recovery.[137] Equally adaptable was Georges Villiers. The new leader of the engineering employers financed the PSF, but kept this from his members and insisted that money was used only for social activities.[138] Big firms such as Gillet promoted the PSF's trade union wing, the SPF, but did not openly support the movement – perhaps because Gillet was from time to time attacked in the PSF press. Other wealthy *marchands de soie*, such as Ariste Potton, hoped that recovery could be achieved without breaking with existing institutions.[139]

The equivocal attitude of big business to the PSF was reciprocated. The party certainly offered something to big business. It was, of course, resolutely anticommunist, and on every practical issue, from the forty-hour week to wages, the PSF agreed with the CGPF.[140] The force of attacks on the CGPF and big business for their lack of 'social' spirit was reduced by the fact that all employers claimed to act in the best interests of workers.[141] And we have seen that the party's *classes moyennes* discourse defined big business as an anonymous clique. Yet in areas other than labour relations the PSF's hostility to big business had a good deal of substance, which became clearer as PSF writers elucidated their ideas. The *profession organisée* was designed to reduce the influence of big business by means of regionalisation.[142] For this reason organisation would be by finished product (such as electrical goods), rather than raw material (such as steel). The business section of the corporation would consist of an equal number of delegates of small, medium and large

---

[136] AN 451 AP 172, Kemlin to Mme de Préval, 11 October 1937; see also Fridenson, *Histoire des Usines Renault*, 260, on the centralisation of business funding of parties in the Rhône.

[137] *Journal d'Henry Morel-Journel*, 26 August 1936, 11 and 15 April 1937.

[138] AN 451 AP 172, 18 December 1938.

[139] Potton, *On a trouvé un chef*; A. Potton and J. Comparat, *La Révolution qu'il faut faire* (Lyon, 1938).

[140] In *Le Volontaire '36*, 28 July and 1 December 1937.

[141] *Ibid.*, 12 February 1937, 11 February 1938.   [142] *Ibid.*, 31 December 1937.

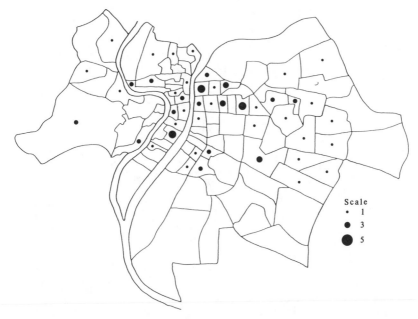

Map 19   Lyon and Villeurbanne: businessmen in the PSF, 1936–9

firms and would be compulsory.[143] This was a far cry from the limited projects designed to give legal backing to employers' organisations favoured by big business.[144] Furthermore, the PSF went as far as to target particular firms. For example it was claimed that organisation of the profession would prevent large crockery firms from using prices to drive medium and small firms out of business.[145]

Big business then saw some potential in the PSF, partly perhaps because of its political isolation in the Rhône, but never dominated it in the way that it once had the Fédération. Rather those businessmen who supported the PSF defined themselves in opposition to the Lyonnais business elite. PSF businessmen preferred the 6th arrondissement and left bank, home of the 'progressive' wing of the industrial bourgeoisie (Maps 19–20). This affiliation was also evident in the fact that engineering employers (who had once favoured the centre-right), were considerably more numerous in the PSF than in the Fédération.[146] Dietz, one of the leaders of a new Syndicat de la petite métallurgie, was a

[143] *Ibid.*, 7 May 1937.
[144] CRCCL, 1936, 190 and PVCCL, 10 November 1936.
[145] *Le Volontaire '36*, 1 April 1938. See also 5 March and 2 July 1937.
[146] Fédération: 5%; PSF: 17% of business supporters.

Map 20   Lyon and Villeurbanne: businessmen in the Fédération républicaine, 1936–9

departmental orator in the PSF. The party also counted in its ranks two *gros façonniers*, another group with a long-standing hostility to the big-business elites. Also numerous were medium firms in the dyeing industry, where concentration in the hands of Gillet made PSF anti-capitalism seem attractive. In this case the Fédération genuinely appeared to be a party of big capital, for on its Comité départemental sat François Balay of Gillet and Jean Vulloid of the second largest dyeing firm in the region. Gillet, moreover, became the scapegoat for the notoriously bad labour problems in the dyeing industry, and was accused by the PSF of entering into a conspiracy with Marxists in order to destroy 'good' capitalists.[147] The emphasis of some PSF writers on a combination of rationalisation and technological progress with quality production and hostility to large firms matched the conceptions of this group.

We have seen that the Fédération too won the support of medium business, and engaged in a moderately populist hostility to the business

[147] *Le Volontaire '36*, 19 July 1937.

elites. But it attracted those more conservative employers, such as the cotton manufacturers of the Monts du Beaujolais and merchant-manufacturers in the silk industry who distrusted rationalisation and often wished to preserve the artisanate. The special attraction of the PSF for the progressive wing of the industrial bourgeoisie had probably not existed in the Croix de Feu. But increasingly, the PSF press became dominated by progressive ideas about business organisation. This may explain why the PSF failed to progress in the Monts du Beaujolais cotton towns, even though the Croix de Feu had possessed a thriving section in Tarare.

The PSF did not recruit small business or artisans in great numbers. Marcel Perdriel failed in an attempt to organise a self-defence group for shopkeepers in the summer of 1936. A subsequent move to create a specialist shopkeeper group also came to nothing.[148] This was partly because of the growing preoccupation of PSF writers with the organisation of large firms. Indeed, Canat argued that in the silk industry artisans should not be allowed to compete with industrial concerns. But the PSF did pay some attention to small business, arguing for example that the organised profession would regulate apprenticeships, prevent overcrowding of trades, encourage 'small inventors' and ensure that the benefits of technological progress were disseminated to the artisanate.[149] This emphasis on technology connected with Canat's attempt to use the idea of 'competence' to draw in the artisanate. But here too the PSF did not encounter a favourable resonance except among the minority of Catholic small traders sensitised to the idea of the professional elite by Catholic Action. Most small businessmen remained anticlerical, while the PSF became ever more Catholic.[150] Thus, the PSF's appeal was limited by a combination of ideological and economic interests.

Engineers

Whereas engineers and senior managers comprised 4% of Fédération sympathisers, they represented 7% of the PSF. Furthermore, those in the Fédération were found in non-industrial sectors, whereas PSF supporters worked in large factories. They also played a significant part in setting the tone of the PSF. Canat de Chizy was the party's social affairs specialist; Paul Cuzin, manager of Textiles du Rhône, ran the

---

[148] ADR 4m 236, 24 July 1937 and 4m 244, campagnes alarmistes.
[149] *Le Volontaire '36*, 20 April 1937.
[150] Catholic Action's specialist branch for small businessmen made some progress in 1937 and 1938, but its influence remained limited.

PSF's Neuville section.[151] Engineers can be seen as taking over the role of big business in local politics, as the latter moved onto the national stage. Engineers were certainly a part of the ruling class. Many, like Cuzin and Paul Lombard, manager of the Rhodiaceta artificial fibre factory, played an important part in the patronal counteroffensive. Yet they saw themselves as a distinct group. True, they were often encouraged to do so by some employers who saw the cadres movement as a front for their own interests. But other factors were also important. Engineers had been encouraged by social Catholic thought to see themselves as representing a middle way between capital and labour, while the bureacratisation of the workplace increasingly separated ownership and control. Thus, for Canat (once of USIC), engineers, heads of department and foremen were better able than employers, and still more workers, to interpret the needs of the enterprise.[152] As a result of June 1936 many added a combination of extreme anticommunism to a sense of having been abandoned by employers isolated in Paris, especially after the 'surrender' of Matignon. Indeed, some had been attacked personally by strikers.[153] These 'frustrated collaborators' mixed radicalism with reaction, and were attracted therefore to the PSF.

Canat de Chizy had belonged to the Croix de Feu, but only in the PSF was he able to develop his ideas on the role of the engineers. He gave them a prominent role in the *profession organisée*, for their intermediacy made them better placed than employers to see the general situation.[154] They would be accorded separate representation alongside employers and workers, and would be consulted before dismissal of workers.[155] André Dominique and Canat were also much influenced by the ideas of the patronal avant-garde, as expressed by Detœuf and the review *Ordre réel*.[156] From such sources they took a belief in technological progress and rationalisation.[157] This created a potential for conflict with the medium-business supporters of the PSF, who often combined rationalisation with a system of production based on quality and flexibility. Symbolically, at least, the conflict would be resolved by the break-up of anonymous large enterprises into federations of semi-autonomous workshops run by engineers. They would thus come to resemble medium firms.[158] There was also an appeal to 'competence' – both engineers and medium businessmen could be seen as gaining

---

[151] On Canat see Hamon, Augustin *Les Maîtres de la France* (3 vols., 1936–8).
[152] *Le Volontaire '36*, 14 January 1936.
[153] Interview with Dr Roger Astruc (1987); *Le Nouvelliste*, 15 July 1936.
[154] *Le Volontaire '36*, 26 February 1937.   [155] *Ibid.*, 31 December 1937.
[156] *Ibid.*, 15 July 1938, 3 March 1939.
[157] *Ibid.*, 5 February and 15 October 1937.   [158] *Ibid.*, 18 June 1937.

expertise and knowledge through their intermediate position and their direct contact with workers.

Workers and white-collar workers

The PSF also articulated the hostility of conservative white-collar workers – the largest single group of its sympathisers – to the establishment.[159] There is no evidence that CFTC activists joined the PSF. But the PSF recruited in areas where the CFTC was strong. Thus few PSF white-collar workers lived in proletarian suburbs, except where they had been able to fasten onto the patronal counteroffensive (for example Gillet employees). Rather they lived in the bourgeois 2nd, 5th and 6th arrondissements. Particularly significant was the 3rd arrondissement, where the PSF was relatively weak, but where a considerable number of white-collar workers supported the party. The explanation is that this had once been a stronghold of the PDP which had drawn heavily on pro-CTFC employees. What is more, the PSF recruited where the more advanced wing of the CFTC had been strong, and not among the white-collar workers of the silk industry resident in the Croix-Rousse. Here the Fédération retained its hold, thanks to the influence of the Œuvre des cercles. On the other hand, the PSF recruited few white-collar workers in the 7th, where the PDP had never established a strong section.

The PSF also resembled the CFTC in that its white collar supporters worked in firms in the centre of the city rather than the large factories of the suburbs. At this point, however, there appears a significant difference between CFTC and PSF support, for PSF supporters worked almost exclusively in small and medium firms whereas CFTC activists were found in the large banks and department stores of the centre as well as in small and medium concerns. The most likely explanation is that in large concerns CFTC activists were more conscious of the distinctive principles of the CFTC and more concerned to distinguish themselves from a distant patronat – perhaps for the first time the CFTC had been able to create a genuine workplace unionism. Much the same pattern applied to working-class support for the PSF, which also came largely from small and medium firms in the centre of the city. The party found it hard to organise openly in areas of large factory production thanks to the extreme hostility of the communists.[160] PSF support in big factories usually depended on the existence of an employer offensive against the CGT. In the left-wing press there were frequent accusations of employer pressure

[159] 30% in the PSF compared to 25% in the Fédération.
[160] AN 451 AP 172, Mme de Préval to Kemlin, 9 October 1937.

to join the PSF.[161] There is more reliable evidence that Paul Cuzin at Textiles du Rhône obliged jobseekers to join the PSF.[162] The Syndicats professionnels français (SPF), the trade union wing of the PSF, made quite significant gains in delegate elections in the Gillet dyeing factories after the failure of a bitter strike in 1937.[163] At the Société lyonnaise de textile, company secretary Canat de Chizy led a section of the SPF.[164]

None of this means, however, that PSF support among manual and white-collar workers can be put down simply to employer pressure. The individuals in our sample of activists not only joined the party, but went to its meetings and had probably been long-standing conservative voters. Moreover, we have seen that the CFTC, on which the PSF drew, had got round the notorious hostility to unions of their employers by basing organisation on the parishes. So to some extent they were beyond the reach of employers. Finally, we have seen that conservative workers and white-collar workers were attracted to the material programme of the Popular Front at a time when the Fédération was undertaking an offensive against social reforms. The PSF seemed therefore to offer a means simultaneously of fighting the left, of protecting material interests and of denouncing a patronat which refused to collaborate.[165] The PSF met these demands first through hostility to the communists and the CGT. Employers would play a part in the choice of workers' delegates to corporate bodies. The right to strike would be limited in the short term to cases of non-observation of a collective contract, and in the long term abolished. The PSF also urged that existing syndicates be reformed along hierarchical lines and 'depoliticised'. They would then become truly professional bodies. This in practice meant either a purge or suppression of the CGT.[166] Conservative workers could hope to gain from the implementation of such measures. Yet the PSF's attitude to the unions remained radical and populist. It aimed not just to defeat the CGT but to take over the leadership of the working-class movement and incorporate it into the nation through a process of mass mobilisation. (It is, however, unclear whether this would be achieved by purging the CGT or by replacing it with the SPF.)

The SPF was thus accorded a certain room for manoeuvre, and in its

[161] B. Beguet, 'Comportements politiques et structures sociales. Le Parti social français et la Fédération républicaine à Lyon, 1936–1939' (mémoire de maîtrise, Lyon II, 1988), 164.

[162] ADR 4m Conseils municipaux, Neuville, Peissel to Angeli, 10 February 1941.

[163] Gillet was the common denominator in the firms mentioned in La Voix du peuple: the Société lyonnaise du textil, the Textiles du Rhône, Rhodiaceta and Rhône-Poulenc.

[164] ADR 3u 316 Parquet de Lyon.

[165] For a contrary view see Soucy, French Fascism: The Second Wave, 129–31.

[166] Le Volontaire '36, 1 December 1936, 14 January 1938.

search for legitimacy in the factories and offices the movement sometimes went beyond the programme of the PSF. The independence of its trade union wing also permitted the PSF to accommodate, in theory at least, the material demands of its own white-collar and working-class constituency. This strategy of mass mobilisation through sectional organisation was in fact typical of authoritarian-populist movements.[167] Thus in the silk industry the SPF claimed credit for the implementation of the forty-hour law, accusing CGT negotiators of deliberately slowing down negotiations to punish those who had not joined the CGT.[168] In the banks the SPF denounced 'the bosses unions, directed by international high finance which is attempting to buy our activists in order to halt their syndical action', and called for index linking of salaries, a demand which appalled employers.[169] Unlike the PSF, the SPF condemned the Daladier decree laws, but typically nevertheless, contributed to the defeat of the general strike which followed.[170] The tensions of the SPF proved, in the end, to be insurmountable. By 1939 its leaders were falling out amongst themselves.[171] Similar conflicts occurred in France as a whole, and in 1939 the PSF created a new organisation, the Propagande ouvrier et commercial (POC), directly under party control. In Lyon, POC leader Darodes wrote of the lack of 'Croix de Feu spirit' in the SPF, and charged the POC with the task of infiltrating and controlling the trade unions.[172] Under the Vichy regime the SPF separated formally from the PSF. In effect the PSF's attempt to incorporate the workers through a sectional organisation had merely imported general social conflict into the party. This was typical of authoritarian-populist movements, which often consisted of an alliance of sectional groupings united by a bond such as paramilitary activism or a leader cult. Both were reduced in efficacy in the PSF.

The peasantry

A combination of anticommunism with hostility to the conservative establishment also explains PSF support in the countryside. The PSF

[167] Jeremy Noakes, 'The Nazi Party and the Third Reich: the myth and reality of the one-party state', in *Government, Party and People in Nazi Germany*, ed. Jeremy Noakes (Exeter, 1980), 13–15.

[168] *SPF des ouvriers et employés de soieries*, 25 May 1937; *La Liberté syndicale*, July 1937.

[169] *Le Nouvelliste*, 4 August 1937.

[170] Mâchefer, 'Les Syndicats professionnels français, 1936–1939', *Mouvement social* 119 (1982), 91–112.

[171] ADR 4m 236, 31 May 1939.

[172] Darodes to Durafour, 20 April 1940, quoted in Boulet, 'Le Parti social français dans le Rhône, 1936–1939 (mémoire de maîtrise, Lyon II, 1975), annexe 2.

represented the first significant challenge to the Fédération in the rural areas since the ALP. But the PSF was very different from the party of de Mun, in which notables had mobilised a passive peasantry through the Church. Indeed, it was the Fédération which recruited in areas of former ALP strength in the Beaujolais and mountains. The PSF recruited more heavily than the Fédération on the plateau, from which Aynard had drawn his strength. But it also made substantial inroads into the mountains – in the *cantonales* of 1937 a PSF candidate came close to defeating Alexandre la Batie, in many ways typical of the absentee landowners who led the Fédération in the mountains. Thus the PSF must be placed in the context of a long-term crisis of notable politics in the countryside. The exception was that the PSF did not establish itself in the Beaujolais wine-growing area. This was partly because of an improvement in wine prices after 1936 and also because in that area it was socialists who had profited from the crisis of the elites. This is why the JAC had not developed in the Beaujolais.

Indeed, it was the JAC, together with Catholic Action in general, which had prepared the way for the PSF. Like the JAC, which had been led by individuals a little on the margins of agricultural society, the PSF was concentrated above all in small towns, especially along the main lines of communication (Map 18). Activists were often drawn from the rural petty bourgeoisie and were less likely than Fédération activists to have been born in the commune in which they resided. PSF activists differed in character from both the notables and representatives of peasant 'bonnes familles' which had supported the Fédération. Nevertheless, the PSF did win substantial peasant support, as the St Laurent election revealed. The fruit of JAC attempts to create a peasant elite was perhaps evident in the fact that peasants were more common in the leadership of the PSF than in the Fédération.

In the countryside the PSF's ideas connected with those of the JAC. This is revealing of the way in which the PSF constituency was shaped simultaneously by social Catholicism and material interest. Thus the PSF agricultural spokesman saw modernisation of agriculture as a means both of putting a stop to the rural exodus and of defending a rural Christian civilisation against the communists. Modernisation could be achieved only through application of Catholic ideas on reform of agricultural syndicates, for which reason it would be necessary first to restore religion to state schools; Catholic France could be saved only by preserving the peasantry.[173] All Catholics would have agreed with the latter. But not everyone agreed that such a goal entailed the purging of

---

[173] *Le Volontaire '36*, 9 April and 4 June 1937, 15 July 1938.

Catholic worthies from the USE. This points again to the populism of the Croix de Feu and to a narrowing of the PSF's potential appeal, as the party's views came more and more to coincide with those of the JAC. Thus the PSF took up the cause of small producers of wheat as the Office du blé was reformed in 1938 and 1939 according to the demands of large growers. That the PSF ended up defending the original socialist version illustrates the tensions within the right caused by the Popular Front.[174] Similarly the PSF saw the corporation as limiting the influence of specialised lobbies dominated by large growers such as the Association générale des producteurs de blé.[175] The PSF declared its intention to 'demolish' existing syndicates if they did not reform themselves, to replace 'vieux dévouements à la cause syndicale' and politicians with a genuine peasant leadership, and to furnish syndicates with a powerful permanent organisation. The PSF also aligned itself with the JAC in approving separate representation for proprietors, tenants, sharecroppers and agricultural labourers within the corporation.[176]

'La famille PSF'

The populism of the PSF can also be seen in its response to a perceived crisis of the family. The conservative press had been horrified by the presence of women in occupied factories and regaled its readers with tales of 'scandals and orgies'.[177] In the following months there was a period of raised consciousness in many sections of the population, women included, and for the first time two women joined the government. This reinforced a pre-existing sense that World War One had upset the normal hierarchy of relations between the sexes, as women took over traditional male roles.[178] Similarly, the Popular Front was seen as responsible for the indiscipline of children. The party saw the murder of the 9-year-old son of a PSF member by a gang of youths in the Croix Rousse as the inevitable result of permitting children to participate in May Day parades.[179]

La Rocque followed majority opinion on the right in seeing the family as a bulwark of the social order and in calling for measures such as a family-based voting system. Where the PSF differed from the old right was in a strategy of politicisation and mass mobilisation through the

---

[174] *Le Volontaire '36*, 21 February 1938, 5 May 1939.   [175] *Ibid.*, 10 March 1939.
[176] *Ibid.*, 20 and 27 January 1939, 3 February 1939.
[177] *Le Nouvelliste*, 17 June 1936.
[178] J. McMillan, *Housewife or Harlot: The Position of Women in French Society* (New York, 1981); Mary Louis Roberts ' "This civilisation no longer has sexes": *La Garçonne* and the cultural crisis in France after World War I', *Gender and History* 4 (1992), 49–69.
[179] *Le Volontaire '36*, 30 April and 7 May 1937.

party section. As the *Volontaire '36* put it: 'the PSF is a political party, but it is also a great family; hence the obligation to have a home (*foyer*)'.[180] Sometimes whole families joined the PSF, where they carried on activities normally confined to private life. Meetings often ended with card games. Children were integrated into the life of the section and learned songs which expressed their fidelity to the party.[181] To reinforce parental discipline the PSF organised physical education through the Sociéte sportive d'éducation sociale (SPES). Even some PSF members had reservations about the 'dryness' of its methods.[182] The president of the 4th section concluded a family evening by addressing 'to all children the paternal salute of the father of the PSF family, La Rocque'.[183] Thus the PSF's response to the crisis of the family was to politicise it. In contrast, the Fédération ensured that politics were the preserve of a small group while boules matches and dances were for the rest. Significantly the jazz band of the Fédération's Foyer de Perrache deserted to La Rocque's party, where it became 'le Jazz band PSF'. In a bid to counter the success of the PSF, the Fédération introduced social activities into political meetings. The Foyer de Perrache was officially taken over by the Fédération in 1938.

Furthermore, La Rocque denied that women could be confined to the role of wives and mothers. Hence the creation of women's sections (Action civique), which operated within a patriarchal vision of society, but also organised women for political action.[184] There was then a fundamental ambiguity in the PSF's attitude to women. On the one hand women were directed into traditionally feminine activities such as distribution of relief to the poor through Action sociale. Or they acted as 'helpers for men in the multiple tasks imposed on them by the PSF'.[185] But on the other hand the goal of Action civique was to prepare women for the vote. To this end they would have access to libraries and participate in study groups. Social activities too provided outlets both for non-working women and for young social workers such as Mlle Frandaz in the 5th arrondissement. Some women were able to rise in the party hierarchy. Madame Ruby, head of Action sociale in the department, was admitted to the inner circles of the PSF in the Rhône and after the war was elected to the Conseil général. Her national counterpart, Madame de Préval, was one of a triumvirate which effectively controlled the PSF.

[180] *Le Nouvelliste*, 4 April 1938; *Le Volontaire '36*, 15 October and 2 April 1937.
[181] *Le Volontaire '36*, 6 January 1939. 'Nous lisons le Petit Journal / Nous nous intéressons à la politique / Nous lisons le Petit Journal / Le quotidien vraiment le plus social.'
[182] AN 451 AP 172, Bruyas to de Préval, 4 February 1939.
[183] *Le Volontaire '36*, 16 December 1938.
[184] La Rocque, *Service public*, 75–6, 155–7.
[185] AN 451 AP 172: statement of the goals of *Action civique* in the 1st arrondissement.

Thus the PSF sought simultaneously to contain and to mobilise women, just as it did the working class. The conflicts of French society were not therefore resolved by the PSF. Rather they were imported into the movement itself. This in turn explains the aggressively male tone of the discourse of the PSF, for it was particularly concerned to guard the unstable frontier between masculinity and femininity. The PSF therefore reversed the traditional counterrevolutionary view, in which France was depicted in terms of suffering femininity and the revolutionaries as lecherous brutes.[186] On the contrary, in the symbolism of the PSF, Joan of Arc was masculinised – a 'male lesson' for the mass of Frenchmen too selfish to think of their country.[187] The other side of the PSF's relatively tolerant attitude to female involvement in politics was the male activism of the EVP.

Many more examples of the kinds of groups which supported the PSF could be given. The important points to emphasise, however, are first that the PSF was a populist movement which brought together a diverse group of interests which defined themselves in opposition to the social elites, to the political system as it was constituted and to the left. Second, as the PSF refined its programme, the movement's constituency became more sharply delimited. Increasingly it was notions of 'competence' and the 'elite', drawn partly from social Catholicism, which defined the PSF. The only significant exception was the attraction to the party of employers from the anticlerical engineering industry. There remained, however, a host of tensions latent within the PSF's constituency, which surfaced as the party moved away from the radical activism of the Croix de Feu. Thirdly, the increasingly narrow appeal of the PSF meant that it failed to win support from the Radicals. And more importantly from our perspective, the PSF came into conflict with its rivals on the right.

The PSF and the right

Given the large membership of the PSF our contention that the PSF's recourse to electoralism narrowed its appeal may seem surprising. Had an election been held in late 1936, the PSF may indeed have had considerable success, as its victory in a by-election in the 2nd arrondissement suggested. In fact, thanks to a (relative) decline in political tension and the Fédération's entrenched political position, the PSF proved less successful at winning by-elections than expected. This was confirmed, both in the Rhône and nationally, by the failure of the PSF to make a

---

[186] *La République lyonnaise*, 25 February 1939.
[187] *Le Volontaire '36*, 5 May 1939.

breakthrough in the local elections of October 1937. This confirms Goguel's conclusion that the PSF would not in the 1940 general elections have had the success upon which it counted.[188] Nonetheless, in eastern and urban France the PSF represented a significant challenge to the Fédération. There is therefore something to be said for Irvine's view that the conflict between the Fédération and the PSF revolved around the electoral challenge of the well-organised PSF to the loosely organised Fédération. It is also true, as Irvine argues, that the PSF's attitude to the reforms of the Popular Front and to the international situation was indistinguishable from that of the Fédération, and that the Fédération was hardly less authoritarian than the PSF.[189] But there was nevertheless more to the conflict between the two parties than electoral rivalry. We have seen that the PSF differed from the Fédération in terms of its social composition, its attitude to the Church and its view of political economy.[190] These differences, moreover, can be detected in the polemics between the two parties and in the views they had of each other.

Victor Perret showed his concern about the hegemonic ambition of the PSF as early as the summer of 1936, and urged that the best way to fight the Popular Front was through an alliance of existing parties.[191] The *Nouvelliste* too envisaged conservative unity in terms of an alliance of parties, together with a new movement grouping people from all parties.[192] Conflict came into the open in November when the PSF won a Conseil d'arrondissement seat from the Fédération in the 2nd arrondissement. The Fédération candidate withdrew in favour of the PSF on the second ballot. But the election over, Victor Perret regretted that there had not been a single conservative candidate.[193] The Jeunesses patriotes and royalist *Lugdunum* also took the side of the Fédération. *Lugdunum*, the descendant of Action française, went as far as to publish the Fédération's election address.

Relations between the PSF and the rest of the right deteriorated nationally in the spring of 1937. As in Lyon there were quarrels over by-elections.[194] Then in March Jacques Doriot proposed a Front de la

---

[188] F. Goguel, 'Les Elections législatives et senatorielles partielles', in *Edouard Daladier, chef de gouvernent*, ed. R. Rémond and J. Bourdin (1977).

[189] Irvine, *French Conservatism in Crisis*, chapter 5.

[190] Louis Marin said that if the PSF programme resembled that of the PSF on the majority of points, 'there are a certain number of points which are purposefully imprecise and which demonstrate an increasing demagogy, a leftwards orientation to which the Fédération is proud never to have succumbed' (AN 317 AP 82, Conseil national of 4 November 1936).

[191] *L'Union républicaine*, 6 August 1936.   [192] *Le Nouvelliste*, 16 and 24 July 1936.

[193] *L'Union républicaine*, 15 November 1936.

[194] Irvine, *French Conservatism in Crisis*, 138–44.

liberté, an alliance stretching from his own PPF to antiPopular Front Radicals. The Front was officially launched in May. It would have a minimum programme, otherwise leaving parties free to pursue their own ideas. Crucially, participants would not put up candidates in seats held by other members of the Front.[195] The PSF rejected an initiative that it rightly saw as an attempt to neutralise it. But Victor Perret welcomed a proposal which matched closely his own views, declaring that nothing could be achieved without the respect of 'situations acquises'.[196] A further round of polemics ensued. The temperature was raised further when in July the ex-Croix de Feu leader, Pozzo di Borgo, alleged that in 1930 Tardieu had subsidised the Croix de Feu out of government funds.[197] At a meeting in Lyon La Rocque denounced Pozzo. Thanks (it was claimed) to the error of a local member La Rocque's comments found their way into the press. As a result Pozzo sued La Rocque for defamation. In September the Lyonnais public were treated to the spectacle of conservative worthies dismantling each others' reputations in a highly publicised trial.

This was not the best preparation for the local elections of November 1937. On the national level the main parties of the right concluded an agreement to present a single candidate in each constituency.[198] In the Rhône negotiations began in May; agreement was announced in August.[199] The upshot was that PSF candidates joined an alliance known as the Républicains social anticommuniste (RSAC). The PSF was confined mainly to seats held by the left. There was some discontent within the PSF.[200] It is indeed surprising that the PSF should have accepted such an inequitable arrangement. The most likely explanation was that the party had been deluded by the presence of a minority of ex-Radicals amongst its activists into thinking that it could win seats from the left. Hence the party's insistence on being allowed to stand in Herriot's constituency.[201] In the end PSF members were disciplined. Those of the Fédération were less so. The main conflict centred on the canton of St Laurent, a safe seat where the Fédération *conseiller d'arrondissement* had stood down to leave the way open for the PSF. But an outraged La Batie stood against the PSF candidate. La Batie was vaguely disowned by Victor Perret, but won narrowly after a bitter

[195] Mâchefer, 'L'Union des droites, le PSF et la Front de la liberté', *Revue d'histoire moderne et contemporain* 17 (1970), 112–26; Irvine, *French Conservatism in Crisis*, 147–9.

[196] *L'Union républicaine*, 23 and 30 May and 6 June 1937.

[197] P. Mâchefer and F. Kupferman, 'Presse et politique dans les années trente: le cas du Petit Journal', *Revue d'histoire moderne et contemporaine* 22 (1975), 7–53. Howlett, 'La Rocque', 248–64. Monnet, *Refaire la République*.

[198] See Howlett, 'La Rocque', 264–7.   [199] *Le Volontaire '36*, 27 August 1937.

[200] *Lyon républicain*, 1 October 1937.   [201] *Le Volontaire '36*, 25 February 1938.

campaign. The PSF/Fédération conflict was not the only problem in this election, for there was a record number of dissident candidates on the right. Bonnevay's supporters refused the patronage of the RSAC because of the presence of the PSF. The PDP split publicly when one of its members urged support for Herriot. *Lyon républicain* commented: 'The battle of the cantonal elections is marked in the reactionary camp by the public airing of clan rivalries and internal schisms.'[202]

Thanks to social tension and the long-term decline of the Radicals in the countryside (a product of the rural exodus) the right nevertheless won two seats on the Conseil général. In consequence the Radicals were eliminated from the majority in this body, which now shifted to the right. But in the wake of the elections intraconservative relations declined to a new low. For the PSF the elections had been a fiasco. Thanks to La Batie's victory in St Laurent the party won no seats. A lengthy controversy over the significance of the result ensued. Perret wrote a series of nine editorials in *L'Union républicaine* attacking the PSF. The nadir came in February 1938 when the PSF broke up Henriot's meeting at the Etoile cinema. Since the elections had been a disappointment nationally for the PSF the party resolved that it would henceforth put up candidates of its own in all constituencies. As a result every by-election in France and the Rhône was the cause of polemic.

But if conflict was precipitated by electoral issues, the polemics between the two parties nonetheless reveal the gulf between an elitist and a populist party. The PSF declared that 'French conservatism failed before the triple problem of peace, economic crisis and social reform'. In June 1936, said the PSF, conservatives reaped the harvest they had sown.[203] Business leaders, too, would have to share the blame for this disaster.[204] In the eyes of the PSF these two groups had in common their commitment to liberalism, a creed which permitted the strong to crush 'les petits'. Their nationalism was merely a cover for self-interest.[205] The mission of the PSF was to sweep away this failed elite. Detached from economic interests, the PSF represented 'the new social elite, which shakes up the old bourgeois cadres'.[206] For Canat, the roots of the Federation's hostility to the PSF lay in 'the insurmountable fear caused by the prospect of the "French social state" which will be created, never doubt it, in a short time, and which will transform the Republic of failures into a clean and healthy state'.[207] Therefore the PSF argued that the defeat of the Popular Front could not come about simply

---

[202] *Lyon républicain*, 2 October 1937; *L'Union républicaine*, 28 November 1937.
[203] *Le Volontaire '36*, 29 April 1938.
[204] *Ibid.*, 22 October 1937.   [205] *Ibid.*, 15 January 1937.
[206] *Ibid.*, 15 October 1937.   [207] *Ibid.*, 26 November 1937.

through a parliamentary alliance such as the Front de la liberté, but must be achieved 'in the country itself'.[208]

The PSF's identification of the Fédération with the business and political establishment was somewhat unfair. The Fédération had been viewed unfavourably by big business since the early 1930s, and was hardly at the centre of parliamentary politics. But this does not alter the fact that the opposition of the PSF to the Fédération was shaped by a host of real social and cultural tensions. The profundity of the conflict between the PSF and the Fédération becomes clearer if we remember that after June 1936 the Fédération became more than ever a party of Catholic landowners, the old bourgeoisie and the Œuvre des cercles. The willingness of Perret to share platforms after June 1936 with royalists, who recruited in the same milieu, is also indicative of the nature of the Fédération.[209] The importance of traditional Catholicism to the Fédération can also be seen in the interest it showed in a Congrès marial held in 1939, just as the PSF was preparing to celebrate the 150th anniversary of the Revolution. Festivities lasted for four days, beginning with the arrival of Madonnas from all the parishes of the diocese, and including immense open-air services, and a reconstruction of the arrival of the missionary St Pothin in Lyon. Perret recognised in the congress an image of the world as it ought to be. There was, he said, no discord and no counterdemonstration. On the contrary, the whole city was united in witnessing 'a magnificent religious drama'. Persons of all classes participated, and were motivated by the spirit of collaboration which softened the life of the less privileged. They were united 'in an act of faith, guided and led by their *leaders in the hierarchy*'.[210]

There was also a consciousness of a socio-cultural opposition in the polemics between the two parties. This was most evident at the time of the disputed by-election at St Laurent. La Batie had been approved by all but one of the canton's mayors – the classic alliance of landowners and peasant notables on which the Fédération depended in the mountains.[211] He also echoed the themes of the Fédération: hierarchy, hard work, self-denial, family, motherland, property and religion. And to counter the PSF's populism he described himself as a representative of Défense paysanne, even though there is no evidence that he was linked to Dorgères's movement. The PSF nevertheless outdid La Batie's appeal to the peasantry, mixing Jacobin rhetoric with the themes of the veterans' movement:

You call yourself an old soldier when you should say career officer, paid before,

---

[208] *Ibid.*, 28 May 1937.   [209] *Ibid.*, 1 December 1936.
[210] *L'Union républicaine*, 1 July 1939 (my emphasis).
[211] *Ibid.*, 9 and 16 January and 17 April 1938.

during and after the war, and granted a pension of several tens of thousands of Francs. You are not the old soldier (*poilu*) earning five sous a day. No, there must be no equivocation, you are a soldier (*combattant*), not what one usually understands as an old soldier (*ancien combattant*).

You claim to defend the peasantry, and you write 'a place for the humble', but through your candidacy you only prove your desire to crush me along with the small and the humble.

The Fédération meanwhile contemptuously dismissed PSF members as upstarts. An anonymous writer in *Union républicaine* described those responsible for the Etoile cinema incident thus:

This gilded youth which had exchanged its cream gloves and embroidered waistcoats for leather jackets and flat caps, exploded into delirious screams which resembled those of wild beasts. . . . The men in leather jackets threw themselves like savages on anything which from near or afar seemed to have a bourgeois air. The great majority of this scum were bourgeois. Think of it! But a bourgeoisie ashamed of itself . . . Long live honour and honesty.

The PSF leaders were 'a devoted pharmacist trained in street fighting and electoral violence [Knersynski] [and] a pale bourgeois from Ainay, shameful of his name [Maintigneux] – one of those social climbers without hope, who always count on the double guarantee of ambition first and cowardice second'.[212]

Perret tried to pretend that nothing divided Federation and PSF. Yet as relations between the two parties deteriorated, other points of view were expressed. Some activists saw the PSF as subversive. Bosse-Platière denounced a movement of *sans culottes*, and claimed that the regimentation of thousands of men in the service of a 'mystique' and in total devotion to a leader was a 'fetishism which could lead to the worst excesses and errors', and promised that the canton of St Laurent would 'defend itself against fascism just as it always had against communism'.[213] Count Guy de Saint-Laumer believed that the exhibition of monster portraits of La Rocque and the holding of tempestuous demonstrations prepared the way for the communists.[214] In sum the Fédération saw the PSF as a group of subversive social climbers.

It could, perhaps, be objected that since the Fédération was willing to collaborate with other leagues, its denunciations of PSF subversion represented an opportunistic cover for its own electoral interests. Indeed, the Fédération's links with other leagues were reinforced. It even merged with the PRNS (formerly the Jeunesses patriotes) in May 1937.[215] The Fédération also collaborated with the PPF in the Front de

---

[212] *L'Union républicaine*, 27 February 1938.
[213] *Le Volontaire '36*, 28 January and 22 April 1938.
[214] *L'Union républicaine*, 13 March 1938.   [215] *Ibid.*, 6 June 1937.

la Liberté. Most successfully, Fédération and PPF joined together in promoting the Union militaire française, an organisation founded in 1938 by the ex-Cagoulard, Loustenau-Lacau, and which was dedicated to the suppression of the Communist Party. Yet it would still have to be explained why the Fédération denounced the PSF in this particular way. Moreover, Perret had always been suspicious of leagues of any type, especially in private.

Conclusion

La Batie and Saint-Laumer regarded the PSF as fascist. In fact the party had changed significantly since the days of the Croix de Feu. It remained anticommunist, antielitist, antiliberal, antiparliamentarian, authoritarian and populist and was based on the cult of a leader said to incarnate the nation. These characteristics made the PSF part of the authoritarian-populist right. Yet it could no longer be described as fascist. The PSF dropped the 'palingenetic' rhetoric and, gradually, the paramilitarism of the Croix de Feu. Indeed, had war not intervened, the PSF might have become a conventional conservative party. The reason for this change was the defeat of June 1936. The victory of the Popular Front, the strikes, and the perceived unreliability of the police made a violent show-down with the left appear risky. Some believed that the methods of the Croix de Feu had served only to cement the unity of the Popular Front.

Nevertheless, the social and political tensions which had led to the growth of the leagues remained and in some respects were aggravated by the Popular Front. Therefore the less authoritarian stance of the PSF, its participation in the electoral process, and the denting of La Rocque's authority as a result of the Tardieu affair, compromised the party's ability to transcend social, ideological and political divisions. Consequently, conflicts which were muted in the sphere of interest politics resurfaced within the PSF and embittered its relations with rival conservative parties. Even the crisis of June 1936 was insufficient to unite the right. Had the elections of 1940 taken place faction fighting may well have reached new heights: the PSF planned to present candidates against sitting Fédération deputies; the centre right had its eye on Fédération seats in the 6th and 2nd arrondissements.[216]

To some extent the divisions of the right were compensated by the increasingly conservative stance of the Radical Party. For Berstein, Radicalism in 1938–9 had occupied the entire political space of the

[216] Fonds Flandin, carton 89.

right.[217] The influence of conservative Radicals, such as finance minister Georges Bonnet, had been evident in the Chautemps ministry which succeeded Blum in June 1937. But it was under Daladier in 1938 that 'neo-Radicalism' triumphed. In October, Daladier used the Munich crisis to break definitively with the Popular Front. He carried out an offensive against the social laws of 1936, provoked and crushed a general strike on 30 November 1938, withdrew police powers from communist municipalities, placed Marseille under administrative rule, and in August 1939 prorogued Parliament for two years, even though war was not yet certain. Daladier had made himself the spokesman of Radical rank-and-file hostility to a Popular Front felt to be too responsive to the needs of the working class. Strikes and the Forty Hour Act were also held to compromise national defence at a time when the Anschluss and Sudeten crises made war seem imminent. Conservative Radicalism, as in the past, found support in the Senate and amongst a minority of deputies. There was also a more fundamental change. For the first time the Radicals took on the leadership of a right-wing government. This transformation was reflected in the party itself, where the reaction against the Popular Front had been spearheaded by the Jeunesses radicaux, a movement which owed something to the authoritarian-populist right. The once tumultuous party congress was reduced to an applause machine for Daladier. As we have seen, even anticlericalism was called into question.

The rightwards shift of the Radicals is a major reason for the failure of the PSF to break into the political 'centre ground', and further qualifies the contention that the commitment of the lower middle class to democracy saved France from fascism. We have seen that in the Rhône too the Radical constituency had been periodically tempted by a rightist Jacobin nationalism. Augagnauer and Elmigar had demonstrated this potential by their victories in general elections in the 3rd arrondissement in 1928 and the 4th in 1936 respectively. Within the Radical Party there had been a strong right-wing faction centred on the two constituencies of the 7th arrondissement. Yet after 1936 the department did not follow the national trend, and indeed became a centre of 'Republican defence'. Elmigar defended laïcité and regarded the special powers granted to Daladier as an offence against the republican credo. He voted consistently with the left against the government.[218] More significantly from our point of view, neo-Radicalism made little headway in the department. Paul Massimi, leader of the neo-Radicals in Lyon, had lost his seat in the Chamber of Deputies in 1936. Camille Rolland was one of

[217] Berstein, *Histoire du Parti radical*, II, 535–90
[218] *Le Nouvelliste*, 20 May 1938; *La République lyonnaise*, 22 October 1938.

only three Radical Senators to favour the innovative financial projects of the second Blum government in June 1938. Justin Godart, another Rhône senator, put himself forward as presidential candidate in 1939 on a platform of republican defence. Most important, Herriot became leader of the pro-Popular Front faction in the party. This surprising evolution was explained by the fact that under Chautemps a more moderate Popular Front had emerged, by Herriot's rivalry with Daladier, and by Herriot's commitment to resist Hitler through collective security and the Soviet alliance.[219] The left-wing orientation of Rhône Radicals was not, however, based on Herriot's prestige alone. The local Jeunesses radicaux rejected the sub-fascism of the parent organisation. Activists had responded to socialist competition by setting up workplace cells, the Amicales radicales-socialistes, which defended the Radical point of view in the CGT. They were especially strong in the civil service and even the police force.[220]

The nature of Radicalism in the Rhône merely underlined the fragility of conservatism locally and nationally. Still fearful of the left and of the possibility of an 'ideological war' against fascism, but too divided to take power for themselves, the right – from the PDP to the PSF – acquiesced in the authoritarian Daladier regime, making a distinction between the patriotism of the prime minister and the sectarianism of his party. The Daladier government looked forward to Vichy. The fall of France in 1940 may have been primarily due to the ineptitude of the military. But the reasons for the response to defeat must be sought in the disintegration of French politics in the 1930s and before.

[219] Berstein, *Herriot*, 249–57.
[220] *Le Démocrate*, 7 May 1935; 4 and 26 June 1938.

10   Conclusion

From the turn of the century until the late 1920s the right in the Rhône was dominated by a Catholic and liberal Progressisme which traced its origins to the Revolution and July Monarchy. It was committed to liberal democracy, market economics and free trade and was rooted in the historic association of Lyon with the manufacture of silk textiles, banking and international trade. Fear of the proletariat encouraged the elites to see the Church as a prop of the social order. Catholicism was also crucial to elite identity and provided a world-view inseparable from perceptions of the social and economic order. Through their domination of Chamber of Commerce and Fédération républicaine, wealthy families like the Aynards, Isaacs and Ribouds ensured that this liberal and Catholic tradition outlived the relative decline of the silk industry after the Great War. In the early 1920s the agricultural syndicate, the USE, was also won over to liberal republicanism. Liberal attitudes were shared by white-collar workers and even some manual workers thanks to the myth of the career open to talent. This was particularly true in the silk industry, where many employees worked in close contact with their bosses and where social mobility was relatively common. Status and social mobility were linked in turn to Catholic values, so that a white-collar worker could attribute perceived success to having adhered to the austere moral code of the Church. Much the same was true of the peasants on the plateau, where the same values could be seen as protecting better-off 'bonnes familles' against land subdivision.

It would be wrong, however, to speak of a Progressiste *hegemony*, and not only because the right remained in a minority throughout our period. The elite combined liberal and Catholic values in such a way as to cut itself off from conservative republicanism in much of France. Progressisme also excluded many of the elites within the department, from integrist Catholics to those who were worried by Aynard's faith in economic progress. Furthermore, the grip of liberal conservatism on the popular constituency of the right was uncertain. Some voted for the Progressistes because there was no alternative; for others loyalty was conditional upon economic prosperity and the tacit backing of the Church for liberal-conservatism. In fact the Church was not a reliable ally. Many senior Catholics retained royalist sympathies into the interwar period, while the Ralliement helped to unleash a popular conservatism which nourished Christian democracy, the radical right and the *Chronique sociale*.

In the 1920s liberal Progressisme entered into crisis. In the country-side the allegiance of peasants to notables, whether Progressistes or Catholic landowners, was undermined by a strengthening of medium peasant proprietors, more developed sociability, increased vulnerability to the market and the development of the JAC. In Lyon the hardening of social barriers and the feminisation of white-collar work coincided with the formation of the CFTC. Both JAC and CFTC promoted an antiliberal corporatist doctrine. Meanwhile the diversification of the Lyonnais economy, greatly accelerated by the war, led to expansion of the engineering industry. Many employers in this sector were recruited from the anticlerical artisanate, which permitted the development of a double hostility, economic and ideological, to the conservative establish-ment. In the late 1920s engineering employers like Weitz preached the value of industrial expansion and social reform. This represented another challenge to traditional liberal individualism, especially as some wealthier factory weavers were sympathetic to modernisation and reform.

These tensions came together in the crisis caused by the reforms of the conservative governments of 1928 to 1932. Reformism was supported by a loose (and politically ineffective) coalition which included the CFTC, Alliance démocratique, PDP, the Fédération left and certain engineering employers. Opposition to reform was led by Victor Perret and the right wing of the Fédération. It won support from some employers in the merchant-manufacturing branch of the silk industry and drew upon the ideological and organisational resources of Catholic integrism, particularly the Œuvre des cercles. The Fédération right was antiliberal and populist in tone, but was dominated by weaker elements of the elites. By 1932 Perret had won control over the Fédération, thereby reducing the influence of the liberal-conservative elite in local politics. The latter sometimes turned to the Alliance démocratique, and also endeavoured to reinforce ties to the bureaucracy in Paris.

With the onset of the economic crisis and the electoral victory of the Cartel in 1932, Perret's popularity rose. Yet the economic crisis also caused sectional conflicts to be pursued with new vigour. Institutions came to be identified with special interests. The Chamber of

Commerce, once seen as the representative of the regional economy, came to be perceived as a lobby for big business. It is true that agreement on corporatism and moderate protectionism now united big business in both the silk and engineering industries. But medium and small firms, as the fiasco of the entente in the silk industry showed, felt that they had been deprived of a voice in professional affairs. Small business, mainly Radical in sympathy, protested on the streets and flirted with the far right. Medium employers in older branches of the economy expressed their hostility to the establishment through the Fédération. Some of the same groups, together with new businesses, voiced their discontent through the Croix de Feu, which through its paramilitary activism was able to obscure differences among its constituency. The Croix de Feu also attracted white-collar workers and peasants, who had been prepared for autonomous political action by social Catholicism. Some sections of the liberal elites also flirted with the league, but were unwilling to provide more than financial support. Doubtless it appeared safer to rely on established political methods than risk bringing the antielitist Croix de Feu to power.

June 1936 represented a further blow to the liberal elite. Ill-suited to the conduct of institutionalised industrial relations, the Chamber of Commerce was marginalised. The focus of the employers' movement was now AICA, which was dominated by a broader big-business group in which the silk industry was merely one element amongst several. In the sphere of labour relations big business was able to win the support of medium and small firms, engineers, white-collar workers and peasants. But unity did not extend beyond opposition to the CGT. Anticapitalism was expressed instead through political parties, including the Radicals, Fédération and PSF. The Fédération more than ever became a movement of the 'old elite' of landowners and merchant-manufacturers. The PSF was a party of younger peasants and white-collar workers touched by social Catholicism, of engineers influenced by USIC and of medium engineering employers, all of whom blamed big business and the political establishment for June 1936. As it abandoned paramilitary activism, the specific grievances of PSF supporters were pursued with greater vigour within the party. The result was conflict within the movement and with the Fédération. By 1939 the big-business Progressiste hegemony was all but extinct. Some big businessmen supported the PSF. But their backing remained discrete, for the party had little prospect of coming to power and it was more and more identified with anticapitalist sectional interests. And as the Popular Front disintegrated it became clear that elite interests could be protected through daily struggle against the CGT in the factories, as Richard Vinen has shown, by manipulation of labour legislation, and by the traditional Union nationale coalition of right and Radicals.

The decline of liberal-conservatism in the Rhône was part of a national crisis of the parliamentary system. But whether the particular form taken by this crisis in the Rhône was paralleled in other parts of France is difficult to say. Little has been published on regional conservative politics, and most of that which has appeared does not ask the questions in which we are interested.[1] We know, however, that the right in Bordeaux had since the nineteenth century been dominated by a moderately anticlerical liberal-conservatism, led by wealthy merchants and winegrowers, and represented in our period by the Alliance démocratique. In the 1920s the liberal right was increasingly hard-pressed by the Catholic populism of deputies abbé Bergey and Philippe Henriot – both had much in common with Perret in the Rhône. But nothing is known of the conditions in which these conflicts occurred, or of the impact of the Croix de Feu/PSF on right-wing politics.[2]

We are a little better informed on the Nord, where there were social and religious tensions similar to those in Lyon. It is, however, unclear how they were related to developments in conservative politics. Here the Fédération was the dominant conservative party, holding eleven out of twenty-four seats in the department in 1932. The Fédération was supported by wealthy coal-owners like Jean Plichon, by the Catholic bourgeoisie of Lille and by the landowners and prosperous tenant farmers of the Flemish-speaking countryside around Hazebrouk – a business/rural alliance similar to that in the Rhône. The Alliance démocratique, which won only one seat in 1932, was backed by many employers in the textile industry. As in the Rhône there were long-standing tensions within the elites between metallurgical and textile employers. In the early 1930s the Fédération underwent a process of renewal analogous to that under Perret in Lyon, perhaps reflecting a parallel hostility to a liberal establishment. Social Catholicism also had an impact on both elites and conservative masses. In 1938 the Catholic and conservative Consortium de l'industrie textile was replaced by an organisation inspired by the social Catholic Bourgeoisie chrétienne. There was also a powerful Catholic trade union movement, doubtless linked to the PDP. The department was also home to important sections of the Croix de Feu/PSF, recruited from the middle and petty bourgeoisie, from miners in the Douai region and the Catholic peasants

---

[1] Passmore, 'Stalemate society or cradle of fascism', 441–8.
[2] Léger, *Opinions politiques*, 73ff; Ginestous, *Histoire politique de Bordeaux*; J. Lagroye, *Société et politique: J. Chaban-Delmas à Bordeaux* (1973).

of Flanders. Most adherents were doubtless right-wing voters, but again it is difficult to relate the PSF more precisely to social and political conflicts.[3]

A study of conservatism in the Calvados department provides a more complete picture.[4] This largely rural department was dominated by deputies linked to the Fédération, most of whom were lawyers or large landowners, sometimes noble. The same individuals were also influential in agricultural unions. Mass support came largely from the peasantry, and as in the Rhône the right profited from the increasing importance in the interwar years of prosperous medium peasants. The first sign of peasant opposition to the notables came in the election of 1928 in the Vire constituency, in the form of the candidacy of the peasant Albert Debon. In his view sitting deputy Lautru, a lawyer, was an inappropriate representative of an agricultural constituency. In the early 1930s prices of milk, meat and cider apples all collapsed. Indebtedness spread amongst the peasantry. Discontent was at first expressed through elite-dominated agricultural unions, then by the populist Défense paysanne from 1932. The two wings of the farmers movement came together in the Front paysan in 1934. The peasant agitation reached a crescendo in 1935, when alcohol distillers (the 'bouilleurs de cru') launched a campaign against government restrictions. Several hundred municipalities resigned in sympathy. The Prefect stressed the inability of local deputies to calm the situation. Meanwhile the Croix de Feu profited from the agitation, forming an alliance with the Front paysan in the summer of 1935. Peasant candidates linked to the far right did well in the elections of 1936. Tensions within the rural conservative electorate were particularly plain in the second Caen constituency, where the peasant demagogue Delaunay battled against Dagorn, a gentleman farmer, and the landowner Baron d'Abouville. Delaunay attacked 'les gros' (in other words d'Abouville), denounced the lawyers, teachers and doctors of the Chamber of Deputies and urged voters to support him as a 'son of the people'. Delauney also depicted agricultural unions as exploiters of the peasantry and urged their replacement by peasant syndicates. Following the victory of the Popular Front in 1936, the Croix de Feu and Défense paysanne collaborated in a

---

[3] P. Chanourdie and G. Obled-Mayeur, 'Le Nord vote en 1936', *De Blum à Daladier: le Nord/Pas-de-Calais 1936–1939* ed. J. Bourgeois *et al.* (Lille, 1979); J.-P. Florin, 'Des Croix de Feu au Parti social français. Une mutation réussie? L'exemple de la Fédération du Nord (1936–1939)', *Revue du Nord* 59 (1977), 233–62; Caudron, 'Du Consortium à la Bourgeoisie chrétienne'; Trimouille, 'La Bourgeoisie chrétienne du Nord (1930–1950)'.

[4] Quellien, *Bleus, blancs, rouges.*

peasant self-defence organisation.[5] Some wealthy notables, such as Jacques Le Roy Ladurie and d'Abouville saw in the Défense paysanne, Croix de Feu and PSF a means of containing the peasant mobilisation. It is possible that because rural Catholic Action was weak in a department where religious practice was relatively low, the peasant movement lacked cadres of its own, and so was more open to such influence. Nevertheless, the emergence of populist peasant discontent represented a rejection of established political leaders and contributed to the emergence of a French fascism in ways that resembled the process described in the Rhône. In the Calvados too it is possible to see the far right as issuing from a climate of antiparliamentarianism, populism, sectionalism and nationalism.

Thanks to the work of Christian Baechler and Samuel Goodfellow, a full comparison is possible with Alsace, although annexation by Germany, the presence of Protestantism and the linguistic divide between French and German speakers made the politics of Haut-Rhin and Bas-Rhin very distinctive.[6] Under German rule there had been an ongoing conflict between a liberal French-speaking Catholic urban elite and a more populist Germanophone middle class which was able, through the Church, to mobilise the Alsatian-dialect-speaking peasantry. The return of Alsace to French rule at first strengthened the Francophone elite, which was able to dominate the new conservative party, the Union populaire républicaine (UPR). Soon, however, the aggressive Gallicisation policy of the government led to criticism of the UPR leadership from German and Alsatian speakers. Within the UPR autonomists like Joseph Rossé and Michel Walter gave expression to the discontent of civil servants and teachers. As in the Rhône, the latter possessed links to Catholic trade unions and to Christian democracy.[7] Meanwhile in the countryside falling prices caused Catholic Alsatian-speaking peasants to turn to the autonomist Bauernbund of Joseph Bilger, a movement which had much in common with that of Dorgères. In Lutheran Bas-Rhin peasants turned to the more pro-German Landespartei. The French-speaking elite had by 1928 been forced out of the UPR.

Thus, as in the Rhône, there was a crisis of the right caused by the mobilisation of rank-and-file conservatives. In Alsace too authoritarianism emerged from this crisis. There were three sources. First, some

---

[5] The PSF leadership forbade contact with Dorgères organisation. *Bulletin d'information du PSF*, 1937.

[6] C. Baechler, *Le Parti catholique alsacien (1890–1939: du Reichsland à la République jacobine* (1982); S. H. Goodfellow, 'Fascism in Alsace, 1918–1940' (Ph.D. dissertation, Indiana University, 1992).

[7] Delbreil, *Centrisme et démocratie chrétienne*, 26, 33, 141, 192.

sections of the French elite reacted to their exclusion from the UPR by turning to the Action française, attracted by its combination of French nationalism and regionalism. Secondly, authoritarianism developed within the autonomist movement. Both Rossé's wing of the UPR and the Bauernbund were tempted by authoritarian-populism. Thirdly, and most importantly, the Croix de Feu won a significant membership in Alsace, largely from the ranks of the UPR, most of which was recruited from the urban Francophone middle class. But the Croix de Feu/PSF was unique among Alsatian political parties in that to some extent it transcended the Franco-German division. Veterans who had fought for Germany in the Great War were permitted to join, and respect for the Alsatian dialect was urged. Doubtless paramilitary activism and refusal to elaborate clear policies also played a part in broadening the appeal of the movement. Both the Alsatian and the Lyonnais Croix de Feu appealed to conservative groups which had already shown hostility to the elites. Thus it was able to attract support from the Bauernbund, autonomists and even pro-German parties. However, the PSF proved less able than the Croix de Feu to transcend the linguistic divide, for after 1936 conflicts between pro-French and antisemitic pro-Nazi elements developed. In sum, the Alsatian example shows a crisis of liberal politics, undermined by conflicts within the elites and by pressure from conservative peasants and white-collar workers influenced by social Catholicism. As in the Rhône these conflicts were expressed first through Christian democracy and then through the fascism of the Croix de Feu.

The story of the right in the Rhône also suggests some provisional conclusions on the major issues with which we began this book: why was the French right so divided, and how much significance should be attached to its divisions? Should we see the right as imprisoned within Rémond's three *mentalités*, or should we follow Marxists in stressing an underlying commitment to the defence of capitalism? The answer suggested here is that although hostility to socialism, however important, did not produce unity, conflicts of material interest were nevertheless central to conservative politics. These struggles were combined with ideological traditions, more diverse and unstable than Rémond allows, to produce a kaleidoscope of conservative groups. The view advanced here is closer to that of Jacques Bainville, who saw Third Republican conservatism as a loose and leaderless agglomeration of interests.

Moreover, conservative politics can be seen as one aspect of a generally fragmented society. Doubt has been cast on the validity of the stalemate society thesis, with its assumption of a widely diffused set of common values. It was certainly true that some sought to create an alliance of business and artisans based on restricted economic growth and social stability. The cotton manufacturers of the Monts du Beaujolais were one example of a group suffused with such a mentality. But the stalemate society thesis is based on the teleological and value-laden concept of modernisation: many cotton manufacturers engaged in quality-based production which looked ahead to flexible modes of industrial organisation, so it is difficult to say whether they were 'traditional' or 'modern'. More importantly from our perspective, the schemes of the cotton manufacturers competed with a host of rival projects, each shaped by a combination of ideology and material interest. They included Aynard's classless society based on economic progress, social mobility and private education; Ernest Mercier's neosolidarist vision of corporate collective bargaining, social reform and technocracy; the PDP's marriage of social Catholicism with democracy; Perret's uneasy synthesis of liberalism, authority and conservative social Catholicism, and Canat's authoritarian-populist version of social Catholicism.

Bainville felt that without a monarch to guide it, such a society must degenerate into its constituent parts. He was half right, for conflict was exceptionally great in France. But societies require neither core values nor an hegemonic power to function. Rather, those in the socialist parties and trade unions who wanted radical restructuring of the system were constrained by the practical obstacles presented by their supporters' lack of cultural and economic power. The elites were able to muster enormous economic and political resources against them, as was demonstrated by the mobilisation of state and business against the general strike of 30 November 1938, and more subtly by the erosion of workers' gains in a daily struggle in the factories. Also the cost of bringing about change was likely to be high for those who sought it, especially given the capacity of the system to generate *some* reward.

There was, then, no stalemate society, no social consensus and no dominant ideology to be internalised by rank-and-file conservatives, let alone the masses. This implies a certain decentring of political power. Parties represented an essential route to local and state power, through state and parliament, and they played a role in socialising *some* sections of the population. But political power was only one of a number of separate but interrelated forms of domination in the Third Republic. Therefore we have contested the Marxist contention that conservative politics were above all explicable in terms of the efforts of big business to secure its power. Certainly business is essential to any understanding of conservative politics. And some parties, like the Progressistes, were dominated by business. Yet in Lyon big business was not inordinately troubled by exclusion from local political influence, for it possessed many other ways of achieving its goals (through lobbying the state, and direct economic power). Conservative parties were related to *all* of the sources of power in the Third Republic. Hence the importance we have accorded to engineers and defenders of the cultural capital represented by Catholic education. Often these components of the right came into conflict. Struggles within the right were further exacerbated by the fact that many rank-and-file supporters occupied contradictory locations in social relations, and in some areas came into conflict with the elites. Conservative peasants and white-collar workers were able to use Catholicism as a form of cultural capital to gain advantages over still lower groups, and simultaneously to articulate grievances against the elites. This led to the emergence of constitutional-popular movements such as the PDP, and of authoritarian-populist movements like the Croix de Feu and PSF. It may be that conservatives sometimes united against the working class, and certainly no-one on the right favoured socialism. But this did not lead to unity in the strong sense of ideological incorporation or hegemony.

The diversity of conservative movements cannot be contained within Rémond's three *mentalités*. His categories of liberal-conservatism, traditionalism and Bonapartism certainly throw some light on conservative politics. But no real political movement fitted neatly into any of these categories. Liberals were divided between Aynard's belief in individualism, social mobility and government by an enlightened elite, and Weitz's view that freely constituted economic associations could contain social conflict. Social Catholics were divided in their attitudes to authority and democracy. And Bonapartism could emphasise either authority or populism. The traditions also overlapped. Perret combined a stress on the stability of family and profession taken from the Catholic ALP with a liberal belief in the market. Similarly, there was a cross-fertilisation of the French tradition of authoritarian-populism with German and Italian fascism. Furthermore, following Rosanvallon, we have also seen that the conservative traditions were transformed by reinscription in new conjunctures. Perret, for example, replaced the liberal idea of economic expansion with the notion that the laws of supply and demand reproduced an essentially static society. Likewise, the belief of many liberals that a unitary nation should be governed by an enlightened elite (Rosanvallon's *libéralisme capacitaire*) fed the authoritarian-elitist conservatism of Tardieu and others. Thus conservatives drew upon a wide variety of ideological materials in order to construct their world-views.

Finally, our study has attempted to throw new light on the question of fascism in France, above all by placing the leagues in their historical context. The emergence of the leagues was made possible by three conditions. Take first the question of social and political instability. Since neither cohesion nor consensus characterise any society, social and political instability cannot constitute a sufficient explanation. Nevertheless, we have argued that such conflicts were particularly profound in France. Economic divisions were not simply about details of policy, but extended to the desirability or otherwise of industrialisation. The slowness and unevenness of economic change meant that opposed positions could become entrenched. Interwar growth made the imbalance in the economy particularly acute. The religious issue was not just about a division within Protestantism, as it was in Britain, but about an institutionalised conflict between intransigent religion and irreligion, nourished by a host of historical grievances. Furthermore, these two problems were connected, so that for every material problem there was a multitude of ideologically shaped solutions, while solutions to religious problems were shaped by class perspectives. In the interwar years conflicting groups were increasingly institutionalised in private and public associations. We have also seen that those who debated the future of French society were not a small elite, but mainstream politicians, business people, trade unionists and others. This was demonstrated by the reforms of the Tardieu years. Tardieu did not fail because he came up against the immovable obstacle of the stalemate society, but because his elitist liberal view of politics prevented him from organising potential support and because he naïvely believed that he could unite French conservatives by focusing on 'neutral' economic measures. What is more, the reforms contributed to the development of a welfare system which was to provoke the emergence of antielitist conservative movements, in the form of Défense paysanne, the Ligue des contribuables and, in the Rhône, Perret's Fédération. These movements did much to prepare the way for the leagues.

Secondly, there was an authoritarian and populist potential within French conservatism. Both liberal and Catholic traditions assumed a unitary society which they felt *ought* to cohere, and were uncomfortable with the notion of *alternance*. The *liberalisme capacitaire* of Morel-Journel shaded into distrust of democracy. Perret's nationalism led him to define his opponents as antiFrench criminals. Christian democratic movements too combined anticommunism and anticapitalism in such a way as to facilitate the passage of some to the far right. This does not, however, mean that the course of French history inevitably led to fascism. Rather, it was a question of authoritarian-populist, sometimes fascist, *potentials*. This point is underlined by the fact that the transformation of the Croix de Feu into the PSF demonstrated that a fascist movement could contain a democratic potential in its populism. In other words, political traditions can lead in multiple directions, depending on context. The notion of a protofascist ideology is too banal to be of use.

In the particular conditions of early 1930s France the exceptionally fragmented nature of French society contrasted with the belief of many conservatives in a unitary nation with a single interest. This was tolerable in the 1920s when the supply of jobs, positions, wages and profits was increasing. But when in the 1930s the economy ceased to expand, sections of the conservative electorate found that their advantages could be preserved only by shifting rewards away from other groups. This transfer would be achieved by a mixture of compulsion and ideological strategies designed to persuade losers that sacrifices were in the 'national interest'. Both could be seen in the campaign for deflation in 1934–5. Yet evocation of the 'general interest' was accompanied by unprecedented political confusion, as competing groups struggled to define the general good in their own way. The divisions of French society also permitted protests on the part of the conservative rank and file against the supposed weakness of the established parties, seen as too divided to implement a deflationary programme, to achieve social harmony, or to resist the German menace. The decisive impetus was imparted by the failure of Doumergue to end the economic crisis, reform the state and exclude the left once and for all from power. This crisis led to a variety of forms of authoritarianism, ranging from the demands of the constitutional right for a stronger state, through Perret's more populist authoritarian-elitism, sectional movements like that of Dorgères, to the fascist Croix de Feu. The latter sought to resolve the contradictions of French society by engaging in a radical drive against the left and the establishment by means of paramilitary activism.

The Croix de Feu, however, had little chance of coming to power. Historians have usually explained this failure in terms of the strength of the Republican tradition in the petty bourgeoisie, which is said to have prevented the middle-class troops of the Radical Party from turning to the far right. The survival of the political centre in turn kept alive the hopes of conservative parliamentarians and social elites that the Radicals could be detached from the Popular Front and incorporated in a right-wing Union nationale majority. Conservative Radicalism also remained in control of the Senate, where it was able to put a brake on Popular Front legislation. These are powerful arguments. But they must be qualified. First the republican tradition of the Radical lower middle class could not prevent the emergence of fascist movements *within the right*.

Large sections of the right-wing constituency were ambiguous in their attitude to the Republic and had little faith in the ability of a parliamentary coalition to resolve the problems confronting them. Second, we have seen that the commitment of the Radical lower middle class to the Republic was not unconditional. In 1932–3 small business, neglected by a Radical government, began to flirt with the far right. But the *active* manipulation of the republican tradition by the antifascist movement, together with proposals for social reform, brought them back into the republican fold. We have also seen that the effectiveness of antifascist action on the streets both deprived the leagues of room for manœuvre and convinced Radical supporters that the leagues represented a threat to order. This argument must not be overstated, for the very formation of the Popular Front is testimony to the importance of the republican tradition. But the initiative for its formation originated at least partly in Moscow. Thirdly, although we have seen that businessmen like Morel-Journel and Fédération deputies like Peissel worked for parliamentary alliance with the Radicals rather than support the Croix de Feu/PSF's bid for power, both nevertheless showed considerable sympathy for the movement. This suggests that emotional commitment to the Republic counted less than calculation of interests.[8] In the circumstances of 1935–6, bringing the Croix de Feu into government must have looked a decidedly risky course of action, given the strength of the left and the uncertainty of La Rocque's programme.

So although France produced a major fascist movement, circumstances remained very different from those in Germany in the period before the Nazi seizure of power. French politicians never concluded, as their German equivalents were to in the winter of 1932–3, that there was no alternative to bringing the Nazis into government. It is more revealing to compare France in February 1934 with Germany in March 1930, a year in which the economic crisis had begun to bite and a left-wing government under Müller had fallen over the question of cuts in unemployment benefit. Authoritarianism was in the air, and was linked to demands for deflation and roll-back of Weimar employment legislation. The political centre had been eroded by sectional parties representing farmers, businessmen and others, a constituency which would later be won by the Nazis. The latter had made advances in local elections at the end of 1929 and would make a breakthrough in the general elections of September 1930. Many of the same features, albeit on a lesser scale, could be found in France in early 1934. But from that point the history of the two countries diverged radically. The Popular

[8] Dobry, 'Février, 1934'.

Front used the democratic tradition to keep the Radicals within the democratic fold, and to build a powerful mass movement which, paradoxically, caused conservatives to turn to authoritarian movements, but also made the employment of force very risky. In Germany and Italy fascism had developed after the defeat of the left, which offered little effective resistance. But in France the Croix de Feu developed in tandem with the Popular Front. The hollowness of the league's claim to be the sole barrier to communism was exposed by the events of April–June 1936. The electoral victory of the Popular Front, together with the strike movement and dissolution of the leagues, constituted a major defeat for French fascism. La Rocque drew the appropriate conclusion and the PSF started to make its way down the road to constitutional conservatism.

The fundamental problems which had plagued the French right persisted under the Vichy regime and beyond. By 1945 most conservatives agreed on the social value of the Church. But some in the Church were less than ever willing to act as tools of the ruling classes, as the affair of the worker-priests in the 1950s showed. Conservatives themselves continued to struggle over the meaning of Catholicism, as in 1945 large sections of the rank and file of the right were mobilised by the Mouvement républicain populaire, while discredited conservative elites returned to liberalism and followed Aynard in combining belief in freedom of conscience with backing for Catholic education. Industrialisation also remained an issue. In the elections of 1951 elements of big business attempted to manipulate small producers through the Groupement de défense des contribuables. As a result they contributed to the emergence of the anticapitalist Poujadist movement.[9] Many of these tensions contributed to the collapse of the Fourth Republic in 1958. In the 1960s, under the authoritarian rule of de Gaulle, a stable conservative majority appeared to have emerged, facilitated by the decline of religious practice and by a new consensus on the value of growth. But May 1968, the disappearance of de Gaulle, a new world economic crisis and above all the victory of Mitterand in 1981 demonstrated how shallow this conservative unity remained.

[9] R. Vinen, 'Business intervention in the 1951 general election: the groupement de défence des contribuables', *Modern and Contemporary France* 1 (1990), 3–16.

Appendix 1
Equations for multiple regression[1]

Non-winegrowing communes

Dependent variable: the right-wing vote

Adjusted R^2	.59922		
Std error	.10215		
F	136.0563	Signif. F	.00000

Independent variables	T	Signif. T
Catholicism	15.018	.0000
Tenants	1.226	.2218

Dependent variable: the Radicals

Adjusted R^2	.53302		
Std error	.09292		
F	40.886414	Signif. F	.0000

Independent variables	T	Signif. T
Pop. diff.	−7.404	.0000
Catholicism	−5.306	.0000
Proprietors	3.531	.0005
Tenants	−3.052	.0026
Wine	2.878	.0045

Dependent variable: the communists

Adjusted R^2	.30422		
Std error	.02208		
F	19.67523	Signif. F	.0000

Independent variables	T	Signif. T
Proprietors	−3.553	.0005
Tenants	−3.014	.0030
Catholicism	−2.061	.0407
Labourers	−1.589	.0646

[1] For an explantion of the method see Norusis, *SPSS-X Introductory Statistics*, 147–186.

Wine-growing communes

Dependent variable: the right

Adjusted R^2	.60824		
Std error	.07991		
F	13.66249	Signif. F	.0000

Independent variables	T	Signif. T
Proprietors	2.678	.0104
Catholicism	1.326	.1916
Wine	−3.4750	.0005
Co-op. members	−3.531	.0010
Pop. diff.	−3.365	.0016

Dependent variable: the Radicals

Adjusted R^2	.18885		
Std error	.09592		
F	5.47112	Signif. F	.0073

Independent variables	T	Signif. T
Tenants	−1.960	.0559
Pop. diff.	−1.870	.0678

Dependent variable: the SFIO

Adjusted R^2	.41456		
Std error	.10982		
F	5.47112	Signif. F	.0073

Independent variables	T	Signif. T
Wine	4.028	.0002
Co-op. members	2.615	.0122
Proprietors	−1.812	.0756
Labourers	−1.794	.0797
Pop. diff.	−1.453	.1533

There are, unfortunately, no department-wide statistics which give the sizes of farms worked by peasants. But useful data on forms of landholding can be obtained from the electoral lists of the Chamber of Agriculture, which distinguishes proprietors, tenants/sharecroppers, agricultural labourers and retired farmers.[2] The lists are not a perfect source. Only those over 25 were allowed to vote in Chamber of Agriculture elections, and there is no guarantee that all those entitled

[2] ADR 7 Mp 36, *Listes électorales de la Chambre d'agriculture*; H. Rollet, *Les Chambres d'Agriculture* (Lyon, 1926), 94–5.

to register actually did so. All the same, the proportion of proprietors in the whole department on the electoral list – 73% – is not too far removed from a figure of 60–70% given by a contemporary national survey.[3] Another problem is the failure to distinguish sharecroppers and tenants. For this reason the fifty-one communes in which the proportion of agricultural land devoted to cultivation of the vine was greater than 30% are analysed separately, on the assumption that these include sharecroppers and not tenants.[4] Analysis of the rest of the department covers 189 communes where less than 20% of cultivatable land was occupied by the vine. As a result twenty-three communes where the confusion of tenants and sharecroppers can be assumed to be greatest are excluded from the analysis. But this was the only way to achieve meaningful results.

Five other variables are examined: first, religious practice. Data are from the 1950s survey of church attendance, hardly an ideal source for analysis of voting behaviour in 1932. But in the countryside at least practice can be assumed to have been relatively stable. Since the breakdown by commune of figures has not survived, it was necessary to read off data from the map of religious practice. Correlations are also blurred by the fact that the figures include female practice. A second variable is difference in population between 1911 and 1936: positive correlations indicate strength of a political movement in communes suffering from depopulation. Third, the number of wine co-operative members as a proportion of those inscribed on the electoral list is a rough guide to the significance of small winegrowers.[5] Fourth, density of population is included as a measure of the strength of the industrial population. Fifth, the proportion of land devoted to the vine is used, again using data from a map rather than raw figures.

---

[3] *Atlas de France. Comité national de géographie; Société français de cartographie*, Map 41. The map also indicates 10–20% tenants and 10–15% sharecroppers.

[4] The source of this information is Garrier, *Paysans du Lyonnais*, Map 42.

[5] The latter figures were obtained from Armand Perrin, 'Les cooperatives vinicoles en Beaujolais', *Etudes rhodaniennes* 19 (1944), 1–20.

Appendix 2
The conservative deputies of the Rhône, 1928–1940

1928 to 1932

Lyon II	Antoine Sallès
l'Arbresle	François Peissel
Givors	Jean-Baptiste Delorme
Tarare	Laurent Bonnevay

1932 to 1936

Lyon II	Antoine Sallès
l'Arbresle	François Peissel
Tarare	Laurent Bonnevay

1936 to 1940

Lyon II	Antoine Sallès
Lyon IV	Alfred Elmigar
Lyon VI	Pierre Burgeot
l'Arbresle	François Peissel
Tarare	Laurent Bonnevay

Constituency boundaries

Constituency	Cantons
Tarare	Tarare, Amplepuis, Thizy, Lamure, Le Bois d'Oingt
Villefranche	Anse, Villefranche, Beaujeu, Belleville, Monsols
l'Arbresle	Neuville, l'Arbresle, Limonest, St Laurent, St Symphorian
Givors	Vaugneray, St Genis Laval, Condrieu, Givors

Select bibliography

PRIMARY SOURCES

ARCHIVES NATIONALES (AN)

BB^{18} Ministère de la justice
F^2 Affairs communaux
F^7 Police générale
Cour de Justice du Rhône
Fonds La Rocque 451 AP
Fonds Louis Marin 317 AP
Fonds Tardieu 324 AP

BIBLIOTHÈQUE NATIONALE (BN)

Fonds Flandin
Fonds de l'Alliance démocratique

ARCHIVES DÉPARTEMENTALES DU RHÔNE (ADR)

1m Fêtes publiques
3m Listes électorales
4m Police politique
6m Listes nominatives du recensement
7m Agriculture
10m Commerce
Cour de Justice
3u Archives du parquet de Lyon
Uncoded dossiers for each national and local election

MUSEE GADAGNE

Fonds Justin Godart

ARCHIVES DE LA CHAMBRE DE COMMERCE DE LYON

Procès verbaux des séances (typed manuscript)

ARCHIVES DE LA CHAMBRE DE COMMERCE DE VILLEFRANCHE
Compte rendu annuel des travaux (printed)

ARCHIVES DE LA CHRONIQUE SOCIALE
Fonds Gonin

PUBLISHED SOURCES

Annuaire de l'Union du sud-est des syndicats agricoles
Annuaire de la compagnie des agents de change de Lyon, 1931–1936 (Lyon, 1936)
Bulletin de l'Union des chambres syndicales lyonnaises
Bulletin des soies
Bulletin du Ministère de travail
Bulletins et documents de l'AICA
Bulletin mensuel de commerce, de l'industrie et de l'agriculture
Bulletin municipal de la ville de Lyon
Bulletin municipal de la ville de Villeurbanne
Compte rendu annuel des travaux de la Chambre de Commerce de Lyon
Compte Rendu Annuel des travaux du Syndicat des fabricants de soieries de Lyon
Indicateur Fournier
Indicateur lyonnais Henry
Journal d'Henry Morel-Journel (Lyon, 1959)
Tout-Lyon Annuaire

PRESS

Action libérale populaire (ALP)
L'Agriculteur du sud-est (USE)
L'Alerte (Jeunesses patriotes)
L'Attaque (PPF)
La Brèche (PPF)
Bulletin des Démocrates populaires du Rhône
Bulletin d'information du PSF
Les Cahiers de Lugdunum (Royalist)
Le Cri populaire de la banlieue (PPF)
La Croix du Rhône
Le Démocrate du sud-est (Radical)
Documents. Edition de l'agence lyonnaise du centre de propagande des républicains nationaux
Droits de la Nation
L'Emancipation du Lyonnais (PPF)
Enfants du Rhône en avant! (PPF)
Le Flambeau (Croix de Feu)
Le Flambeau du sud-est (Croix de Feu)
La Flèche (Front social)

Journal de Villefranche
La Liberté de la Croix Rousse (PPF)
La Liberté syndicale (SPF)
Lyon républicain
Le Nouveau Journal
Le Nouvelliste
La Patrie de Lyon
Le Petit montagnard de Tarare
Le Progrès
La Relève (Croix de Feu)
La République lyonnaise (Action française)
Réveil du Beaujolais
Salut public
Semaine religieuse de Lyon
Solidarité française du sud-est
SPF des Ouvriers et employés de soieries. Bulletin Mensuel (SPF)
Le Sud-est républicain (Alliance démocratique)
La Tradition légitimiste
Trait d'Union des Démocrates populaires du Rhône
L'Union. Organe des militants de l'Union des artisans de la région lyonnaise
L'Union française (1928–30) (Jeunesses patriotes)
L'Union française (1938–9) (Fernand Sape)
L'Union républicaine (Fédération républicaine)
L'Union royaliste
La Voix du peuple (PCF)
La Voix sociale (CFTC)
Le Volontaire '36 (PSF)

SECONDARY SOURCES

Abrahams, D., *The Collapse of the Weimar Republic: Political Economy and Crisis* (New York, 1986)

Abercrombie, N., Hill, S. and Turner, B. S. *The Dominant Ideology Thesis* (1980)

Albitreccia, A., 'L'Industrie du coton', *Annales de géographie* 8 (1933), 233–47

Albout, C., 'Démographie et industrialisation d'une région rurale de la fin du XVIIIe siècle à nos jours: le canton de Tarare' (mémoire de maîtrise, Lyon II, 1970)

Anderson, M., *Conservative Politics in France* (1974)

Archer, J., 'La Naissance de la IIIᵉ république à Lyon (4–15 Septembre, 1870)', *Cahiers d'histoire* 16 (1971), 5–25

Atlas de France, Comité national de géographie: Société français de cartographie (1930)

Augé-Laribé, M., *La Politique agricole de la France* (1942)

Aynard, E., *Discours prononcés à la Chambre des députés pendant la législature de 1889 à 1893* (no date)

    Discours prononcés à la Chambre des députés pendant la législature de 1893 à 1913 (no date)

Baechler, C., *Le Parti catholique alsacien (1890–1939): du Reichsland à la République jacobine* (1982)

Bainville, J., *The French Republic* (1935)

Barral, P., *Les Agrariens français de Méline à Pisani* (1968)

'Les Syndicats bretons de cultivateurs-cultivant', *Mouvement social* 67 (1969), 147–71

Beguet, B., 'Comportements politiques et structures sociales. Le Parti social français et la Fédération républicaine à Lyon, 1936–1939' (mémoire de maîtrise, Lyon II, 1988)

Béraud, H., *Ciel de suie* (1933)

Berger, S., *Peasants against Politics: Rural Organisation in Brittany, 1911–1967* (Cambridge, Mass., 1972)

Berl, E., *La Politique des partis* (1931)

Bernard, P. and Dubief, H., *The Decline of the Third Republic, 1914 to 1938* (Cambridge, 1988)

Berstein, S., *Histoire du Parti radical*, 2 vols. (1980, 1982)

Edouard Herriot, ou la République en personne (1985)

Berstein, S. and Rudelle, O. (eds.), *Le Modèle republicain* (1992)

Bertrand, H., *Soierie lyonnaise: chardonne et soie ordinaire. Evolutions récentes; situation actuelle* (Lyon, 1930)

Bienfait, J., 'La Population de Lyon à travers d'un quart de siècle de recensements douteux (1911–1936)', *Revue de géographie de Lyon* 1–2 (1968), 63–132

Billiard, R., *Vigneronnage et vigneron beaujolais* (Villefranche, 1938)

Birnbaum, P., *'La France aux français': histoire des haines nationalistes* (1993)

Blinkhorn, M. (ed.), *Fascists and Conservatives: The Radical Right and the Establishment in Twentieth Century Europe* (1990)

Boltanski, L., *The Making of a Class: Cadres in French Society* (Cambridge, 1987)

Bonnevay, L., *Histoire politique et administrative du conseil général du Rhône*, II: *1790–1940* (Lyon, 1946)

Le Six février (1934)

Bonneville, M., *Naissance et métamorphose d'une banlieue ouvrière: Villeurbanne. Processus et formes d'urbanisation* (Lyon, 1978)

Bordas, H., 'Tarare', *Annales de géographie* 33 (1930), 40–9

Boulet, H., 'Le Parti social français dans le Rhône, 1936–1939' (mémoire de maîtrise, Lyon II, 1975)

Bourgeois, J. et al., *De Blum à Daladier: le Nord/Pas-de-Calais 1936–1939* (Lille, 1979)

Bourgeon, M.-L., 'Répartition des métiers de tissage de la soie au service de la fabrique lyonnaise en 1937–8', *Etudes rhodaniennes* 14 (1938), 215–34

Bouvier, J., *Le Crédit lyonnais* (1961)

Brun, G., *Technocrates et technocratie en France (1914–1945)* (1985)

Brunet, J.-P., *Jacques Doriot: du communisme au fascisme* (1986)

Buché, J., *Essai sur la vie et l'œuvre d'Edouard Aynard (1837–1913)* (1921)

Burel, J., 'La Vignoble beaujolais' (thèse de droit, Lyon, 1941)

Burrin, P., *La Dérive fasciste: Doriot, Déat, Bergery* (1986)

Caron, F., *An Economic History of Modern France* (1979)

Caudron, A., 'Du Consortium à la Bourgeoisie chrétienne' *Revue du Nord* 73 (1991), 411–15

Cayez, P., *Métiers Jaquard et hauts fourneaux* (Lyon, 1978)

Chaix, M., *Juliette: chemin des cerisiers* (1976)
    Les Lauriers du lac de Constance (1974)

Chaline, N.-J., *Des Catholiques normands sous la Troisième république: crises, combats, renouveaux* (Roanne, 1985)

Chauvy, G., *Lyon, 40–44* (1985)
    Lyon, des années bleus: libération, épuration (1987)

Chevallier, G., *Clochemerle* (1934)

Cholley, A., 'Quelques remarques sur la culture et la commerce des fruits dans la banlieue de Lyon', *Études rhodaniennes* 3 (1927), 83–107

Cholvy, G., 'Religion et politique en Languedoc méditeranéen et Roussillon à l'époque contemporaine', in *Droite et gauche de 1789 à nos jours* (Montpellier, 1975)

Chopine, P., *Six ans chez les Croix de Feu* (1935)

Christiane, G., 'La Fabrique lyonnaise de soieries et la Grande dépression, 1929 à 1934' (mémoire de maîtrise, Lyon II, 1969)

Christophe, P., *1936: Les catholiques et le Front populaire* (1980)

Clague, M., 'Vision and myopia in the new politics of André Tardieu', *French Historical Studies* 8 (1972), 105–29

Coston, H., *Partis, journaux et hommes politiques* (Paris, 1960)

Dansette, A., *Histoire religieuse de la France contemporaine* II: *sous la Troisième république* (1952)

Davallon, J., Dujardin, P. and Sabatier, G. (eds.), *Le Geste commémoratif* (Lyon, 1994)

Delbreil, J.-C., *Centrisme et démocratie-chrétienne en France: le Parti démocrate populaire des origines au MRP* (1990)

Delpech, F., 'La Presse et les partis à Lyon de l'avènement des républicains à l'esprit nouveaux', *Cahiers d'histoire* 16 (1971), 27–38

Demaison, A., 'Visites à la presse de province (V), Bourgogne et région lyonnaise', *Revue des deux mondes* (1929)

Dobry, M., 'Février 1934 et la découverte de l'allergie de la société française au fascisme', *Revue française de sociologie* 30 (1989), 511–33

Douglas, A., *From Fascism to Libertarian Communism: Georges Valois against the Third Republic* (Berkeley, 1993)

Drieu la Rochelle, P., *Secret Journal and Other Writings* (Cambridge, 1973)

Dupraz, J., *Regards sur le fascisme* (Lyon, 1935)

Durand, J.-D., *et al.* (eds.), *Cent ans de catholicisme social à Lyon et en Rhône-Alpes* (Lyon, 1992)

Eatwell, R. and O'Sullivan, N. (eds.), *The Nature of the Right: American and European Politics and Political Thought Since 1789* (1989)

Ehrmann, H. W., *Organised Business in France* (Princeton, 1957)

Eley, G., *Reshaping the German Right: Radical Nationalism and Political Change after Bismarck* (1980)
    'What produces fascism: preindustrial traditions or crisis of the capitalist state?', *Politics and Society* 12 (1983), 53–82

Ellis, Jack D., *The Physician Legislators of France: Medicine and Politics in the Early Third Republic, 1870–1914* (Cambridge, 1990)

Elwitt, S., *The Making of the Third Republic: Class and Politics in France, 1868–1884* (Baton Rouge, 1975)

The Third Republic Defended: Bourgeois Reform in France, 1880–1914 (London and Baton Rouge, 1986)

Estève, C., 'Le Souvenir de la Révolution dans le Cantal. L'exemple du Ralliement et son échec partiel', *Revue historique* 187 (1992), 391–417

Fine, M., 'Toward corporatism: the movement for capital–labour collaboration in France, 1914 to 1936' (Ph.D. thesis, Wisconsin, 1971)

Fleuret, A., 'L'Extrême Droite dans le Rhône, 1929–39' (mémoire de maîtrise, Lyon II, 1979)

Florin, J.-P., 'Des Croix de Feu au Parti social français. Une mutation réussie? L'exemple de la Fédération du Nord (1936–1939)', *Revue du Nord* 59 (1977), 233–62

Folliet, J., *Notre Ami, Marius Gonin* (Lyon, 1944)

Fougère, E., *L'Effort industriel de Lyon pendant la guerre* (Lyon, 1919)

Fridenson, P., *Histoire des Usines Renault* I: *naissance de la grande entreprise* (1972)

Garcin, S., 'La Fabrique lyonnaise de soieries de 1900 à 1929' (mémoire de maîtrise, Lyon II, 1969)

Gardin M. et. al., *Paroisses et communes de France: le Rhône* (1978)

Garrier, G., 'L'Union du sud-est des syndicats agricoles avant 1914', *Mouvement social* 67 (1969), 17–38

Paysans du Lyonnais et du Beaujolais (Grenoble, 1973)

Garrigues, J., 'Léon Say: un libéral sous la Troisième République', *Revue historique* 579 (1991), 119–41

Gayet, G., 'L'Union du sud-est des syndicats agricoles' (mémoire de maîtrise, Lyon II, 1972)

Geni, F., 'L'Organisation professionnelle de la fabrique lyonnaise de soieries: étude historique et critique' (thèse de droit, Grenoble, 1942)

Gibson, R., *A Social History of French Catholicism* (1989)

Giddens, A., *The Constitution of Society* (Cambridge, 1984)

Gillet, P., *Edmund Gillet 1873–1831: industriel, régent de la Banque de France* (Lyon, 1932)

Ginestous, E., *Histoire politique de Bordeaux* (Bordeaux, 1945)

Goguel, F., *La Politique des partis sous la Troisième République* (1946)

Géographie des élections françaises sous la troisième et la quatrième république (1970)

Goodfellow, S. H., 'Fascism in Alsace, 1918–1940' (Ph.D. dissertation, Indiana University, 1992)

Gordon, D. M., 'Liberalism and socialism in the Nord: Eugène Motte and Republican politics in Roubaix, 1898–1912', *French History* 2 (1989), 312–43

Liberalism and Social Reform: Industrial Growth and Progressiste Politics in France, 1880–1914 (Westport, Connecticut, 1996)

Gratton, P., *Les Paysans contre l'agrairisme* (1972)

Greene, N., *Crisis and Decline: The French Socialist Party in the Popular Front Era* (Ithaca, 1969)

Grelon, A. (ed.), *Les Ingénieurs de la crise* (Paris, 1986)

Gric, P., pseudonym of G. Rieussec, *Les Courants politiques du Rhône: types et silhouettes* (Lyon, 1934)

Griffin, R., *The Nature of Fascism* (1992)

Guéneau, L., *La Soie artificielle* (1928)

Guicherd, G. and Ponsart, C., *L'Agriculture du Rhône en 1926* (Lyon, 1927)

Guiot, P., *Thurins: démographie d'une commune rurale de l'ouest lyonnais* (1949)

Hagtvet, B., Ugelvik, S. and Myklebust, J. P. (eds.), *Who Were the Fascists?* (Oslo, 1980)

Herriot, E., *Lyon pendant la guerre* (Lyon, 1919)

Lyon n'est plus (Lyon, 1939)

Higgs, D., *Nobles in Nineteenth Century France* (Baltimore and London, 1987)

Hoare Q. and Nowell Smith, G. (eds.), *Selections from the Prison Notebooks of Antonio Gramsci* (1971)

Hoffman, S. *et al.* (eds.), *In Search of France* (New York, 1963)

Hoisington Jr, W., *Taxpayer Revolt in France* (Stanford, 1973)

Houssel, J.-P., *La Région de Roanne et le Beaujolais textil face à l'économie moderne*, 2 vols. (Lille, 1979)

Howlett, G., 'La Rocque, the Croix de Feu and the Parti Social Français' (D.Phil. thesis, Oxford, 1986)

L'Industrie dans la région de Roanne, Thizy, et Cours (Roanne, 1929)

Irvine, W. D., *French Conservatism in Crisis: The Republican Federation of France in the 1930s* (Baton Rouge and London, 1979)

The Boulanger Affair Reconsidered (Oxford and Baton Rouge, 1990)

'Fascism in France. The strange case of the Croix de Feu', *Journal of Modern History* 63 (1991), 271–95

Irving, R. E. M., *Christian Democracy in France* (1973)

Isaac, A., 'Les Cahiers de l'industrie française. La soie', *Revue des deux mondes* (1930), 89–106

Jackson, J., *The Politics of Depression in France 1932–1936* (Cambridge, 1985)

The Popular Front in France (Cambridge, 1988)

Jankowsky, P., *Communism and Collaboration: Simon Sabiani and Politics in Marseille, 1919–1944* (New Haven, 1989)

Jauffret, L., 'Quelques grands bourgeois lyonnais' (mémoire de maîtrise, Lyon II, 1987)

Jeanenney, J.-N., *Leçon d'histoire pour une gauche au pouvoir: la faillite du Cartel* (1975)

François de Wendel en république (1976)

'La Fédération républicaine', in *La France et les françaises*, ed. R. Rémond and J. Bourdin (1979)

L'Argent caché (1981)

Jeantet, R. and Willemain, J., 'La Banlieue maraîchère et la commerce des légumes à Lyon jusqu'en 1939', *Etudes rhodaniennes* 16 (1940), 221–74

Jessner, S., 'Edouard Herriot in Lyons: some aspects of his rôle as Mayor', in *From Ancien Régime to Popular Front*, ed. C. K. Warner (New York and London, 1969)

Joly, J. (ed.), *Dictionnaire des parlementaires françaises* (7 vols., 1962–72)

Jomand, J., *Chaponost en lyonnais* (Lyon, 1966)

Judt, T., *Socialism in Provence* (Cambridge, 1979)

Kemp, T., 'French economic performance: some new views reconsidered', *European History Quarterly* 15 (1985), 473–88

Kergoat, J., *La France du front populaire* (1986)

Kleinclausz, A. *et al.*, *Histoire de Lyon*, 3 vols. (Lyon, 1952)

Kolboom, I., 'Patronat et cadres: la contribution patronale à la formation du groupe des cadres', *Mouvement social* (1982), 71–95

La Revanche des patrons: le patronat français face au Front populaire (1986)

Kuisel, R. F., *Ernest Mercier, French Technocrat* (Los Angeles, 1967)

'Auguste Detœf, conscience of French industry', *International Review of Social History* 20 (1975), 149–74

Capitalism and the State in Modern France: Renovation and Economic Management in the Twentieth Century (Cambridge, 1981)

Lachapelle, G., *L'Alliance démocratique* (1935)

Laclau, E., *Politics and Ideology in Marxist Theory* (1977)

Lafferère, M., *Lyon, ville industrielle: essai de géographie et de techniques industrielles* (1960)

Laffey, J., 'Lyonnais imperialism in the Far East, 1900–1938', *Modern Asian Studies* 10 (1970), 225–40

'Municipal imperialism in decline: the Lyon Chamber of Commerce, 1914–1925', *Journal of European Economic History* 4 (1975), 95–120

'Municipal imperialism: case of the Lyon Chamber of Commerce, 1925–1938', *French Historical Studies* 9 (1976), 329–53

Lagardette, H., *Impressions beaujolais: de la résistance à la vigne* (Lyon, 1931)

Lagroye, J., *Société et politique: J. Chaban-Delmas à Bordeaux* (1973)

Laperrière, G., *La Séparation à Lyon (1904–1908): étude d'opinion publique* (Lyon, 1973)

Larkin, M., *Religion, Politics and Preferment in France since 1890* (Cambridge, 1995)

La Rocque, E. and La Rocque, G., *La Rocque, tel qu'il était* (1962)

La Rocque, Lt Colonel de, *Service Public* (1934)

Latreille A. (ed.), *Histoire de Lyon et du lyonnais* (Lyon, 1956)

Launay, M., 'Le Syndicalisme chrétien en France, 1885 à 1940' (thèse d'état, Paris, 1980)

La CFTC: origines et développement, 1919–1940 (1986)

Le Baron, J., 'La Vie politique à Lyon aux lendemains de la Libération: le tournant de 1946' (thèse de 3ᵉ cycle, 2 tomes, Lyon II, 1985)

Le Bras, G., 'Notes statistiques et d'histoire religieuse', *Revue d'histoire de l'Eglise de France* 6 (1933), 503–5

Introduction à l'histoire de la pratique religieuse en France, 2 vols. (1942 and 1945)

Lebovics, H., *The Alliance of Iron and Wheat in the Third French Republic, 1860–1914: The Origins of the New Conservatism* (Baton Rouge and London, 1988)

Lefranc, G., *Les Organisations patronales en France du passé au présent* (1976)

Léger, B. M. E., *Les Opinions politiques des provinces françaises* (1934)

Léon, P., *Géographie des fortunes et des structures sociales à Lyon au XIXe siècle (1815–1914)* (Lyon, 1969)

Lequin, Y., *Les Ouvriers de la région lyonnaise (1848–1914)* (1972)

Lévy-Leboyer, M. (ed.), *Le Patronat de la seconde industrialisation* (1979)

Locke, R. R., *French Legitimists and the Politics of Moral Order* (1974)

Mâchefer, P., 'Les Croix de feu (1927–1936)', *L'Information historique* 34 (1972), 28–33

'Le Parti social français en 1936–7', *L'Information historique* 35 (1972), 74–80

'Les Syndicats professionnels français, 1936–1939', *Mouvement social* 119 (1982), 91–112

Mâchefer, P. and Kupferman, F., 'Presse et politique dans les années trente: le cas du Petit Journal', *Revue d'histoire moderne et contemporaine* 22 (1975), 7–53

Magondeaux, O. de., *Les Ententes industrielles obligatoires en France* (1937)

Maier, C. S., *Recasting Bourgeois Europe: Stabilization in France, Germany and Italy after World War One* (Princeton, 1975)

Margairaz, M., 'La Droite française face à la crise: incompétence ou choix politique?', *Cahiers d'histoire de l'institut Maurice Thorez*, 20–1 (1977), 69–88

'La Droite et l'état en France dans les années trente', *Cahiers d'histoire de l'institut Maurice Thorez* 20–1 (1977), 91–136

Martelli, R., 'Peut-on connaître la droite? Approches critiques', *Cahiers d'histoire de l'institut Maurice Thorez* 20–1 (1977), 15–19

Martelli, R. and Wolikow, S., 'Unité et différention de la droite: le cas de l'Entre-deux-guerres', *Cahiers d'histoire de l'institut Maurice Thorez* 20–1 (1977), 230–48

Martin, B. F., *Count Albert de Mun: Paladin of the Republic* (Chapel Hill, NC, 1978)

Massoubre, E.-S., *Les Ententes professionnelles dans le cadre national et la doctrine économique* (1935)

Maurice, M., 'L'Evolution du travail et du syndicalisme chez les cadres', *Mouvement social* 61 (1967), 47–64

Mayeur, F., *L'Aube: étude d'un journal d'opinion, 1932–1940* (1966)

Mayeur, J.-M., *L'Abbé Lémire* (1966)

'Catholicisme intransigeant, catholicisme social, démocratie chrétienne', *Annales ESC* 27 (1972), 483–99

'Les Catholiques Dreyfusards', *Revue historique* 261 (1979), 337–60

La Vie politique sous la Troisième République, 1870–1940 (1984)

Mesliand, C., 'Le Syndicat agricole vauclusien', *Mouvement social* 67 (1969), 39–60

Meuret, B., *Le Socialisme municipal: Villeurbanne, 1880–1982* (Lyon, 1982)

Milza, P., *Le Fascisme français: passé et présent* (1987)

Moissonier, M., 'Le Cartel du bâtiment à l'heure de l'unité syndicale (1933–1936)', *Cahiers d'histoire de l'institut Maurice Thorez* 15 (1983), 6–30

'Front populaire et identité communiste à Villeurbanne (1933–1936)', *Cahiers d'histoire de l'institut de recherches marxistes* 24 (1986), 56–67

Moissonnier, M. and Boulmier, A., 'La Bourgeoisie lyonnaise aux origines de l'Union civique de 1920?', *Cahiers d'histoire de l'institut de recherches marxistes* 14 (1980–1), 106–31

Moissonnier, M. and Pinol, J.-L., 'Le Parti communiste français dans la région lyonnais (fin 1938–fin 1940)', *Cahiers d'histoire* 30 (1985), 3–31

Monnet, F., *Refaire la république: André Tardieu, une dérive réactionnaire* (1933)

Montclos, X. de. and Latreille, A. (eds.), *Eglises et chrétiens dans la deuxième guerre mondiale: la région Rhône-Alpes* (Lyon, 1978)

Morel-Journel, H., *Notes sur la Chambre de Commerce de Lyon à l'usage de ses membres* (Lyon, 1937)

Morel-Journel, H., *Journal d'Henri Morel-Journel* (Lyon, 1957)

Müller, K.-J., 'French fascism and modernisation', *Journal of Contemporary History* 9 (1976), 75–107

Murphy, R., *Social Closure: The Theory of Monopolisation and Exclusion* (Oxford, 1988)

Noiriel, P., *Les Ouvriers dans la société française xixe–xxe siècles* (1986)

Nord, P., *Paris Shopkeepers and the Politics of Resentment* (Princeton, 1986)

Olin Wright, E., *Capital, Crisis and the State* (1978)

Ory, P., 'Le Dorgèrisme. Institution et discours d'un colère paysan', *Revue d'histoire moderne et contemporaine* 22 (1975), 168–90

Parkin, F., *Marxism and Class Theory: A Bourgeois Critique* (1979)

Les Parlementaires du Rhône à Vichy: manifeste des huit résistants (1944)

Passmore, K., 'The French Third Republic. Stalemate society or cradle of fascism?', *French History* 7 (1993), 417–49

'Business, corporatism and the crisis of the French Third Republic. The example of the silk industry in Lyon', *Historical Journal* 38 (1995), 959–87

' "Boy-scouting for grown-ups?" Paramilitarism in the Croix de Feu and PSF', *French Historical Studies* 19 (1995), 527–57

'Business, corporatism and the crisis of the French Third Republic. The example of the silk industry in Lyon', *Historical Journal* 38 (1995), 959–87

'The Croix de Feu. Bonapartism, national-populism or fascism', *French History* 9 (1995), 93–123

'Class, gender and populism: the Parti populaire français in Lyon' in *The French Right*, ed. N. Atkin and F. Tallet (1997)

Paul, H. W., *The Second Ralliement: The Rapprochement between Church and State in France in the Twentieth Century* (Washington, 1967)

Payant, J.-P., 'Etude démographique d'une cellule industrielle en Haut Beaujolais: Thizy et Bourg-de-Thizy de 1836 à nos jours' (mémoire de maîtrise, Lyon II, 1974)

Perret, J., 'Dans la banlieue industrielle de Lyon: Vaulx en Velin', *Etudes rhodaniennes* 13 (1937), 24–33

Perrin, A., 'Le Mont d'Or lyonnais et ses abords', *Etudes rhodaniennes* 3 (1927), 55–81

Petitfils, J.-C., *La Droite en France de 1789 à nos jours* (1973)

Peyronnet, M., *La Dynastie des Gillets: les maîtres de Rhône-Poulenc* (1979)

Pin, A., 'Un Notable paysan de l'entre-deux-guerres: Jean-Marie Parrel' (mémoire de maîtrise, Lyon II, 1989)

Pinol, J.-L., *Espace sociale et espace politique: Lyon à l'époque du Front populaire* (Lyon, 1980)

'Mobilités et immobilismes d'une grande ville: Lyon de la fin du XIXe siècle à la seconde guerre mondiale' (doctorat ès lettres, Lyon II, 1989)

Pinton, A., 'La Soie artificielle à Lyon', *Etudes rhodaniennes* 6 (1930), 242–3

'La Soie artificielle à Lyon en 1935', *Etudes rhodaniennes* 12 (1936), 104–7

Plumyène, J. and Lasierra, R., *Les Fascismes français, 1923–36* (1963)

Ponson, C., *Les Catholiques lyonnais et la Chronique sociale* (Lyon, 1979)

Potton, A., *On a trouvé un chef* (Lyon, 1937)

Potton, A. and Comparat, J., *La Révolution qu'il faut faire* (Lyon, 1938)

Prévosto, J., 'Les Elections municipales à Lyon de 1900 à 1908', *Revue d'histoire moderne et contemporaine* 36 (1979), 51–78

Prost, A., *Les Anciens Combattants et la société française*, 3 vols. (1977)
Quellien, J., *Bleus, blancs, rouges: politique et élections dans le Calvados, 1870–1939* (Caen, 1986)
Raymond-Laurent, J., *Le Parti démocrate populaire* (Le Mans, 1965)
Rémond, R., *Les Catholiques, le communisme et les crises* (1960)
   Les Droites en France (1981)
Rémond, R. and Renouvin, P. (eds.), *Léon Blum: chef de gouvernement* (1966)
Rigby, S. H., *English Society in the Late-Middle Ages: Class, Status and Gender* (1995)
Rivet, F., *Le Quartier de Perrache: étude d'histoire et de géographie urbaine* (Lyon, 1951)
Robert, F., 'Trayvou 1909–39. Qualification, rationalisation et mobilité ouvrière' (mémoire de maîtrise, Lyon II, 1986)
Rollet, H., *Les Chambres d'agriculture* (Lyon, 1926)
Rosanvallon, P., *Le Moment Guizot* (1985)
Rougerie, J., 'Faut-il départementaliser l'histoire de la France?', *Annales ESC* 21 (1966), 178–93
Sabel, C. and Zeitlin, J., 'Historical alternatives to mass production: politics, markets and technology in nineteenth century industrialisation', *Past and Present* 108 (1985), 173–6
Saint-Loup, *Marius Berliet, l'inflexible* (1962)
Sansom, R., 'L'Alliance démocratique', in *La France et les français en 1938–39*, ed. René Rémond and Janine Bourdin (1978)
Sauvy, A., *Histoire économique de la France entre les deux guerres*, 4 vols. (1965–75)
Schmidt, M., *Alexandre Ribot: Odyssey of a Liberal in the Third Republic* (The Hague, 1974)
Schweitzer, S., *De l'Engrenage à la chaîne: les Usines Citröen, 1913–1935* (Lyon, 1983)
Scott, J., *Gender and the Politics of History* (New York, 1988)
Shapiro, D. (ed.), *The Right in France 1890–1914*. St Anthony's Papers (London, 1962)
Siegfried, A., *Tableaux des partis en France* (1930)
Sirinelli, J.-F. (ed.), *Histoire des droites en France*, 3 vols. (1992)
Smith, M., *Tariff Reform in France, 1860–1900: The Politics of Economic Interest* (Cornell, 1980)
Soucy, R., 'The nature of fascism in France', *Journal of Contemporary History* 1 (1966), 27–55
   French Fascism: The First Wave, 1924–1933 (Yale, 1986)
   'French fascism and the Croix de Feu: a dissenting interpretation', *Journal of Contemporary History* 26 (1991), 159–88
   French Fascism: The Second Wave, 1933–1939 (Yale, 1995)
Soulié, M., *La Vie politique d'Edouard Herriot* (1962)
Sternhell, Z., *La Droite révolutionnaire: les origines françaises du fascisme* (1978)
   Ni Droite ni Gauche: l'idéologie fasciste en France (1983)
Stone, J., *Bourgeois Reform in France* (1984)
Tombs, R. (ed.), *Nationhood and Nationalism in France from Boulangism to the Great War* (1991)
Trimouille, P., 'La Bourgeoisie chrétienne du Nord (1930–1950)', *Revue du Nord* 73 (1991), 415–27

Vaucelles, L. de, *Le Nouvelliste de Lyon et la défense religieuse, 1879–1889* (1971)

Vavasseur-Desperrier, J., 'L'implantation locale d'un grand notable du Pas-de-Calais, Charles-Célestin Jonnart (1857–1927)', *Revue du Nord* 288 (1990), 907–27

Velu, H., 'Villefranche en Beaujolais', *Études rhodaniennes* 14 (1938), 46–71

Vidélier, P., *Vénissieux d'A à Z* (Lyon, 1984)

Vinen, R., *The Politics of French Business, 1936–1945* (Cambridge, 1991)

Ward, S. (ed.), *The War Generation: Veterans of the World War* (New York, 1975)

Weber, E., *Action française: Royalism and Reaction in Twentieth Century France* (Stanford, 1969)

Weng Ting Lung, 'L'Historique et la doctrine des Croix de Feu et du Parti social français' (thèse de droit, Nice, 1970)

Wileman, D. G., 'P.-E. Flandin and the Alliance républicain démocratique, 1929–1939', *French History* 4 (1990), 139–73

Wilson, S., 'The antisemitic riots of 1898 in France', *Historical Journal* 19 (1976), 787–806

Winock, M. (ed.), *Histoire de l'extrême droite en France* (1993)

Wolf, D., *Doriot: du communisme au collaboration* (1971)

Zdadtny, S., *The Politics of Survival: Artisans in Twentieth Century France* (Oxford, 1990)

Zeldin, T., *France, 1848–1945*, 2 vols. (1977)

Index